*The Snake and the Mongoose*

# The Snake and the Mongoose

## *The Emergence of Identity in Early Indian Religion*

NATHAN MCGOVERN

OXFORD
UNIVERSITY PRESS

OXFORD
UNIVERSITY PRESS

Oxford University Press is a department of the University of Oxford. It furthers the University's objective of excellence in research, scholarship, and education by publishing worldwide. Oxford is a registered trade mark of Oxford University Press in the UK and certain other countries.

Published in the United States of America by Oxford University Press
198 Madison Avenue, New York, NY 10016, United States of America.



CIP data is on file at the Library of Congress
ISBN 978-0-19-064079-8

1 3 5 7 9 8 6 4 2

Printed by Sheridan Books, Inc., United States of America

*For my parents*

# *Contents*


*Acknowledgments* ix

*Abbreviations* xiii

1. Introduction 1
2. The Snake and the Mongoose at the Horizon of Indian History 39
3. Taming the Snake and the Mongoose of Indian History 65
4. The Brahman as a Celibate Renunciant 85
5. The Brahman as the Head of a Household 133
6. The Emergence of the Snake and the Mongoose 165
7. Losing an Argument by Focusing on Being Right 193
8. Conclusion 217

*Notes* 225

*Bibliography* 293

*Index* 305

# *Acknowledgments*

THIS BOOK HAS been shaped by a serendipitous series of events that have passed over the course of the last decade and a half. Although this book reflects the interest in early Indian Buddhism with which I entered grad school, it is also informed by my experiences in Thailand while conducting research there in the years that followed. I was from the very beginning intrigued by the pervasiveness of Hindu themes within Thailand's living Buddhist culture. In even the most casual tour of the capital Bangkok, one encounters statues and reliefs of Hindu deities, Sanskritic references to Hindu mythology in the names of prominent institutions, the painting of the *Rāmāyaṇa* along the inside wall of the Temple of the Emerald Buddha, and even a temple for Brahmans employed by the king just across the street from city hall. This interest led to my master's research, which was on the pervasive worship of Brahmā by Thai Buddhists. When I ultimately decided to return to the study of early Indian Buddhism for my dissertation research, I was profoundly influenced by what I had learned in Thailand. Seeing how problematic the distinction between "Hinduism" and "Buddhism" is in modern Thai society, I became curious about the dynamic between "Buddhism" and "Brahmanism" in early Indian society and consequently obsessed with the category *Brahman* in the early Buddhist literature. My dissertation explored the formation of early Buddhist identity vis-à-vis the category *Brahman*, and this book expands and generalizes the argument made there to completely rethink our conception of the formation of religious identity in ancient India.

Many people have helped me to bring this book to fruition. First of all, thanks must go to my two main advisors in graduate school—Vesna Wallace and David White—who, in training me in Indian Buddhism and Hinduism, respectively, have each molded me to become the scholar that I am today. My two other advisors in grad school, Bill Powell and Justin McDaniel, also greatly informed my scholarly development, and I owe in particular an enormous debt of gratitude to the latter for his continued guidance and friendship up until today. In addition to these advisors, I have been particularly influenced in my training by Barbara Holdredge and José Cabezón, both of whom mentored me since my earliest days at UCSB and gave useful advice and criticism in my latter days there. Given the textual nature of my research, I also owe a great debt of gratitude to my language teachers, who in my opinion are the great unsung heroes of the university. First and foremost, I am eternally grateful to Greg Hillis, who introduced me to both Sanskrit and Tibetan and also provided much useful insight on matters language-related and un-related while I was working on my dissertation. During my last few years in graduate school, Evelyn Wade taught me German, and her brilliance in doing so will make me a better scholar and, through her example, has already made me a better teacher. In Chinese, I have been blessed with too many wonderful teachers to count, much less name. At UCSB, I wish in particular to thank Jennifer Hsu, whose pedagogical energy and tenacity forced my brain, spoiled as it was by the study of Sanskrit and Thai, to contend with the very different grammatical and written world of Chinese. At ICLP in Taipei, I had many different excellent instructors, but I would like in particular to thank Liu Xiaoping, who helped me to work through my very first "encounter dialogs" in Chinese. In addition to those already mentioned, many people have provided useful advice, criticism, and support in one way or another over the course of the past decade as I was thinking through and working on this project. These include Michael Jerryson, Nathaniel Rich, Joel Gruber, Paul Harrison, Luis Gómez, Bhikkhu Sujāto, Emily Schmidt, Mark McLaughlin, David McMahan, Alyson Prude, Robert DeCaroli, Kerry San Chirico, Rahuldeep Singh Gill, Amanda Lucia, Jason Schwartz, Chris Austin, Stefan Baums, Charles DiSimone, Jinkyoung Choi, Johannes Bronkhorst, Anālayo Bhikkhu, Joseph Walser, Jens Schlieter, Timothy Lubin, Claire Maes, and Lauren Bausch. Special thanks to Ruth Gamble, whose key advice allowed me to make this book a reality, as well as Cynthia Read, the staff at OUP, and the anonymous reviewers, who brought the book to fruition. All of these people and others have helped to make this a better book in one way or another; I of course take full responsibility for all weaknesses and errors that remain. Finally, I would like to thank my colleagues at Franklin and Marshall College, Ludwig-Maximilians Universität München, Dalhousie University, and the University of Wisconsin-Whitewater, as well as my friends at ICLP, whose support, professional guidance, and friendship has been invaluable in allowing me to write this book while engaging in the itinerant life of a beginning scholar.

Of course, no one is able to become a scholar without the love and support of those who are closest to them. In my case, I am increasingly, as I get older, in awe of one particular gift that my parents gave to me when I was a child—the gift of reading. Their tireless reading of bedtime stories (or, as I sometimes requested, readings from a college-level world history textbook) gave me a love and ability for reading that truly must be understood as the most important condition for the writing of this book to have been possible. Thanks must also go to Helen, who cleverly leveraged her role as the doting aunt to subsidize my personal library by taking me to bookstores whenever we had the chance to visit with one another. Finally, I owe an eternal debt of gratitude, one that can only be repaid over the course of lifetimes, to my beloved wife Nanda, who, among other things, has kept me sane long enough to see this book to completion.

# *Abbreviations*

| | |
|---|---|
| *AB* | *Aitareya Brāhmaṇa* |
| *ĀDhS* | *Āpastamba Dharma Sūtra* |
| *AN* | *Aṅguttara Nikāya* |
| *Ap.* | *Apadāna* |
| *ĀS* | *Āyāraṅga Sutta* |
| *AVŚ* | *Atharva Veda Saṃhitā, Śaunaka* Recension |
| *BĀU* | *Bṛhad Āraṇyaka Upaniṣad* |
| *BDhS* | *Baudhāyana Dharma Sūtra* |
| *BS* | *Bṛhat Saṃhitā* |
| *Bv.* | *Buddhavaṃsa* |
| *ChU* | *Chāndogya Upaniṣad* |
| *Dhp.* | *Dhammapada* |
| *DN* | *Dīgha Nikāya* |
| *GDhS* | *Gautama Dharma Sūtra* |
| *Iti.* | *Itivuttaka* |
| *Jāt.* | *Jātaka* |
| *JB* | *Jaiminīya Brāhmaṇa* |
| *MBh.* | *Mahābhārata* |
| *MDhŚ* | *Mānava Dharma Śāstra* |
| *Mil.* | *Milinda Pañha* |
| *MN* | *Majjhima Nikāya* |
| *Mvu.* | *Mahāvastu* |
| *Nidd.* | *Niddesa* |
| *Paṭis.* | *Paṭisambhidāmagga* |
| *Peṭ.* | *Peṭakopadesa* |
| *Pv.* | *Peta Vatthu* |
| *RV* | *Ṛg Veda Saṃhitā* |
| *RVKhil.* | *Ṛg Veda Khilāni* |
| *ŚB* | *Śatapatha Brāhmaṇa* |

| | |
|---|---|
| *Sn.* | *Sutta Nipāta* |
| *SN* | *Saṃyutta Nikāya* |
| *Sūyag.* | *Sūyagaḍaṃga Sutta* |
| *Ther.* | *Theragāthā* |
| *Therī.* | *Therīgāthā* |
| *TS* | *Taittirīya Saṃhitā* |
| *Ud.* | *Udāna* |
| *VDhS* | *Vasiṣṭha Dharma Sūtra* |
| *Vin.* | *Vinaya* |

# 1

# *Introduction*

I FIRST ENCOUNTERED the image of the snake and the mongoose as a child in a public elementary school I attended in a suburb of Memphis, Tennessee, when we were shown the animated short *Rikki-Tikki-Tavi*.[1] This half-hour-long 1975 film, written and directed by Chuck Jones and narrated by Orson Welles, is adapted from a story found in Rudyard Kipling's *The Jungle Book*. It tells the tale of Rikki-Tikki-Tavi, a mongoose who defends a little English boy named Teddy and his family from two cobras, Nag and his wife Nagaina. Although we were shown the film several times, we were never given any context for its story. We were not told what Teddy and his family were doing in India in the first place, nor of the ideology of white supremacy that lay behind Rudyard Kipling's depiction of their life. As mostly white and African American children living in the American Mid-South, we could not help but be struck by the image of battle between what to us seemed like two very exotic animals, the mongoose and the cobra.

Perhaps in part because of this particular encounter with what we might term the "banality of Orientalism" (to play on Hannah Arendt's famous expression) that I experienced as a child, it seems striking to me that the image of the snake and the mongoose has become associated in the modern scholarly and pedagogical imagination with the origin of the major Indian religions. It is a commonplace in the contemporary teaching of Indian religions to refer to the struggle between two groups of religious specialists in ancient India, the *śramaṇa*s and the Brahmans. The Brahmans were the ancient priests of India, purveyors of the Vedic scriptures and associated sacrifices, going back to the late 2nd millennium

BCE with the first Indo-Aryan migrations to the Indian subcontinent. The *śramaṇas*, on the other hand, were upstarts whose movement first arose during the so-called second urbanization in India, which occurred in the Ganges Valley beginning in the middle of the 1st millennium BCE. Their name, coming from the Sanskrit root *śram*, "to toil," referred to their austere religious practices, which involved renunciation of the comforts of ordinary householder life. The *śramaṇa* movement, according to this narrative, was opposed to the ancient religion of the Brahmans, rejecting the Brahmans' claims to social superiority, the authority of the Vedas, and the efficacy of the Vedic rituals. It gave rise to the "non-Brahmanical" religions of Ājīvikism, which died out after only a few centuries; Jainism, which still exists in India today; and Buddhism, which mostly died out in India in the early 2nd millennium CE, but spread beyond India to Central Asia, East Asia, and Southeast Asia, where it is still practiced today. Brahmanism, on the other hand, became the basis for Hinduism, the majority religion of modern India.

In relating this narrative of early conflict between *śramaṇas* and Brahmans that led to the rise of the major Indian religions, modern scholars often make reference to a surprising source: an ancient treatise on Sanskrit grammar. As one scholar writes, "Patañjali the grammarian refers to the hostility between Brahmanism and Sramanism as innate as is that between the snake and the mongoose."[2] This same assertion has been made or repeated by several other scholars.[3] There is a particular vividness to the image of the snake and the mongoose that perfectly captures a particular way of thinking about the origins of Indian religions, and of religions in general, for which reason I have chosen it as the title of this book. First, the use of an animal metaphor implies a sort of "naturalness" to the relationship between the two parties. This implication of innateness in the hostility between the *śramaṇa* and the Brahman is then reinforced by the particular choice of animals, the snake and mongoose, who in real life engage in a form of combat that is somewhat rare in its symmetrical hostility—not of predator and prey, but of two predators who each have the real chance of killing the other when they fight. Moreover, although this was certainly not the intention of any of the scholars who have evoked it, the image of the snake and the mongoose happens to play into the Orientalist imaginary, via the general "exoticness" of mongooses to Western audiences, the more specific staging of fights between snakes and mongooses by "snake charmers" in South Asia, and of course the Kipling character Rikki-Tikki-Tavi.

The most apt way in which the Patañjali-derived image of the snake and the mongoose represents the received narrative about the origins of Indian religions is that, while having just enough relationship to facts to sound plausible, it is not technically true. Patañjali never made this comparison. The source of the analogy is supposed to be his mid-2nd-century BCE *Mahābhāṣya*, a commentary on Pāṇini's foundational treatise on Sanskrit grammar, the *Aṣṭādhyāyī*. But at no point in this work does he compare the relationship between the *śramaṇa* and the Brahman to that between the snake and the mongoose, nor does he ever mention the compound "snake and mongoose" (*ahi-nakula*) in conjunction with the compound "*śramaṇa* and Brahman" (*śramaṇa-brāhmaṇa*).[4] What he does do is give "*śramaṇa* and Brahman" as an example of a certain type of compound defined by Pāṇini in rule 2.4.9: an "oppositional compound" (*virodha-dvandva*), that is, a compound of two elements "between whom there is constant strife" (*yeṣāṃ ca virodhaḥ śāśvatikaḥ*). Indeed, some scholars have made note of this example given by Patañjali as illustrating an antagonism between *śramaṇas* and Brahmans, without referring to any comparison to the snake and the mongoose.[5]

So where did the image of the *śramaṇa* and Brahman as being like the snake and mongoose come from? Although Patañjali does not mention the compound "snake and mongoose" (*ahi-nakula*) in his commentary on Pāṇini's rule 2.4.9, the much later Jain grammarians Jayāditya and Vāmana do give this compound as an example of Pāṇini's rule in their 7th-century commentary on the *Aṣṭādhyāyī*, the *Kāśikāvṛttī*. Unlike Patañjali, however, they do not give "*śramaṇa* and Brahman" as an example of this same compound. There is thus no comparison of the relationship between the *śramaṇa* and the Brahman to that between the snake and the mongoose, even implicit, in either Patañjali or the much later commentary by Jayāditya and Vāmana. Apparently the two commentaries on Pāṇini's rule 2.4.9 were conflated at some point by a modern scholar (although it is not entirely clear when or how this happened), and the conflation was then propagated in scholarship from there.

It is of course not my purpose in this book simply to nitpick as to whether the comparison of the relationship between the *śramaṇa* and the Brahman and the relationship between the snake and the mongoose is actually attested in the ancient literature. Rather, my purpose is to critique a model of religious origins that I believe this comparison aptly represents. This received model for the origins of the major Indian religions of Buddhism, Jainism, and Hinduism can be characterized as metahistorical: That is, it implicitly posits an essential characteristic for the Indian religions that explains their development throughout Indian history. That essential characteristic is an intrinsic dichotomy between the "Brahmanical" and the "non-Brahmanical." Most often, this intrinsic dichotomy is implicated in the study of early Buddhism, which will indeed be a focal point of this study. Buddhism is presented as having arisen in opposition to a preexisting Brahmanism, and this opposition then explains the competition that existed between Buddhism and Hinduism throughout Indian history. The intrinsic dichotomy applies in the same way to Jainism, as a fellow *śramaṇic* religion. It also is implicated, though, in the study of Hinduism, insofar as Hinduism is often understood as deriving from ancient Brahmanism, while subsuming within it, or accommodating itself to, countervailing non-Brahmanical beliefs and practices.

What I will argue in this book is that we should abandon the metahistorical assumption of an intrinsic dichotomy between Brahmanical and non-Brahmanical in Indian religions, such as is implied by the usual narrative of the *śramaṇa* movements as having arisen in opposition to a preexisting Brahmanism. This narrative, for one, privileges Brahmanism. While Brahmanism of course has its roots in the Vedas many centuries before the rise of the *śramaṇa* movements, it is now increasingly understood to have a complex history, with many of what were once considered its "essential" characteristics having arisen after the *śramaṇa* movements. In addition, this narrative lacks explanatory power: It explains the hostility that came to be shown toward Brahmans in early Buddhist and Jain texts in terms of a hypothetical "*śramaṇa* movement" from which they derived, but of which they are in fact the only two examples for which we have substantive evidence. I will argue that instead of understanding Buddhism and Jainism as metahistorically opposed to a preexisting Brahmanism, which latter then reacted to their challenge to create Hinduism,[6] we should understand all three traditions as having emerged out of a period of dialectical identity formation. In particular, I will argue that Buddhism, Jainism, and Brahmanism/Hinduism emerged out of a period of contestation over the category *Brahman*, which all of them sought to claim. Buddhism and Jainism were not intrinsically "non-Brahmanical" simply by virtue of being *śramaṇa* traditions; rather, they both sought, but ultimately failed, to articulate a vision of Brahmanhood rooted in *śramaṇic* ideals of renunciation. Similarly, Hinduism is not rooted in "the" Brahmanism of ancient India; rather, it is rooted in one particular ancient articulation of Brahmanhood that (1) sought but ultimately failed to reject *śramaṇic* ideals of renunciation but (2) did succeed in arrogating the category *Brahman* to itself.

The implications of my critique of the model of Indian religions based on a metahistorical dichotomy between Brahmanical and non-Brahmanical go beyond the narrow academic discourse on ancient Indian religions. My critique forces us to rethink modern discourses in India that are predicated on the naïve acceptance of "the Brahman" as a stable and self-evident agent in Indian history. It also forces us to rethink our understanding of religion more broadly, since the model of Indian religions is inextricably intertwined with the modern construction of "world religions," predicated as it is on the Western category of "religion" itself.

## *The Snake and the Mongoose in Modern Scholarship*

Modern theories on the emergence of the major Indian religions of Hinduism, Buddhism, and Jainism out of a foundational struggle between "the Brahmans" and "the *śramaṇa* movement" are inextricably tied up in the way that Indology developed over the past 200 years as a Western Orientalist field of knowledge, including the eventual birth of Buddhology as an autonomous field. A good deal of interesting and critical work has been done recently on the history of Western Indology and Buddhology and their implication within the larger Orientalist project; while I will be referring to this work in what follows, it is not my intention to give a full history of these disciplines, a task far beyond the scope of this book. Rather, I will focus on key themes within the history of Indology and Buddhology that have laid the foundation for the current consensus on the emergence of the early Indian religions. I will begin with Eugène Burnouf, who established the chronological priority of Brahmanism over Buddhism and thus lay the seeds for the assumption of its metahistorical priority. I will then trace the rise and fall of the "Lutheran model" of Buddhist origins, which in spite of having been refuted by Hermann Oldenberg, still lives on in a modified form in the so-called *śramaṇa* movement. Next, I will discuss the emergence of Buddhology as an autonomous discipline, which led to an institutional separation between those studying Buddhism and those studying Brahmanism/Hinduism, reflected in the assumption of a fundamental dichotomy between Brahmanical and non-Brahmanical in ancient India. Finally, I will survey the recent resurgence of interest in the relationship between Buddhism and Brahmanism in ancient India, which has coalesced around a consensus that Buddhism and the other *śramaṇa* movements arose in opposition to a preexisting Brahmanism, but with important dissenting voices as well.

## Establishing the Chronological Priority of Brahmanism to Buddhism: Eugène Burnouf

As the work of several recent scholars has shown, the modern vocabulary of "religion" and "religions" is the product of many centuries of increasing contact between Europeans and the rest of the world, which only fully coalesced in the 19th century.[7] Already by the end of the 18th century, Europeans had become aware of the existence of a single religious tradition, dubbed Buddhism, unifying a number of "idolatrous" (in the parlance of early European discourse) cults across Asia. Nevertheless, it took several decades for scholars to come to a consensus about the exact context in which this "Buddhism" had arisen. In large part this was due to the vicissitudes of history. Because Buddhism had long-since died out in India by the time European colonialists came there, the latter faced a lack of social and institutional knowledge to help them contextualize Buddhism in its land of origin. During the late 18th and early 19th centuries, Western scholars struggled to answer basic questions, such as whether there had been one or two Buddhas; whether the Buddha (or Buddhas) was indigenous to India or came from Africa[8]; and which was chronologically prior, Buddhism or Brahmanism.[9]

Resolution of these issues, though not absolute and certainly not immediate, was nonetheless effectively achieved with the publication of Eugène Burnouf's *Introduction à l'histoire du Buddhisme indien* in 1844. This incredibly influential book was based on a study of original Indian Buddhist texts discovered and sent to Burnouf by Brian Hodgson, a novel development in the study of Buddhism that Burnouf portrayed as central to his thesis and to his understanding of the history of Buddhism. As Lopez and Buffetrille argue in the introduction to their translation of Burnouf's book, "Perhaps the most important sentence in the entire volume occurs on the first page of the foreword, where Burnouf declares that the belief called Buddhism is completely Indian, literally 'a completely Indian fact' (*un fait complètement indien*)."[10] For Burnouf, the discovery of Buddhist texts in the Indian language of Sanskrit confirmed once and for all that Buddhism was born in India, developed in India, and could be explained completely on Indian terms, without reference to outside influences.

Burnouf came to a similarly strong conclusion on the question of the chronological relationship between Buddhism and Brahmanism. On the basis of his reading of the Sanskrit manuscripts that had been sent to him by Hodgson, in which he finds numerous references to Brahmanical gods, Burnouf concludes "that at the time when Śākyamuni traveled through India to teach his law, Brahmanical society had reached its highest degree of development."[11] He finds this conclusion to be secure regardless of the dating of the manuscripts at his disposal:

> [T]he sūtras that attest to the existence of Brahmanical society were either written around the time of Śākya, or a very long time after him. If they are contemporary with Śākya, the society they describe existed then, because one could not imagine why they would have spoken in such detail of a society that was not the one in which Śākya appeared. If they were written a very long time after Śākya, one does not understand any better how the Brahmanical gods and personages occupy so vast a place there, because long after the Buddha, Brahmanism was profoundly separated from Buddhism, and because these two cults had but a single ground on which they could meet, that of polemic and war.[12]

We see in this argument an extension of Burnouf's broader argument that, among the Sanskrit texts at his disposal, there are "primitive" *sūtra*s (those in question here) that are "closest to the preaching of Śākya, [and] remain shielded from the double influence that the system of celestial buddhas and bodhisattvas and the category of tantras or most especially of dhāraṇīs . . . exercised on the developed sūtras."[13] These "primitive" *sūtra*s, he argued, were more historical, less fantastical, and thus more useful than the later *mahāvaipulya* (Mahāyāna) *sūtra*s for understanding the historical context in which Buddhism arose.[14]

There are two major observations we should make about Burnouf's conclusions regarding the chronological relationship between Buddhism and Brahmanism. The first is that, in retrospect, we now see that Burnouf's reasoning was flawed. The "primitive" *sūtra*s Burnouf used to come to the conclusion that Buddhism emerged in an already well-developed Brahmanical society—from the *Divyāvadāna*—were in fact not particularly old[15]; their position as "primitive" in the 19th-century scholarly quest for the origins of Buddhism was quickly rendered obsolete as the texts of the Pali Canon were more carefully examined after Burnouf's death. Indeed, far from the presence of Brahmanical gods and personages being "inexplicable" if the texts in question are late, we find now, with our more complete understanding of the chronology of Indian Buddhist texts, that in some senses there is an *increase* in references to Brahmanical culture in later texts—a fact that is not surprising given our increasing awareness of the lateness of certain elements of classical Hinduism.[16]

The second observation we should make is that the flaws in Burnouf's argument have no bearing on the influence they have had. As Buffetrille and Lopez simply put it, Burnouf's *Introduction* "was the most influential work on Buddhism to be written during the nineteenth century. In important ways, it set the course for the academic study of Buddhism, and especially Indian Buddhism, for the next century."[17] One of the ways in which it did so was by setting Buddhism firmly in not only an Indian but a *Brahmanical* Indian context. This legacy, in particular, is felt still to this day. By this I do not mean to imply that Burnouf's legacy is simply another Orientalist sin of our forebears to be expunged from current scholarship. The flaws of Burnouf's argument notwithstanding, his conclusion has withstood the test of time, insofar as the discovery of even older texts in Pali has failed to turn up evidence for a "pre-Brahmanical" Buddhism.[18] More importantly, though, Burnouf's conclusion, when understood within the framework of the scholarly discourse of his day, represents a *real advance* in our understanding of the history of Indian religions. Prior to Burnouf, scholars struggled to answer the simple question of which came first: Buddhists or Brahmans. Although this is a problematic question, and more recent scholarship (to which this book will add) has necessarily explored the theoretical issues implicated within it, on a certain very basic level of chronology there is a simple answer, namely that arrived at by Burnouf: there were Brahmans before there were Buddhists. What is problematic is not this chronological statement per se, but rather the unwarranted and uninterrogated assumption that has followed from it: that Brahmans and Brahmanism are therefore metahistorically prior to Buddhism.

## The Rise, Fall, and Afterlife of the "Lutheran Model"

One of the earliest ways in which Europeans elaborated upon the conclusion that Brahmanism existed prior to Buddhism was by superimposing a European religious narrative—namely, Protestantism's narrative of its own origins—on the situation in early India. In his *British Discovery of Buddhism,* Philip Almond argues that in 19th-century England "[i]t was perhaps inevitable that the Buddha, *qua* religious reformer, should be compared with Martin Luther, and that Buddhism should be compared with the Protestant Reformation."[19] Once it became established that Brahmanism was historically prior to Buddhism, it became easy to construct a narrative with the Buddha serving as the Luther of India. The Brahmans were a priestly class; they were associated both in ancient literature and in modern practice with ritual; and the Buddha in some sense rejected the "pretensions" of the Brahmans. As Almond argues, this narrative served as an anti-Catholic polemic at a time when anti-Catholic sentiment in England was particularly high.[20] It also laid the basis for an Orientalist discourse in which Hinduism was painted in a negative light as an analogue to the "popery" of European Catholicism, and an essentialized portrait of Buddhism based on a selective reading of early texts was used to criticize by comparison both Hindu practice and the "degenerate" practices of contemporary Buddhists.

In his *Introduction,* Burnouf had already warned against a simplistic portrayal of the Buddha as a social reformer who abolished caste.[21] A real turning point in the scholarly discourse on the Buddha as reformer[22] was not achieved, however, until Hermann Oldenberg, in his *Buddha: His Life, His Doctrine, His Order,* argued forcefully against the comparison of the Buddha to Martin Luther:

> Above all it must be borne in mind that Buddha did not find himself like other reformers face to face with a great, united power, capable of resistance, and determined to resist, in which was embodied the old which he attacked and desired to replace by the new.
>
> People are accustomed to speak of Buddhism as opposed to Brahmanism, somewhat in the way that it is allowable to speak of Lutheranism as an opponent of the papacy. But if they mean, as they might be inclined from this parallel to do, to picture to themselves a kind of Brahmanical Church, which is assailed by Buddha, which opposed its resistance to its operations like the resistance of the party in possession to an upstart, they are mistaken. Buddha did not find himself in the presence of a Brahmanical hierarchy, embracing the whole people, overshading the whole popular life.
>
> Thus Brahmanism was not to Buddha an enemy whose conquest he would have been unable to effect. He may often have found

> the local influence of respected Brahmans an obstacle in his path, but against this a hundred other Brahmans stood by him as his disciples or had declared for him as lay members. Here no struggle on a large scale has taken place.[23]

Almond notes that after Oldenberg's book was translated into English in 1882, the scholarly literature records repeated references to his work as having conclusively proven that the Buddha was not a social or political reformer. Almond argues that this rather dramatic change in scholarly opinion was "the result of an attempt to protect the Victorian Buddha from being perceived as an early proponent of those forms of socialism that were perceived by many as threatening the structure of English society from the beginning of the 1880s especially."[24] Regardless of the specific reasons why Oldenberg's argument became so widely accepted, on its own merits it represents the addition of a significant level of nuance to the scholarly understanding of Buddhism's Brahmanical context. Burnouf had perhaps inadvertently laid the basis for the "reformer" narrative by emphasizing so emphatically the thoroughly Brahmanical character of the world in which Buddhism arose. Oldenberg's contribution is to point out that, while there is ample evidence that Brahmanism was present when Buddhism came into being, it hardly represented a monolith. His argument is not so much that the Buddha was not a reformer per se (and therefore he cannot be used as a champion of socialism), but rather that Brahmanism did not represent the sort of widespread, hegemonic institution that one could reform in the first place.

Indeed, even though scholars generally no longer explicitly compare the Buddha to Martin Luther and are aware of the pitfalls of seeing the Buddha as a "reformer," especially with respect to the institution of caste, the Lutheran model lives on, in attenuated form, in the contemporary model of early Indian religions. No longer do we have a single reformer, the Buddha, standing up in opposition to a corrupt and monolithic Brahmanical Church. Instead, we have the upstart *śramaṇa* movement, including the Buddhists, the Jains, the Ājīvakas, and any number of other nameless groups, who were opposed to and rejected the pretenses of the Brahmans. These latter were not institutionalized into a Church, nor were they a monolith, but they were older, as first established by Burnouf, and thus have been assumed to have a metahistorical priority. Thus, we retain the basic model of one preexisting group being opposed by other, newer groups.

Even for the Protestant Reformation itself, this model is extremely limited. On the one hand, Protestant Reformers were very much a product of the Catholic Church of their day, and Protestantism even now remains firmly rooted in the theological, ritual, historical, and cultural heritage of Western Christianity. On the other hand, the modern Catholic Church is not simply a continuation of the pre-Reformation Church; it is, through the Council of Trent and the Counter-Reformation, as much a product of the Reformation as Protestantism is. If the "Lutheran model" is limited in its explanatory power even for the Reformation itself, then, it certainly is limited in its explanatory power for ancient Indian religions.

## The Emergence of Buddhology as an Autonomous Discipline

Although the early 19th-century figure Eugène Burnouf is often called the father of modern Buddhist Studies, Buddhism continued to be studied in the context of Indology more broadly through the 19th century. Oldenberg, for example, made significant contributions not only to the study of Buddhism, but to the Vedas as well.[25] This situation began to change in the early 20th century, which saw an increase in the number of scholars more narrowly focused on Buddhism. First and foremost among this group was Thomas William Rhys Davids, founder of the Pali Text Society. A space for the emerging discipline of Buddhology was cleared by Rhys Davids' cleverly titled *Buddhist India*, published in 1903. The title, which appears at first glance to simply present the book's topic (Buddhism in India, or Buddhist aspects of India), quickly reveals itself to be a polemical expression of Rhys Davids' thesis. For Rhys Davids sets out in this book not simply to explore the Buddhist contributions to Indian culture, but to argue that ancient India can be primarily understood through a Buddhist lens, that India in ancient times was very much a *Buddhist*, and not a *Brahmanical*, India. In this work, Rhys Davids' main criticism of previous scholarship is that scholars have relied too heavily on Brahmanical texts in reconstructing the history of early India. He believes that the polemical and "normative" (to use a more modern term) character of these texts gives the false impression "that the only recognised, and in fact universally prevalent, form of government was that of kings under the guidance and tutelage of priests. But the Buddhist records, amply confirmed in these respects by the somewhat later Jain ones, leave no doubt upon the point."[26] Rhys Davids argues that just as much, and in many ways more, can be learned about early India from the Pali Buddhist texts, which contain a wealth of information on ordinary customs and religious practices, unencumbered by a totalizing Brahmanical ideology.[27]

The conclusion that Rhys Davids comes to by constructing an understanding of early Indian society on the basis of Pali Buddhist texts instead of Brahmanical texts is that the viewpoint offered by the Brahmanical texts is little more than polemic. He writes,

> The fact is that the claim of the priests to social superiority had nowhere in North India been then, as yet, accepted by the people. Even such books of the priests themselves as are pre-Buddhistic imply this earlier, and not the later, state of things with which we are so much familiar. They claim for the north-western, as distinct from the easterly, provinces a most strict adherence to ancient custom. The ideal land is, to them, that of the Kurus and Panchalas, not that of the Kasis and Kosalas. But nowhere do they put forward in their earlier books those arrogant claims, as against the Kshatriyas, which are a distinctive feature of the later literature. The kings are their patrons to whom they look up, from whom they hope to receive approval and rewards. And it was not till the time we are now discussing that they put forward claims, which we find still vigorously disputed by all Kshatriyas—and by no means only by those of noble birth (a small minority of the whole) who happen also to be Buddhists.[28]

The widespread acceptance of Brahmanical ideology, its hegemony over Indian social discourse, should not be read back into the early Indian context. This does not mean that Brahmans or Brahmanical claims were not present in early India, only that they were more claims than reflections of reality:

> It is difficult to avoid being misunderstood. So I would repeat that the priests were always there, were always militant, were always a power. Many of them were learned. A few of them, seldom the learned ones, were wealthy. All of them, even those neither learned nor wealthy, had a distinct prestige . . . .But it is a question of degree. *Their own later books persistently exaggerate, misstate, above all (that*

> *most successful method of suggestio falsi) omit the other side. They have thus given a completely distorted view of Indian society, and of the place, in it, of the priests.* They were not the only learned, or the only intellectual men, any more than they were the only wealthy ones. The religion and the customs recorded in their books were not, at any period, the sole religion, or the only customs, of the many peoples of India.[29]

With Rhys Davids, therefore, we have come full circle from Burnouf. Where Burnouf rightly established the chronological priority of Brahmanism, Rhys Davids just as rightly pointed out that chronological priority does not imply hegemony.[30]

Rhys Davids' insight that ancient India was far less "Brahmanical" than Brahmanical texts make it appear has unfortunately (with the notable exception of the work of Johannes Bronkhorst, about whom more below) yet to be fully embraced by scholars of ancient Indian religions, even after over 100 years. Instead, the most immediate legacy of Rhys Davids' work may have been simply to open a space for Buddhist Studies as its own discipline, to be studied on its own terms and apart from Brahmanism or Hinduism. Indeed, whereas nineteenth century scholarship had been very much preoccupied with the question of the relationship between Buddhism and Brahmanism, Monsignor Étienne Lamotte's 1958 *Histoire du Bouddhisme Indien*—a monumental work on early Indian Buddhism that is still fruitfully consulted today—has comparatively little to say about the issue. In this work of nearly 800 pages, a mere 7 are devoted at the beginning of the book to a discussion of "Vedic antecedents." The rest of the book is devoted to a discussion of the development of Indian Buddhism on its own terms, with only infrequent reference to any non-Buddhist context. The final paragraph of the section on Vedic antecedents, in which Lamotte cites approvingly the words of his teacher Louis de La Vallée Poussin, provides a concise theoretical justification for such an approach:

> This movement of ideas, a compromise between two civilizations, developed during the seventh-sixth centuries in the region of the Middle Ganges. Being situated more to the east, the lands which were to be the cradle of Buddhism escaped it for the most part. This explains why the preoccupations of early Buddhism are relatively remote from the speculations originated by the Hinduized brāhmins. It can be said, as did L. de La Vallée Poussin, that the "brāhmanism

> from which Buddhism sprang is not the brāhmanism of the *Brāhmaṇa* and the *Upaniṣad*," but represents, even better than the latter, the ancient Indian *yoga*.[31]

This statement reflects an increased awareness of the geographical diversity of early India (most importantly between an "orthodox" Brahmanical west and a "heterodox" east), a more finely nuanced picture of early Indian chronology (in particular the slow development and spread of Vedic texts and schools, with a gradual movement from west to east), and a particular conclusion derived from this increased understanding of the early Indian data that there is a fundamental *separateness* between the Buddhist and Brahmanical traditions that allows the former to be understood largely independently of the latter.

The emergence of Buddhist Studies as an autonomous discipline has left a mixed legacy. On the one hand, the autonomy of Buddhist Studies has, not surprisingly, led to a deeper understanding of Indian Buddhism. Even more importantly, by defining its disciplinary boundary in terms of Buddhism, a tradition spanning multiple regions of Asia and over 2,000 years of history, rather than India, Buddhist Studies has given rise to a damning critique of the assumptions of the 19th-century Indological study of Buddhism. Increasingly, scholars of Buddhism have come to realize that Tibetan Buddhism, East Asian Buddhism, Southeast Asian Buddhism, and even Western Buddhism are worthy of study on their terms, without privileging Indian Buddhism as somehow more original or authentic. Likewise, within the study of Indian Buddhism, which remains quite robust, there has been an increasing interest in later forms of Buddhism, in particular Buddhist Tantra, that were once considered corrupt deviations from "primitive" Buddhism and thus not worthy of study.[32] Buddhist Studies, as articulated most famously by Gregory Schopen,[33] has now firmly rejected the earlier assumption that Indian forms of Buddhism, chronologically prior forms of Buddhism, and written (as opposed to practiced) forms of Buddhism are somehow more authentic. These assumptions are now recognized as a legacy of an unwarranted privileging of the "original" and the "textual," derived from Protestant theology, as well as an unwillingness to take seriously living Buddhist actors in Asia, derived from Orientalism.

Another legacy of the emergence of Buddhist Studies as an autonomous discipline, however, has been less positive. That is, it has led to an institutional bifurcation between those who have expertise in Buddhism and those who have expertise in Hinduism/Brahmanism. This development is inevitable in an ever-increasingly specialized academy and can be considered positive insofar as it allows for more detailed study of developments within Indian Buddhism and Hinduism. At the same time, though, it can lead to a lack of necessary consideration of the interactions between Buddhists and Brahmans (or more broadly, "Hindus"), who did, after all, occupy the same spaces in India for approximately 1500 years. This tendency is exacerbated by the fact that, in many cases, the primary evidence scholars are working with are normative texts, authored in either Buddhist or Hindu traditions, that participate in an *imaginaire* that constructs a Buddhist or Hindu world, respectively, while deliberately excluding the other. Normative texts that ignore the existence of religious others are particularly common in the Brahmanical tradition, especially from the centuries around the turn of the era, which make no mention of Buddhists, Jains, or other "heterodox" groups. The intensive study of these texts has led to historical questions about seemingly innovative ideas (such as *karma* and rebirth) and tensions in the Brahmanical tradition (in particular between this-worldly and renunciatory values) that are difficult to answer when Brahmanical texts are studied in isolation. Answers to these questions have tended to take one of two approaches: The "orthogenetic" approach, which emphasizes the continuity in Indian religions from the *Ṛg Veda* onwards, and the "heterogenetic" approach, which explains changes in the Hindu tradition, in particular, by appealing to outside influences.[34] Both of these approaches, however, are premised on the problematic assumption of a metahistorical dichotomy between Brahmanical and non-Brahmanical in Indian history.

## Recent Scholarship

To summarize what we have seen so far, the early development of modern scholarship in the nineteenth century has left three main legacies that contribute to the "snake and mongoose" model of Indian religions. First, Eugèṇe Burnouf's conclusive discovery that Brahmanism predated Buddhism, while constituting a pivotal advance in our understanding of the chronology of Indian religions, has led to a too-often unexamined assumption in subsequent scholarship that Brahmanism is therefore metahistorically prior to Buddhism and the other *śramaṇa* traditions. Second, anti-Catholic sentiment in the 19th century, and the prevailing myth of Protestant origins, led to frequent comparisons of the Buddha to

Martin Luther. Although Hermann Oldenberg refuted this comparison as simplistic, the general theory of one religious tradition arising in protest against a preexisting one lives on in the prevailing model that Buddhism, Jainism, and Ājīvikism arose out of the *śramaṇa* movement, which was defined by rejection of the key tenets of a preexisting Brahmanism. Finally, the emergence of Buddhist Studies from Indology as an autonomous discipline, while allowing for increased specialization, has also served to institutionalize a division between Buddhism and Hinduism, thus reinforcing the sense that the two traditions are intrinsically separate.

The fact that the study of Buddhism and Hinduism has to a certain extent become institutionally separated does not mean, however, that there have been no attempts to study the relationship between the two traditions, or more specifically the shared space between Brahmanism and the *śramaṇa* movements in early India. Indeed, there has been a robust scholarly discourse from the late 19th century to the present on the relationship between Buddhism and Hinduism, with a particular interest in the interrelationships in meditative traditions and related philosophical ideas between early Buddhism, the Upaniṣads, Sāṃkhya, and Yoga.[35] I will focus here on the most recent developments in the study of Brahmanism and early Buddhism that, I would argue, are undermining the assumptions behind the "snake and mongoose" model of Indian religions and thus will particularly inform my methodological approach in this book.

One of the most important developments in recent scholarship has been an increasing recognition that many of what were once considered essential features of Brahmanism in fact developed relatively late, in many cases after the rise of Buddhism and the other *śramaṇa* movements. This has led to the slow but steady replacement of Brahmanism as a metahistorical agent in Indian history with Brahmanism as itself being a historical process that continually underwent profound changes between the composition of the Ṛg Vedic hymns in the late 2nd millennium BCE and the rise of classical Hinduism in the early 1st millennium CE. Important work has been done by Michael Witzel[36] and Jan Heesterman[37] on the development of the Vedic texts and associated ritual systems, by Romila Thapar on the concomitant rise of states in early India,[38] and by Brian Black on the late-Vedic Upaniṣads.[39] The monumental work of Patrick Olivelle on the post-Vedic Dharma literature has led to a more robust understanding of the development of Brahmanical ideology in these texts, in particular the *āśrama* system.[40] Although much work remains to be done on other post-Vedic Brahmanical literature, the recent work of Timothy Lubin on the Gṛhya Sūtras has raised important questions about the history of the concept of "twice-born," Vedic initiation, and, concomitantly, the institution of Brahmanhood itself.[41] Recent work on the *Mahābhārata*, in particular by Alf Hiltebeitel, James Fitzgerald, and Madeleine Biardeau, has resulted in an increasing consensus that India's great epic was initially composed around the Śuṅga period, after the fall of the Mauryas, and that it was composed in deliberate response to the anti-Brahmanical policies of the emperor Aśoka.[42]

While the works just mentioned each focus on specific texts or genres of text relevant to the history of Brahmanism, other work has contributed to the historicization of Brahmanism by defining epochal changes relevant to Brahmanism's development. Particularly notable in this regard is the work of Sheldon Pollock in defining the "Sanskrit cosmopolis," a cosmopolitan world defined by the use of classical Sanskrit that did not arise until close to the turn of the Era, after the rise of Buddhism and Jainism.[43] In addition, a conference held at the University of Texas, and the resulting volume edited by Patrick Olivelle, helped to define the period "Between the Empires" (300 BCE to 400 CE) as a significant period of change in India.[44] Finally, Johannes Bronkhorst's most recent trilogy of books, which we will be examining in more detail shortly, has constructed a compelling narrative of Brahmanism as an ideological movement that, driven eastward by cataclysmic invasions, succeeded in perpetuating itself by absorbing new ideas and constructing a narrative universe in which Brahmans and Brahmanical ideals are and have always been dominant.[45] All of this work has served to fatally undermine the earlier understanding of Brahmanism, based in part on Brahmanism's self-representation, as a timeless essence going back to the earliest period in Indian history.

While scholarship in Indology has brought an increasing awareness of the relatively late development of many key features of Brahmanism, other scholarship, much though not all of it coming from Buddhist Studies, has brought a renewed focus on the ways in which Brahmanism and early Buddhism inhabited a shared world in the late 1st millennium BCE. In part, this has consisted of a continuation of the early 20th-century debates over the relationship between Buddhism, the Upaniṣads, Sāṃkhya, and Yoga, but with a particular focus on the diversity of teachings on meditation found in early Buddhist sources and what these suggest about the relationship of the early Buddhist tradition to Yoga.[46] In addition, many important contributions to the study of Buddhism and Brahmanism in recent scholarship have taken the form of close studies of specific references to Brahmanism in the early Buddhist texts.[47]

Other works have taken a sociological approach to early Buddhism that, following the methodological approach set by Narendra Wagle in his *Society at the Time of the Buddha*,[48] makes use of the early Buddhist scriptures to understand the social world of early Buddhism but with the more specific goal of situating Brahmans and Brahmanism within that world. In her *Social Dimensions of Early Buddhism*, Uma Chakravarti undertakes a comprehensive analysis of all recorded social class statuses of people mentioned in the Pali Canon. She finds that Brahmans make up the largest single social group within both the *saṅgha* (i.e., monks and nuns) and the laity (i.e., those who take refuge in the Buddha, but do not ordain), which leads her to conclude that many Brahmans, due to the fact that they were already a "religious group," were attracted to Buddhism in spite of the general antagonism of Brahmans to asceticism.[49] Tsuchida Ryutaro, on the other hand, suggests that there are in fact two distinct types of Brahmans found in the early Buddhist texts—rich householders (*brāhmaṇagahapatika*) and matted-hair ascetics (*jaṭila*)—and that while the Buddha was highly critical of the former, he was generally sympathetic to the latter. Moreover, even rich Brahman householders were welcome to become followers of the Buddha as long as they recognized the authority of his teaching.[50] In *The Sociology of Early Buddhism*, Greg Bailey and Ian Mabbett argue that the way in which Brahmans are treated in the early Buddhist texts, including the frequent mention of Brahmans entering the *saṅgha* or becoming lay followers, can be understood as "marketing" to present the Buddhist *saṅgha* as a better alternative in the competition with Brahmans for royal patronage. This marketing strategy they define as "the deliberate application of a panoply of techniques to parade, in an intentionally persuasive manner, the ideology each group claimed to embody and its corresponding lifestyle."[51]

As innovative as the recent work that has been done on the shared context of early Buddhism and Brahmanism has been, most of this work has been focused specifically on explicating the *Brahmanical* context of Buddhism. That is, while representing a much-welcome overcoming of the institutional forces encouraging the segregated study of Buddhism on the one hand and Hinduism/Brahmanism on the other, it has ignored the insight of Rhys Davids that Buddhism did not arise in a thoroughly Brahmanical world, and rather has represented a continuation of the assumption, present since Burnouf, that the chronological priority of Brahmanism implies a metahistorical priority as well. This position, that Buddhism must be understood as having arisen in a Brahmanical context, has been articulated and defended most explicitly and at length by Richard Gombrich.[52] In particular, Gombrich argues in *How Buddhism Began* that to properly understand the Buddhist teaching on *anātman,* we must understand the Upaniṣadic doctrine of *ātman* to which it was a response.[53] Likewise, Gombrich argues that the Buddhist doctrine of *karma,* which is identified with "intention" (as opposed to its literal meaning of "action"), is "the Buddha's answer to brahmin ritualism,"[54] and he sees "dependent origination as the Buddha's answer to Upaniṣadic ontology."[55] In *How Buddhism Began,* Gombrich argues that the central metaphor of early Buddhism—that of fire, which is used by the Buddha in his third sermon to refer to the senses and is intrinsic to the idea of *nirvāṇa* (lit., "blowing out") itself—is a deliberate response to the central role that (literal) fire plays in Brahmanical ritual.[56] Finally, in "The Buddha's Book of Genesis," Gombrich argues that the cosmogony found in the *Aggañña Sutta* was not originally meant to be taken literally, as it was taken by the later Buddhist tradition, but was intended as a satire of the Brahmanical cosmogony found in the *Bṛhadāraṇyaka Upaniṣad.*[57]

One recent scholar has taken a radically different approach from that exemplified by Gombrich, which insists on placing the origins of Buddhism firmly in a Brahmanical context. In his most recent trilogy of books, Johannes Bronkhorst has given new life to Rhys Davids' insight that ancient India was not thoroughly Brahmanical. In the first volume of the trilogy, *Greater Magadha,* Bronkhorst argues that in the late first millennium BCE we can speak of a distinct geographical region in the eastern Gangetic basin, which he calls "Greater Magadha," that was characterized by a distinct culture and set of religious traditions separate from those of the Vedic Brahmans, who were originally from a more westerly region. According to Bronkhorst, some of the features of Greater Magadhan religion, in particular the belief in an *ātman,* karmic retribution, and rebirth, were adopted *later on* by Brahmans as they entered into Greater Magadha—a region that before the time of Manu was regarded as un-Āryan—and thus came into classical Brahmanical doctrine from the outside, and not from within the Vedic tradition.[58] In the third book of his trilogy, *How the Brahmins Won,* Bronkhorst argues that this process was set in motion by foreign invasions in the northwest of the subcontinent. These invasions drove the Brahmans eastward and, together with the hostility of the

Nandas and Mauryas, fostered an existential crisis that gave birth to the Brahmans' uniquely inward-looking ideology.[59]

Bronkhorst addresses the relationship between Brahmanism and Buddhism most directly in the second book of his trilogy, *Buddhism in the Shadow of Brahmanism*. He begins from the assumption, contra Gombrich and most other scholars, that Buddhism was not a reaction against Buddhism, because, although he admits that many Vedic texts already existed in oral form at the time of the Buddha, "the bearers of this tradition, the Brahmins, did not occupy a dominant position in the area in which the Buddha preached his message, [so] this message was not, therefore, a reaction against brahmanical thought and culture."[60] Bronkhorst argues that the references to Brahmans in the early Buddhist *sūtras* (i.e., frequently cited *suttas* from the Pali Canon) are probably relatively late and in any case represent an early Buddhist response to what he calls "the new Brahmanism."[61] The ideological content of this new Brahmanism was not simply a continuation of the old Vedic tradition:

> The Brahmanism that succeeded in imposing itself, and its language, on regions that had thus far never heard of it was a reinvented Brahmanism. It was not a simple continuation of the vedic priesthood, but something new that proposed far more than simply executing sacrifices for rulers who needed them. Brahmanism had become a socio-political ideology, but one that disposed of a number of tools in the service of the one ultimate goal: establishing the superiority of the Brahmins in all domains that the ideology claimed were theirs.[62]

Brahmanism reinvented itself in two ways. First, it wrote itself into the past—even to the point of giving itself a role in administration of the Mauryan, and most certainly anti-Brahmanical, king Candragupta—with the intent of lending itself an air of trans-historical importance.[63] Second, it borrowed heavily from the ascetic traditions of the *śramaṇic* movements, in particular by developing the literary trope of the *āśrama*, or "hermitage," in order to better appeal to wealthy political leaders as a worthy recipient of patronage.[64] As Brahmanical ideology became increasingly normalized in Indian society, Buddhism itself became "Brahmanized." Earlier Buddhist works portrayed the Buddha as living in a non-Brahmanical world, with Brahmanical ideas criticized and marginalized. Later works, however, most notably the *Buddhacarita* of Aśvaghoṣa, portrayed him as living in a *thoroughly* Brahmanical world, imbued with Brahmanical customs, philosophy, and ideas about society and kingship.[65]

Bronkhorst's concept of the new Brahmanism represents perhaps the most important contribution to the study of early Indian religion made by his trilogy. I will make frequent reference to this concept, although, with all due respect to Prof. Bronkhorst's original nomenclature, I will prefer to use the term *Neo-Brahmanism*. The reason for this is twofold. The first reason is simply a matter of economy in writing: "Neo-Brahmanism" is a bit shorter than "the new Brahmanism" and definitely more grammatically versatile when used repeatedly in academic prose. The second reason is that I think the *Neo-* nomenclature, as exemplified by terms such as *Neo-conservative, Neo-liberal, Neo-Classical,* and *Neo-Confucian,* captures perfectly what Bronkhorst is referring to in speaking of the "new Brahmanism": a movement-cum-ideology that styles itself after an older concept but re-envisions it so radically that (1) it bears little resemblance to the older concept but (2) successfully arrogates to itself that concept to such an extent that the "Neo-" ideology is, from then on, erroneously read back into the older concept in the past.[66]

Bronkhorst's work represents another continuity with older scholarship, however, that is more problematic, namely, a retention in somewhat modified form of the assumed dichotomy between Brahmanical and non-Brahmanical in ancient Indian religions. While Bronkhorst rejects the prevailing theory that Buddhism arose in opposition to a Brahmanical context, he nonetheless draws a sharp contrast between Vedic and non-Vedic traditions by divorcing Buddhism and the other religions of what he calls "Greater Magadha" entirely from what at times appears to be an essentialized Brahmanism. Bronkhorst convincingly argues that there was a culture in the general area around Magadha that was discernible from the Vedic culture in the east, and that this region only came to be recognized as *āryavarta* in Brahmanical texts after the turn of the era, thus implying a late process of "Brahmanization." Indeed, a similar argument has been made independently by Geoffrey Samuel, drawing on the unpublished work of Thomas Hopkins.[67]

Less convincing, however, is Bronkhorst's attempt to show that the concepts of *ātman, karma,* and *saṃsāra,* and ascetic technologies for effecting release from *saṃsāra,* are wholly products of the Greater Magadhan religious milieu that came to Brahmanism from outside. Since others have provided critiques of this aspect of Bronkhorst's Greater Magadha thesis, there is no need to repeat them here.[68] What I would add to these critiques is that Bronkhorst's assumption of a sharp divide between a Brahmanical West and Greater Magadhan East does not accord well with the Buddhist evidence. As many scholars have shown, Brahmanical terminology is *utterly pervasive* throughout the Buddhist texts, including the earliest strata. If Brahmans were simply loath to venture as far east as Greater Magadha prior to the time of Patañjali, and the encounter between Brahmans and Greater Magadhan religion occurred mostly after that point, that is, around the turn of the era, then we would expect to find Buddhist polemic against Brahmans suddenly appearing in somewhat late *sūtras* such as those discussed by Bronkhorst, reflecting the late entrance of Brahmans into Greater Magadha. Instead, as I will demonstrate in this book, what we find is a progression from a virtual identification on the part of Buddhists with the Brahmanical tradition to an increasingly antagonistic position in the later literature. In a personal communication, Bronkhorst has pointed out to me that he has been careful never to argue that there were no Brahmans at all in Greater Magadha during the Buddha's time and shortly thereafter. Rather, he argues only that this region was marginal to Brahmanical culture and ruled by regimes hostile to it, and thus Brahmanism could not have set the hegemonic context in which Buddhism arose.[69] This point is well taken, but it also undermines the fundamental geographical dichotomy that underlies Bronkhorst's Greater Magadha thesis. What we need is a theory of early India that incorporates the insight, first formulated by Rhys Davids and now revived by Bronkhorst, that Buddhism did not arise in the context of a metahistoric Brahmanism, but without sweeping the equally problematic assumption of a fundamental dichotomy between "Brahmanical" and "non-Brahmanical" under the carpet of geography or anything else.

## *A New Methodology for the Study of Early Indian Religions*

What I am proposing in this book is that we should set aside, once and for all, the distinction between Brahmanical and non-Brahmanical as a metahistorical principle for the interpretation of early Indian religions. Given recent trends in scholarship, I believe that this is a paradigm shift whose time has clearly come. In spite of the institutional division between the study of Buddhism and the study of Hinduism/Brahmanism, there has been an increasing interest in the intersections between these two traditions, and this scholarship has shown conclusively that the two traditions cannot be studied in isolation from one another. In addition, scholarship focused specifically on the Brahmanical tradition has pulled back the veil of ahistorical eternality that shrouds it, exposing it as having a rich history over the course of its over 1000-year existence prior to the coalescence of classical Hinduism in the Gupta age. More specifically, this historicization of the Brahmanical tradition has shown that many of its key features were relatively late developments—not preexisting the *śramaṇa* movements but rather responding to them, such that we are justified in speaking, as I will in this book, of a highly innovative and reactionary Neo-Brahmanism that was just as much a product of the massive changes taking place in North India in the mid- to late 1st millennium BCE as Buddhism and Jainism were. Recent scholarship has thus eroded the foundation of the Brahmanical/non-Brahmanical distinction; what remains is the final renunciation of this distinction as a metahistorical principle in interpreting ancient Indian history.

In practice, abandoning the metahistorical distinction between Brahmanical and non-Brahmanical means that we can no longer explain particular actors, movements, groups, or events in ancient India by saying, "This is Brahmanical," "This is non-Brahmanical," or "This is some sort of interaction between Brahmanism and something non-Brahmanical." Instead, we must interpret all contributions to ancient Indian discourse as creative and dynamic articulations of identity vis-à-vis other articulations of identity at a particular time and place. In taking this approach, I am influenced by Jean-François Bayart. In *The Illusion of Cultural Identity*, Bayart has argued that the cultural identities we take for granted in the modern world are not primordial, as they claim to be, but rather fabrications of the recent past, reflecting particular contingencies therein, rather than essences deriving from some distant origin.[70] What I am proposing, then, is that the illusory nature of identity is just as operative in ancient times as it is in the modern world. The ancient Indian discourse that we study does not reflect preexisting, metahistorical identities such as Brahmanical or non-Brahmanical; instead, ancient Indian discourse is the raw material out of which such identities emerge—both, over time, within the discourse itself and for those of us in the present who study that ancient discourse from historical distance. *In other words, identity does not precede discourse; discourse precedes identity.*

As modern observers of ancient Indian discourse, we are at both an advantage and a disadvantage in seeing past the illusion of identity. On the one hand, we are not embedded within ancient Indian discourse, so we are in a position to view ancient Indian discourse in toto and thus discern changes within it. On the other hand, we are still subject to the beguiling aura of the present, which creates the illusion of identity by projecting present circumstances onto the past. Given the particular conception of Brahmanhood that exists today—a product in part of British colonial policies in the recent past, but also of thousands of years of discourse on Brahmanhood—it is difficult to even read the word *Brahman* in an ancient text without the baggage of the modern conception of Brahmanhood coloring our interpretation of that text.

I will argue in this book that, by abandoning the hermeneutic of a metahistorical distinction between Brahmanical and non-Brahmanical, we arrive at a more nuanced understanding of ancient Indian religion than that of the "snake and mongoose" model. In order to accomplish this objective, we will need to take seriously *all* articulations of Brahmanhood in ancient India rather than interpreting them through the lens of a pre-determined distinction between Brahmanical and non-Brahmanical. Scholars have long realized that early Buddhist texts often used the word *Brahman* to refer to the Buddha or the Buddhist ideal person in the abstract. The same is true, although it has been less often pointed out, of early Jain texts; that is, early Jain texts also use the word *Brahman* to refer to Mahāvīra or the Jain ideal person in the abstract. Because of the uninterrogated assumption of a metahistorical Brahmanical identity that by definition excluded Buddhists and Jains, scholars have assumed that these Buddhist and Jain references to themselves as Brahmans must have been merely polemical, a rhetorical device intended to delegitimize the "actual" Brahmans by claiming that either the Buddhists or Jains better embodied the ideals of Brahmanhood. What I will argue is that we should take the early Buddhists and Jains seriously as Brahmans. That is, we should interpret Buddhist and Jain articulations of Brahmanical identity as just that—articulations of identity like any other—without prejudicing the issue by assuming that they were not "really" Brahmans. In the process, we will find that the Jain and Brahmanical articulations of Brahmanical identity, although certainly not primordial, do show important continuities with the past, in particular through their embrace of the celibate state of *brahmacarya*.

Concomitantly with taking seriously all ancient articulations of Brahmanical identity, we must problematize the one articulation of Brahmanical identity that has hitherto been taken seriously to the exclusion of all others—namely, the one found in what we now call the Brahmancial literature. In particular, given the time period we are interested in, this articulation of Brahmanical identity is most clearly expressed in the Dharma Sūtras. I will argue that by decentering this particular articulation of Brahmanical identity, we will find that it does not provide the "natural" definition of Brahmanhood, much less the primordial one. Rather, the articulation of Brahmanical identity found in the Dharma Sūtras was unique among all articulations of Brahmanical identity of its day in rejecting celibate renunciation as the basis for Brahmanhood and instead arguing that the true Brahman can, indeed according to some of its proponents must, be a householder. Although certainly rooted in an ancient tradition of Vedic sacrifice, the Neo-Brahmanism represented by the Dharma Sūtras was not so much conservative as it was reactionary. The Vedic literature contains references to practices that are both world-affirming and world-abnegating, but the second urbanization in India had created opportunities for wealth accumulation that accentuated the contrast between renunciation and non-renunciation, thus exacerbating the already existing tension within the tradition. Neo-Brahmanism defended its unique embrace of the non-celibate, non-renunciant householder lifestyle by (1) using the innovation of the *āśrama* system to sequester and deemphasize the traditional but problematic celibate practice of *brahmacarya* and (2) codifying and systematizing the *varṇa* system to divorce Brahmanhood from celibate renunciation and base it instead on birth.

When Brahmanical identity in ancient India is viewed in this way—not as a timeless essence, but as a series of articulations, employed in different ways at different times by different groups—the relationship between the categories *Brahman* and *śramaṇa* takes on a different shape than that implied by the "snake and mongoose" model. The categories *Brahman* and *śramaṇa* were not, as a matter of principle or definition, mutually exclusive or intrinsically opposed to one another. On the contrary, many groups in ancient India claimed to be Brahmans, and among them, most were also *śramaṇas*—that is, they articulated a Brahmanhood that was based on renunciation. One group in particular, however, rejected *śramaṇa* lifestyles and articulated a Brahmanhood that not only accommodated itself to the householder lifestyle but declared it to be the only legitimate lifestyle. This latter group was then so successful in arrogating to itself the category "Brahman" that, over time, the *śramaṇas* were forced to abandon the category. The result, rather than the cause, of this process was the opposition between the *śramaṇa* and the Brahman spoken of by Patañjali in the 2nd century BCE, and the distinction between "Brahmanical" and "non-Brahmanical" spoken of by scholars today.

At this point, it may be worth delimiting my argument and establishing a couple of things that I am *not* saying. First, in rejecting the metahistorical priority of Brahmanism in Indian history and taking early Buddhists and Jains seriously as Brahmans, I am not saying that there was no such thing as Brahmans or Brahmanism in some sense prior to the second urbanization, the rise of the *śramaṇa* movements, and the subsequent reactionary rise of Neo-Brahmanism. Obviously *Brahman* is a very old category in the Indian tradition, going back to the earliest strata of the Vedic literature dating to the late 2nd millennium BCE. What I am saying is that the principle of Brahmanhood as based solely or primarily on birth, to whatever extent it may have existed, was neither universal nor uncontested. We should take seriously the early Buddhist and Jain claims to the category *Brahman* on the basis of principles other than birth that were made most likely in the century or so prior to the foundation of the Mauryan Empire in the late 4th century BCE, rather than accepting at face value the Neo-Brahmanical arrogation of the category. In making this argument, I am not denying that Buddhism and Jainism were in certain ways substantively new and represented clear breaks with earlier Brahmanical practice; instead, I am drawing attention to the fact that the Neo-Brahmanical tradition was also substantively new. It represented clear breaks with earlier Brahmanical practice and thus should not be privileged as uniquely representing continuity with the Brahmanical past.

Second, although I am critical of recent scholarship that accepts the metahistorical distinction between Brahmanical and non-Brahmanical, especially in interpreting Buddhist references to themselves as Brahmans, I do not mean to reject the conclusions of that scholarship out of hand. I accept that there came to be a distinction between Brahmanical and non-Brahmanical in ancient India. I am not arguing that there is no evidence of such a distinction; instead, I am arguing that it emerged out of contestation over the category *Brahman*, rather than being the explanation for why people contested that category. In addition, because of the nature of the evidence at our disposal, in some particular cases that have been studied by scholars, there is already a sense that the category *Brahman* belongs properly to the proponents of what I call Neo-Brahmanism, and the Buddhists or Jains are simply polemicizing against this category in claiming to themselves be Brahmans. I argue that the reason for this is that the literature as it has come down to us, after centuries of oral transmission, has been shaped by the "emergence of the snake and the mongoose"—that is, the emergence of a distinction between the categories *śramaṇa* and *Brahman*.

Thus, an important part of my task in this book will be to show that there is evidence of Buddhists and Jains at one time claiming to be Brahmans without polemicizing against an external group of "actual" Brahmans, as well as to trace and explain the transformation of these early discourses of Brahmanhood into polemics against the Neo-Brahmanical movement that proved so successful in arrogating the category *Brahman* to itself.

## *Broader Implications*

"The Brahman," not simply as a real social actor but as a monolithic figure in Indian history, has been a crucial structuring principle in modern Indian religious, social, and political discourse. The fashioning of "Hinduism" as a modern "world religion" was predicated, in one way or the other, on the monolithic status of "the Brahman" in Indian history. Hindu nationalism has its basis in the Orientalist construction of Hinduism as a world religion through the privileging of the Brahman as a central figure in Indian history and of Brahmanical texts as defining the "orthodoxy" of that religion in imitation of Christianity.[71] But a critique of "the Brahman" also played a significant role in the "Hindu Renaissance." Rammohan Roy, the founder of the Brahmo Samaj and "father of modern India," was himself a Brahman and saw his crusade against "idolatry" in Indian religion as one of rectifying a "perversion" in Brahmanism.[72] Dayananda Saraswati, who is often seen as the progenitor of more exclusionary aspects of modern Hindu nationalism, was even more critical of "the Brahman" in his articulation of a "purified" Hinduism. Echoing the anti-Catholic rhetoric found in English discourse, he blamed what he saw as the degeneration in Hinduism in his day on a "corrupt priesthood," and thus he rejected caste and the ritual services of Brahmans. The organization that he founded, the Arya Samaj, used *shuddhi* rites to initiate members of lower castes and even Christians and Muslims into Vedic practice. As C. S. Adcock has argued, the modern shift from caste identity to religious identity as a structuring principle in Indian society and politics, and the concomitant rise of Hindu nationalism, was thus predicated on a narrative of the Brahman as a monolithic corrupting influence in Indian history.[73]

The critique of "the Brahman" was carried on by critics of the emerging Hindu nationalism in such a way as to, ironically, even more deeply entrench the Brahman as a monolithic figure in Indian history. Jyotirao Phule, founder of the Satyashodak Samaj that opposed Brahman power and led boycotts of Brahmans in the 19th century, subscribed to the Aryan invasion theory and used it to portray Brahmans as foreign invaders that oppressed the original inhabitants of India.[74] The Tamil activist Iyothee Thass also subscribed to the Aryan invasion theory and promoted a vision of Indian history as being characterized by conflict between Buddhists and Brahmans. He argued that the Tamils were originally Buddhists that were then reduced to low-caste status within the Hinduism imposed by the Brahmans. This belief led him to convert to Buddhism with the help of Henry Steel Alcott, who himself had pioneered the idea that untouchables were the descendants of Buddhists that had been subjugated by the Brahmans.[75] Thass's conversion to Buddhism was later followed by the more famous conversion of Ambedkar. Although he did not subscribe to the Aryan invasion theory, Ambedkar did, like Thass, promote a vision of Indian history as characterized by struggle between Buddhists and Brahmans.[76]

Other prominent figures fostered similar narratives of the Brahman as a monolithic antagonist in Indian history without turning to Buddhism as a solution. Maraimalai Adigal, a Tamil Shaiva, argued that the Aryan Brahmans were originally barbaric nomads who were culturally inferior to his own caste of agricultural Vellalars. While his ultimate goal was to replace Brahman supremacy with the supremacy of Vellalar Shaivism, he also valorized Buddhism as having made the attempt earlier in India's history to "civilize" the Brahmans.[77] Periyar E. V. Ramasamy, a former *sādhu* who became disgusted with what he saw as the corruption of Hinduism, abandoned religion altogether, became an atheist, and founded the Self-Respect Movement to fight caste inequality. He critiqued Hinduism, Brahmanism, and nationalism as one and the same.[78] This sentiment was echoed in the "Non-Brahmin Manifesto" of 1916, which broke from Congress's push for Home Rule, declaring that rule by the British was preferable because Home Rule would be equivalent to rule by Brahmans. This manifesto led to the establishment of the Justice Party, which opposed Brahman domination of government ministries and promoted caste reservations. Under the leadership of Ramasamy, the Justice Party was later transformed into the Dravidar Kazhagam, which in turn gave birth to the major Dravidian parties in Tamil and Indian politics.[79]

Colonialism, the hegemonic influence of Western modernity, and the emerging power of the Non-Brahmin Movement as a force in Indian electoral politics have all contributed to a transformation of the Brahman as a social figure in modern Indian life. As scholars such as Aditya Nigam, Ramesh Bairy, and M. S. S. Pandian have argued, Brahman castes adapted to modernity by privatizing their Brahmanness while cultivating a modern, secular public persona through education, embracing the English language and Western norms, and entering the civil service. The public embrace of modern norms therefore allows Brahmans to defend their success as meritocratic, especially in opposition to caste reservations, while at the same time their private Brahmanness can be cited as a source of cultural superiority that explains why Brahmans are so preponderant in this success. Concomitantly, the success of the Non-Brahmin Movement has ironically created a new sense of solidarity among various Brahman castes that, according to traditional norms, would have had little sense of common identity.[80]

The modern status of the Brahman in India therefore shows the same sort of malleability and constant reformation of identity that I am arguing for in ancient India in this book. The historical shock of British colonialism and the hegemony of Western norms that have followed it have led members of Brahman castes to privatize their Brahmanness and embrace the Western discourses of secularism and modernity, which has enabled them to maintain their real power in society but in a different form. In this book, I will argue that a similarly radical transformation in Brahman identity took place in the late first millennium BCE in India, as urbanization led to a bifurcation between renunciatory and non-renunciatory articulations of Brahman identity, with the latter side in this controversy winning the battle over identity in part by giving in to the emerging valorization of renunciatory values. The ancient transformation of Brahman identity, like the modern transformation of Brahman identity, is but an example of the constant articulation and re-articulation of Brahman identity that has taken place throughout history. It is perhaps ironic, then, that the modern transformation of Brahman identity has been shaped in large part by discourses that assume the Brahman to be a monolithic, even metahistorical, figure in Indian history.

In addition to its relevance to modern discourses on Brahmanhood in India, this study also has broader implications for our understanding of religion in general. Through the work of Tomoko Masuzawa, Talal Asad, and others, there has been an increasing realization that the "world religions" paradigm is a modern construction and that the word *religion* itself is not a natural category but a product of a particular Western and largely Christian history.[81] The word *religion* comes from the Latin *religio* and appears in ancient, pre-Christian Roman times to have referred to the traditional practices of various ethnic groups in the known world, especially as they pertained to the gods, but without any implication of mutual exclusivity between them. This changed with the adoption of Christianity as the religion of the empire. Since Christianity styled itself the "true religion" to the exclusion of all others, it introduced an assumption of mutual exclusivity into the category *religion*.[82] Concomitantly, the category *religion* became colored by a host of features characteristic of monotheism in general and Christianity in particular. This included the centrality of a single, all-powerful higher being; an institutional structure with a distinction between clergy and laity; a valorization of "history" over "myth"; and programs for policing boundaries primarily on the basis of *correct belief* (orthodoxy) rather than *correct practice* (orthopraxy). The Christian emphasis on belief over practice was reinforced even further by Luther's doctrine of salvation by faith alone and the subsequent devaluation of ritual by later Reformers. In addition, the Protestant Reformation introduced into the category of religion an emphasis on scripture as the most important authority for determining "true religion," as well as the quintessentially modern idea of the individual, rather than the community, as the locus of religious agency.

Almost simultaneously with the Protestant Reformation and the emergence of Western modernity, colonialism led to the spread of the category *religion* around the world as European colonizers sought to categorize the various beliefs and practices they encountered that struck them as "religious." Scholars of Asian religions in particular have emphasized that this was not a process of *discovery* but rather a process of *construction*. That "religion" was not a natural, trans-cultural category is made obvious by the often arbitrary way in which this category came to be translated into Asian languages. Most of the languages of Southern Asia, for example, used a Sanskrit term to translate "religion," but different languages chose different Sanskrit terms to use for this purpose: for example, *dharma* in several Indian languages, *āgama* in Sinhala and Indonesian/Malay, and *śāsana* in Thai (which conversely uses *āgama* to refer to "magic"!). The colonial naturalization of the category *religion* led to the modern paradigm of "world religions," but, as scholars of religion have increasingly come to realize, this paradigm is based on an implicit Christian paradigm for what constitutes a "religion." Much of the work in studying religion in non-Western contexts now consists of deconstructing the Christian baggage carried by the category *religion* so as to uproot problematic assumptions about the nature of religion that plagued earlier scholarship on Asian religions.

Buddhism played an important role in the construction of the "world religions" paradigm, and it is now playing an equally important role in the critique thereof. As Philip Almond, Donald Lopez, Richard King, and others have shown,[83] early modern Europeans who came into contact with beliefs, practices, and institutions we would now categorize as "Buddhist" did not conceive of them as such, nor were they confronted with a pan-Asian discourse, analogous to the medieval European discourse of "Christendom," that would force them to do so. Rather, the category *Buddhism* was constructed, largely during the 19th century and through the collaboration of colonial administrators who obtained Buddhist texts and scholars who studied them in Europe. Indeed, as Masuzawa has shown, the construction of Buddhism was pivotal in the construction of "world religions" in general, as certain characteristics imputed to it, including a historical founder (the Buddha), a clerical institution (the *saṅgha*), and an effort to spread through "missionary" activity, made it similar enough to Christianity to convince Western scholars that *religion* could be understood as a universal category.[84]

The actual construction of Buddhism, however, was a product of the problematic confluence of two forces: Protestant Christian assumptions about the nature of religion and Orientalism. On the one hand, Western scholars, following Protestant models, located "true" Buddhism within the Buddhist scriptures, and in particular the earliest scriptures (thus preferring the Pali Canon to later Mahāyāna *sūtras* and especially *tantras*), and reading those scriptures selectively to emphasize the philosophical ideas found within them (*dharma*) rather than the practices they prescribed (*vinaya*). On the other hand, when confronted with evidence of actual practices among Buddhists in Asia, they dismissed these practices as a "degeneration" in the Buddhist tradition—echoing, of course, anti-Catholic polemics in the West, but amplified by Orientalist prejudices that constructed the "Oriental" as infantile, irrational, overly fanciful, and thus not capable of understanding and properly transmitting, in the case of Buddhists, their own religion. Thus, from the very beginning Buddhism was constructed as part of a larger program (the construction of "world religions") that projected Western and in particular Christian assumptions about the nature of religion, as well as intra-Christian polemics, onto universal categories.

This study, as a critique of modern understandings of Buddhist and related Indian religious identities, therefore necessarily takes part in a much larger critique of the category *religion* itself and the deconstruction of Western/Christian/Protestant assumptions that were written into the modern discourses of "religion" and "world religions." In particular, I am interested in critiquing an understanding of religious identity that is based on an assumption of mutual exclusivity rooted in the historical Christian practice of policing boundaries, both internal and external, on the basis of an exclusivist emphasis on orthodoxy. I should emphasize that in doing so I am not simply rejecting the assumption that Indian religious traditions police boundaries in the same way as Christianity historically has. This critique has already been ably integrated into Buddhist Studies and Indology through the adoption of Paul Hacker's concept of "inclusivism" as the operative principle structuring religious identity in India.[85] Thus, for example, Buddhism need not, as did Christianity,[86] reject the existence of local deities or even supreme deities such as the sectarian gods Viṣṇu and Śiva; instead, it "includes" them within its system by acknowledging their existence and to a certain extent their power, but making them mortal and therefore *saṃsāric* beings who are incapable of bringing one to *nirvāṇa* and are therefore ranked below the Buddha. Various sectarian movements within the broader rubric of Hinduism have done the same sort of thing to each other, with Śaivas "including" Viṣṇu as a subordinate god within their mythology, Vaiṣṇavas "including" Śiva as a subordinate god within theirs, and both "including" Brahmā as a subordinate god.[87] Likewise, Vaiṣṇavas have even "included" Buddhism by making the Buddha an avatar of Viṣṇu.

My study in this book goes a step farther than this, benefiting from and contributing to an increasing realization that the Christian self-understanding of its identity, which it has subsequently projected on the "world religions," is itself a mirage rooted in the discourse of orthodoxy. In this respect, I have been particularly influenced by the work of Daniel Boyarin, who has argued that "Christian" and "Jewish" identities were not naturally given, but rather imposed from above through the work of elite heresiologists who worked to create mutually exclusive Christian and Jewish identities. His work is made possible by the increasing realization by scholars that, contrary to the model given by Eusebius, "orthodoxy" is not the natural given, with "heresies" later arising as deviations from it; rather, orthodoxy and heresy are constructed simultaneously with one another, through a selection process, as elites seek to valorize one understanding of a religion to the exclusion of all others.[88] The implication of Boyarin's work is that religious identity is not "natural" or metahistorical, but rather emerges through contestation between various religious actors.

Similar arguments in favor of a model of religious identity as emergent rather than given can be found in the work of scholars working on other traditions as well. Fred Donner, for example, has argued that the early Muslim community did not possess an identity exclusive of other monotheistic identities (Christian and Jewish) but rather, such an exclusive identity emerged over the course of the century after Muhammad's death as the various Arab conquests consolidated into an "Islamic" empire.[89] Likewise, Maria Dakake has argued that early Shi'ites did not conceive of themselves as a separate "sect" of Islam but rather as a movement within Islam based on particular values.[90] Even the traditional narrative of the Reformation as an abrupt rupture within Western Christianity, which as I argued above continues to haunt narratives of early Indian religions, has increasingly come to be replaced with an understanding of the Reformation as a long process within Western Christianity that both was the product of forces within and had a profound effect on Western Christianity as a whole.[91] Insofar as I am arguing in this book that the distinction between *śramaṇa* and *Brahman* was not natural, but rather emerged over time through contestation over the category *Brahman*, my work is indebted to these earlier scholars and contributes to what I hope will be a continuing trend to understanding religious identity as an emergent property.

## *Outline of the Book*

This book is divided into seven chapters. In this first, introductory chapter, I have laid out the rationale for critiquing the "snake and mongoose" model, and I have presented an alternative model for early Indian religions. This model understands the opposition between the categories *śramaṇa* and *Brahman* not as a metahistorical given, but as having emerged out of a period of contestation over the category *Brahman*. Carrying out this project, however, is made difficult by the nature of the sources at our disposal. Aside from the edicts of Aśoka and the testimony of a few Greek writers such as Megasthenes who visited India in the wake of Alexander's abortive invasion in 327 BCE, sources for Indian history in the late first millennium BCE cannot be dated beyond an educated guess with an uncertainty of a century or more. Complicating matters further, one of the most useful bodies of evidence, the early Buddhist texts preserved in the Pali Canon and in certain parallel versions in Chinese and other languages, were originally composed and transmitted orally over the course of several centuries. Thus, in the form they come down to us, they do not always reflect the situation in the earliest Buddhist community. In Chapter 2, I review the basic chronology and sources available for studying religious identity in India during the late first millennium BCE. I argue that Alexander's invasion, which was followed not long after by compositions on Indian society in Greek, as well as the indigenous testimony of the inscriptions of Aśoka, forms a sort of "horizon" to Indian history, at which point we find some evidence for the conception of *śramaṇa* and *Brahman* as separate categories. The task then becomes to trace how this distinction arose *prior* to the imperial unification of India, but this is made difficult by the oral nature of the most useful source for the task, the early Buddhist texts. I argue that we can peer across this horizon in two ways: first, by examining the evidence synchronically for evidence that contradicts the prevailing "snake and mongoose" narrative, and second, by making use of the early Buddhist texts, the *Aṭṭhaka* and *Pārāyaṇa*, in conjunction with commentaries and narrative framings of them, to examine diachronically how Buddhist treatments of the category *Brahman* changed over time.

I then begin in Chapter 3 with a synchronic examination of the evidence, including *sutta*s of the Pali Canon but also early Jain texts and the edicts of Aśoka. I show, first, that in spite of the frequent citation of Patañjali by modern authors as demonstrating an opposition between the categories *śramaṇa* and *Brahman*, the relevant rule that Patañjali is commenting on is not even followed in the vast majority of instances of the compound *śramaṇa-brāhmaṇa* ("*śramaṇa*s and Brahmans") found in the extant literature. Moreover, when read in context, this compound is not used to refer to *śramaṇa*s and Brahmans as separate groups; rather, it is used to refer to collectively to religious practitioners in general—either negatively, to refer to those with "wrong views," or positively, to refer to those who are worthy recipients of gifts. This lack of evidence for mutual exclusivity in the treatment of the categories *śramaṇa* and *Brahman* in the literature, I argue, suggests that the assumption that the *śramaṇa*s arose in opposition to the Brahmans is overly simplistic.

The diachronic examination of the evidence begins in Chapter 4 and continues through the rest of the book. In Chapter 4, I examine what are likely among the oldest texts of the Buddhist literature, the *Aṭṭhaka Vagga* and *Pārāyaṇa Vagga* of the *Sutta Nipāta*, together with what are likely the oldest texts of the Jain literature, the first books, respectively, of the *Āyāraṅga Sutta* and the *Sūyagaḍaṃga Sutta*. I show that they refer to the ideal (i.e., enlightened) person of the respective Buddhist and Jain traditions as a Brahman, without any polemical comparison to a Brahmanical "other." In contradistinction with earlier scholarship, especially in Buddhist Studies, I argue that we should take these early Buddhist and Jain articulations of Brahmanhood seriously rather than assuming they are merely polemics on the basis of an assumption of the metahistorical priority of the Brahmans of the "Brahmanical" tradition. Moreover, I argue that these Jain and Buddhist articulations of Brahmanhood as being rooted in the practice of renunciation and celibacy were not outlandish or entirely novel, but indeed rooted in Vedic references to the practice of *brahmacarya*. Instead of being opposed to a Brahmanical "other" per se, the early Buddhists and Jains were Brahmans who were opposed to any conception of "the Brahman" that was not rooted in celibate renunciation.

In Chapter 5, I examine just such a conception of Brahmanhood, as articulated in the Dharma Sūtras. Instead of reading these texts as the work of "the" Brahmans, I decenter them by reading them coequally with the early Buddhist and Jain texts as articulations of Brahmanhood that demonstrate both innovations and continuities with the past. In particular, the Neo-Brahmanism of these texts sought to articulate Brahmanhood as rooted in a world-affirming, child-producing, householder lifestyle. They did so, I argue, by introducing two ideological tools. First, the *varṇa* system served to sever any possible connection between Brahmanhood and celibate renunciation by tying it instead to birth. Second, the *āśrama* system served to catalog all the religious lifestyles found in Indian antiquity, with the purpose of valorizing one, the householder lifestyle, as the best or even only proper lifestyle. I argue that the Neo-Brahmanical authors of the Dharma Sūtras were successful in arrogating the category *Brahman* to themselves, such that Buddhists and Jains ceased to seriously claim the category but in the process lost the battle over renunciation, being forced over the course of time to make accommodations to renunciatory lifestyles.

I conclude my diachronic examination of the evidence in Chapters 6 and 7 by showing how the Buddhists, in particular, came to abandon their claim to Brahmanhood. In Chapter 6, I show that the abandonment of the category *Brahman* by the early Buddhists can be seen diachronically in the evidence. Whereas in the early *Aṭṭhaka* and *Pārāyaṇa* the category *Brahman* is used as a natural category for the Buddhist ideal, later commentaries and narrative framings of these texts introduce comparisons to the proponents of Neo-Brahmanism, thus transforming the Buddhist use of the category *Brahman* into a mere polemic. Then, in Chapter 7, I present a model for how the Buddhist abandonment of the category *Brahman* came about. I argue that the Buddhists' penchant for explicitly rebutting the claims of the householder Brahmans in a genre of texts I call "encounter dialogs" ultimately proved counterproductive. On the one hand, it gave the claims of the householder Brahmans "free press," while the householder Brahmans not only did not reciprocate; they almost completely ignored their ideological opponents. On the other hand, encounter dialogs set up a narrative structure that opposed the categories *śramaṇa* (in the form of the Buddha) and *Brahman* (in the form of his interlocutor), thus naturalizing an opposition between these categories even while it was being argued against.

Finally, in Chapter 8, I summarize the argument of the book and revisit its broader implications for modern discourses on the Brahman in India and the general discourse on world religions.

Over the course of this book, I make use of a variety of textual sources preserved in the Buddhist, Brahmanical, and Jain traditions. Since searchability was critical in the research I conducted for this book, all citations of primary texts are taken from searchable electronic editions. All Pali texts are taken from Ven. Yuttadhammo's *Digital Pali Reader* (available at pali.sirimangalo.org), which makes use of a Burmese edition of the *Tipiṭaka*. Brahmanical and Jain texts in Sanskrit and Ardhamāgadhī are taken from the *Göttingen Register of Electronic Texts in Indian Languages* or GRETIL (gretil.sub.uni-goettingen.de). The Buddhist text *Yìzújīng* preserved in Chinese is taken from the *CBETA Chinese Electronic Tripiṭaka Collection* (www.cbeta.org). Primary texts are generally cited according to the various chapter, section, and/or verse numbers found in the edition used. For Pali *suttas*, I have simply cited according to the *sutta* number; I only make use of PTS citations for Vinaya texts, where there might otherwise be ambiguity. All translations are my own unless otherwise noted.

Throughout this book, I refer to texts in Sanskrit, Pali, and Ardhamāgadhī, which share a common vocabulary but each with unique spellings. It was not always easy to decide which spelling to use in a particular instance. Generally speaking, I use the Sanskrit spelling unless I am referring specifically to the use of a word in a Pali or Ardhamāgadhī text. Still, it was impossible to be completely consistent, and the reader may find it confusing when different spellings are used for the same word. In particular, the reader should note that *samaṇa* is simply the Pali spelling of *śramaṇa,* and *sutta* is the Pali spelling of *sūtra.* To avoid littering the text with more italicized foreign words than it already is, I avoid using the Sanskrit/Pali word *brāhmaṇa,* using in its stead *Brahman,* which has become an English word in its own right.

# 2

# *The Snake and the Mongoose at the Horizon of Indian History*

IT IS MY central contention in this book that the categories "Brahman" and *śramaṇa* were not intrinsically opposed to one another, and thus we cannot assume an opposition between these two groups in order to explain the development of early Indian religions. But this is not the same as saying that no opposition ever came to exist between the categories "Brahman" and *śramaṇa* in ancient India. Indeed, there is an abundance of evidence that such an opposition did arise, even in ancient times. The oft-quoted passage from the 2nd-century BCE grammarian Patañjali is an example of such evidence. Patañjali did not in fact compare the relationship between the *śramaṇa* and the Brahman to that between the snake and the mongoose, but he did apparently see the two categories as being opposed in some way, enough to give them as an example of an "oppositional compound." Modern scholars who conflate these two sources—the 2nd-century BCE *Mahābhāṣya* of Patañjali that refers to "*śramaṇa* and Brahman" as an example of an oppositional compound and the 7th-century-CE *Kāśikāvṛttī* of Jayāditya and Vāmana that gives "snake and mongoose" as an example of the same—therefore may be technically incorrect, but in the process lend a vivid image to an actually antagonistic relationship that arose in ancient India.

My contention in this book is that the antagonistic relationship between the *śramaṇa* and the Brahman—symbolized, as it has come to be, by the snake and the mongoose—was not *intrinsic* but rather arose through a period of contestation between different groups, all of whom claimed to be Brahmans. What exactly I mean by this will become clear in subsequent chapters. In this chapter, I want to focus on the evidence for an antagonistic relationship between the *śramaṇa* and the Brahman—the snake and the mongoose—itself. If this antagonistic relationship emerged in some way, then it behooves us to begin by showing how far back the evidence for it actually goes.

Unfortunately, tracing the antiquity of the "snake and the mongoose" in ancient Indian history is made difficult by the nature of the evidence. Ancient evidence for the categories *śramaṇa* and *Brahman* is not lacking per se—on the contrary, it is quite abundant—but much of this evidence is difficult or impossible to date with any certainty. Texts that survive from antiquity in India often do not have a named author, and even when they do, such as in the case of Patañjali, they are not dated, and thus scholars are left to guess the date on the basis of internal evidence and comparison to other texts that are themselves lacking in a firm date. As if this situation were not bad enough, one of the most important sources for studying the relationship between the categories *Brahman* and *śramaṇa*, the Buddhist *Tripiṭaka*, is not really a "text" at all, but rather a vast corpus of oral literature that was passed down for centuries before being written down. Since this early Buddhist oral tradition is unlikely to have been static over the course of its multi-century transmission, the antiquity of any particular trope within it is not simply a matter of a single text whose date must be inferred from internal and external evidence. Rather, it is a matter of an untold number of individual passages or even words that may have been added, deleted, or subtly modified over the course of oral transmission.

In this chapter, I will examine the evidence we have for dating the emergence of the "snake and mongoose" of Indian history. I will begin with the most firmly datable evidence, all of which is from the Mauryan period or shortly before—the inscriptions of Aśoka and the testimony of Greek authors going back to the conquest of Alexander the Great, who crossed the Indus in 326 BCE. I will then turn to the early Buddhist literature, which potentially contains parts that are up to a century older, assuming that we date the Buddha to the 5th century BCE, but which is difficult to date because of its original oral transmission. I will argue that firmly datable evidence in the form of Greek testimony and Aśoka's inscriptions provides a horizon for Indian history in the Mauryan period, but that by making judicious use of oral Buddhist sources, we can peer over this horizon to get a glimpse at the emergence of "Brahman" and *śramaṇa* as mutually exclusive and antagonistic categories.

## *The Horizon of Indian History: Evidence from the Mauryan Period*

In the study of ancient Indian history, the most important signpost for establishing some semblance of a reliable chronology is the reign of Aśoka Maurya from approximately 274 BCE to approximately 232 BCE. Even these dates are not entirely certain, and modern scholars have proposed dates for both Aśoka's accession and his death that vary by a few years in either direction.[1] Nevertheless, Aśoka Maurya is of unique importance to the study of ancient Indian history because he left behind a large corpus of inscriptions. These inscriptions are, aside from the much earlier and still undeciphered script of the Indus Valley Civilization, the earliest known evidence of writing on the Indian subcontinent,[2] and they are also the earliest historical documents from India that can be dated with any degree of certainty. Indeed, they serve as a sort of chronological Rosetta Stone for ancient India since they name five contemporaneous Hellenic kings ruling over various remnants of Alexander's empire, the dates of whom are known exactly from Western records.[3]

Aśoka refers frequently to "Brahmans and *śramaṇas*" in his inscriptions, indicating that the use of these two categories in tandem with one another was found in North Indian discourse in the 3rd century BCE. As we will see in the next chapter, however, nearly every time Aśoka refers to "Brahmans and *śramaṇas*," he does so in a way that treats them as referring to a single class of people who are worthy of gifts. Never do we find an explicit statement, like that in Patañjali's 2nd-century BCE *Mahābhāṣya*, to the effect that Brahmans and *śramaṇas* were "opposed" to one another. Indeed, only once do we find a statement that might be interpreted as showing that the two categories were understood to represent *separate* groups. In the Thirteenth Rock-Edit at Kālśī, Aśoka writes, "There is no country where these (two) classes [*nikāyā*], (viz.) the Brāhmaṇas and the Śramaṇas, do not exist, except among the Yōnas."[4] Even this statement is somewhat ambiguous: The listing of two groups with different names need not imply that they are completely separate. A good counterexample would be the "clergy and religious" of the Catholic Church. There are some clergy (ordained men) who are not members of religious orders and some members of religious orders who are not ordained, but there are also some men, such as Pope Francis, who are both ordained and members of religious orders, thus both clergy and religious.

Even earlier evidence than that of Aśoka is provided by Greek sources that resulted from the contact between Hellenic and Indian culture in the wake of Alexander's invasion of India in 326 BCE.[5] Since these sources were written by foreigners describing a culture unfamiliar to their readers, they are more explicit in describing the precise relationship between *śramaṇas* and Brahmans. The most well-known of the post-Alexandran Greek accounts of India is that of Megasthenes, who was the ambassador of Seleukos Nikator to the court of Aśoka's grandfather Candragupta Maurya around 302 BCE.[6] Unfortunately, Megasthenes' book *Indika* does not survive, but extensive quotations from this work are found in the writings of later writers of the ancient Western world. According to Strabo, Megasthenes divided Indian society into seven social groups,[7] of which the first, the philosophers, are divided into two groups: the *Βραχμᾶναι* and the *Γαρμᾶναι* (probably a corruption of *Σαρμᾶναι* = *śramaṇa*).[8] Strabo also records the testimony of Kleitarchos, who accompanied Alexander the Great in his Asian conquest and wrote a history of it.[9] According to Kleitarchos, "The Pramnai [*Πράμναι*: again, probably a corruption of *śramaṇa*] are philosophers opposed to the Brachmanes, and are contentious and fond of argument. They ridicule the Brachmanes who study physiology and astronomy as fools and imposters."[10] Taken together, this evidence indicates that by the time of Candragupta Maurya (late 4th c. BCE) there was in general colloquial discourse a conception of *śramaṇas* and *brāhmaṇas* as separate, perhaps even mutually antagonistic groups.

Unfortunately, with the Greek sources dating to Alexander's invasion and the reign of Candragupta Maurya in the last quarter of the 4th century BCE, we hit a wall in tracing the antiquity of the "snake and mongoose" in Indian history, since there are no sources that can be firmly dated prior to this time. Indeed, the Mauryan period, coming as it did in the wake of contact with the West and producing the very first examples of indigenous writing on the Indian subcontinent, serves, at least from a chronological perspective, as a sort of horizon for Indian history. Prior to this time, we simply do not have contemporaneous historical documents that can be dated with any sort of certainty. In this respect, it is impossible to see clearly into Indian history prior to the Mauryan period.

## *Peering Beyond the Horizon of Indian History: The Early Buddhist Oral Literature*

This is not to say, however, that we cannot see at all. Indeed, there is an abundant oral literature in India dating back to the late 2nd millennium BCE, when the earliest portions of the *Ṛg Veda* were likely composed. If we are to peer beyond the horizon of Indian history to trace the emergence of the "snake and mongoose," we must find some way of making sense of the pre-Mauryan oral literature. This task is simplified somewhat by the fact that the categories *śramaṇa* and *Brahman* are generally speaking not used in tandem with one another at all in Brahmanical literature, the famous quote from Patañjali being a rare exception. The category *Brahman* by itself is of course quite common in Brahmanical literature, from the *Ṛg Veda* onwards, but the category *śramaṇa* is surprisingly rare, even in relatively late texts. The earliest instances of the word *śramaṇa* in the Brahmanical literature, as identified by Olivelle, are in two late Vedic texts, the *Taittirīya Āraṇyaka* (2.7) and the *Bṛhadāraṇyaka Upaniṣad* (4.3.22), which probably predate Aśoka by a couple of centuries.[11] Overall, though, the term *śramaṇa* is exceedingly rare in Brahmanical texts, a paradox that we will explore more fully in later chapters.

Where we do find abundant use of the terms *śramaṇa* and *Brahman* in tandem with one another is in the early oral literature of the Buddhists. This is an important piece of information, but it also raises difficult questions. On the one hand, it means that there is no evidence for two mutually exclusive, antagonistic groups known as *śramaṇas* and Brahmans prior to the time of the Buddha. The Buddhist literature itself, by definition, dates from the Buddha's time or later, and the only Indian literature older than the oldest Buddhist literature, namely, the Vedas, makes scarcely any mention of *śramaṇas* at all, much less of any antagonism between *śramaṇas* and Brahmans. It is of course not impossible that the notion of "Brahman" and *śramaṇa* as mutually exclusive and antagonistic predates the Buddha, but there is simply no evidence for this. This fact has been ignored in the modern model of Buddhism, which takes Buddhism as having arisen in the context of antagonism between two competing religious groups, the *śramaṇas* and Brahmans. Such a model for Buddhism's origins simply projects a situation attested in Greek sources and inscriptions from the Mauryan period onto an earlier time.

Of course, if there is no evidence that the "snake and mongoose" predates the Buddha, this immediately raises the question of when the Buddha lived. Unfortunately, the dates of the Buddha are far less certain than those of Aśoka. Traditionally, in Theravāda Buddhist countries, the Buddha is understood to have died in 543 BCE. This date, often referred to as the "long chronology," is based on the Pali textual tradition of the Theravāda school. According to this textual tradition, the Buddha died 218 years before the accession of Aśoka—which, based on what we now know about the dates of Aśoka, should place the Buddha's death in the early 5th century BCE, rather than the middle of the 6th century BCE. Modern scholars, beginning with George Turnour in the early 19th century, recognized that the traditional Theravāda date for the Buddha's death was based on a miscalculation of the dates for Aśoka, and therefore revised the "long chronology" to place the death of the Buddha around 486 BCE.[12] This date held as the consensus in modern scholarship until quite recently, in spite of the existence of another old Buddhist textual tradition, from the Sarvāstivāda school, that placed the Buddha's death only around 100 years before the accession of Aśoka. Although this "short chronology" was long dismissed by scholars in favor of the supposedly more reliable "long chronology," the consensus changed definitively in 1988 when Heinz Bechert held a conference on the question of the date of the Buddha. Numerous scholars who participated in this conference and contributed to the resulting printed volumes[13] questioned the reliability of the "long chronology," especially given the lack of corroborating evidence, possible errors in the Pali textual tradition itself, the potential archaeological implausibility of such an early date for the Buddha, and the equal plausibility of the short chronology found in Sarvāstivāda sources. Although there is no way to know for sure when the Buddha died, at least given the present evidence available to us, scholars today tend toward a later rather than an earlier date for the Buddha's death, with 400 BCE, give or take a couple of decades, often given as a best guess.[14]

If the Buddha did die around 400 BCE, then he was active during the last half of the 5th century BCE. This is about a century before the invasion of Alexander in 326 BCE, which is the earliest reliable date for which we have evidence of two mutually antagonistic groups known as *śramaṇa*s and Brahmans, namely the Greek evidence examined above. A century may not seem like a long time in retrospect, but it does constitute several generations during which the "snake and mongoose" could have emerged in North Indian discourse. In addition, this century was a century of *massive* changes in North Indian social and political life, seeing a transition from small, lineage-based proto-states (*janapada*s) to the expansive, dynastic empires of the Nandas and Mauryas[15]—not to mention the rise of the major *śramaṇa* movements themselves, including those of the Buddhists, Jains, and Ājīvakas. The Buddha himself, therefore, lived in a totally different context than that experienced by Greek writers who visited India in the wake of Alexander's invasion; at the same time, the Buddha played an important role in creating the Indian world that Hellenistic visitors were later exposed to. Insofar as the early Buddhist oral literature is the earliest Indian literature that refers to *śramaṇas* and Brahmans in tandem with one another, it is our best hope to allow us to peer beyond the horizon of Indian history to see the emergence of the "snake and mongoose" in the century between the time of the Buddha and the foundation of the Mauryan empire.

Unfortunately, the early Buddhist oral literature poses problems of dating far greater even than that of the Buddha's death. For here it is not simply a matter of determining one particular date; indeed, the very nature of oral literature,[16] as well as the vastness of the Pali *Tipiṭaka* and its partial parallels preserved in Chinese, Tibetan, and Sanskrit,[17] implies a long period of time, perhaps on the order of centuries. The current consensus that the Buddha lived in the late 5th century BCE provides an approximate *terminus post quem* for the early Buddhist oral literature; specifying a *terminus ante quem*, on the other hand, is more controversial. In theory, the *terminus ante quem* for the early Buddhist oral literature would be the point (or points) at which it was written down and became fixed. Early Buddhist oral literature has survived to the present day in several textual forms, but the Pali *Tipiṭaka* of the Theravāda school is the most complete (indeed the only complete *Tripiṭaka* from any early Buddhist *nikāya*) and therefore the most important for historical inquiry. Unfortunately, due to the humid climate in South and Southeast Asia, manuscripts of the Pali *Tipiṭaka* do not survive from anywhere close to ancient times,[18] so the manuscript tradition cannot be used to determine when the Pali *Tipiṭaka* became fixed. Instead, we must rely on conjecture based on internal evidence within the *Tipiṭaka* and external historical evidence.

Perhaps the most conservative view on how early we can date the fixing of the Pali *Tipiṭaka* is that of Gregory Schopen, who argues that we cannot know for certain that the *Tipiṭaka* was fixed until the 5th century CE, when the great Theravāda scholar Buddhaghosa compiled Pali commentaries on it.[19] This stance is probably overly skeptical, however. To begin with, Buddhaghosa did not write his commentaries de novo, but rather compiled them from earlier commentaries; these commentaries included the views of certain named Buddhist elders, none of whom is later than the 1st century CE.[20] Likewise, the *Parivāra*, the last book of the Pali Vinaya, which was written in Sri Lanka and serves as an appendix to the Vinaya proper, refers to a lineage of Vinaya masters that ends in the 1st century CE.[21] These two pieces of evidence accord well with the tradition, recorded in the Pali chronicle the *Dīpavaṃsa*, that the texts of the *Tipiṭaka* were first written down in Sri Lanka in the 1st century BCE.[22] We thus can be relatively certain that the Theravādin *Tipiṭaka* was fixed and a commentarial tradition upon it was being developed by about the turn of the era.

This leaves, in theory, a period of nearly 400 years for the development of the early Buddhist oral tradition. The turn of the era only represents a rough guess of when the Theravāda tradition made the transition from oral transmission to writing and commentary, however; there is further evidence to indicate that much of the actual *content* of the *Tipiṭaka*, even if not entirely fixed due to oral transmission, was composed closer to the Buddha's time than to the Common Era. To begin with, written versions of early Buddhist *sūtra*s from sectarian traditions other than the Theravāda, especially in the Āgamas preserved in Chinese,[23] show a remarkable consistency in general content and doctrine, differing mostly in the exact wording and use of oral formulas. This suggests that the Buddhist oral literature developed fairly early in the *saṅgha*'s history and that the oral lineages that passed it down were sufficiently conservative to result in comparable texts being produced in the widely separated contexts of 1st-century BCE Sri Lanka and 4th- and 5th-century CE China.[24] In addition, there is epigraphic evidence for the institutionalized oral transmission of early Buddhist literature going back to the 2nd century BCE, written in Brāhmī during the Śuṅga era, immediately following the Mauryan period. This includes numerous references to "reciters" (*bhāṇaka*s) and "knowers of the *sūtras*" (*sutaṃtika*) at Bhārhut and Sāñcī, as well as a reference at Bhārhut to a *peṭakin*, presumably a *bhāṇaka* who is versed in an entire basket (*piṭaka*) of the *Tipiṭaka*.[25] These references to specialists in oral transmission, as well as the numerous depictions of Jātaka tales and other canonical themes at Bhārhut and Sāñcī from the early to mid-1st century BCE,[26] would imply that the Buddhist oral tradition was quite well developed a century or so after Aśoka.

An inscription left by Aśoka himself, however, indicates that this institutionalized Buddhist oral tradition was by no means a wholly post-Mauryan innovation. Although Aśoka never refers to *bhāṇaka*s or other terms for monastic specialists in oral transmission, he does, in his Bhābrā edict, refer to specific Buddhist *texts* that he recommends listening to. The names he gives for these texts, however, do not correspond to the names of *sutta*s or other canonical texts in the Pali *Tipiṭaka* as it has come down to us. This has led to controversy over which particular texts Aśoka is referring to in his edict, although plausible suggestions have been made.[27] More importantly for our purposes, the somewhat ad hoc list given by Aśoka and the difficulty in unambiguously identifying the texts named within it has led to controversy over the extent to which the Bhābrā edict proves or does not prove the existence of the Buddhist Canon by the reign of Aśoka in the 3rd century BCE. T. W. Rhys Davids long ago argued strongly that Aśoka's list demonstrates the antiquity of the Buddhist Canon:

> As was pointed out a quarter of a century ago[28] it is a critical mistake to take these titles as the names of books extant in Asoka's time. They are the names of edifying passages selected from an existing literature. It is as if an old inscription had been found asking Christians to learn and ponder over the Beatitudes, the Prodigal Son, the exhortation to the Corinthians on Charity, and so on. There are no such titles in the New Testament. Before short passages could be spoken of by name in this familiar manner a certain period of time must have elapsed; and we should be justified in assuming that the literature in which the passages were found was therefore older than the inscription.[29]

Rhys Davids is quite insightful here in recognizing that the "texts" named by Aśoka are not really texts as such, but rather certain edifying passages within early Buddhist texts. Indeed, this accords well with the identifications that have generally been made by modern scholars for the names given by Aśoka. Moreover, since these identifications have been made with passages found in the *Aṅguttara Nikāya, Sutta Nipāta, Dīgha Nikāya, Itivuttaka*, and *Majjhima Nikāya*,[30] thus representing a wide swath of the extant *Sutta Piṭaka*, we can surmise that a wide variety of *sūtra* texts were in oral circulation during the reign of Aśoka.

Nevertheless, caution is due, and I think Rhys Davids goes too far in his otherwise insightful comparison to edifying passages in the Christian New Testament. The Christian New Testament is a written text, or rather a collection of written texts, all of which can, quite independently of any hypothetical epigraphic evidence, be dated with fair certainty to the 1st century CE. It thus makes some sense to see references to "edifying passages" such as the Beatitudes, the Prodigal Son, etc., as being indicative of a stage in which New Testament texts have been circulating for some time.[31] The early Buddhist literature, however, was an oral literature, and of such a nature that certain stock passages could be (and the evidence shows, were) reused and inserted in various contexts in different *sūtras*. Therefore, although Aśoka's list of edifying passages does suggest that a wide variety of *sūtra* texts[32] were being circulated orally in the 3rd century BCE, it by no means proves that all *sūtra* texts that came to be included in the written *Tipiṭaka* had been composed by that time, nor that those that had been composed by that time were being recited in entirely the same form in which they came to be written down.

Indeed, although much of the early Buddhist literature was probably already in circulation well before Aśoka's accession, there is reason to suspect that at least some *sūtra* texts specifically reflect the imperial context of Aśoka and his immediate predecessors. Bronkhorst has argued that the *Assalāyana Sutta* could only have been composed after the time of Alexander the Great in the late 4th century BCE, that is, nearly a century after the Buddha's death. In the *Assalāyana Sutta*, the Buddha says that among the Yonas and Kambojas there are only two classes of people, slaves and masters. The Kambojas are a people who lived in the extreme northwest of the Indian subcontinent, and "Yona" refers to Greeks, who also lived in the extreme northwest of the Indian subcontinent after Alexander's invasion.[33] It thus seems likely that this passage in the *Assalāyana Sutta*, if not the *sutta* as a whole, was composed in the aftermath of Alexander's invasion, when Candragupta Maurya established an empire that spread right up to the doorstep of the Hellenistic kingdoms that succeeded Alexander's empire.

Likewise, the theme of the *cakravartin* (P. *cakkavatti*), or world-conquering monarch, found in several early Buddhist *sūtras*, would seem to imply an imperial context. The concept of the *cakravartin* would come to be integral to the ideology of Buddhist kingship right up to the present day,[34] in particular through the theme of the "Marks of a Great Man" (Skt. *mahāpuruṣalakṣaṇāni*; P. *mahāpurisalakkhaṇāni*), which has its origins in the early Buddhist literature but then became a staple of the later written biographies of the Buddha.[35] According to this theme in the early Buddhist literature, Vedic Brahmans versed in physiognomy are able to recognize 32 physical marks that together characterize a "Great Man." Such a "Great Man" is destined either to become a Buddha or to become a *cakravartin*, a world-conquering monarch. Although this homologization between Buddhahood and kingship would become integral to the ideology of Buddhist kingship beyond India, more important for our present purposes is the way in which the concept of the *cakravartin* is articulated in the early Buddhist literature, and the fact that it is articulated at all.

This can be seen most clearly in the *Cakkavatti-sīhanāda Sutta* ("The *Sūtra* on the Lion's Roar of the *Cakravartin*"), in which the Buddha describes *cakravartin* monarchs of the distant past and future. The very fact that this and other early Buddhist texts would describe a monarch who is more than an ordinary king (*rājā*) by virtue of having conquered the known world (lit. "conqueror of the four quarters": *cāturanto vijitāvī*) suggests a context in which such monarchs exist. The earliest such monarchs are the Nandas, who immediately preceded the Mauryas in the 4th century BCE, conquering much of North India from their base in Magadha, and the Mauryas themselves, who in the late 4th century and 3rd century BCE expanded the Magadha-based empire to an even greater extent, reaching its apogee during the reign of Aśoka. Indeed, an empire of the extent first achieved by Aśoka would seem to be implied by the description of the *cakravartin* in the *Cakkavatti-sīhanāda Sutta*. The area conquered by the *cakravartin* is here described as "this earth bound by the ocean" (*imaṃ pathaviṃ sāgarapariyantaṃ*); Aśoka was the first Indian monarch, and indeed one of the few throughout history, to establish an empire that covered most of the Indian subcontinent. Moreover, the entire ideology of kingship espoused by the *Cakkavatti-sīhanāda Sutta* seems suspiciously similar to that expressed by Aśoka himself in his edicts. The *cakravartin* in this *sutta* does not conquer by force of arms, but rather by the *dhamma*, which is physically represented by a wheel that precedes his armies as he proceeds throughout the four quarters and various peoples submit to him without a fight. Of course, in real life Aśoka did conquer by force of arms, but he explicitly expresses regret for this and, like the Buddhist *cakravartin*, repeatedly refers to his desire to rule through *dhamma* rather than force, as well as making use of the symbolism of the wheel.[36] These close similarities between the Buddhist concept of the *cakravartin* and Aśoka's known ideology of kingship all suggest that the concept of the *cakravartin* arose during the reign of Aśoka himself, or perhaps afterward as his model of peaceful *dhamma*-based kingship fell apart.[37]

Further hints at an imperial context can be found in the *Mahāparinibbāna Sutta*, which records the final events in the Buddha's life leading to his death and *parinibbāna*. In this *sutta*, the Buddha visits a village in Magadha called Pāṭaligāma, and while there he prophesies to Ānanda, "Throughout the Ariyan realm, to the extent of the trade routes, this will become the chief city, Pāṭaliputta, spreading its seed."[38] This prophecy would seem to be referring to a time no earlier than the Nandas, who made Pāṭaliputra the capital of Magadha for the first time and from there created the first pan–North Indian empire. Prior to the Nandas, Magadha was simply one kingdom among many, and its capital was Rājagṛha rather than Pāṭaliputra;

it is this earlier situation that is uniformly depicted as the context of the Buddha throughout the early Buddhist literature.

A less conclusive but nonetheless suggestive hint at an imperial context for the *Mahāparinibbāna Sutta* as it comes down to us is found at the very end of the *sutta*. After the Buddha dies and is cremated, several different groups lay claim to the relics, and in the end, the relics must be divided into eight portions, with the urn and the embers from the funeral pyre going to two additional groups. "Thus," according to the *sutta*, "there were eight *stūpas* for the relics, a ninth for the urn, and a tenth for the embers."[39] But this is then followed by a curious statement: "Thus it was in the past."[40] Although there is no direct evidence in Aśoka's inscriptions, later Buddhist legend claims that Aśoka opened the original *stūpas* containing the Buddha's relics, divided them further, and then built 84,000 *stūpas* around his realm.[41] Is it possible that the last line of the *Mahāparinibbāna Sutta* is alluding to this "event"? Although the story of Aśoka building 84,000 *stūpas* is likely legendary or at the very least exaggerated, the final line of this *sutta* does seem to imply that the Buddha's relics are no longer contained in a mere ten *stūpas*. Historically, Aśoka's reign would surely have been a turning point in the proliferation of Buddhist *stūpas*, given the Constantine-like role that Aśoka played in the spread of Buddhism, both through his direct patronage of the *saṅgha* and through his establishment of a pan-Indian empire.

Let me now summarize what I see as a basic chronology for the development of the early Buddhist literature to use as a guideline in going forward. The early Buddhist literature likely began developing in the 4th century BCE, if we take 400 BCE as the approximate date of the Buddha's death. By the turn of the era, the transition was likely being made, at least in the Theravāda tradition, from an institution of oral transmission to a written tradition with accompanying commentaries. This leaves about 400 years for the development and transmission of the early Buddhist oral tradition. Nevertheless, this oral tradition was most likely already quite well developed and robust by the 2nd century BCE, when terms for specialists in oral transmission such as *bhāṇakas* were recorded in inscriptions at Buddhist monuments. Indeed, looking even earlier to the 3rd century BCE, there must have been a fairly wide oral circulation of *sūtra* literature, since Aśoka refers to passages from throughout the *Sūtra Piṭaka* in his Bhābrā edict. At the same time, though, it is unlikely that even the *sūtra* literature, much less the Vinaya and Abhidharma literature, was fully developed in Aśoka's day in the form that has been preserved in the later textual traditions. As we have seen, certain Pali *suttas* contain clues that point to an imperial context for their composition, which would indicate that the early Buddhist oral tradition was still in the process of formation during the Mauryan period.

This leaves us with a bit of a conundrum in our attempt to trace the emergence of the "snake and mongoose" in Indian history. We have already seen that there is firm evidence for a conception of the Brahman and *śramaṇa* as separate and opposed from the time of Alexander's invasion in 326 BCE, just prior to the foundation of the Mauryan dynasty. We have also seen that there is no evidence for such a conception prior to the Buddha, since the early Buddhist oral literature is the earliest Indian literature that refers to such a conception. But we have also just seen that the early Buddhist literature, including the *sūtra* literature that we are most concerned with, was likely still in the process of development during the Mauryan period. How then are we to use it to peer beyond the horizon of Indian history? When we find evidence relating to the conception of the relationship between the Brahman and *śramaṇa* in the early Buddhist literature, how, in other words, will we know if we are peering beyond the horizon of Indian history . . . or just seeing a reflection of the Mauryan period or an even later time?

In order to answer this question, I will begin in the next section by examining evidence in the early Buddhist literature for a conception of the relationship between the Brahman and *śramaṇa* that agrees with the separate and oppositional one for which we have evidence as far back as the Mauryan period. This evidence takes the form of what is often referred to as the trope of the "true Brahman"—that is, the frequent statement found in the early Buddhist literature that the Buddha and other enlightened monks are Brahmans. After reviewing the usual interpretation of this trope in the early Buddhist literature, I will then outline a different approach that does not presuppose a metahistorical opposition between the categories *śramaṇa* and *Brahman*.

## *The Buddhist "Brahman" as Polemic*

As it comes down to us, in the Pali Canon, Chinese Āgamas, and other fragmentary textual sources, the early Buddhist oral literature reflects the oppositional conception of the Brahman and the *śramaṇa* for which we have independent attestation from the Mauryan period. Most especially, the "snake and mongoose" is reflected in what is often referred to in modern scholarship as the trope of the "true Brahman." This curious use of the word *Brahman* to refer to the Buddha or the ideal Buddhist person in general is arguably the centerpiece of the theory that the authors of the early Buddhist texts (or the Buddha himself) engaged in "marketing" by appropriating Brahmanical terms and redefining them with new Buddhist meanings. *Brahman*, after all, would appear on its face to be the most quintessential of all Brahmanical terms, and thus any use of the term to refer to anyone other than a "real" Brahman—that is, a Brahman by birth—is self-evidently ironical or metaphorical. Such a reading of the Buddhist use of the word *Brahman* of course assumes a clear dichotomy between Brahman and non-Brahman, such that one can assume an unambiguous distinction between literal and non-literal uses of the term. Gombrich articulates his position in terms of this assumption quite succinctly:

> The Buddha was not a brahmin in the literal sense, i.e. born as one, but the *Sutta Piṭaka* contains several passages in which he argues that brahmin, properly understood, is not a social character but a moral one, referring to a person who is wise and virtuous.[42]

Gombrich concedes that "the Buddha" was engaging in a reasoned argument over the meaning of the word *Brahman*—in other words, that the term was contested. However, by characterizing the "social" understanding of the word as "literal," he privileges that understanding over the one presented in the Buddhist texts and implies that it is prior and even more legitimate. Bailey and Mabbett articulate this assumption even more directly in reference to what they call the "almost obsessive mapping of Buddhist teachings upon the structure of brāhmaṇical tradition,"[43] of which the term *Brahman* is a central example:

> A heterodox or minority tradition needs to relate itself to the orthodox or mainstream practice; almost necessarily, Buddhism mapped itself upon a structure supplied by the Brahmins, defining itself by reference to what it was not; a series of systematic oppositions identified its relationship to the pre-existing orthodoxy.[44]

But as I am arguing in this book, we should *not* assume that the Brahmanism in whose context Buddhism arose was a "pre-existing orthodoxy"; rather, Brahmanical orthodoxy grew slowly over a period of many centuries and was still in a state of flux at the time that Buddhism arose.

If we adopt the methodology advocated here and drop the assumption that there was a clearly defined, preexisting Brahmanical orthodoxy prior to the rise of Buddhism, how does this affect our understanding of the use of the word *Brahman* to refer to the Buddhist ideal in early Buddhist texts?

In order to answer this question, we must first acknowledge that there are many cases in which the use of the word *Brahman* in the early Buddhist literature does clearly imply a distinction between the meaning understood by the advocates of Neo-Brahmanism and that being presented as the word of the Buddha. The most explicit examples are those in which the Buddha explicitly contrasts the Neo-Brahmanical understanding of Brahman with his own in narrative format. An example of this is found in a *sutta* of the *Sutta Nipāta* (1.7), in which the Buddha encounters a Brahman named Aggikabhāradvāja, who is in the midst of making a fire offering. This *sutta*, at least in the form in which it comes down to us, with a short prose narrative frame encompassing the verses that make up the bulk of the narrative, can be considered an example of what I will refer to in this book as an "encounter dialog"—an encounter between the Buddha and an interlocutor, with the Buddha identified as a *samaṇa* and the interlocutor as a Brahman. In this particular encounter dialog, however, the very binary by which this genre of early Buddhist narrative is defined is problematized by the content of the Buddha's teaching within it. When the Buddha approaches the Brahman's house, the latter verbally abuses him, saying, "Stop right there, *muṇḍaka*! Stop right there, *samaṇaka*! Stop right there, *vasalaka*!"[45] I have refrained from translating the three terms of abuse since their connotation and denotation are nearly impossible to simultaneously translate into English. All three use the diminutive *-ka* suffix to convey a dismissive attitude toward the Buddha. The first term, *muṇḍa*, simply means "shaved," and thus refers to the fact that the Buddha, as a wandering mendicant, has shaved his hair. (Often *muṇḍaka* is therefore translated as "shaveling.") The second term, *samaṇa*, refers to the Buddha's identity as a *samaṇa*, here clearly intended as an insult. Finally, the third term, *vasala* (Skt. *vṛṣala*), is itself intrinsically a term of abuse; it refers to a little or contemptuous man—although Norman translates it as "outcaste," which seems like an appropriate translation given the way it is used later in the *sutta*.[46]

The Buddha responds in such a way as to turn the Brahman's insult on its head by ethicizing the last of these three terms of abuse. Over the course of 20 verses (*Sn.* 116–135), the Buddha describes various types of morally inferior people—thieves, murderers, liars, and the like—and equates them with the "outcaste" or *vasala* with the words *taṃ jaññā vasalo iti* ("He is to be known as a *vasala*"). He then concludes by saying,

> Not by birth does one become a *vasala*; not by birth does one become a Brahman.
> By action does one become a *vasala*; by action does one become a Brahman.[47]

In order to illustrate this point, the Buddha concludes by recounting the case of a certain *caṇḍāla* named Mātaṅga who, in spite of his social status as a *caṇḍāla*, was reborn in *brahmaloka* (*brahmalokūpago*) because of his meritorious deeds.[48] The Buddha notes further that in spite of their high birth and knowledge of the Vedas, some Brahmans perform evil deeds and receive the due recompense in their next life. Thus, in this *sutta* the Buddha redefines the word *Brahman* by first ethicizing *vasala*, the socially loaded term of abuse with which the Brahman reviled him, and then by logical extension ethicizing the term *Brahman* itself.

Another encounter dialog presents a similar example in which the Buddha ethicizes the term *Brahman*, except that here the Brahman interlocutor himself participates in the ethicization. In the *Soṇadaṇḍa Sutta* (*DN* 4), a Brahman named Soṇadaṇḍa ("Dog-Stick"[49]) living in Campā, which had been given to him by King Bimbisāra of Magadha as a *brahmadeyya* land grant, visits the Buddha after hearing that he is in the area and is asked by the latter what it is that makes one a Brahman.[50] Soṇadaṇḍa answers by saying that there are five characteristics a Brahman must have:

1. He is well-born on both sides, on his mother's and his father's, of pure descent up to the seventh generation of ancestors, undisturbed, blameless with respect to the matter of birth.[51]
2. He is a scholar, a bearer of the *mantras*, perfected in the three Vedas—together with their vocabularies and rituals, with their phonology and etymology, and the oral tradition (*itihāsa*) as a fifth—skilled in philology and grammar, not lacking in the Lokāyata and marks of a Great Man.[52]
3. He is handsome, good-looking, pleasing (to look at), endowed with supreme beauty of complexion, having the complexion of Brahmā and the body of Brahmā, having an appearance that is not small to behold.[53]
4. He is endowed with morality, of increasing morality, endowed with increasing morality.[54]

5. And he is wise, intelligent, the first or the second of those holding out the sacrificial ladle.[55]

Clearly, these characteristics, especially the first, second, and fifth of them, are central to the definition of the Brahman advanced by the proponents of Neo-Brahmanism. The narrative continues, however, with the Buddha asking if any of these characteristics can be set aside as inessential. Soṇadaṇḍa, much to the dismay of his fellow Brahmans who have come along to witness his meeting with the Buddha, one-by-one admits that the first three characteristics are inessential. When the Buddha asks him if either of the other two can be eliminated, Soṇadaṇḍa answers no, "for wisdom . . . is purified by morality; morality is purified by wisdom."[56] The Buddha then gives a long sermon that defines wisdom and morality in Buddhist terms. Thus, the overall effect of the dialog is to take a Brahmanical understanding of the word *Brahman* and redefine it in Buddhist terms, first by eliminating those characteristics deemed totally inessential (birth, knowledge of the Vedas, and appearance) and then by explicating the remaining two in terms proper to the *dharma* advanced in the early Buddhist texts.

While the *Soṇadaṇḍa Sutta* rather subtly navigates from a definition of Brahman that derives from the agenda of Neo-Brahmanism to an ethicized one based on Buddhist teachings, yet another encounter dialog, the *Vāseṭṭha Sutta* (*MN* 98=*Sn.* 3.9), presents the contrast between these two definitions in much more stark relief. This *sutta* begins with two Brahman students (*māṇava*) named Vāseṭṭha and Bhāradvāja debating over which of precisely these two definitions of the word *Brahman* is correct. Here the Neo-Brahmanical position, attributed to Bhāradvāja, is reduced to the single criterion of birth:

> If he is well-born on both sides, on his mother's and his father's, of pure descent up to the seventh generation of ancestors, undisturbed, blameless with respect to the matter of birth, then he is a Brahman.[57]

Vāseṭṭha, on the other hand, takes the position that morality defines the Brahman: "And if he is endowed with morality and endowed with vows, then he is a Brahman."[58] Neither being able to convince the other, they go to the Buddha to settle the dispute. The Buddha does so in an extended sermon in verse that places him firmly on the side of Vāseṭṭha. He begins by noting that while various species of plants and animals have marks (*liṅga*) to distinguish them from one another, human beings do not (v. 600–611). Then he lists a variety of occupations, from farmer to king, and states that each such person should be known by his occupation and not as a Brahman (v. 612–619). The obvious implication is that people who call themselves Brahmans often undertake occupations that are not proper to their *varṇa*. Therefore, the Buddha does not acknowledge Brahmanhood simply on the basis of birth (v. 620). With this, the Buddha launches into a 28-verse description (v. 620–647) of the qualities that *do* characterize a Brahman. The virtues extolled in each of these verses describe a person who has attained Awakening according to the generally accepted tenets of the early Buddhist texts—he is free of sensual pleasures, is endowed with wisdom, is non-violent, has put an end to rebirth, does not steal, is purified, is without possessions, has destroyed the *āsavas*, and is even explicitly called an *arhat*. Moreover, each of the verses follows a formula: They each end with the words *tam ahaṃ brūmi brāhmaṇaṃ* ("Him *I* call a Brahman")—with the emphatic nominative pronoun *ahaṃ* included, even though it is grammatically unnecessary, to emphasize the contrast between the Buddha's definition of a Brahman and the definition based on birth. The *sutta* ends with the Buddha summarizing his argument (v. 648–656) that designations based on birth are mere social conventions and that therefore one truly becomes a Brahman by action and not by birth.[59]

Aside from these three major discourses that present in explicit and extensive detail the contrast between the Brahman by birth and the Buddhist conception of the Brahman, casual references to the Brahman as an ideal are found scattered throughout various texts of the Pali Canon, usually in verses. Many of these verses are collected in the last *vagga* of the *Dhammapada* and the first *vagga* of the *Udāna*. While some of these cannot be unambiguously interpreted as contrasting a Buddhist conception of the Brahman to a Neo-Brahmanical conception of the Brahman,[60] at least one *Dhammapada* verse explicitly contrasts these two conceptions of the Brahman within the verse itself:

> Not by matted hair, not by *gotra*, not by birth does one become a Brahman.
> In whom there is truth and *dharma*, he is pure and he is a Brahman.[61]

Verses in the *Udāna* are given prose frame stories, and these frame stories often serve to make explicit a contrast between the Brahman by birth and the Buddhist conception of the Brahman found in the verse. Thus, for example, in *Ud.* 1.4, a Brahman of the "*huṃhuṅka* type" (*huṃhuṅkajātiko*)[62] approaches the Buddha and asks him what makes one a Brahman, and the Buddha answers with the following verse:

> He who is a Brahman, in the state of sin warded off,
> Not a huṃ-huṃ-er, without *āsavas*, self-controlled,
> Gone to the end of the Veda, having lived *brahmacariya*,
> Should rightly proclaim the *brahma*-doctrine,
> Who has no distinguishing qualities anywhere in the world.[63]

Likewise, in *Ud.* 1.9, the Buddha encounters a group of *jaṭilas* at Gayā performing water ablutions and fire offerings, and he comments on the scene in the following verse:

> One is not purified by water, (yet) many people bathe here.
> In whom there are truth and *dhamma*; he is pure and he is a
> Brahman.[64]

As we will see below, references to the word *Brahman* are often situated in a context that draws out an explicit contrast between a "literal" Brahman by birth and a Buddhist conception of the Brahman through the use of just such prose frame narratives.[65] What is important to note for the moment, though, is that there do exist texts within the Pali Canon that, either through extended narrative or through contextual framing, set up a clear contrast between the Brahman defined by birth and the Brahman defined by deeds, and to that extent therefore are well explained by a model of polemical "marketing."

What the marketing model fails to take account of, however, is the fact that the Pali Canon and other textual versions of the early Buddhist literature that have come down to us are not ordinary texts, written all at once at a particular time and place. Instead, they are textualizations of a living oral tradition made after that oral tradition had developed and been transmitted for many centuries. As we saw above, the early Buddhist oral tradition was not substantially textualized until at least the 1st century BCE, nearly 400 years after the death of the Buddha. This oral tradition may have been substantially complete and stable by the 2nd century BCE, but in the 3rd century CE, during the reign of Aśoka Maurya, even the early *sūtra* portion of this tradition was almost certainly still in the process of development. Since we have independent evidence of a conception of the Brahman and *śramaṇa* as oppositional from the Mauryan period, it is hardly surprising that an oral literature that was still in the process of formation at that time would include evidence of such a conception as well. The question is, does it also preserve evidence of an earlier conception of the relationship between the Brahman and the *śramaṇa*? And does it contain evidence of how the conception of the Brahman and the *śramaṇa* as mutually exclusive and opposed to one another came about?

## *Treating the Early Buddhist Oral Literature Diachronically*

Unfortunately, treating the early Buddhist oral literature diachronically, that is, as reflecting a long period of development that straddles the horizon of Indian history, is easier said than done. For our purposes, though, it is not necessary to establish a full theory of the development of the early Buddhist literature, which may in any case be impossible. Instead, we can focus specifically on finding evidence of the emergence of the conception of the *śramaṇa* and Brahman as opposed categories in the early Buddhist literature, armed with the knowledge that that literature developed over the period of time when the emergence of this concept likely occurred. One strategy we can use in doing this is to simply look for evidence of a non-oppositional conception of the *śramaṇa* and the Brahman in the early Buddhist literature, without worrying specifically about the relative antiquity or lateness of that evidence. After all, we should not expect the "snake and mongoose" conception of the Brahman and *śramaṇa* to have emerged and become universal all at once; therefore, the presence of a non-oppositional conception of their relationship in the early Buddhist literature at all will be telling. This is the approach we will take in Chapter 3, where we will find that the treatment of the Brahman and the *śramaṇa* as non-oppositional was far more common in Indian antiquity than is generally realized.

Still, given the centrality of the early Buddhist literature as a body of evidence and its precarious position straddling the horizon of Indian history, it will be useful to find some way to explore changes in that literature over time and the place of the conception of the *śramaṇa* and Brahman within those changes. For this purpose, I will be focusing on the *Aṭṭhaka* and *Pārāyaṇa*, which are preserved as the fourth and fifth *vaggas* of the

Pali *Sutta Nipāta*, respectively, and, in the case of the former, in a Chinese version as well. The reason for focusing on these two short collections of verses is that they are likely to be among the oldest Buddhist texts extant, and in any case older than the bulk of the *Sutta Piṭaka* as it has come down to us.

There are four major reasons to think that the *Aṭṭhaka* and *Pārāyaṇa* are of relative antiquity. First, A. K. Warder has argued on the basis of metrical analysis that the verses of the *Aṭṭhaka* and *Pārāyaṇa* are older than those found in other Pali texts.[66] Second, the *Aṭṭhaka* and *Pārāyaṇa* are commented upon by the *Niddesa*, a text that is itself sufficiently old to be considered canonical (unlike most Pali commentaries, which are post-canonical). Although the *Niddesa* is not strictly speaking the only "commentary" found within the canonical texts of the Pali tradition,[67] it is fairly unique as a self-contained, free-standing canonical text[68] that serves solely as a technical commentary on other canonical texts.[69] The third reason for believing in the antiquity of the *Aṭṭhaka* and *Pārāyaṇa* is closely related to the second: Both of these collections are referred to by name elsewhere.[70] In addition, as Norman has noted, while several *suttas* or portions thereof from the first three *vaggas* of the *Sutta Nipāta* are reproduced elsewhere in the Canon, none of the texts from the *Aṭṭhaka Vagga* (*Sn.* 4) or *Pārāyaṇa Vagga* (*Sn.* 5) are. "This would seem to imply," he argues, "that these two vaggas were regarded as a whole at the very earliest period of Buddhism, and had already been given a status of 'original and indivisible.' "[71] The fourth and final reason for regarding the *Aṭṭhaka* and *Pārāyaṇa* as particularly old is the unique ideas found within them that do not accord well with the standard doctrines found throughout the more "mainstream" texts of the Pali Canon (and corresponding Chinese Āgamas). The classic scholarly work addressing the unusual doctrines of the older texts of the *Sutta Nipāta* is Luis Gómez's 1976 article "Proto-Mādhyamika in the Pāli Canon,"[72] and more detailed analyses of the apparently pre-canonical doctrines of the *Aṭṭhaka* and *Pārāyaṇa* have been taken up by Tillmann Vetter,[73] Alexander Wynne,[74] and Grace Burford.[75]

None of these reasons taken in isolation is sufficient to unequivocally establish the antiquity of these two collections, but taken together, I believe that they make it difficult not to come to the conclusion that they are among the oldest Buddhist texts extant. Gombrich has noted rightly the remarkable consistency in the teachings found in the early Buddhist texts[76]—a consistency that extends to the Chinese Āgamas as much as to the texts of the Pali Canon—although *contra* Gombrich I would attribute this consistency to a normativizing tendency within whatever segment of the Buddhist *saṅgha* (possibly the Sthavira branch[77]) produced the "mainstream" texts of the Nikāyas/Āgamas, rather than the putative genius of the Buddha himself. Insofar as the *Aṭṭhaka* and *Pārāyaṇa* do not conform to this normativizing tendency, they were likely composed and accepted in much the same form as we have them today *before* those normative forces came into play.

For our purposes, though, it is not important that the *Aṭṭhaka* and *Pārāyaṇa* are literally *the* oldest Buddhist texts extant, nor exactly how they were formed. Ultimately, what is important for our purposes is that the *Aṭṭhaka* and *Pārāyaṇa* are relatively old and have been preserved in a relatively archaic state up to the present. In addition, the fact that they were commented upon, and narratively framed, during the time when the early Buddhist oral tradition was developing gives us the opportunity to observe changes in early Buddhist thinking about the relationship between the categories *śramaṇa* and "Brahman" within a secure diachronic framework. Burford's method of comparing the verses of the *Aṭṭhaka* to later commentaries upon them, both in the *Niddesa* and in the post-canonical commentary,[78] provides a useful model for performing a diachronic analysis of themes in the early Buddhist oral tradition. The early Buddhist oral tradition as a whole may resist detailed diachronic analysis because the written artifacts of it that come down to us reflect hundreds of years of development in the oral tradition, with few clues as to what is early or late. But with the *Aṭṭhaka* and *Pārāyaṇa*, we have the equivalent of archaeological test holes—two likely old texts that can be compared to two layers of commentarial tradition, providing clearly demarcated diachronic strata that can be used in the analysis of any particular theme found within them, including the conception of the relationship between the *śramaṇa* and the Brahman.[79]

## *Conclusion*

In this chapter, we have explored the historical issues involved in, and evidence available for, tracing the emergence of the "snake and mongoose" in Indian antiquity. Early Indian texts are notoriously difficult to date, and as a result the earliest firmly datable historical documents on India are Greek writings dating from Alexander's invasion in 326 BCE and the inscriptions of Aśoka that followed shortly thereafter in the 3rd century BCE. I have therefore referred to the Mauryan period, which began almost immediately after the invasion of Alexander, as the horizon of Indian history, beyond which it is difficult to see due to a lack of firmly datable evidence. As I have shown, there is evidence that a conception of the *śramaṇa* and Brahman as mutually opposed already existed at this horizon of Indian history. This evidence has been used by modern scholars to construct the model of Buddhism and Jainism as having arisen in the context of a fundamental conflict between two opposed groups, the *śramaṇas* and the Brahmans. But this model simply projects the situation in late-4th and 3rd-century BCE North India, which was the *product*, in part, of the rise Buddhism, Jainism, and related *śramaṇa* movements, onto what must have been the very different, pre-imperial situation of the 5th century, when these movements likely arose.

In order to trace the emergence of the "snake and mongoose," we must find some way to peer beyond the horizon of Indian history at the beginning of the Mauryan period. Crucial in this task is the early Buddhist oral literature, which, given the near total lack of mention of *śramaṇas* in the Vedic literature, is our oldest evidence for conceptions of the relationship between *śramaṇas* and Brahmans in ancient India. Unfortunately, situating this evidence historically is made difficult by the fact that it was originally an oral literature that developed over a period of centuries. Moreover, that development most likely straddled the horizon of Indian history in the Mauryan period. That is, while the early Buddhist oral tradition had nearly 100 years to develop from the death of the Buddha to the foundation of the Mauryan empire and thus provides a means to peer beyond the horizon of Indian history, it is likely that it was still in the course of development during the reign of Aśoka. Thus, in the written forms in which it comes down to us, it also reflects the later imperial context.

As I have shown in this chapter, the early Buddhist literature in places reflects an oppositional conception of the *śramaṇa* and the Brahman, completely consonant with the conception of their relationship in sources firmly datable to the Mauryan period and later. One way to see if the early Buddhist literature preserves evidence for the emergence of this oppositional conception prior to the Mauryan period is to simply look for evidence of non-oppositional conceptions of the relationship between the Brahman and the *śramaṇa*. This is the approach we will take in the next chapter. Indeed, we will find that such evidence is abundant—even more abundant, in fact, than the evidence for an oppositional conception of their relationship. I will show that, even when including known later evidence like the inscriptions of Aśoka, the vast majority of references to the *śramaṇa* and Brahman in ancient Indian literature do not portray them as mutually exclusive, opposed categories.

Ultimately, however, this approach is not fully satisfying because it does not allow for a diachronic analysis of the evidence. Although mapping the early Buddhist oral literature diachronically is fraught with difficulties, I have argued that two texts, the *Aṭṭhaka* and *Pārāyaṇa*, can play a key role in a diachronic analysis of the conception of the relationship between the categories *śramaṇa* and "Brahman." The reason for this is that these two texts appear to have been composed and taken on a relatively stable form relatively early in the Buddhist tradition. In Chapter 4, I will therefore examine their use of the word *Brahman* and argue that it differs in a significant way from the use of the polemical use of that word in the early Buddhist literature at large. In addition, due to their early composition, the *Aṭṭhaka* and *Pārāyaṇa* have been subjected to early commentary in the *Niddesa* and implicit commentary through narrative framing, in addition to the ordinary commentary found in the post-canonical literature. This affords us a unique opportunity, which I will pursue in Chapter 6, to examine, through well-defined strata in the tradition, the way in which the conception of the relationship between the categories *śramaṇa* and Brahman changed over time.

In this chapter, I have focused on discussing the early Buddhist literature because of its unique ability to offer us a window into the emergence of the "snake and mongoose" prior to the horizon of Indian history in the Mauryan period. Jain literature is less useful in this regard because even the earliest Jain literature is generally understood to be somewhat later than the earliest Buddhist literature. Nevertheless, I will make some reference to the earliest Jain literature when it provides useful supporting evidence. In particular, the first book of the *Āyāraṅga Sutta* and the first book of the *Sūyaḍaṃga Sutta* are most likely the very oldest Jain texts extant,[80] and they bear remarkable similarities to the Buddhist *Aṭṭhaka* and *Pārāyaṇa* in their treatment of the category *Brahman*, which I will have occasion to refer to, especially in Chapter 4. In addition, in spite of almost completely ignoring the category *śramaṇa*, Brahmanical texts are central to my argument about how the conception of the Brahman and *śramaṇa* as mutually exclusive, opposed categories arose. In particular, I will be making use of the Dharma Sūtras, post-Vedic texts that were likely composed from the late 3rd century BCE to the 1st century BCE.[81] These will be discussed in detail in Chapter 5, in which I argue that they were articulations of a novel, anti-*śramaṇ*ic conception of Brahmanhood that was so successful, it led to the abandonment of the category *Brahman* by *śramaṇa*s and thus the bifurcation between the categories *śramaṇa* and Brahman.

# 3

# *Taming the Snake and the Mongoose of Indian History*

IN THE PREVIOUS chapter, we saw that "the snake and the mongoose" of Indian history—the conception of the Brahman and the *śramaṇa* as mutually exclusive and antagonistic categories—can be dated fairly reliably to the beginning of the Mauryan dynasty in the late 4th millennium BCE. This is nearly a century after the death of the Buddha, which, even with the tendency of recent scholarship to prefer a later rather than an earlier date, probably occurred no later than about 400 BCE. This of course does not mean that the categories of *Brahman* and *śramaṇa* could not have been understood as antagonistic to one another prior to the accession of Candragupta Maurya, but it does mean that there is no a priori reason why antagonism between Brahmans and *śramaṇas* should be accepted as a preexisting context for the rise of Buddhism and Jainism. On the contrary, we must assume that the conception of Brahmans and *śramaṇas* as separate and mutually antagonistic groups developed over time prior to the founding of the Mauryan dynasty. Moreover, given that the Buddhists and the Jains were the most successful of what came to be known as "the *śramaṇas*," it seems quite likely that they played an important role in the contestation that led to the rise of "the snake and the mongoose," and that that contestation would be preserved in their earliest texts.

In addition, as we saw, there is reason to believe that much of what we find in the early Buddhist *sūtras* represents an imperial context fairly removed from the time of the Buddha. Ultimately, we will want to perform a diachronic analysis that shows how the conception of the relationship between the *śramaṇa* and the Brahman changed over time.

This task will be saved for later in this book. In this chapter, we will begin with a simpler task. The early Buddhist *sūtras*, which were not written all at once but rather composed and passed down orally over the course of many centuries, presumably do preserve elements that date to an earlier time than any of our reliably datable written sources (i.e., the Greek sources and inscriptions of Aśoka cited previously). Thus, it is worthwhile to simply look at them in the form they come down to us and ask if they (or, for the sake of comparison, the earliest Jain texts) preserve any evidence of the process that led to the concept of the Brahman and the *śramaṇa* as being opposed to one another like the snake and the mongoose. In other words, do these texts, which by their oral nature allow us to peer over the horizon of Indian history, preserve uses of the categories of *Brahman* and *śramaṇa* that do not imply mutual exclusivity or antagonism?

We will find not only that the early Buddhist and Jain texts preserve such non-oppositional references to the Brahman and the *śramaṇa*, but that the overwhelming majority of references to these two categories as a paired couple in early Indian literature—including the amorphously oral early Buddhist and Jain texts, but also the securely datable written inscriptions of Aśoka—do not imply mutual exclusivity or antagonism at all. As we saw in the last chapter, much has been made of the fact that the 2nd-century BCE grammarian Patañjali gave *śramaṇa-brāhmaṇa* ("*śramaṇa*s and Brahmans") as an example of an "oppositional compound." Therefore, we will begin by looking at the way these two words are actually used in compound with one another in the Buddhist, Jain, and Aśokan texts, and find that they do not even follow Pāṇini's rule. Then, we will turn to the way in which the compound *śramaṇa-brāhmaṇa* is used rhetorically in the same texts and find that it is used in two ways, both of which treat it as effectively a single category. First, "*śramaṇa*s and Brahmans" is used in early Buddhist and Jain texts as a unified "other" against which to construct one's own identity. Second, it is used in early Buddhist texts and the inscriptions of Aśoka to refer to a uniform class of individuals who are worthy of receiving gifts from ordinary householders. Finally, given this overwhelming evidence for a conception of *śramaṇa*s and Brahmans that is not antagonistic and perhaps not even mutually exclusive, I will ask where the concept of the "*śramaṇa*s and Brahmans" came from in the first place, if not from a metahistorical opposition between two mutually exclusive groups. This will lay the groundwork for our further investigations in the rest of the book.

## *Snake–Mongoose: The Grammar of an Opposition*

As discussed in the Introduction, modern scholars have often cited the 2nd-century BCE Sanskrit grammarian Patañjali as demonstrating, through an obscure grammatical rule, that *śramaṇas* and Brahmans were considered to be antagonistic groups in ancient India. Some have also claimed that Patañjali compared the "*śramaṇa* and the Brahman" to the "snake and the mongoose," but as we saw, this is incorrect. The use of the example "snake and mongoose" is actually found in the much later (7th century CE) *Kāśikāvṛttī* by the Jain grammarians Jayāditya and Vāmana, which, like Patañjali's *Mahābhāṣya*, is also a commentary on the classic work of Sanskrit grammar, Pāṇini's *Aṣṭādhyāyī* (ca. 4th c. BCE). Even if the dramatic comparison to the snake and mongoose does not date to the 2nd century BCE, however, Patañjali's implicit assertion that the *śramaṇa* and the Brahman are characterized by "constant strife" does. It therefore behooves us to look more closely at the context in which Patañjali makes this statement. This of course entails first understanding the grammatical rule for which Patañjali gives "*śramaṇas* and Brahmans" as an example. Then, we will go a step further and ask a question that almost seems too obvious to ask: Did anybody in the real world actually follow this rule when talking about *śramaṇas* and Brahmans?

The grammatical rule for which the Jain grammarians Jayāditya and Vāmana gave "snake and mongoose" (*ahi-nakula*) and Patañjali much earlier gave "*śramaṇa* and Brahman" (*śramaṇa-brāhmaṇa*) as examples is rule 2.4.9 of Pāṇini's *Aṣṭādhyāyī*: "And between whom there is constant strife" (*yeṣāṃ ca virodhaḥ śāśvatikaḥ*). Given the pithy aphoristic style of the *Aṣṭādhyāyī* as a member of the *sūtra* genre, this rule is to be read as an elaboration on rules above it. The context provided by these preceding rules shows that this particular rule is to be understood as referring to a specific class of *dvandva* compounds. A *dvandva* compound in Sanskrit is a sort of compound not generally found in English in which a pair of two words are simply linked together instead of using a conjunction; a somewhat similar example in English (but still retaining the conjunction) is the proverbial game of *cat-and-mouse*. In the context of this particular rule, the types of *dvandva* compounds being enumerated are all to be inflected in the singular grammatical number, in spite of being dual in meaning. Indeed, Patañjali spells this out in his commentary on the rule, saying, "Those between whom there is constant strife take the singular number in a *dvandva*" (*yeṣām ca virodhaḥ śāśvatikaḥ teṣām dvandve ekavacanam*). Although he does not give the specific example "snake and mongoose," he does give a couple of other animal examples: the crow and the owl (*kākolūkam*) and the dog and the jackal (*śva-sṛgālam*).[1]

Remarkably, in spite of their proclivity for citing Patañjali's listing of *śramaṇa-brāhmaṇa* as an example of this rule, scholars have failed to notice that in the actual use of this compound in the literature, the rule is never followed. Indeed, I have not come across a single example of *śramaṇa-brāhmaṇa* inflected in the singular in my perusal of the early Buddhist and Jain *sūtras* and the inscriptions of Aśoka. Even if an example of the compound in the singular exists somewhere, it is clear that in the overwhelming abundance of cases, the compound is inflected in the plural (*śramaṇa-brāhmaṇāḥ* according to Sanskritic spelling conventions).

If the compound *śramaṇa-brāhmaṇa* as it is used in actual practice does not follow Pāṇini's rule for oppositional *dvandva* compounds as Patañjali says it does, then what does it actually mean? Is it even a *dvandva* compound at all? One could hypothetically, as Bailey and Mabbett have suggested,[2] interpret it as a *karmadhāraya* compound, that is, a compound in which the first element is an adjective describing the second. According to this interpretation, the compound would mean "a Brahman who strives" (since the word *śramaṇa* literally means "striving"), rather than "*śramaṇas* and Brahmans."

In some cases, the context is ambiguous, and the compound could potentially be read grammatically in this way. When, for example, early Buddhist texts refer in Pali to *eke samaṇa-brāhmaṇā* and an early Jain text refers in the corresponding Ardhamāgadhī to *ege samaṇa-māhaṇā* (*Sūy.* 1.1.1.6), this could be read as either "some *śramaṇas* and Brahmans" or "some striving Brahmans." A couple of other examples from the same Jain text seem to support the latter interpretation. At *Sūy.* 1.1.2.14 and 1.1.3.8, references to "*māhaṇā samaṇā ege*" appears, given the absence of any conjunction, to refer to "some Brahmans" who are described by an adjective *samaṇā* ("striving").

Overall, however, most contexts support the interpretation of *śramaṇa-brāhmaṇa* as a *dvandva* compound, referring grammatically to two groups of people. The Aśokan inscriptions, for example, show a preference for the compound *brāhmaṇa-śramaṇa* (spelled variously according to the local Prakrit), with *brāhmaṇa* listed first. Since *brāhmaṇa* cannot conceivably be understood as an adjective describing *śramaṇa*, this compound is most plausibly interpreted as a *dvandva*.[3] Likewise, the early Jain texts show a rather unsystematic pattern of splitting up *samaṇa-māhaṇā* into its constituent components, but in various ways often use conjunctions to join them as two parallel categories: "*samaṇā ya māhaṇā ya*" (*Āy.* 1.4.2.3), "*māhaṇaṃ va samaṇaṃ vā*" (*Āy.* 1.8.4.11), "*samaṇā māhaṇā ya*" (*Sūy.* 1.6.1, 1.12.11). Given this lack of systematicity, the examples given above where no conjunction is used may simply be idiosyncratic.

The early Buddhist texts, on the other hand, are quite systematic in their treatment of the words *samaṇa* and *brāhmaṇa*, and taken together they point conclusively to the interpretation of *samaṇa-brāhmaṇā* as a *dvandva*, referring to two groups of people. The general rule appears to be that when the two elements *samaṇa* and *brāhmaṇa* are joined conjunctively ("and"), they are given in compound, but when they are joined disjunctively ("or"), they are split up and joined by the conjunction *vā*. In addition, these conjunctive and disjunctive combinations of the two categories correspond to the plural and the singular, respectively.

An example from the first *sutta* in the Canon, the *Brahmajāla Sutta* (*DN* 1), will suffice to illustrate. This *sutta* consists primarily of an enumeration of wrong practices and views, which are ascribed to "some *samaṇas* and Brahmans" (*eke samaṇa-brāhmaṇā*). Generally speaking, these wrong practices and views are ascribed to other ascetics and Brahmans in precisely this way, that is, conjunctively and in the plural, but sometimes a more detailed enumeration of views is given, and then there is a switch to the disjunctive, singular usage. Thus, at a certain point the Buddha states, "There are, monks, some *samaṇas* and Brahmans who are eternalists, who declare in four ways the self and the world to be eternal" (*santi, bhikkhave, eke samaṇabrāhmaṇā sassatavādā, sassataṃ attānañca lokañca paññapenti catūhi vatthūhi*). In enumerating each of these "four ways," however, the Buddha begins with the stock phrase, "Here, monks, a certain *samaṇa* or Brahman . . . " (*idha, bhikkhave, ekacco samaṇo vā brāhmaṇo vā . . .* ). There thus is a rhetorical shift from thinking about a group of people who share a certain type of wrong view, broadly construed, to thinking about a particular individual within that group who holds a particular wrong view within the broader category. Given that, grammatically, the shift from plural to singular is accompanied by a shift from the conjunctive to the disjunctive in relating the two categories *samaṇa* and *brāhmaṇa* to one another, we can see that, at least on the grammatical level, these two categories are understood to be categories of individuals that are treated together as an aggregate but that apply in some way separately to a particular individual.

None of the early texts, Buddhist, Jain, or epigraphic, follows Pāṇini's rule for "oppositional compounds" when talking about "*śramaṇas* and Brahmans," as Patañjali's commentary suggests one should. This opens up the question of what the compound *śramaṇa-brāhmaṇa* actually meant in ordinary usage—that is, whether it referred to two groups of people at all. Although in some contexts the meaning is ambiguous, in most cases the compound must be treated, grammatically at least, as a *dvandva* joining two categories. In other words, the early texts of the Buddhists and Jains, as well as the inscriptions of Aśoka, do refer to two groups of people, *śramaṇas* and Brahmans, and when read in light of the evidence dating from the imperial period, it seems reasonable to interpret these as separate and opposed groups. When we stop reading them through the lens of this later evidence as we are attempting to do here, however, we must ask what exactly the relationship between the two categories is. In terms of a Venn diagram, are we talking about two completely separate circles? Or are the two circles overlapping, concentric, or even coterminous?

In order to answer this question, we need to move beyond technical issues of grammar and look at the way in which the compound *śramaṇa-brāhmaṇa* is used rhetorically in early Indian texts. What we find is that, in early Jain and Buddhist texts as well as the inscriptions of Aśoka, it is treated as a *single* category with absolutely no meaningful reference to a distinction between *śramaṇas* and Brahmans. As such, the compound is used in two ways. First, as we will see in the next section, it is used in early Buddhist and Jain texts as a uniform "other" against which to construct Buddhist or Jain identity, respectively. Second, as we will examine in the section following, it is used in early Buddhist texts and the inscriptions of Aśoka to refer to a unified class of individuals who are "worthy," in particular of receiving gifts from ordinary householders. These two uses clearly point to a Venn diagram in which the two circles have significant overlap.

## *Teachings on Wrong Views:* "Śramaṇas *and Brahmans" as a Unified "Other"*

Numerous scholars have pointed to teachings within the early Buddhist texts that appear to be a response to or argument against specific teachings found in Brahmanical texts.[4] Central among these is the teaching of "not-self" (*anattā*), which Norman and Gombrich, among others, have argued was directed against the teaching about the self, or *ātman*, found in the early Upaniṣads.[5] According to this argument the Brahmanical tradition, through philosophical speculations that found their culmination in the latest Vedic texts, the Upaniṣads, developed the concept of a permanent, unchanging "self" (referred to in Sanskrit, awkwardly as in the English translation, using the reflexive pronoun *ātman*) that is the real being behind all human individuals. This *ātman*, because it is eternal, survives the death of the body and takes on a new body; this is the basis of the concept of reincarnation. The Buddha, while accepting that living beings reincarnate when they die, rejected this "Upaniṣadic" explanation of reincarnation as having no basis in experience. That is, we, as individual subjects, have no empirical evidence of a permanent, unchanging, and blissful self, but only of five "aggregates" (Pali: *khandhas*) of form, feelings, perceptions, volitions, and consciousness, which are impermanent, painful, and beyond our complete control. For this reason, according to the Buddha, they can only be considered "not-self" (Pali: *anattā*; Skt.: *anātman*). This became an incredibly important doctrine in Buddhism and, according to this explanation, its origins lay in a specific polemic against a preexisting Brahmanical doctrine of the *ātman*.

This narrative has been vociferously questioned, however, by Johannes Bronkhorst, who instead argues that the teaching of the *ātman* was native to the "Greater Magadha" area in which Buddhism and Jainism arose, and that Brahmans, who came from the West, only later incorporated into their Upaniṣads when they encountered this Eastern culture.[6] In other words, when the early Buddhist texts talk about *anattā*, they are not engaging with Brahmans at all; instead, they are engaging with a local "Eastern" concept of a permanent, transmigrating *ātman* that was originally foreign to the religion of the Brahmans, who came from the West. The concept of reincarnation and the *ātman* was adopted by Brahmans as they moved East, but only slowly and hesitantly, eventually becoming a central concept within popular Hinduism. According to this narrative, then, the concept of *ātman* that the Buddha argued against is best represented not by the Brahmanical Upaniṣads, which were only borrowing the concept, but by the Jains, who, like the Buddhists, came from Greater Magadha but, unlike the Buddhists, accepted the concept of the *ātman*.

Many scholars have questioned Bronkhorst's overall "Greater Magadha" thesis,[7] and I myself argue that it, like the narrative it critiques, is predicated on a problematic dichotomy between "Brahmanical" and "non-Brahmanical." Nevertheless, Bronkhorst's thesis is based in part on an astute and undeniable observation about the treatment of Brahmans on the one hand, and philosophical debates on the other, in the early Buddhist texts. That is, as a general rule, the early Buddhist literature portrays the Buddha engaging in debate with interlocutors called "Brahmans" only when arguing against the tenets of what Bronkhorst calls the "new Brahmanism" (and what I call Neo-Brahmanism)—that is, householder supremacy, the *varṇa* system, and the value of Vedic ritual. When engaging in debate about the nature of the self and other philosophical issues, the interlocutor, when there is one, is not identified as a Brahman, and opposing viewpoints are not ascribed to Brahmans.[8] For the sake of clarity, I will refer to these two different types of Buddhist *sūtras* as belonging to different "genres," which I refer to as "encounter dialogs" and "teachings on wrong views" respectively.

While encounter dialogs, whose significance we will discuss in a later chapter, define the Buddha as a *samaṇa* and his interlocutor as a *brāhmaṇa*, the use of the compound *samaṇa-brāhmaṇa* is mostly restricted to a different class of *suttas* in which the Buddha discusses wrong views and practices. These *suttas* may or may not consist of a dialog between the Buddha and an interlocutor, and when they do involve an interlocutor, more often than not that interlocutor is identified as a *paribbājaka* ("wanderer") rather than as a Brahman.[9] In these *suttas*, which I will refer to as "teachings on wrong views," the compound *samaṇa-brāhmaṇa* is used in the plural to refer to a whole class of individuals against whom as an aggregate the author of the *sutta*, using the voice of the Buddha, seeks to construct a Buddhist identity. This is as true in *suttas* such as the *Brahmajāla Sutta*, in which the compound *samaṇa-brāhmaṇā* is sometimes split up into the disjunctive *samaṇo vā brāhmaṇo vā* for use in the singular, as it is in other *suttas* in which we find only the compound. That is, regardless of whether the compound is technically a *dvandva* or nominally refers to two separate groups of individuals, the compound is used rhetorically to refer to a single class of individuals against which the Buddha, as a literary character, seeks to define himself. What matters is not the distinction between *samaṇas* and *brāhmaṇas*, much less to which category the Buddha and his followers belong, but rather the distinction between the Buddha and his followers on the one hand, and the whole lot of *samaṇa-brāhmaṇā* on the other.[10]

The extent to which the distinction between *samaṇa* and *brāhmaṇa* often does not matter in the use of the compound *samaṇa-brāhmaṇa* in the Pali Canon can be seen in the *Saṅgārava Sutta* (*MN* 100), in which the Buddha speaks to a Brahman student (*māṇavo*) named Caṇḍalakappa, who is incredulous about the faith of a certain Brahman woman (*brāhmaṇī*) in such a "shaveling ascetic" (*muṇḍaka samaṇaka*).[11] When Caṇḍalakappa meets the Buddha, he says,

> There are, O Gotama, some *samaṇa-brāhmaṇā* who promise the fundamental *brahmacariya* having attained accomplishment and perfection of super-knowledge in this world. So which, O Gotama, of those *samaṇa-brāhmaṇā* who promise the fundamental *brahmacariya* having attained accomplishment and perfection of super-knowledge in this world is the Venerable Gotama?"[12]

Caṇḍalakappa is asking the Buddha where he places himself within the broad category of *śramaṇas* and Brahmans who claim (to put it more simply) to have attained enlightenment.

Now, this would be a perfect opportunity for the Buddha to self-identify as a *samaṇa,* even if just cursorily to say, "I am a *samaṇa* who has actually attained enlightenment in this very life." But this is not what the Buddha does. Instead, he begins by dividing "*samaṇas* and Brahmans" into three groups whose distinction effectively ignores the distinction between *samaṇas* and Brahmans. The first group are "traditionalists. They, having attained accomplishment and perfection of super-knowledge in this world by means of tradition, promise the fundamental *brahmacariya*—just like the *tevijja* Brahmans."[13] The second group are those who, "having attained accomplishment and perfection of super-knowledge in this world only by mere faith, promise the fundamental *brahmacariya*—just like the logicians and investigators."[14] The third group are those who, "having attained accomplishment and perfection of super-knowledge in this world by the super-knowledge, completely by themselves, of a *dhamma* among *dhammas* that were not passed down traditionally in the past, promise the fundamental *brahmacariya*."[15] The Buddha then identifies himself, as we would expect, as a member of the third group, as someone who has *actually* attained enlightenment through super-knowledge rather than one who teaches about it merely on the basis of faith or oral tradition.

What is interesting here is that each group is invariantly referred to as "some *samaṇas* and Brahmans" (*eke samaṇa-brāhmaṇā*). This includes the first group, which we find out at the end of the description, actually refers to "Brahmans of the Triple Veda" (*brāhmaṇā tevijjā*).[16] In other words, even those whom we would refer to as "the" Brahmans are referred to as "some *samaṇas* and Brahmans," and even though they are identified specifically as Brahmans, the Buddha feels it necessary to add the adjective *tevijja* ("of the Triple Veda") to make clear what group of "Brahmans" he is talking about. Even more interestingly, however, the Buddha fails to identify *himself* as either a *samaṇa* or a Brahman; instead, he says,

> Now, Bhāradvāja, I am among those *samaṇa-brāhmaṇā* who, having attained accomplishment and perfection of super-knowledge in this world by the super-knowledge, completely by themselves, of a *dhamma* among *dhammas* that were not passed down traditionally in the past, promise the fundamental *brahmacariya*."[17]

Thereupon he recounts the story of how he left home and attained enlightenment.[18] Thus, the Buddha ultimately answers Caṇḍalakappa's question regarding his place within those *samaṇas* and Brahmans who teach about enlightenment not by identifying himself, even implicitly, as a *samaṇa*, but simply by saying that he is one of those *samaṇas* and Brahmans who have actually attained enlightenment.

A closely related example of how the compound *samaṇa-brāhmaṇā* is used in such a way that the presumable distinction between the two elements of the compound is effectively ignored is the treatment of what are often called in English the "six heretical teachers." Although often the early *sūtras* use "*samaṇas* and Brahmans" in the abstract as a foil against which to construct a Buddhist identity, sometimes these six non-Buddhist teachers appear, together and more or less as stock characters, to personalize the "other" against which Buddhist identity is constructed. The most detailed explanation of the doctrines of these six teachers is given in the *Sāmaññaphala Sutta* (*DN* 2), in which King Ajātasattu of Magadha goes to the Buddha and recounts to him conversations he had had previously with the six teachers. Of the six, two are easily identifiable from the Jain scriptures: Nigaṇṭha Nātaputta is Mahāvīra, revered by Jains as the last Tīrthaṅkara, and Makkhali Gosāla is a student of Mahāvīra who parted ways with him over the issue of burning off existing karma and became a leader of the Ājīvikas.[19] Pūraṇa Kassapa, who in the *Sāmaññaphala Sutta* is presented as teaching a doctrine of non-action (i.e., that there are no karmic results of good or bad actions), also appears to have been associated with the Ājīvikas. He is said to be "chief of five hundred Ājīvikas" (*pañcamātrāṇām ājīvikaśatānām pramukhaḥ*) in the *Saṅghabhedavastu* of the Mūlasarvāstivādins,[20] and is mentioned by name in a Tamil text as having been held in high esteem by the Ājīvikas.[21] Ajita Kesakambalī teaches a doctrine of materialism, which, like that of Pūraṇa Kassapa, denies the efficacy of karma but explains the non-efficacy of karma in terms of the breakup of the body (and thus the final end of the human individual) into its constituent elements at death.[22] Pakudha Kaccāyana also appears to deny the efficacy of karma, but does so on the basis of a theory of atomism; Basham argues that this theory "follows logically from Makkhali [Gosāla]'s determinism" and notes that it forms part of the teaching of the Ājīvikas as described in Tamil texts.[23] Finally, Sañjaya Belaṭṭhaputta refuses to commit to any position on questions of controversy, in words that elsewhere (*DN* 1) are attributed to the "eel-wrigglers" (*amarāvikkhepikā*).[24]

What is important to note about these six "heretical" teachers is that none of them appears to be a "Brahman" according to a dichotomous understanding of Brahman versus non-Brahman. That is, none is a person born into a specific lineage who promotes the Brahmanical ideology of *varṇa,* sacrifice, and Vedic knowledge, as do the Brahmanical interlocutors found in encounter dialogs. Indeed, two of them (Nigaṇṭha Nātaputta and Makkhali Gosāla) are well-known leaders of the "non-Brahmanical," śramaṇ*ic* Jain and Ājīvika sects; Pūraṇa Kassapa appears to have also been a leader of the Ājīvikas; Pakudha Kaccāyana's teaching of atomism appears to be associated with the Ājīvikas; Ajita Kesakambalī's teaching of non-action explicitly rejects the efficacy of sacrifice; and Sañjaya Belaṭṭhaputta's skepticism has no apparent connection to the ideology of the householder Brahmans, or any other ideology for that matter. What we appear to have here is six rivals to the Buddha exclusively from within the *śramaṇa* movement. But this is not how they are presented in the early Buddhist texts. In the *Sāmaññaphala Sutta,* King Ajātasattu describes his previous encounters with the six heretics after he poses a question to the Buddha and is asked by the latter in return, "Do you admit, Great King, that you have asked other *samaṇa*s and Brahmans this question?"[25] In four other *sutta*s spread throughout the Canon (*DN* 16, *MN* 30, *SN* 1.3.1.1, *Sn.* 3.6),[26] the six heretics are introduced using a stock formula that identifies them, again, not specifically as *samaṇa*s but as *samaṇa-brāhmaṇā*:

> O Gotama, these *samaṇa-brāhmaṇā* have *saṅgha*s, have *gaṇa*s, are teachers of *gaṇa*s, are known, famous ford-makers, highly respected by many people—namely, Pūraṇa Kassapa, Makkhali Gosāla, Ajita Kesakambala, Pakudha Kaccāyana, Sañcaya Belaṭṭhaputta, Nigaṇṭha Nāṭaputta.[27]

The six heretics, therefore, represent a clear example of how the compound *samaṇa-brāhmaṇā* can be used in such a way that, not only does the distinction between *samaṇa* and *brāhmaṇa* not matter, but only one of the two categories (when understood as distinct) appears to be present at all.

The depiction of the "six heretical teachers" in the *Sāmaññaphala Sutta* can fruitfully be compared to an early Jain text that, in parallel to the Buddhist texts, seeks to define Jain identity against various non-Jain teachings. The first "lecture" (*samayajjhayaṇe*) of the *Sūyagaḍaṃga* consists of an enumeration of various wrong teachings, framed by the correct teaching that one must not kill under any circumstances. In format and structure, it is somewhat different from the *Sāmaññaphala Sutta*. It is not given in a narrative format, does not attribute the wrong teachings it discusses to specific named teachers, and in general is less systematic in its written structure than the corresponding Buddhist text. Nevertheless, it does fulfill the same narrative function of defining a "correct" teaching (in this case, the total eschewing of all killing) by contrasting it to various "wrong" teachings.

The *Sūyagaḍaṃga* is a less clearly structured text than the *Sāmaññaphala Sutta* and it is therefore difficult in some cases to determine where one "wrong teaching" ends and another begins. Nevertheless, it is clear that some of these wrong teachings are similar if not identical to wrong teachings enumerated in the *Sāmaññaphala Sutta*. We find references to materialists who reduce the entire universe to five (1.1.1.7–10) or four (1.1.1.18) elements, annihilationists who declare that the self (*āyā*) is destroyed at death (1.1.1.11–14), eternalists who declare that all is eternal (1.1.1.15–16), and fatalists who declare that pleasure and pain are determined solely according to fate (1.1.2.1–3). The text also appears to refer to Buddhists in a criticism of those who preach a doctrine of five *skandhas* (1.1.1.17: *pañca khandhe*) and the "view of the *kriyāvādins*" (*kiriyāvāidarisaṇaṃ*) who contend that intention be taken into account in determining the sinfulness of an act. And lastly, it criticizes teachings that we now associate with Brahmanism: the creation of the world by gods or Brahmā (1.1.3.5: *devautte ayaṃ loe, bambhautte i āvaṛe*), by Īśvara (1.1.3.6: *īsareṇa kaḍe loe*), by Svayambhū (1.1.3.7: *sayaṃbhuṇā kaḍe loe*), or from an egg (1.1.3.8: *aṇḍakaḍe*).

The *Sūyagaḍaṃga* makes even less of an effort to clearly attribute the wrong teachings it criticizes to specific groups than does the *Sāmaññaphala Sutta*. In most cases, it simply attributes them to "some" (*ege*). When it does elaborate on who these people are with more specific social categories, it does so by referring either to "some *samaṇas* and

Brahmans" (1.1.1.6: *ege samaṇamāhaṇā*; 1.1.2.14, 1.1.3.8: *māhaṇā samaṇā ege*)[28] or simply to *samaṇas* (1.1.2.10, 32; 1.1.3.2). These two phrasings appear to be used interchangeably, and in any case there is absolutely no attempt to distinguish between *samaṇas* and Brahmans. In fact, in the section that refers to what we in retrospect might call "Brahmanical" doctrines of creation of the world by a god or cosmic egg, the phrase used is "some *samaṇas* and Brahmans" (or "some striving Brahmans": 1.1.3.8, *māhaṇā samaṇā ege*). The Jain *Sūyagaḍaṃga*, therefore, like the *Sāmaññaphala Sutta* and other early Buddhist texts, uses the categories of *śramaṇa* and Brahman together as an amorphous body of "others" against which to construct its own identity.

## "Śramaṇas *and Brahmans" as Undifferentiated Worthy Recipients*

So far we have been looking at uses of the compound *śramaṇa-brāhmaṇā* in a negative sense, as a negatively portrayed "other" against which to construct one's own identity. This, as already noted, is by far the most common way in which the compound is used in the early Buddhist and Jain *sūtras*. There is also, however, in the Buddhist texts a subset of cases in which the compound is used in a positive sense to refer to a class of persons who are worthy of honor, praise, and in particular gifts (*dāna*). As we will see, this positive use of *śramaṇa-brāhmaṇā*, like the negative, refers to *śramaṇas* and Brahmans as a single class and essentially ignores any distinction between them.

One way in which the compound is used in a positive sense is to refer to the "fact" (in the eyes of the authors of the early Buddhist texts) that some people have indeed attained enlightenment and thus put an end to the cycle of rebirth. Possibly the earliest example of this is found in one of the earliest Buddhist texts to have come down to us, the *Pārāyaṇa Vagga* of the *Sutta Nipāta*. This text consists of a series of short dialogs between the Buddha and various interlocutors; in one of these dialogs, a certain Nanda asks the Buddha about "*samaṇas* and Brahmans" who "say purity is by means of what is seen or heard, say purity is by means of morality and vows, say purity is by means of various (things)."[29] The Buddha responds by criticizing such *samaṇa-brāhmaṇāse*,[30] saying that they "have not crossed over birth and old age."[31] If it ended here, this would simply be another example of the use of the compound *samaṇa-brāhmaṇā(se)* as a foil against which to construct Buddhist identity, but the Buddha qualifies his answer by saying, "Not all *samaṇa-brāhmaṇāse* do I say are enveloped by birth and old age"; rather, those who give up what is seen and heard and the like are without *āsavas* and "have indeed crossed the flood."[32] Now, presumably these "good" ascetics and Brahmans are the Buddha and his disciples, but regardless they are still referred to as *samaṇa-brāhmaṇāse,* as if that were the most basic category by which to identify them.

Elsewhere in the Pali Canon,[33] this concept—namely, that some *samaṇas* and Brahmans have indeed escaped from *saṃsāra*—is generalized and made a part of "right view" (*sammādiṭṭhi*). This is expressed through the following formula:

> There exists what is given; there exists what is offered; there exists what is sacrificed; there exists the fruit, the result of meritorious and demeritorious actions; there exists this world; there exists the other world; there exists mother; there exists father; there exist spontaneously arisen beings; there exist in the world *samaṇa-brāhmaṇā,* rightly gone, gone on the right path, who, having realized by themselves through super-knowledge, declare this world and the other world.[34]

"Wrong view" (*micchādiṭṭhi*), on the other hand, is defined as the precise converse:

> There does not exist what is given; there does not exist what is offered; there does not exist what is sacrificed; there does not exist the fruit, the result of meritorious and demeritorious actions; there does not exist this world; there does not exist the other world; there does not exist mother; there does not exist father; there do not exist spontaneously arisen beings; there do not exist in the world *samaṇa-brāhmaṇā,* rightly gone, gone on the right path, who, having realized by themselves through super-knowledge, declare this world and the other world.[35]

Again, presumably those *samaṇas* and Brahmans who have "realized by themselves through super-knowledge" are the Buddhists themselves, although the phrasing of this formula leaves this ambiguous. In any case, those who have attained the highest goal, whoever they are, are identified once again by the category *samaṇa-brāhmaṇā,* and recognition of their attainment, in terms of this category and without regard to any putative distinction between *samaṇas* and Brahmans, is written into the definition of right view itself.

Closely related to this formulation of right view is a theme, found several times in the *Dīgha Nikāya* (26, 30, 31), the *Aṅguttara Nikāya* (3.1.4.6, 5.1.5.2, 5.5.3.7, 5.5.3.8, 8.1.4.8, 8.1.5.6, 8.1.5.8), and also in a Jātaka (457), that situates *samaṇa-brāhmaṇā* within the context of lay *dharma*. These texts generally list support (i.e., *dāna*) for *samaṇa-brāhmaṇā* together with other types of support a layperson would be expected to provide—such as to one's parents, children, slaves, and other dependents. The Jātaka text puts this quite bluntly: Those by whom their parents and *samaṇa-brāhmaṇā* are "well-honored" (*susammānitā*) go to heaven, while those who do not so honor them go to hell. Again, no attempt is made to distinguish between *samaṇas* and *brāhmaṇas*, much less to situate a particular "worthy" group of religious specialists (i.e., Buddhist monks) within this broad category; rather, the entire category is presented as worthy of respect.

So far in this chapter, we have been making use of early Jain and Buddhist texts to peer across the horizon of Indian history. The texts as they come down to us probably date from the imperial period, after the first securable dates in Indian history marked by the inscriptions of Aśoka. Nevertheless, we have viewed them as providing a glimpse, however obscured, of India prior to the imperial period, since they speak about events prior to the rise of unification of northern India under the Nandas and were transmitted orally for centuries before being written down. Interestingly, the particular trope of encouraging support for *śramaṇas* and Brahmans as a group is also found in the written source that defines the horizon of Indian history itself: the inscriptions of Aśoka.

Throughout his inscriptions, Aśoka defines *dhamma* in terms of generosity toward *śramaṇas* and Brahmans, along with other "dependent" groups such as one's parents or the aged. In some inscriptions, Aśoka notes that "[i]n times past, for many hundreds of years, there had ever been promoted the killing of animals and the hurting of living beings, discourtesy to relatives, (and) discourtesy to Śramaṇas and Brāhmaṇas," but that "now, in consequence of the practice of morality on the part of king Dēvānāṃpriya Priyadarśin, the sound of drums has become the sound of morality."[36] Elsewhere, Aśoka defines this *dhamma* directly, writing, "Herein the following (are) comprised, (viz.) proper courtesy to slaves and servants, reverence to elders, gentleness to animals, (and) liberality to Śramaṇas and Brāhmaṇas; these and other such (virtues) are called the practice of morality."[37] Aśoka instructs his officials to go throughout his dominion and teach the people about *dhamma* in similar terms that include giving to *śramaṇas* and Brahmans,[38] and he even presents himself as an example by "visiting Śramaṇas and Brāhmaṇas and making gifts" to them in his "*dhamma*-tours" (*dhaṃma-yātā*).[39]

Now, as we have already seen in the last chapter, Aśoka certainly had a conception of *śramaṇas* and *brāhmaṇas* as two discernible groups (*nikāya*), and he was also certainly aware of individual groups that could be classified under *śramaṇa-brāhmaṇā*, including Brahmans.[40] Indeed, this is to be expected given the evidence we have seen for a conception of separate categories of *śramaṇa* and Brahman as early as the reign of Candragupta. Moreover, Bronkhorst has recently argued convincingly that Aśoka's policies, in spite of the ecumenical tone of his edicts, were very much hostile to the interests of Brahmans (i.e., Vedic ritualists).[41] Nevertheless, we *still* find in the Aśokan inscriptions, much more prevalently than any rhetoric of sectarian division, repeated reference to *śramaṇa-brāhmaṇā* as a single class of persons who are worthy of respect and donations, just as we find in the early Buddhist texts. This shows that the tendency to treat *śramaṇa-brāhmaṇā* rhetorically as a single category remained even after the two subcategories are known to have been recognized as distinct and perhaps even antagonistic.

The evidence presented so far in this chapter shows that, in spite of an apparent grammatical treatment of *śramaṇa-brāhmaṇā* as a *dvandva*, which would imply a conjunction of two distinct categories, the compound is treated rhetorically throughout early Jain and Buddhist texts and even the inscriptions of Aśoka as if it were a single category. This is sometimes the case even when the compound is not present and the two elements *śramaṇa* and *brāhmaṇa* are given separately as distinct words. A recurrent formula found throughout the Buddhist *Saṃyutta Nikāya* effectively equates the two categories in the following terms:

> And, monks, whatever *samaṇas* or Brahmans understand [here is inserted whatever doctrinal elements are taken as the subject of the *sutta*], monks, those *samaṇas* or Brahmans are regarded by me as *samaṇas* among *samaṇas* and Brahmans among Brahmans, and moreover those venerable ones dwell having realized and attained in this world for themselves by super-knowledge the advantage of being a *samaṇa* and the advantage of being a Brahman.[42]

Within the context of this formula, the particular terminology one uses to refer to the religious life—whether it be *samaṇa* or Brahmans—is not important; in either case, the goal is reached by understanding a particular point of Buddhist doctrine.

A similar theme is found in the *Mahāsīhanāda Sutta* of the *Dīgha Nikāya* (8), in which the Buddha encounters a naked ascetic (*acelo*) named Kassapa and shows him the worthlessness of the practice of going without clothes. As a refrain in his sermon to Kassapa, the Buddha says the following three times:

> When, Kassapa, a monk cultivates non-hatred, non-malevolence, a mind of loving-kindness, he dwells, without *āsavas* due to the wasting away of the *āsavas*, having realized and attained for himself in this world by super-knowledge the liberation of mind, the liberation by wisdom. This monk, Kassapa, is called both a "*samaṇa*" and a "Brahman."[43]

By following this quintessentially Buddhist practice, therefore, one is called both a *samaṇa* and a Brahman. This practice is contrasted with that of the naked ascetic, which is so easy that "it would have been possible for a householder or a householder's son—even a slave-girl who brings water—to do this,"[44] and it is for this reason that "this is a common saying . . . in the world: 'Being a *samaṇa* is hard; being a Brahman is hard.' "[45] Likewise, in an *udāna* (4.8), the people of Sāvatthi, having been tricked by some jealous non-Buddhist wanderers into thinking that Buddhist monks had had sex with and then murdered a woman, disparage the *samaṇā sakyaputtiyā*[46] in the following terms:

> These *samaṇā sakyaputtiyā* are shameless, devoid of morality, of sinful character, speakers of falsehood, not *brahmacārins*. They may claim to be practitioners of *dhamma*, practitioners of peace, *brahmacārins*, speakers of truth, endowed with morality, of good character, (but) they do not possess the quality of being a *samaṇa*; they do not possess the quality of being a Brahman. Perished is their quality of being a *samaṇa*; perished is their quality of being a Brahman. Whence do they have the quality of being a *samaṇa*? Whence do they have the quality of being a Brahman? These are those whose quality of being a *samaṇa* is departed; these are those whose quality of being a Brahman is departed. For how indeed could a man do the duty of a man and deprive a woman of life?[47]

Thus we see, not only put into the Buddha's mouth as a pro-Buddhist polemic but also put into the mouths of ordinary laypeople as a colloquial expression, a rhetoric of *samaṇa* and Brahman that, while treating the two categories separately, treats them as effectively synonymous, as two equivalent ways of referring to the ideal religious practitioner.

## *Conclusion*

As we saw in the Introduction, scholars have constructed a narrative of the origins of the early Indian religions that assumes a metahistorical opposition between *śramaṇa*s and Brahmans, symbolized by the comparison to the snake and the mongoose. Looking across the horizon of Indian history as we have in this chapter, however, shows that the categories *śramaṇa* and Brahman were not always or even usually conceived of as being discrete and oppositional. There is, to be sure, ample evidence that they were conceived as such from the time of Candragupta onward, based on Greek testimony, the inscriptions of Aśoka, and of course the grammarian Patañjali's oft-quoted commentary on Pāṇini's rule about "oppositional" *dvandva* compounds. But the actual use of the compound *śramaṇa-brāhmaṇa* in all the sources we have looked at does not conform to Pāṇini's rule. Close inspection of these sources shows that, generally speaking, the compound is treated grammatically as a *dvandva*, that is, of two conjoined categories, but rhetorically speaking, it is treated as a unified category—either of others against whom to construct a self-identity, or of those who are worthy of gifts.

But if the earliest uses of the compound *śramaṇa-brāhmaṇa* were not oppositional, and the idea that *śramaṇa* and Brahman were separate and mutually exclusive categories arose only through time, then why did the people of North India in the mid- to late 1st millennium BCE come to speak of "*śramaṇa*s and Brahmans" in the first place? Why not simply refer to "Brahmans," as had been done since the time of the *Ṛg Veda*? In other words, why did the additional and possibly redundant category of *śramaṇa* come to be added to this?

However we are to answer this question, it cannot be through appeal to an extra-Vedic or "non-Brahmanical" source. Indeed, as has been shown by Patrick Olivelle, the oldest extant uses of the word *śramaṇa* are found in Brahmanical texts. This is not surprising given that the verb root √*śram* and its nominal derivative *śrama* are common in the Vedic literature going back to the *Ṛg Veda*. They refer to striving, exertion, or toil, both in terms of ordinary human life and in terms of the creative actions of the gods and the "labor" that goes into performing a sacrifice.[48] The earliest use of the form *śramaṇa* specifically is in the *Taittirīya Āraṇyaka*, which refers to so-called *vātaraśana ṛṣis* as *śramaṇas* and celibates (*ūrdhvamanthinaḥ*).[49] As Olivelle argues, this use of the word *śramaṇa* probably does not refer to a category of persons, but rather is an adjective ("striving") that describes the *vātaraśana ṛṣis*.[50] The word *śramaṇa* is, however, found in the *Bṛhadāraṇyaka Upaniṣad* as referring to a class of persons.[51] The context of this passage is somewhat ambiguous: Since it is listed together with both mother and father on the one hand and abortionists and *cāṇḍālas* on the other, it is difficult to say whether the *śramaṇa* is conceived of as "good" or "bad," or, to put it differently, as "Brahmanical" or "non-Brahmanical."[52] The use of the close derivative *śrāmaṇaka* in the Dharma Sūtras is equally ambiguous. It is used in three *sūtras* (*BDh* 2.11.15, *GDh* 3.27, *VDh* 9.10) in the description of the *āśrama* of the forest hermit to refer to, according to Olivelle's interpretation, a "special procedure for establishing the sacred fire."[53]

Overall, however, the specific form *śramaṇa* is rare in the texts of the Brahmanical tradition. This is somewhat surprising given that the term is used quite frequently in the early Buddhist and Jain texts, as well as the inscriptions of Aśoka, which implies that it was a commonly used colloquial term in North India in the late 1st millennium BCE. Instead what we find, beginning with the Dharma Sūtras, is the etymologically related term *āśrama*, which is used to refer to four different ways of life—those of the life-long celibate student, the householder, the forest-dweller, and the wanderer. Now, as Olivelle has pointed out, the more common use of the term *āśrama* in early Indian literature is to refer to a place of intensive religious practice.[54] This latter usage, incidentally, has passed into modern English as the word *ashram*, used frequently to refer to Hindu (and sometimes non-Hindu) centers of religious or "spiritual" practice. Since this is the more common usage, Olivelle has argued convincingly that it is the original usage, and the use of the same word in the Dharma Sūtras is a technical one restricted to the authors of those texts and their intellectual successors.[55]

Based on his assumption of a fundamental dichotomy between "Brahmanical" and "non-Brahmanical," however, Olivelle has also argued that *āśrama* in both senses of the term was a Brahmanical concept and thus not associated originally with celibate *śramaṇa* lifestyles, but with the intensive practice of specially committed Brahman householders.[56]

In order to address this argument and answer the question of how the category *śramaṇa* arose, it will be necessary first to reexamine the rhetorical strategies used by Jains, Buddhists, and "Brahmans" in the mid- to late 1st millennium BCE, without viewing them through the dichotomy of Brahmanical versus non-Brahmanical and thus privileging the ideological position of one over the others. What we will see is that their rhetorical strategies, when viewed in tandem with one another, evince not a challenge to a pre-established Brahmanism but rather a debate over what Brahmanhood consisted of. This debate centered on the question of the proper lifestyle for a person worthy to be called a Brahman: Should a Brahman live as a householder and have children, or should a Brahman forsake the householder's life and remain celibate? The next two chapters will take up these two positions in turn. First, we will look at the position of the Buddhists and Jains, which rejected the householder's life and advocated celibacy. Then we will look at the Neo-Brahmanical position, which embraced the householder's life and rejected celibacy as inconsistent with the Vedas.

# 4

# *The Brahman as a Celibate Renunciant*

THE EARLY LITERATURE of the Jains and Buddhists is replete with claims that the founder of the respective monastic community (Mahāvīra of the former or the Buddha of the latter), as well as monks and nuns[1] who successfully follow his example in attaining liberation, are Brahmans. As we have seen, this fact, especially with respect to the Buddhist literature, has long been noted by scholars and has been explained by various theories of "borrowing" and "marketing." According to such theories, Buddhists and Jains simply called themselves Brahmans as a polemic or marketing strategy against the "actual" Brahmans of their day. In part, as I have shown, this explanation is due to a historical accident in the development of Western Buddhology—the fact that Eugène Burnouf formulated his theory of the priority of Brahmanism on the basis of relatively late Sanskrit Buddhist texts that reflect the Brahmans' successful "colonization of the past."[2] Concomitantly, I have argued that once the chronological priority of Brahmanism was established, scholars have succumbed to the methodological error of assuming that Brahmanism was *metahistorically* prior to Buddhism and Jainism. Only in recent decades have scholars begun to chip away at this methodological fallacy, with the increasing awareness that many of the characteristics of Brahmanism actually developed fairly late and were anachronistically projected into the distant past, both by Brahmanical authors and by modern scholars who depended on later Brahmanical texts to interpret earlier ones.

Of course, another problem has been posed by the state of the earliest Buddhist and Jain literature as it comes down to us. The early collections of Buddhist and Jain *suttas*, i.e., the *Sutta Piṭaka* of the Buddhists and the Jain *aṅgas*, both include references to the ideal person as "Brahman" alongside references to a particular group of outsiders known as "Brahmans." This juxtaposition gives the impression that the former references to the ideal person as "Brahman" are *merely* a polemic or marketing strategy against a fixed social group to whom this appellation properly belonged. Indeed, at times the claims that the founder of the monastic community and his liberated followers are Brahmans seem *self-consciously* to be made as a polemic against Brahmans as a social category. But as we saw in Chapter 2, the early collections of Buddhist and Jain *sutta*s as they come down to us are the product of a long process of oral transmission and elaboration stretching from the time of the Buddha and Mahāvīra themselves to well after the initial adoption of writing in or just before the Mauryan period. If we are to peer over the horizon of Indian history, we must make some effort, as we have done, to identify the oldest parts of the early Buddhist and Jain literature and contrast them critically with the overall tenor of the early collections as a whole.

As I argued in the last chapter, the opposition between the categories *śramaṇa* and *Brahman* has been overblown, and in any case must be understood as the *product* of a period of contestation between different groups rather than the metahistorical cause of that contestation. The contestation I have in mind, of course, is over precisely what it means to be a Brahman. Does being a Brahman consist of leaving the world, through the lifestyle of renunciation and celibacy and the soteriological goal of liberation? Or does being a Brahman consist of embracing, supporting, and even participating in the construction of the world, through householdership, marriage, the production of children, and the performance of ritual?

In this chapter, we will set aside the assumption of a fundamental dichotomy between "Brahmanical" and "non-Brahmanical" and ask ourselves, what do early Buddhism and Jainism look like if we take seriously their claim to present a path to becoming a Brahman? I will argue that, even in the form that they come down to us, the early texts of the Buddhists and Jains do present a coherent case for understanding their systems as "Brahmanisms," albeit Brahmanisms that posit the "Brahman" as a celibate renunciate. I will begin by examining the very oldest texts that we can identify in the Buddhist and Jain literature and show that they, in quite similar terms, make the claim that the founder of the monastic order and his liberated followers are Brahmans, and that these are contrasted not with the "actual" Brahmans (i.e., the proponents of Neo-Brahmanism), but rather with *śramaṇas*. Looking more broadly at the early Buddhist and Jain literature, we will then see that what Buddhist and Jain monks *do*, which is known in both traditions as *brahmacarya*, has clear antecedents in the Vedic literature, and the Buddhist/Jain interpretation of *brahmacarya*—lifelong celibacy and studentship—is not inconsistent with those antecedents. This would suggest that the early Buddhists and Jains were indeed advancing coherent theories of Brahmanhood that were based on celibacy and renunciation. This supposition is supported by the fact that the rival group that the Buddhists in particular most closely identified with was not (according to the distinctions made by modern scholarship) a fellow *śramaṇa* group such as the Jains, but rather the *jaṭilas*, whom I identify with the *vānaprasthas* of Brahmanical literature and who modern scholars typically classify as Brahmanical. The group that the early Buddhists and Jains most clearly distinguished themselves from was neither "Brahmans" nor even one another, but rather householders. Although both Buddhist and Jain monks certainly relied on householders for material support, the householder represented an absolute other to their own identity as Brahmans because they assumed that the Brahman must renounce the world and remain celibate. Finally, I will argue that the early articulations of the Buddhist and Jain monastic communities as "Brahmanisms" helps to explain the significance of the novel category of *śramaṇa*, which we left as an open question at the end of the previous chapter.

## *Buddhists and Jains as Brahmans*

As they come down to us, the early collections of the Jains and Buddhists (the *aṅgas* and *Sutta Piṭaka*) bear features indicating some remove from the time of the founders of the respective monastic communities. Nevertheless, in each case there are two texts that appear to be of the greatest antiquity in the collection and that reflect ideas deviating from the doctrinal standards in the collection as a whole. These are, for the Buddhists, the *Aṭṭhaka Vagga* and core verses (omitting the frame narrative) of the *Pārāyaṇa Vagga*, and for the Jains, the first book of the *Āyāraṅga Sutta* and the first book of the *Sūyagaḍaṃga Sutta*. In both cases, the latter text is likely a bit less old than the former text, but still older than the bulk of texts in the canonical collection. While studies of these texts, especially the two Buddhist ones, that have argued for their antiquity have focused on general doctrinal differences from the canonical norm, we are interested here more specifically in how they treat the category *Brahman* differently from later texts. What we will find is evidence in both traditions of an early articulation of a Brahmanical identity: a vision of a monastic community that was founded by a "Brahman" and that leads people on the path to becoming a Brahman.

The tendency in the oldest Buddhist texts, the *Aṭṭhaka* and the *Pārāyaṇa*, to refer to the Buddha or the ideal person as a Brahman, has already been noticed by both Luis Gómez and Tilmann Vetter. In discussing the differences between the *Pārāyaṇa* and the *Aṭṭhaka*, Gómez notes that the *Pārāyaṇa* prefers to use the word *bhikkhu* to refer to the ideal person, whereas in the *Aṭṭhaka* the word *brāhmaṇa* is more common.[3] He does not elaborate on the significance of this, though, and he consistently translates *brāhmaṇa* as "true Brahman,"[4] indicating that he reads the references to the ideal person as a Brahman as being somehow metaphorical, as in other cases in the Canon already discussed in Chapter 2. Vetter also notes the prevalence of references to the ideal person as a Brahman in the *Aṭṭhaka*, and he notes further a certain degree of correlation between those *suttas* that refer to the ideal person as a Brahman and those that he includes in his reckoning of the "core" of the *Aṭṭhaka* on the basis of their doctrinal content.[5] Unlike Gómez, however, Vetter does not interpret these references to the ideal person as a Brahman as metaphorical in the same sense as found elsewhere in the Canon:

> Pasūra (in 828) and Cūḷabyūha (in 883-4, 890) denounce the quarrelsome ascetics *(samaṇa)* and (only Cūḷabyūha 891-2) the sectarians *(?titthyā)*. Here we get the impression that the Brāhmaṇa as the person accomplishing the mystical way is opposed to the Samaṇa and not to the Brāhmaṇa by birth, the latter opposition being a common theme in other parts of the canon, but not in any way alluded to here . . . [6]

In other words, Vetter recognizes that the word *Brahman* is used in the *Aṭṭhaka* in an unusual way that does not correlate well to the metaphorical way it is often used throughout the rest of the Canon, that is, in explicit contrast to Brahmans by birth.[7]

I would like to expand this insight to show that it does not apply only to a single text in the Buddhist tradition, but to the earliest articulations of Buddhist and Jain identity as a whole. We will begin with the oldest text in each tradition, the *Aṭṭhaka Vagga* and the *Āyāraṅga Sutta*, which articulate this vision most clearly, followed by a discussion of the somewhat younger texts, the *Pārāyaṇa Vagga* and the *Sūyagaḍaṃga Sutta*. With the exception of the single use of the word in the compound *samaṇabrāhmaṇā* (v. 859), all instances of the word *Brahman* in the *Aṭṭhaka* refer to the ideal person. Most of these are found within the *suttas* that Vetter identifies as the "core" of the *Aṭṭhaka*, and thus take as their theme the non-dual teaching that Gómez described in his article. The Brahman is accordingly described in fairly negative terms—in terms, that is, of what does *not* define him. For example, according to one verse from the *Suddhaṭṭhaka Sutta* (4),

> A Brahman does not say that purity is from something else, in what is seen, in what is heard, in morality and vows, or in what is thought.
> [He is] unsmeared with respect to merit and evil, rejecting what has been taken up, not doing [anything] in this connection.[8]

Gómez has convincingly argued that this verse advocates a non-dual position,[9] which we may add is used to define the Brahman as an ideal. This is confirmed by the final verse of the same *sutta*:

> The Brahman is beyond boundaries. There is nothing cognized or seen that is seized by him.
> He is not empassioned by passion; he is not empassioned with dispassion. Nothing else is taken up by him here.[10]

A similarly negative description pointing to a non-dual ideal is found in the immediately following *Paramaṭṭhaka Sutta* (5):

> With respect to what is seen, heard, or felt here, there is not even the slightest apperception formed by him.
> Who here in the world could have doubts about that Brahman who has not taken a view?
> They do not form [apperceptions]; they do not honor [one over another]; and *dhammas* are not accepted by them.
> A Brahman is not to be inferred by morality or vows. Gone to the far shore, such a one does not return.[11]

In all three of these verses, the Brahman is described in terms of a non-dual ideal, according to which one's excellence cannot be determined by any of the characteristics that might ordinarily determine excellence—morality (*sīla*), vows (*vata*), or merit (*puñña*)—and therefore, as v. 795 puts it quite bluntly, he is "beyond boundaries" (*sīmātigo*).

Two other *suttas* in the *Aṭṭhaka* define the Brahman in similarly non-dualistic terms, but focusing more specifically on his avoidance of disputes by eschewing all views. Verse 907 of the *Mahābyūha Sutta* (13) begins much as v. 790, saying, "There is for the Brahman nothing that needs to be taught by another," but then turns to the question of views rather than morality and vows:

> having considered that which is grasped among *dhammas*.
> Therefore, he has gone beyond disputes, for he sees no other
> *dhamma* as best.[12]

The *sutta* continues for a few verses with the Buddha describing the folly of those who adhere to views; then, in v. 911, he once again defines the Brahman as the antithesis of this folly:

> The Brahman cannot properly be defined; he is not a follower of
> views, nor is he attached to knowledge.
> And having known common conventions, he is indifferent,
> (thinking), "Surely they (will) take it up."[13]

A verse of the *Māgandiya Sutta* (9) puts the non-entry of the Brahman into disputes into the context of his (ideal) inability to make distinctions:

> Why would that Brahman say, "True"? Or with whom would he
> dispute, [saying,] "False"?
> For whom there is neither equal nor unequal, with whom would
> he enter into an argument?[14]

The Brahman, according to these two *suttas*, therefore, refuses to embrace any particular view, and thus is not drawn into any disputes—since obviously one cannot take part in an argument unless one takes a side.

There remains only one more reference to the ideal person as a Brahman in the *Aṭṭhaka*, which, unlike the ones we have looked at so far, lies outside of the "core" *suttas* identified by Vetter. As such, the Brahman in this verse is defined in almost the opposite terms as the ones we have just looked at:

> Not having deviated from the truth, the sage stands on dry ground,
> a Brahman.
> Having given up everything, that one indeed is called "calmed."[15]

The Brahman here is called "calmed" because, following the "desire" theme delineated by Burford, the *Attadaṇḍa Sutta* (15) in which this verse is found focuses on the abandonment of desire as the means to attaining the goal. Unlike the "anti-*diṭṭhi*" *sutta*s we have just been looking at—and more in concert with the rest of the Canon—this *sutta* does not disparage knowledge but uses it to define the ideal person. The immediately following verse, in fact, can be taken as the mirror image of the anti-*diṭṭhi* passages we have been looking at:

> That one indeed is knowledgeable; he has attained knowledge.
> Having found out the *dhamma*, he is independent.
> Behaving properly in the world, he does not envy anyone.[16]

Thus, the Brahman in this *sutta* is defined in terms more in keeping with what we might find elsewhere in the Canon—as an ideal person who is defined as such by his attainment of knowledge—rather than the non-dualistic ideal *à la* Gómez that disparages knowledge, as is found in the other *Aṭṭhaka* we will look at. Nevertheless, the *pattern* according to which the word *brāhmaṇa* is used is the same as in the other *Aṭṭhaka* passages. The ideal person is simply referred to as a Brahman, without any apparent comparison or contrast to a social group going by the same name—only in contrast, rather, to those, whoever they may be, who do not fit the ideal.

The first book of the Jain *Āyāraṅga Sutta* is striking in the similarity it bears to the Buddhist *Aṭṭhaka Vagga* in its use of the category *Brahman*. With the exception of two verses in which the word *māhaṇa* (the Ardhamāgadhī spelling of Brahman) is coupled with the word *samaṇa* (*ĀS* 1.4.2.3, 1.8.4.11), every use of the word *māhaṇa* is a reference to the ideal person. There are a total of eleven such uses of the word in this text. Overall, the first book of the *Āyāraṅga* can be read as an exhortation to follow the path to liberation, through non-killing of all creatures, non-attachment, and so on. Three times in the text, the word *māhaṇa* is simply used to refer in the abstract to the person who follows this path. In the first of these three, the ideal person is exhorted not to engage in killing: "[T]he Brahman follows the unrivalled . . . . He should not kill, nor cause others to kill, nor consent to the killing of others."[17] The other two are found within a chapter of the *Āyāraṅga* (1.7.8) that constitutes the oldest instructions for undertaking what is known in classical Jainism as *sallekhanā*, or religious death.[18] Since the purpose behind such a form of death is to bring an end to all forms of action, the person undergoing it, who is referred to as a Brahman, must find a piece of ground on which to do so without inadvertently killing any living creatures: "Having examined a spot of bare ground he should remain there; stay O Brâhma*n*a!"[19] Shortly thereafter, the chapter ends by referring to the Brahman dying in this state and thus attaining *nirvāṇa* (*ĀS* 1.7.8.24–25).

The other eight references to the ideal person as a Brahman in the *Āyāraṅga Sutta* are all specifically to Mahāvīra, the founder of the Jain order. Although "Mahāvīra," along with "Jina," came to be the preferred epithet for the founder of Jainism, just as "Buddha" came to be the preferred epithet for the founder of Buddhism, a variety of epithets, including "Brahman," are used fairly interchangeably in this text. Context makes clear that the founder of the order is being referred to. For example, one verse declares, "By the Brahman, the wise . . . three vows have been enjoined."[20] A later verse in the same chapter similarly attributes a teaching encouraging donations to the Jain monastic order to this same "Brahman":

> Know the law declared by the wise Brâhma*n*a: one should give to one of the same faith food, &c., clothes, &c., and one should exhort him (to give) or do him service, always showing the highest respect. Thus I say.[21]

The fact that specific rules or teachings are being laid down in these verses makes it clear that the "Brahman" being referred to is Mahāvīra.

The remaining references to Mahāvīra as a Brahman are all found in the very last chapter of the first book of the *Āyāraṅga Sutta*, which consists of a short hagiography of Mahāvīra. It begins with him giving up the wearing of clothing and then follows him as he wanders through North India, meditating and maintaining his composure as he suffers numerous hardships and insults from people who are shocked by his appearance. Throughout this chapter, Mahāvīra is referred to with a variety of names and epithets, including "sage" (1.8.1.9: *muṇī*), "son of Jñātṛ" (1.8.1.10: *nāyaputte*), "Great Hero" (1.8.1.13: *mahāvīre*), "Blessed One" (1.8.1.15: *bhagavaṃ*), *śramaṇa* (1.8.2.3: *samaṇe*), and of course "Brahman." This last epithet is given some prominence in the text, since it is the one chosen for a refrain found at the end of each of the four sections into which this chapter is divided:

> This is the rule which has often been followed by the wise
> Brâhma*n*a, the Venerable One, who is free from attachment:
> thus proceed (the monks).
> Thus I say.[22]

In addition, on two occasions in this chapter, Mahāvīra is described with the following phrase: "[T]he Brâhma*n*a wandered about, speaking but little."[23]

What is striking about all these uses of the word *Brahman* in the *Aṭṭhaka* and the *Āyāraṅga* that we have reviewed so far is that they refer simply and straightforwardly to the ideal person. In the examples we looked at from other parts of the Buddhist *Sutta Piṭaka* in Chapter 2, when reference is made to the Buddhist ideal person as a Brahman, it is done so in contrast—either explicitly or else implicitly through narrative framing—to "literal" Brahmans—that is, members of a particular social group that claim Brahmanhood by birth. In the *Aṭṭhaka* and *Āyāraṅga*, no such comparison is found. *Brahman* is simply used as a word for the ideal person, together with other words such as *bhikkhu* and *muni* that lack the historical baggage that the word *Brahman* has acquired, and thus appear to us as more naturally "śramaṇ*ic*." We can even say that these and other such terms are used interchangeably with one another. Thus, there is nothing about the use of the word *Brahman* that seems to privilege it over or distinguish it from other honorific terms; all are simply used to refer to the ideal person.

Moreover, this straightforward honorific use of the word *Brahman* to refer to the ideal person is almost the only way in which the word is used at all in the *Aṭṭhaka* and *Āyāraṅga*. As already noted above, there is only one exception in the *Aṭṭhaka* and two in the *Āyāraṅga*. All three of these exceptions involve using the word *Brahman* in tandem with the word *samaṇa*. In this respect, these three exceptions are consistent with later canonical usage. But as we saw in the last chapter, the overwhelming tendency throughout early Indian literature, whenever the words *Brahman* and *śramaṇa* are used in tandem with one another, is for them to be used in a non-oppositional way. These sparing examples in the *Aṭṭhaka* and *Āyāraṅga* are no exception. The *Purābheda Sutta* of the *Aṭṭhaka* (10) uses the compound *samaṇabrāhmaṇā* to refer to people *other* than the ideal person being described by the *sutta*:

> That by which ordinary people, as well as *samaṇa*s and Brahmans,
> might speak of him

> Is not esteemed by him; therefore, he does not shake in the midst of doctrines.[24]

Likewise, a verse in the Jain *Āyāraṅga* refers to "*śramaṇa*s and Brahmans" (*samaṇā ya māhaṇā ya*) who teach a wrong view:

> Many and several in this world, Brâhma*n*as or *S*rama*n*as, raise this discussion: We have seen, heard, acknowledged, thoroughly understood, in the upper, nether, and sidelong directions, and in all ways examined it: all sorts of living beings may be slain, or treated with violence, or abused, or tormented, or driven away. Know about this: there is no wrong in it.[25]

"*Śramaṇa*s and Brahmans" is used in these two examples, much as we found elsewhere in the canonical texts in the last chapter, as a foil against which to construct one's own identity. Finally, one additional reference is found to "a Brahman or a *śramaṇa*" in the *Āyāraṅga*:

> When a Brâhma*n*a or *S*rama*n*a, a beggar or guest, a *K*â*nd*âla, a cat, or a dog stood in his way, [w]ithout ceasing in his reflections, and avoiding to overlook them, the Venerable One slowly wandered about, and, killing no creatures, he begged for his food.[26]

As in the previous two examples, any distinction between the *śramaṇa* and the Brahman here is irrelevant; they are grouped together as a class of people to be opposed to the ideal person, in this case, Mahāvīra himself.

When looked at in comparison with the *Aṭṭhaka Vagga* and the *Āyāraṅga Sutta*, the *Pārāyaṇa Vagga* and the *Sūyagaḍaṃga Sutta* include a greater number of uses of the word *Brahman* that are in conformity with typical canonical uses. This is understandable given that these latter two texts were probably composed a bit later than the former two. In several cases in the *Pārāyaṇa* and *Sūyagaḍaṃga*, the word *Brahman* is used in tandem with the word *samaṇa*, like the examples we just saw from the *Aṭṭhaka* and *Āyāraṅga*, as a unified class of "others" against which to construct one's own identity. We already looked at the examples from the *Sūyagaḍaṃga* in Chapter 3, so it is not necessary to review them here. A similar example can be found in the *Nandamāṇavapucchā* of the *Pārāyaṇa* (7). The interlocutor of the *sutta*, Nanda, asks the Buddha about "whatever *samaṇabrāhmaṇāse* say that purity is by means of what is seen or heard, say that purity is by means of ceremonial observances, say that purity is by various means."[27] The Buddha confirms that such people do not escape from rebirth. Here again, *samaṇabrāhmaṇāse*[28] serve collectively as a foil against which to construct the Buddhist ideal. The Buddha continues, however, by noting that not all *samaṇabrāhmaṇāse* fail to escape from rebirth:

> I do not say that all *samaṇabrāhmaṇāse*
> Are enveloped in birth and old age.
> Whosoever, having given up here what is seen or heard or felt, as well as ceremonial observances,
> Having given up all the various forms, having thoroughly known thirst, are without *āsavas*.
> I say that they indeed are men who have crossed the flood.[29]

Thus, once again, *samaṇabrāhmaṇāse* are treated collectively, as a group, some members of whom have "crossed the flood" of rebirth. As in the many canonical uses of the compound *samaṇabrāhmaṇā* treated in Chapter 3, the distinction here between *samaṇa* and *brāhmaṇa* is irrelevant; the only relevant distinction is between those who have escaped from rebirth and those who haven't.

Unlike the *Aṭṭhaka* and *Āyāraṅga*, the *Pārāyaṇa* and *Sūyagaḍaṃga* also contain clear references to the Brahmans as a social group—that is, the Vedic Brahmans who claimed Brahmanhood on the basis of birth and practiced sacrifice. The *Puṇṇakamāṇavapucchā* of the *Pārāyaṇa* (3) refers three times to "*khattiyas* [=Skt. *kṣatriyas*] and Brahmans who each offered sacrifices to deities here in the world."[30] Here the reference is clearly to Brahmans as a social category, recognized along with *khattiyas* as prominent individuals who perform sacrifices (*yañña*). The *sutta* as a whole is a criticism of the practice of sacrifice, which is said not to lead to escape from rebirth, unlike stilling desire, which does. In this *sutta*, therefore, the word *brāhmaṇa* is not used to refer to a Buddhist ideal at all—instead, it refers to a social group that is criticized. This is the only such example found in the *Pārāyaṇa*,[31] but there are several references to the Brahmans as a social group in the *Sūyagaḍaṃga*. We find, for example, a reference to Brahmans as a class of beings who must eventually (upon death, it is implied) "leave their rank and suffer."[32] We also find Brahmans paired with *kṣatriyas* as a high-ranking social group that may try to "seduce" a Jain monk (*Sūyag*. 1.3.2.15). We even find a reference to Brahmans in a list of social groups that includes all four *varṇas* (*Sūyag*. 1.9.2) and a reference to monks who are "Brahman[s] or *kṣatriya*[s] by birth" (*Sūyag.* 1.13.10: *je māhaṇe khattiyajāyae vā*) but are told not to take pride in their *gotra*. All of these references, especially those in the *Sūyagaḍaṃga*, show a continuity with the canonical literature at large, which is increasingly concerned with explicitly positioning Buddhist or Jain identity with respect to Neo-Brahmanical conceptions of birth.

Nevertheless, there are other passages in the *Pārāyaṇa* and *Sūyagaḍaṃga* that show a remarkable continuity with the honorific use of the word *Brahman* in the earlier *Aṭṭhaka* and *Āyāraṅga*. In the *Dhotakamāṇavapucchā* of the *Pārāyaṇa* (5), a certain Dhotaka approaches the Buddha to ask him about *nibbāna*, and praises him in the following terms:

> I see in the world of gods and men a Brahman wandering about
> with nothing.
> Therefore, I bow to that one who is all-seeing. Release me, Śākya,
> from my doubts.[33]

The Buddha responds that he cannot release a person from doubts, only teach him the "best *dhamma*" (*dhammañ ca seṭṭhaṃ*). Dhotaka then asks him to do so:

> Having pity, Brahmā, teach me the *dhamma* of detachment, that
> I may understand,
> (And) being unchanging just like space, calmed, I may wander
> right here unattached.[34]

This *sutta* is unique among the Buddhist *suttas* we are examining here in having the Buddha's interlocutor refer to the Buddha himself as a Brahman; however, in this respect it parallels many similar passages that we have already seen from the *Āyāraṅga* that refer to Mahāvīra as a Brahman. Note here as well that there is no comparison, explicit or implicit, to a "real" or "literal" Brahman—that is, a Brahman by birth. Dhotaka simply refers to the Buddha as a Brahman as if that is a natural word to describe him. As such, he refers to the Buddha using the vocative *brahme* ("Brahmā"), and this appears to be interchangeable with the other vocatives he uses to describe him—namely *bhagavā* ("Blessed One") and *mahesi* ("Great Seer"). In calling the Buddha a Brahman, Dhotaka does describe him as "having nothing" (*akiñcanaṃ*), but this serves simply as an attributive describing the noun *brāhmaṇaṃ*. What Dhotaka seems to be saying, therefore, is that he sees a Brahman—namely, the Buddha—and is impressed by him because he "has nothing"—and that is why he has approached him to "release me from my doubts."

This particular association between the Brahman and "having nothing" recalls the final lines of the immediately preceding *sutta* in the *Pārāyaṇa*, the *Mettagūmāṇavapucchā* (4). This *sutta*, like the *suttas* we already looked at from the *Aṭṭhaka*, uses the term *brāhmaṇa* abstractly to refer to the ideal person. In this *sutta*, the Buddha's interlocutor, Mettagū, asks him about how to cross the "flood" (*ogha*) of birth and old age, and he responds by saying that one must not have "attachment" (*upadhi*). After answering Mettagū's questions, the Buddha summarizes, saying,

> Whomever one would recognize as a Brahman, having knowledge,
> without possessions, unattached to sensual pleasure and
> existence,
> He has certainly crossed this flood and, having crossed over to the
> far shore, is without defect, without doubt.[35]

The ideal Brahman spoken of here is said to be *vedagū*—a word with a problematic etymology, but generally agreed to mean "having knowledge."[36] In describing the Brahman in this way, the Buddha is effectively calling himself a Brahman, since at the very beginning of their dialog, Mettagū had announced that he thought the Buddha was *vedagū* (v. 1049).

We also find the Brahman associated with knowledge, in this case designated by *ñāṇa*, in yet another *sutta* of the *Pārāyaṇa*, the *Posālamāṇavapucchā* (14):

> Having known the origin of nothingness, [he thinks,] "Enjoyment
> is a fetter."
> Understanding this thus, therefore he sees clearly with respect
> to that.
> This is the true knowledge of that perfected Brahman.[37]

This difficult verse has been commented upon by Wynne, who argues that the Buddha is saying that one moves beyond the state of nothingness (*ākiñcañña*) by having the insight (*vipassati*) that it has its origin in the "fetter 'delight'" (*nandī saṃyojanaṃ iti*).[38] Regardless of how exactly one interprets this verse and the short dialog in which it is found, it is clear that the Buddha and his interlocutor Posāla are engaging in a rather technical discussion about meditative techniques. Within this context, the Buddha uses the word *Brahman*, without any immediately apparent comparative intent, simply to refer to the person who has attained the meditative goal he is describing.

In spite of its preoccupation with the social category of Brahman that we saw above, the first book of the *Sūyagaḍaṃga* also contains a number of passages that show continuity with the *Āyāraṅga*'s earlier emphasis on *Brahman* as an honorific for the ideal person. Two chapters begin with a nearly identical sentence that refers to Mahāvīra as a Brahman: "What is the Law [or Path] that has been preached by the wise Brâhma*n*a?"[39] In addition, the second chapter of the first book of the *Sūyagaḍaṃga* describes the ideal person abstractly at some length, referring to that ideal person several times as a Brahman. The first instance can be taken as typical:

> As a bird covered with dust removes the grey powder by shaking itself, so a worthy and austere Brâhma*n*a, who does penance, annihilates his Karman.[40]

The next section of the text refers to the ideal monk as a Brahman so many times that Jacobi simply leaves them out of his translation.[41] These passages praise the Brahman for not being proud of his *gotra* (1.2.2.1), for being detached (1.2.2.5–6, 1.2.2.22), and for not indulging in various passions (1.2.2.29).

Thus, to summarize, the oldest texts that have come down to us from the Buddhist and Jain literatures are characterized by a pervasive trope of referring to the ideal person—either in the abstract or specifically to the founder of the monastic order himself—as a Brahman. Unlike in later canonical usage, such references are made without contrasting the Jain or Buddhist Brahman to the Vedic Brahmans, those who claim Brahmanhood on the basis of birth. Instead, *Brahman* is simply used as an honorific, often interchangeably with other honorifics such as *muni* and *bhikkhu*. Moreover, in the very earliest of these texts, the first chapter of the Jain *Āyāraṅga Sutta* and the Buddhist *Aṭṭhaka Vagga*, this honorific usage of the word *Brahman* is virtually the only way in which the word is used. There are a very small number of non-oppositional references to "*śramaṇa*s and Brahmans," but none to Brahmans as a social group defined by birth. The somewhat later first chapter of the Jain *Sūyagaḍaṃga* and the core verses of the Buddhist *Pārāyaṇa* are more in line with later canonical trends in including more references to "*śramaṇa*s and Brahmans," as well as to Brahmans by birth. But even they contain several passages that show continuity with the earlier texts in using the word *Brahman* as a straightforward honorific for the ideal person.

What this evidence suggests is that although the Buddhist and Jain traditions became increasingly concerned over the course of time with defining themselves against a group that arrogated to itself the term *Brahman* on the basis of birth, this was not a concern in the earliest texts. Instead, we find the early Jains and Buddhists quite comfortable in owning the term *Brahman* for themselves. In other words, *the earliest identity we find articulated by the Buddhists and Jains is a self-consciously Brahmanical identity*. Instead of reading into these early articulations of Buddhist and Jain identity the conflict that later developed between them and the proponents of Neo-Brahmanism, we will here take these alternative articulations of Brahmanhood seriously. But this immediately raises the question: On what basis did the early Buddhists and Jains claim to be Brahmans? The answer to this question, I will argue, is simple: Early Buddhists and Jains called themselves Brahmans because they practiced *brahmacarya*.

## *Brahmacarya as a Brahmanical Way of Life*

After the term *brāhmaṇa* itself, *brahmacarya* is perhaps the most important "Brahmanical" term that is also used by the early Buddhists and Jains. Within a "reaction" model of Buddhism's relationship to Brahmanism, *brahmacariya* would be, a priori, an example of a Brahmanical term that was appropriated by early Buddhism and given a Buddhist sense; indeed, Norman lists it as one of the "[t]erms taken over by the Buddha but used with new senses."[42] One can of course extend this argument to Jainism as well. The "new sense" supposedly given to this particular term is "celibacy." The Pali word *brahmacariya* and its Ardhamāgadhī equivalent, *bambhacera*, do, in fact, generally take this seemingly narrow and specialized meaning in the Buddhist and Jain canonical texts, and accordingly, the negative form *abrahmacariya* takes the meaning of "non-celibacy."

Within the Buddhist texts, this narrow meaning is clear, for example, in *DN* 24, in which the Buddha quotes a certain naked ascetic (*acelo*) embarking upon his religious career by making seven vows, one of which is as follows: "As long as I live, I will be a *brahmacārī*; I will not indulge in sexual intercourse."[43] The use of *brahmacārī* to refer specifically to celibacy is also expressed in the common formula, "Having abandoned *abrahmacariya*, he becomes a *brahmacārī*, living far from, abstaining from the village custom of sexual intercourse."[44] Elsewhere, the reference to sexual intercourse is not explicit but is clearly implied. For example, on several occasions, people are criticized for being *abrahmacārī*—that is, not celibate—even though they have vowed to be *brahmacārī*.[45] Frequently, we also find the compound *accantabrahmacārī*, which means "perpetual" *brahmacārī* and thus implies a lifelong commitment to abstaining from sexual intercourse.[46] Numerous other instances of the word *brahmacārī* or *abrahmacārī* can be understood from context to refer to celibacy or non-celibacy, respectively.[47]

We also frequently find the terms *bambhacera* (=Skt. *brahmacarya*) and *bambhacārī* or *bambhayārī* (=Skt. *brahmacārin*) used in the early Jain texts to refer to the practice of celibacy. An excellent example is the 16th chapter of the *Uttarajjhāyā*, which lists "the ten conditions of perfect chastity," according to the translation by Jacobi.[48] The word that Jacobi translates here as "chastity" is *bambhacera*, and the context makes it particularly clear that this specific meaning is meant. Every one of the ten conditions listed in the chapter is directed toward minimizing the possibility that a Jain monk will lapse from his vow not to engage in sexual intercourse. The first six conditions all involve avoiding women or the thought of women in one form or another. The ninth condition states that the monk should not ornament himself, and this is explicitly explained as necessary to avoid attracting women to oneself. The seventh, eighth, and tenth conditions refer less directly to women or sexual intercourse, but given the context are clearly intended to reduce the possibility of lustful states of mind arising: A monk should not eat "well-dressed food"; he should not eat or drink excessively; and he should "not care for sounds, colours, tastes, smells, and feelings."[49]

It would be a mistake, however, to think that the words *brahmacārī* and *brahmacarya* in Buddhist and Jain texts can be reduced to a single, narrow meaning of "celibacy." The earliest Jain texts, the first book each of the *Āyāraṅga* and the *Sūyagaḍaṃga*, refer several times to the *bambhacera*,[50] but in no case does this word refer unambiguously to celibacy. Instead, the word seems to refer to the lifestyle of a Jain monk in general, which, although it certainly centers on celibacy, also goes beyond that. For example, in *Āyāraṅga* we find the following description of the difficulty of *bambhacera*:

> Though some know the misery of the world, have relinquished their former connections, have given up ease, live in [*bambhacera*], and, whether monk or layman, thoroughly understand the law, they are not able (to persevere in a religious life). The ill-disposed, giving

up the robe, alms-bowl, blanket, and broom, do not bear the continuous hardships that are difficult to bear.[51]

Certainly celibacy is among the hardships that some are unable to bear in this sort of lifestyle, but this passage is clearly referring to these hardships in general and not just celibacy. Likewise, the 14th chapter of the *Sūyagaḍaṃga* begins with a reference to the *bambhacera* of a monk,[52] but this does not serve as a prelude to a discussion of celibacy, but rather as a prelude to the discussion of the importance of obeying one's teacher so as to properly learn the monastic discipline. Again, celibacy is certainly central to monastic discipline, but not wholly constitutive of it.

Turning now to the Buddhist texts, the most common use of the word *brahmacārī* in the Pali Canon is in the compound *sabrahmacārī*, which, roughly speaking, can be translated as "co-religionist."[53] Although this word certainly implies celibacy, this implication is somewhat trivial, as the emphasis is on a *relationship* between human individuals based on a common pursuit that has to do with much more than simple abstinence from sexual intercourse. Moreover, the relationship implied is generally quite close, as of companions who know one another personally; what we are dealing with here is not an imagined community of ancient Indian "Promise Keepers" linked merely by putative celibacy, but members of local, face-to-face communities linked by common teachers, practices, and systems of belief that go far beyond celibacy, although celibacy would have certainly played a part. An excellent example of the use of the word *sabrahmacārī* is with reference to Bharaṇḍu Kālāma, who is mentioned in a *sutta* (*AN* 3.127) as a former *sabrahmacārī* of the Buddha himself (*bhagavato purāṇasabrahmacārī*). The Buddha stays at Bharaṇḍu Kālāma's hermitage (*assama*) while in Kapilavatthu and (in an exchange that is somewhat obscure) slights Kālāma in the presence of Mahānāma, a prominent Sakyan, thus forcing the former to leave the city. According to the commentary, Bharaṇḍu Kālāma is called a former *sabrahmacārī* of the Buddha because, prior to the Buddha's Awakening, they had both been disciples of Āḷāra Kālāma.[54] The use of this word in such a context clearly implies living a celibate life of study under the tutelage of a teacher.

Indeed, a passage from the *Dīgha Nikāya* emphasizes the importance to perfecting *brahmacariya* of having a good teacher. After hearing about the disarray among the Jain monks (Nigaṇṭhas) after the death of their leader, the Nigaṇṭha Nātaputta (Mahāvīra), the Buddha addresses a novice named Cunda about what will keep the Buddhist *saṅgha* strong and in accord. In doing so, he says,

> Moreover, Cunda, the *brahmacariya* is endowed with these qualities: The teacher is not a recognized elder long-gone-forth, getting-on, attained to old-age. Thus the *brahmacariya* is imperfect in this case. But since, Cunda, the *brahmacariya* is endowed with these qualities—the teacher is a recognized elder long-gone-forth, getting-on, attained to old-age—thus the *brahmacariya* is perfect in this case.[55]

The Buddha then goes on to explain, in the same terms, the importance of senior monk disciples (*therā bhikkhū sāvakā*), monk disciples of middle standing (*majjhimā bhikkhū sāvakā*), junior monk disciples (*navā bhikkhū sāvakā*), senior nun disciples (*therā bhikkhuniyo sāvikā*), nun disciples of middle standing (*majjhimā bhikkhuniyo sāvikā*), junior nun disciples (*navā bhikkhuniyo sāvikā*), and various types of lay disciples.[56] Finally, he says that *brahmacariya* itself must be "prosperous, opulent, extensive, public, well-spread, well-proclaimed by gods and mortals, and attained to the highest gain and fame."[57] The *brahmacariya* being described in these terms is clearly not only celibacy but the entire enterprise the author of this text envisions the Buddhist *saṅgha* being engaged in. Moreover, since the interlocutor with whom the Buddha is engaging here is a Nigaṇṭha (Jain monk), it is clear that this expansive understanding of *brahmacarya* is one shared by the early Buddhists and Jains.

It should not be surprising that early Buddhists and Jains would articulate what it was they were doing using the term *brahmacarya*. The Buddhist Vinaya provides for a monk to be assigned both a preceptor (*upajjhāya*) and a teacher (*ācariya*) upon ordination.[58] Positions by these same names are also known within the Jain monastic orders, and although the preceptor has become a fairly rare position, the teacher (Skt. *ācārya*) remains an important position of rank within Jain monastic communities.[59] In addition, the Buddhist scriptures repeatedly cast the Buddha in the role of teacher (P. *satthā*, Skt. *śāstṛ*) and, as already discussed above, use the word *sāsana/śāsana* ("teaching" or "instruction") to describe in the abstract what members of the *saṅgha* submit themselves to. Jain scriptures also place great emphasis on obedience to one's teacher, sometimes in the same terms.[60] Given this extensive rhetoric of education, together with the requirement of celibacy, the similarities to the Bramanical institution of *brahmacarya* are obvious.

Nevertheless, interpretation of Buddhist and Jain uses of the word *brahmacarya* have been colored by the Brahmanical *āśrama* system, the system of four "orders of life," which became, together with the system of four *varṇas*, one of the cornerstones of classical Hindu *dharma*. In its classical form, first articulated in the *Mānava Dharmaśāstra* ("The Laws of Manu"), the *āśrama* system is a series of four stages of life, to be undertaken in succession. The first of these is called *brahmacarya*, which in this context refers to Vedic studentship, to be completed prior to getting married and becoming a householder (the second stage). Patrick Olivelle has shown that in fact the earliest articulation of the *āśrama* system, found in the Dharma Sūtras, is different: Here, each *āśrama* is a lifelong vocation, and one must choose one of the four rather than completing all in succession. In this context, the first *āśrama*, called *brahmacarya*, refers to lifelong celibacy under a teacher and is distinct from Vedic studentship.[61]

Nevertheless, the association of *brahmacarya* with Vedic studentship in the classical system can give the misleading impression that *brahmacarya* is a properly "Brahmanical" term. Because of this, it might seem more natural to label the early Buddhists and Jains as *parivrājakas* ("wanderers," the fourth *āśrama* in the system), and not as *brahmacārins*. On the one hand, the similarities between the early Buddhists and Jains and the āśramic descriptions of the *parivrājaka* are clear, and the category *parivrājaka* does not play a central role in Brahmanical ideology. On the other hand, the category *brahmacarya* is colored by its equation with the Brahmanical institution of Vedic studentship in the classical system. Viewed in this way, the tendency of the early Buddhist and Jain texts to identify with the category of *brahmacārī* could be understood simply as a strategic move to coopt the prestige of the Brahmans. This would, of course, be an example of "marketing" as the term is used by Bailey and Mabbett.

We will be looking at the *āśrama* system more closely in the next chapter as a central element of the articulation of a world-affirming, househoulder-supremacist vision of Brahmanhood. Nevertheless, since *brahmacarya* has come in modern scholarship to be associated so closely with the Brahmanical *āśrama* system, it behooves us to address its relevance to our discussion of *brahmacarya* with respect to the Buddhist and Jain traditions here. I believe that an uncritical acceptance of the Brahmanical *āśrama* system has the potential to color our perception of non-Brahmanical uses of the categories found therein, in three ways. First, the very taxonomization of ways of life into four categories itself can give the false impression that these four categories are mutually exclusive. Indeed, it seems difficult to deny that

Buddhist and Jain monks would have been considered *parivrājakas*, given that they were celibate, shaved (or plucked) their heads, subsisted off of alms obtained through begging, and wandered except for a retreat of fixed residence during the rainy season. Indeed, both groups used a verb closely related to the verbal root of *parivrājaka* (Skt. *pari* + *vraj*) to refer to the initial stage of a monk's ordination, the "going forth" (Skt. *pravrajyā: pra* + *vraj*).[62] At the same time, however, it certainly seems plausible to locate the Buddhist and Jain monks under the category of *brahmacārin*, insofar as they were celibate, underwent a ritual of initiation (which Jains even refer to as *dīkṣā*![63]), and studied under the tutelage of more senior monks and, ultimately, the Buddha or Mahāvīra himself. There is no reason to assume that the categories *parivrājaka* and *brahmacārin* were, in colloquial speech, mutually exclusive. While the *āśrama* system does set them up as separate categories, we will see in the next chapter that that system is contrived to serve a particular agenda—namely, the Dharmaśāstric agenda of taxonomizing social custom.

This brings me to the second way in which we must be careful not to be misled by the *āśrama* system. The introduction of the concept of the *āśrama* system itself, and the inclusion of lifelong *brahmacārya* within it, represents a *particular* ideological representation of a concept with roots far more ancient than the system of *āśrama*. In his study of the *āśrama* system, Olivelle warns against confusing the two, writing that "[t]he four *āśramas* . . . are not coextensive with the respective social institutions classified by the system" and that "[t]he history of the system, therefore, is quite distinct from the history of these institutions taken individually or collectively, and the study of the former should not be confused with that of the latter."[64]

What then can we say about *brahmacarya* as it was understood, even within Vedic texts, prior to its incorporation into the *āśrama* system? The earliest usage of the word *brahmacārin* is found in the tenth book of the *Ṛg Veda*, where its purport is unfortunately rather obscure. It occurs in the context of a hymn (*RV* 10.109) calling for the return of a Brahman's abducted wife. In the course of this brief and rather cryptic narrative, the following verse is included:

> A *brahmacārin* lives as a servant serving intently; he becomes one limb of the gods.
> In that way, Bṛhaspati found his wife (who had been) taken by Soma, like the gods (found) the sacrificial ladle (when it was taken by Soma).[65]

According to Wendy Doniger O'Flaherty, a parallel is being drawn here between a human Brahman appealing to the king to return his wife and a myth in which Bṛhaspati's wife is abducted by Soma.[66] It is not entirely clear whether the *brahmacārī* who is the subject of the verb *carati* is a human Brahman, the god Bṛhaspati, or perhaps both. What is somewhat clear is that being a *brahmacārin* involves "working" or "serving" (*veviṣat*[67]) as a "servant" (*viṣa*).

Other slightly later Vedic *saṃhitā* texts make equally brief and cryptic references to the *brahmacārin* or *brahmacarya*. The *Taittirīya Saṃhitā* refers to a son of Manu named Nābhānediṣṭha, who is deprived by his father of his inheritance, as a *brahmacārin*, but no further background about this appellation is provided.[68] There is one other reference to *brahmacarya* and the *brahmacārin* in the *Taittirīya Saṃhitā*, in the following verse:

> Even while being born a Brahman is born with three debts: with [the debts of] *brahmacarya* to the *ṛṣis*, sacrifice to the gods, [and] offspring to the ancestors. On the other hand, he is without debt who has sons, sacrifices, and dwells as a *brahmacārin*.[69]

This is a fairly well-known verse because it became the basis of the "theology of debts" in later Brahmanical orthodoxy.[70] It does not, however, give any real sense of what *brahmacarya* is or what it means to "dwell" as a *brahmacārin*.[71] The *Atharva Veda* makes several references to the *brahmacārin*, most of which are equally cryptic. One reference, included in a hymn asking for success in throwing dice, appeals to the speaker's having lived in *brahmacarya* (perhaps in fulfillment of the debt spoken of in *TS* 3.1.9.4?) in asking the gods for help with the dice.[72] Two other references associate the *brahmacārin*, unsurprisingly, with *brahman*.[73] Another verse refers to the *brahmacārin* "of" Death, for whom he procures a man (*puruṣa*)—perhaps in reference to the practice of a *brahmacārin* begging on behalf of his teacher.[74]

The *Atharva Veda* also contains, however, an entire hymn extolling the virtues of *brahmacārin*, constituting what may be the earliest text to address the *brahmacārin* and *brahmacarya* at length. Given the significance of this hymn, I will quote it here in full:

> The *brahmacārin* wanders impelling both heaven and earth. The
> gods are of one mind with respect to him.
> He holds earth and heaven; he protects the teacher with *tapas*. (1)

The fathers, those born of the gods, the gods one-by-one—all go to the *brahmacārin*.
The *gandharvas* came to him—thirty-three, three hundred, six thousand—he protects all the gods with *tapas*. (2)
Bringing the *brahmacārin* near, the teacher makes him an embryo within.
He bears him in his belly for three nights; the gods approach to see him born. (3)
This piece of fuel is the earth; the second is the sky; and the atmosphere he fills with fuel.
The *brahmacārin* protects the worlds with fuel, his girdle, toil, and *tapas*. (4)
First born of the *brahman*, the *brahmacārī*, wearing sunshine, stood up by means of *tapas*.
From him were born the Brahman, the most excellent *brahman*, and all the gods, along with immortality. (5)
The *brahmacārin* goes kindled with fuel, wearing the skin of the black antelope, consecrated, with a long beard.
He goes at once from the lower to the higher sea; he grasps the worlds and brings them to himself over and over again in an instant. (6)
The *brahmacārin*, generating the *brahman*, the waters, the world, Prajāpati, Parameṣṭhin, Virāj,
Became an embryo in the womb of immortality, and then having become Indra, crushed the *asuras*. (7)
The teacher fashioned both "clouds," the wide, deep earth and heaven.
The *brahmacārin* protects them with *tapas*; with respect to him the gods are of one mind. (8)
The *brahmacārin* at first brought this land, the earth, as alms—and heaven.
Having made them into fuel, he attends upon them; all beings are dependent on them. (9)
The one here, the other beyond—the two treasures of the Brahman are deposited secretly behind the sky.
The *brahmacārin* protects them with *tapas*; that alone the one with knowledge makes into *brahman*. (10)
The one here, the other there—two fires from the earth come together between these two "clouds."

Upon them are fixed firm rays; the *brahmacārin* ascends them
using *tapas*. (11)
Roaring, thundering, a large ruddy, whitish penis enters into
the earth.
The *brahmacārin* sprinkles semen on the summit, on the earth; by
means of that the four quarters live. (12)
In fire, in the sun, in the moon, in the air, in the waters, the
*brahmacārin* deposits fuel.
Their flames go one-by-one in the cloud; their clarified butter is
man, rain, water. (13)
The teacher (was) death, Varuṇa, Soma, plants, milk.
The clouds were attendants; by them this sun was brought. (14)
Varuṇa, having become the teacher, makes his own ghee at home.
Whatever he desired from Prajāpati, that the *brahmacārin* offered
as a friend from his own self. (15)
The teacher is the *brahmacārin*; the *brahmacārin* is Prajāpati.
Prajāpati rules; Virāj became the ruler Indra. (16)
A king guards his kingdom with *brahmacarya*, with *tapas*.
A teacher seeks a *brahmacārin* with *brahmacarya*. (17)
By *brahmacarya* a maiden finds a young man (to be her) husband.
By *brahmacarya* an ox (or a) horse seeks to go to pasture. (18)
By *brahmacarya*, by *tapas*, the gods destroyed death.
Indra then used *brahmacarya* to bring the sun to the gods. (19)
Plants, the past and the future, day and night, the tree,
The year with (its) seasons—they were born of the
*brahmacārin*. (20)
Those animals that are of the earth, of the sky, wild and
domesticated,
Without wings and with wings—they were born of the
*brahmacārin*. (21)
All individually bear the breaths of Prajāpati in themselves.
The *brahman* brought in the *brahmacārin* protects them all. (22)
Elicited by the gods, this wanders unmounted, shining.
From it were born the Brahman, the most excellent *brahman*, and
all the gods, along with immortality. (23)
He bears the shining *brahman* (over that all the gods are woven
together),
Generating the in- and out-breaths and then the circulating breath,
speech, mind, heart, *brahman*, (and) intelligence. (24)

Put eye, ear, fame in us, food, semen, blood, belly. (25)
Arranging those, the *brahmacārin* stood generating *tapas* on the surface of the water in the ocean.
He, bathed, tawny, (and) ruddy, shines much on the earth. (26)[75]

There are several interesting features worth noting about the description of the *brahmacārin* in this hymn. First, he has a teacher (*ācārya*). No mention is made of a curriculum that the *ācārya* teaches the *brahmacārin*, however; instead, in v. 3, the *ācārya*, "bringing" the *brahmacārin* "near" (*upanáyamāno*, which is derived from the same root and prefix as *upayana*, the Brahmanical rite of initiation), makes him an "embryo within" (*gárbham antáḥ*) and "bears him in his belly three nights" (*táṃ rā́trīs tisrá udáre bibharti*), after which the *brahmacārin* is "born" (*jātáṃ*). What exactly is "born" or what this "birth" entails is not entirely clear, although twice (v. 5, 23) the "most excellent *brahman*" (*bráhma jyeṣṭháṃ*) of the Brahman (*brā́hmaṇaṃ*)[76] is said to be "born from that" (*tásmāj jātáṃ*). Although no mention is made of the *ācārya* "teaching" his *brahmacārin* anything in the ordinary sense, the *brahmacārin* clearly serves his *ācārya*, bringing in v. 9 "alms" (*bhikṣā*), which are then used as fuel, presumably in the sacrificial fire. Repeated mention is made of the *brahmacārin*'s *tapas*, and of the seemingly immense power that the *brahmacārin* possesses as a result of it. The *brahmacārin*'s *tapas* appears, in v. 17–19, to be equated with *brahmacarya* itself as a power by which great things can be accomplished. It allows a king to defend his kingdom, an *ācārya* to seek a *brahmacārin*, a maiden to win a husband, an animal to obtain food, the gods to destroy death, and Indra to bring heaven to the gods. Although it is not stated so explicitly, it is likely that this "power" referred to as *brahmacarya* is derived from celibacy, since it is equated with *tapas* (a concept associated throughout Indian history with control over seminal emissions) and attributed to many types of people other than just *brahmacārins*—in particular, a young woman, whom we can assume wins herself a husband on the basis of her virginity.

When described in these terms, *brahmacarya* and the *brahmacārin* hardly seem like inappropriate categories for describing the Buddhist or Jain *bhikkhu*. To begin with, the Buddhist *bhikkhu*, upon entering the *saṅgha*, has both an *upajjhāya* and an *ācariya*, whom he serves,[77] and Jain monks had similarly named preceptors and teachers as well. The *bhikkhu* in both orders obtains sustenance by begging for alms; indeed, the word *bhikkhu* (Skt. *bhikṣu*) itself is derived from the verb root meaning to beg (*bhikṣ*). The *bhikkhu* is celibate, and the word *brahmacariya,* as we have seen above, refers both to celibacy per se and more broadly and abstractly to the endeavor that he is engaged in. Finally, although the language about the *ācārya* "birthing" his *brahmacārin* that we find in the *Atharva* passage is not, generally speaking, paralleled in the early Buddhist and Jain literature; nonetheless, the identity that the *bhikkhu* is expected to assume as the result of his training is expressed using the same word found in this and other Brahmanical texts: *Brahman.*

Indeed, as Timothy Lubin has suggested, it is possible that undergoing *brahmacarya* was originally what *made* one a Brahman, and that the idea of being born (i.e., through natural birth) into a particular *varṇa* came later.[78] This appears to at least be hinted at in *AVŚ* 11.5. As already noted, the teacher makes his *brahmacārin* into an embryo (*garbha*) for three nights, after which he gives "birth" to him. Although no direct connection is made, the "most excellent *brahman* of the Brahman" (*brā́hmaṇaṃ bráhma jyeṣṭháṃ*) is also said to be born in the process. A more direct connection is made in an extended discussion of the *upanayana* in the *Śatapatha Brāhmaṇa.* In this passage (*ŚB* 11.5.4), it is said that a teacher (*ācārya*) teaches his *brahmacārin* the *sāvitrī,* but that in the past he did so only after a year, the rationale being that "children are indeed born the measure of a year."[79] Progressively shorter intervals of time are then given for waiting to teach the *sāvitrī* (*ŚB* 11.5.4.7–10), each being correlated in some way with the normal gestational period of "one year" for a human child. This culminates in an interval of three days, which is said to correspond to a year because there are three seasons in the year (*ŚB* 11.5.4.11). The *brāhmaṇa* then continues,

> Also concerning that, they sing a *śloka*: "The teacher becomes pregnant after laying his right hand [on the *brahmacārin*]. / On the third [night] he is born with the *sāvitrī* as a Brahman. //"[80]

This passage clearly parallels the *Atharva* passage examined above, which also speaks of the *ācārya* becoming pregnant with his *brahmacārin* for a period of three nights. Here, however, it is clear that the "birth" that results is the birth of a Brahman.

The idea that an *ārya* is "born again" through the *upanayana* is a well-known element of classical Hindu doctrine, and the term *dvija,* "twice born," is used in reference to that idea. In classical Hinduism, all three *ārya varṇas* (*brāhmaṇa, kṣatriya,* and *vaiśya*) are eligible for the *upanayana* and thus *dvija.* The idea that they are born twice is simply a perfunctory reference to the *upanayana* metaphorically conceived of as a second birth; all it serves to do is distinguish them from *śūdras*, who are ineligible for initiation. Lubin has noted, however, that the word *dvija* was not used to refer to the *three* higher *varṇas* until rules of initiation for all three of those *varṇas* were laid out in the Gṛhya Sūtras. Prior to that time, the word *dvija* was used only to refer to Brahmans, and the person who undergoes *upanayana* and *brahmacarya* is assumed to be a Brahman. In fact, even in the Gṛhya Sūtras, Lubin notes, discussions of the *upanayana* sometimes seem to assume that the initiate is a Brahman. On the basis of these observations, Lubin argues that, starting with the Gṛhya Sūtras, Brahmans tried to inculcate Brahmanical piety in the broader population by making Vedic initiation and study accessible to and incumbent upon *kṣatriyas* and *vaiśyas*, as well as Brahmans.[81]

Following Bronkhorst, however, I would argue that we must be wary of assuming a preexisting *varṇa* system in interpreting texts such as the Gṛhya Sūtras Lubin is looking at; indeed, as Bronkhorst has convincingly argued, the very idea that society could be divided into four *varṇas* was as much a part of the agenda of Neo-Brahmanism as any other new idea introduced in late Vedic and early post-Vedic texts—such as, say, that there are *three dvija* classes who are all eligible for *upanayana.* If *brahmacarya* was indeed, as the texts we have looked at suggest, originally the way in which one became a Brahman, and that process was conceived of in terms of rebirth, then the term *dvija* would naturally have been applied to Brahmans precisely because they had been reborn, *as Brahmans.* The innovation of the Gṛhya Sūtras, then, would not simply have been an *extension* of the right to *upanayana*, and thus *dvija* status, to two other classes, but rather a total *reformulation* of the purpose of *upanayana* and *brahmacarya.* Whereas before it had been the means by which a person was reborn and therefore became a Brahman, now all people were born (naturally) into a particular *varṇa. Upanayana* became merely a marker of elite status within that system, and *brahmacarya* an opportunity to educate these elites in an increasingly sophisticated body of Vedic knowledge. The metaphor of rebirth was retained in the term *dvija,* but merely as a relic of the old system.

This brings me to the third and final way in the *āśrama* system can obscure our understanding of the categories found therein. Insofar as the *āśrama* system was used as an ideological tool of Neo-Brahmanism, it encourages us to see the categories it brings into its orbit in terms dictated by Neo-Brahmanism—namely, the vision of society as divided into four *varṇas* determined by birth, with the Brahmans as custodians and executors of Vedic knowledge at the top. I have already argued that, as a matter of methodology, we should not assume that the advocates of Neo-Brahmanism owned the word *brāhmaṇa* and that all others who used it, such as the early Buddhists, did so only derivatively as a "reaction" or "marketing." The same is true of the terms *brahmacarya* and *brahmacārin*. As I have shown, the earliest references to *brahmacarya* in the Brahmanical literature make reference to features that are shared by Buddhist monks—including celibacy, collecting alms, serving a teacher, and the goal of becoming a Brahman.

The only aspect of Buddhist/Jain *brahmacarya* that might possibly be considered innovative, insofar as it makes it impossible to repay one's debt to the gods by producing progeny (*TS* 6.3.10.5, cited above), is that it is (ideally) lifelong. Even here, however, the evidence for ancient practice is ambiguous. Most of the passages we have looked at, including the extended discussions of *brahmacarya* in the *Atharva Veda* and the *Śatapatha Brāhmaṇa*, say nothing about how long it is to be practiced. Some other texts do clearly define it as temporary. There is another interesting extended discussion of the *brahmacārin* in the *Śatapatha Brāhmaṇa*, for example, that at least alludes to the end of *brahmacarya* by saying that the *brahmacārin* should no longer beg for alms once he has bathed.[82] Two passages in the *Chāndogya Upaniṣad* (4.10.1, 6.1.2) describe *brahmacarya* as lasting 12 years. Elsewhere, however, there are stories of people or gods who undertake much longer periods of *brahmacarya*. A story in the *Taittirīya Brāhmaṇa* (3.10.11) has Bharadvāja remaining in *brahmacarya* until age 75. Likewise, according to *Chāndogya Upaniṣad* 8.11.3, Indra underwent a *brahmacarya* of 101 years.[83] One passage of the *Chāndogya* even describes a type of *brahmacārin* who "settles himself permanently in the family of a teacher"[84]—which is precisely the practice described as one of the four *āśramas* in the earliest descriptions of the system in the Dharma Sūtras.

While there are therefore clear lines of continuity between early conceptions of *brahmacarya* as evinced in the Vedas and Buddhist/Jain *brahmacariya*, conversely there were, as we will explore in more detail in the next chapter, clear and important innovations with regard to *brahmacarya* in the Brahmanical tradition—innovations that were tied to the incorporation of *brahmacarya* into the *āśrama* system and the subsequent development of that system. For now, suffice it to say that by incorporating into the system the problematic practice of *brahmacarya* as a lifelong vocation of celibacy, the proponents of Neo-Brahmanism sequestered it, thus creating space for the construction of a normative *brahmacarya* that was dedicated to Vedic study, and most importantly temporary, which in turn allowed for the assumption of householdership and the production of children. Then, with the development of the classical system, lifelong *brahmacarya* was eliminated entirely by replacing it with the normative period of Vedic study.

This is not to say that *brahmacarya* as practiced by the early Buddhists and Jains was actually more faithful to the "primitive" concept of *brahmacarya* than *brahmacarya* as it came to be defined in the orthodox Brahmanical tradition. The Buddhist/Jain formulation of *brahmacarya* was just as much an innovative construction based on historical antecedents as was the orthodox Brahmanical formulation. What I am arguing, however, is that we should not privilege the orthodox Brahmanical understanding of *brahmacarya* over the Buddhist/Jain simply because *brahmacarya* "really" belongs to the Brahmanical tradition. Early Buddhism, Jainism, and Neo-Brahmanism were all equally innovative and equally rooted in tradition; their unique understandings of *brahmacarya* are both derived from this interplay between historical precedent and innovation.

## *Celibate Renouncers Positioning Themselves vis-à-vis One Another*

As we saw in the last chapter, the assumption of a fundamental dichotomy between *śramaṇa*s and Brahmans is not borne out by the vast majority of the early evidence in which the categories *Brahman* and *śramaṇa* appear. In this chapter, we have now seen evidence that the earliest Jains and Buddhists actually saw *themselves* as Brahmans and articulated a path to Brahmanhood rooted in *brahmacarya*—which for them meant lifelong celibacy under the guidance of a teacher or teachers. Still, one might argue that it is precisely *this* that separates the *śramaṇa*s from the "real" Brahmans—namely, the articulation on the part of the former of a pseudo-Brahmanhood based on celibacy. But such an objection faces a key problem: From an etic[85] perspective, there is no way to clearly circumscribe "Brahmanism" in such a way as to exclude lifestyles based on celibacy. In particular, in ancient India there was a class of religious practitioners who were committed to performing Vedic sacrifices—so committed, in fact, that they sequestered themselves in the forest to do so—but also, at least in some cases, practiced celibacy.[86] These practitioners are referred to by most of the Dharma Sūtra authors as *vānaprasthas*,[87] literally, "forest dwellers." In spite of their strong commitment to Vedic sacrifice, however, it is precisely this group of ascetics that Buddhist texts treat as most closely related to their own. One might assume, based on a model positing a fundamental dichotomy between Brahmanical and non-Brahmanical, that the early Buddhists would have seen their own views most closely approximated in another "non-Brahmanical" group, such as the Jains or Ājīvakas. Instead, we find that they most closely identify with the *vānaprasthas*, or as they referred to them, the *jaṭilas*.[88]

It should be noted at the outset that the word *vānaprastha* itself is not found in the Pali Canon.[89] I would argue, however, that the same type of religious practitioner referred to by the Dharmaśāstric literature as *vānaprastha* (and apparently known to Megasthenes as such[90]) is referred to in the Pali Canon as *jaṭila*. The word *jaṭila* refers to the hair of these ascetics, which was not shaved off, as in the case of Buddhist monks and perhaps most other *parivrājaka* groups, but worn long and matted or braided in some fashion. Three of the Dharma Sūtras (*GDhS* 3.34, *BDhS* 2.11.15, *VDhS* 9.1) use the same word *jaṭila* to describe the hair of the *vānaprastha*. It is thus possible that the authors of the early Buddhist texts used the word *jaṭila* to refer to *vānaprastha*-like ascetics as a sort of "slang"—perhaps derived from colloquial usage, although it is impossible to know for sure.

This conclusion would appear to be confirmed by a post-canonical text, the commentary on the *Jātaka*.[91] Both the term *jaṭila* and the sorts of practices that are associated with the *vānaprastha* in the Dharma Sūtras are there found much more often than in the canonical texts of the Pali Canon, and they appear to be correlated with one another. The portrayal of *jaṭilas* in the Jātakas is generally negative; in fact, most often *jaṭila* characters appear as wily rogues referred to as *kūṭajaṭila* or "deceitful *jaṭila*."[92] Nevertheless, reference to them is useful for our purposes, because *kūṭajaṭilas* often are described as living in the same way as the Dharma Sūtras describe of the *vānaprastha*. All four Dharma Sūtras state clearly that the *vānaprastha* (or *vaikhānasa*) should not only live in the forest but should live off of it. Unlike the *parivrājaka*, who wears rags and eats alms from the village (both of which involve a connection to human culture), the *vānaprastha* wears clothes taken from the wild (such as bark or animal skins) and eats gleanings (such as roots and fruits).[93]

Little mention is made of the clothing of *jaṭila*s, either in the *Jātaka* or elsewhere in the early Buddhist texts, but in *Jāt.* 138, the external characteristics of a *kūṭajaṭila*—namely, his matted locks (*jaṭāhi*) and his garment made of skin (*ajinasāṭiyā*)—are criticized by the Bodhisatta as worthless if the inside is impure. More often, we find reference to the practice of living off of gleanings in the forest. In *Jāt.* 313, the Bodhisatta is born as a Brahman but goes off to live in the forest, "nourishing himself with various fruits" (*phalāphalena yāpento*). Later in the story he encounters a king, who refers to him derisively as a *kūṭajaṭila*. Likewise, in *Jāt.* 344, a *kūṭajaṭila* builds an *assama* (Skt. *āśrama*) near a river and lives off of ripe mangoes that fall from the trees in a nearby mango grove. In *Jāt.* 283, interestingly, we find a story whose main characters are a tiger and a boar, but a *kūṭajaṭila* is also mentioned who "eats the meat obtained" (*gahitamaṃsakhādako*) by the tiger. This would appear to parallel a provision in Baudhāyana, who says that a *vānaprastha*, in addition to eating roots and fruits, "may also make use of the flesh of an animal killed by a predator."[94] Finally, in *Jāt.* 505, a certain *jaṭila* practices gardening and sells what he grows in the market. He is criticized by the Bodhisatta (in this story taking the form of a prince), who says to himself, "This *kūṭajaṭila*, rather than doing the duty of a *samaṇa* for himself, does the work of a green-grocer."[95] This would seem to imply that the *jaṭila* should not be growing his own food; this is paralleled by language found in three of the Dharma Sūtras, which specify that the *vānaprastha* should not even set foot on plowed land, much less engage in gardening himself.[96]

Sometimes, generic ascetics, usually termed *tāpasa*, appear as characters in Jātakas and and have some of the same characteristics as *jaṭila*s in the early Buddhist texts or *vānaprastha*s in the Dharma Sūtras. For example, in *Jāt.* 532, a whole family, including parents and children, go to live in an *assama*; they have matted hair, and the children gather fruits for their parents to eat. Likewise, in *Jāt.* 526, a certain *tāpaso* lives in an *assama* and offers fruits and berries, which he has presumably acquired through gleaning, to a guest.[97] A similar situation is found in *Jāt.* 444, in which two Brahmans go to the Himalayas, build an *assama*, and "nourish themselves with various roots and fruits of the forest" (*vanaphalāphalena yāpentā*). Later, they separate, and the one who remains, Maṇḍabya, is framed for a robbery when a robber breaks into a nearby house, steals something, and then drops the thing he has stolen in front of Maṇḍabya's hut. Interestingly, Maṇḍabya is introduced in this story as a *tāpasa*, but when the owners of the house discover's the stolen item outside of his hut, they say, "Eh, wicked *jaṭila*, you work as a robber by night, [but] by day you go about with the form of a *tāpasa*."[98]

This statement, taken together with the other evidence we have accumulated from the Jātakas, confirms my hypothesis that *jaṭila* is a slang term used to refer to the type of ascetic referred to in the Dharma Sūtras as a *vānaprastha*. As we have seen, ascetics referred to as *jaṭila* or *kūṭajaṭila*, aside from the obvious fact that they have matted hair, also find sustenance in the same way as *vānaprastha*s—that is, by gleaning rather than by growing their own food or begging. In other cases, ascetics who live in this way are simply called *tāpasa*, but the householders' reaction in *Jāt.* 526, when they discover that Maṇḍabya is the robber (or so they think), shows that these are no different than *jaṭila*s, and that in fact *jaṭila* was a term of derision. For in *Jāt.* 526, Maṇḍabya is generally referred to as a *tāpasa*, and it is only when the householders "discover" that he is the robber that they in anger (indicated by the rude interjection *are*) refer to him as a "wicked *jaṭila*" (*duṭṭhajaṭila*).

Now that we have established, on the basis of this evidence from the Jātakas, that *jaṭila* was a slang term used to refer the same sort of ascetic referred to by the Dharma Sūtra authors as the *vānaprastha*, we can return to the canonical texts themselves, where we find more extended stories about *jaṭila*s and the Buddha's interaction with them. By far, the most prominent practice with which *jaṭila*s are associated in the Pali Canon is the tending of a sacred fire. A rule in the *Vinaya* exempting *jaṭila*s from the ordinary probationary period for members of other sects who wish to ordain in the *saṅgha*, which we will examine in more detail shortly, refers to them as *aggikā jaṭilakā* to indicate their association with fire.[99] Likewise, a short anecdote in the *Udāna* has the Buddha encounter *jaṭila*s who "bob up and bob down in the Gayā, perform upward and downward bobbings, sprinkle [themselves with water],[100] and *offer oblations to Agni*"[101]; the Buddha criticizes them for thinking that purity comes from such actions. This again confirms our conclusion that *jaṭila* is slang for a *vānaprasṭha*-like ascetic, because all four of the Dharma Sūtras describe the *vānaprastha*, uniquely among the three celibate *āśrama*s, as maintaining a sacred fire.[102]

The few extended narratives that feature *jaṭila*s as characters within them associate them closely with fire as well. A parable told by Kumāra-Kassapa to Prince Pāyāsi of Kosala (*DN* 23) describes an *aggika jaṭila* who lives in a leaf-hut located in the wilderness (*araññāyatane paṇṇakuṭiyā*) and adopts a baby whom he finds abandoned and raises him as his own.

The parable centers on the stupidity of the child, who when left alone allows the sacred fire to go out and then uses a series of ineffective methods to try to relight it. Likewise, according to an anecdote in the *Vinaya* (IV.108–110), the Buddha, while wandering in Ceti near Bhaddavatikā, is warned by people not to go to Ambatittha because there is a *nāga* who lives there in the *āśrama* of a *jaṭila* (*jaṭilassa assame*). The Buddha himself does not go to Ambatittha, but one of his monks, a certain Sāgata, does go there. He enters the "fire-room" (*agyāgāraṃ*) of the *āśrama,* sits in meditation, and then battles with and ultimately defeats the *nāga* by producing "heat" (*tejo*). In a similar and better-known story, the Buddha converts the three Kassapas and their 1,000 *jaṭila* disciples after spends the night in the fire-room (*agyāgāre*) of the *āśrama* (*assama*) of Uruvelakassapa and uses his "heat" (*tejo*) to defeat the *nāga* that lives there (*Vin.* I.24–35). After the mass-ordination of these *jaṭila*s, the Buddha preaches the "Fire Sermon," which is known in the Theravāda tradition as the Buddha's third sermon because it is the third teaching given by the Buddha in the *Mahāvagga* narrative, after the *Dhammacakkappavattana* and the sermon on *anattā*. This sermon famously inverts the value placed on fire by the *jaṭila*s, transforming it from a sacred object into a metaphor for *saṃsāra.* Fire is no longer something to be tended and cared for, but something to grow "weary" of and abandon.[103]

Narratives about *jaṭila*s are more common in the post-canonical narrative portions of the Jātakas, and there too make reference to the worship of fire in the forest. In two Jātakas (144 and 162), the Bodhisatta is born into a "northern Brahman family" (*udiccabrāhmaṇakule*); when he turns 16, his parents take his "birth fire" (*jātaggiṃ*) and give him two choices: Either he can learn the three Vedas and live in a house, or he can take his birth fire into the woods and worship it there. In both cases, the Bodhisatta decides to take his fire into the forest to worship it there, but in both cases disaster convinces him to abandon fire worship. Now, in neither of these Jātakas is the Bodhisatta explicitly identified as a *jaṭila,* but he *is* identified as a Brahman, and his life follows a course similar to that outlined by the Dharma Sūtras in their descriptions of the *āśrama* system; that is, once he reaches a certain age, he is given a choice between living as a householder or going out into the forest to live an alternative lifestyle of singular devotion to the sacred fire. As in the Dharma Sūtras, and unlike the later classical texts, this is presented as a lifelong decision—and in fact, even after abandoning the fire, the Bodhisatta does not return home but lives out the rest of his life as a homeless ascetic.

The fact that the Bodhisatta is portrayed in these two Jātakas as engaging in a *jaṭila*-like practice of worshiping fire in the forest after being born as a Brahman is paralleled by links with Brahmanical identity found in narratives about *jaṭilas*. In the story of the conversion of the Kassapa brothers already discussed above, for example, Uruvelakassapa is at one point referred to as a Brahman.[104] A more substantive link is found in the one major narrative about a *jaṭila* that we have not already discussed, the story of the *jaṭila* Keṇiya. This story is found in two versions. We will focus on the version in the *Sela Sutta* (*MN* 92) and reproduced at *Sn*. 3.7, since it contains the most extensive links between *jaṭila*s and Brahmans.[105] In this version of the story, a *jaṭila* named Keṇiya hears of the fame of Gotama[106] and therefore goes to see him and offers to feed him and his entire entourage of 1,250 monks. The Buddha responds to this offer by objecting that, on the one hand, his entourage is quite large (and therefore would be difficult to feed) and, on the other, Keṇiya is "devoted to the Brahmans" (*brāhmaṇesu abhippasanno*). This devotion to the Brahmans is borne out later in the story, when, after the Buddha finally accepts Keṇiya's invitation, Keṇiya is busy preparing the meal, and a certain Brahman named Sela comes by and asks Keṇiya what he is doing. While Keṇiya is described simply as a *jaṭila*, Sela is labeled explicitly as a Brahman and described with a formula exalting his Vedic learning.[107] This encounter between Sela and Keṇiya is not by chance, however; the text reports that "at that time Keṇiya the *jaṭila* was devoted to Sela the Brahman."[108] The relationship between Keṇiya and Sela is unfortunately not discussed in any further detail. Sela, impressed by what Keṇiya tells him about the Buddha, decides to visit the Buddha and ultimately ordains in the *saṅgha* together with his entourage and attains Awakening. Keṇiya, quite separately, continues with his preparations and feeds the *saṅgha*, after which we hear nothing more about him.

As always, however, imposing a binary between Brahmanical and non-Brahmanical can obscure more than it reveals in trying to understand categories such as *jaṭila*. On the one hand, *jaṭila*s as they are depicted in the early Buddhist texts appear to be closely related to Vedic Brahmans—most obviously, of course, their practice is centered on making offerings to a sacred fire. But they are also, as we have seen, referred to as Brahmans, as in the case of Uruvelakassapa, and depicted as being devoted, as in the case of Keṇiya, to a Brahman schooled in the three Vedas. On the other hand, we will see in the next chapter that the Dharma Sūtras demonstrate that however close the *jaṭila*s might have been to the category *Brahman* or how close their relationship might have been to Brahmans educated in the Vedas, their relationship to the proponents of Neo-Brahmanism was tenuous at best. That is, at least insofar as they practiced celibacy, they were branded *vānaprasthas* and either denied legitimacy completely or frowned upon as inferior to the *gṛhastha*.

For their own part, the early Buddhists seem to have been unconcerned with any binary between Brahmanical and non-Brahmanical in situating themselves vis-à-vis other *samaṇabrāhmaṇa* groups. We have already seen that the early Buddhist texts, like those of the Jains, embrace the category *brahmacārī*, not unreasonably, as reflecting the *bhikkhu* as a celibate student. We have also seen that the early texts are critical of a wide variety of particular rival groups and seek to define the Buddha's teaching against them; this is as true of the *jaṭilas* as it is of the Nigaṇṭhas (Jains) and Ājīvikas. Nevertheless, the *Vinaya* (I.71) singles out *jaṭilas* as the one group of rival sectarians who did not have to undergo a four-month probationary period (*parivāsa*) if they wanted to ordain as Buddhist monks. The ordinary rule for members of other sects (*aññatitthiyapubbā*) who wanted to ordain was that they had to wait four months; this was to ensure that new converts were committed to being Buddhist monks and would not switch allegiances back and forth. The reason the Buddha gives for exempting *jaṭilas* from this rule is that they are *kammavādino* and *kiriyavādino*.

What exactly does this mean? According to the commentary, it means that "they do not ward off causative action (*kiriyaṃ*); they are of the view that action (*kamma*) and the result of action exist."[109] If this is taken to refer simply to the belief in *karma*, then it is not clear why *jaṭilas* would be singled out in this respect and other groups, such as the Jains, would be excluded, since the latter also believe in *karma*. Nevertheless, this distinction on the basis of being *kammavādī* and *kiriyavādī* is maintained consistently in other texts. For example, a *sutta* in the *Aṅguttara Nikāya* (6.57) reports that Pūraṇa Kassapa, one of the "six heretical teachers" already discussed above, categorizes people in six groups, in which *bhikkhū* are identified as *kammavādā* and *kiriyavādā*, and other groups including the Jains are not:

> Reverend sir, six species are made known by Pūraṇa Kassapa—the black species is made known, the indigo species is made known, the red species is made known, the yellow species is made known, the white species is made known, the supremely white species is made known.

> With respect to that, reverend sir, this is the black species made known by Pūraṇa Kassapa: sheep-butchers, fowlers, deer-hunters, hunters, fishermen, robbers, killers of robbers, jailers, or whoever else follows a bloody trade.
>
> With respect to that, reverend sir, this is the indigo species made known by Pūraṇa Kassapa: *bhikkhus* of the thorn-practice and whoever else propounds action (*kammavādā*) and causative action (*kriyavādā*).
>
> With respect to that, reverend sir, this is the red species made known by Pūraṇa Kassapa: one-cloth *nigaṇṭhas*.
>
> With respect to that, reverend sir, this is the yellow species made known by Pūraṇa Kassapa: house-dwelling, white-clad disciples of naked ascetics.
>
> With respect to that, reverend sir, this is the white species made known by Pūraṇa Kassapa: male and female Ājīvikas.
>
> With respect to that, reverend sir, this is the supremely white species made known by Pūraṇa Kassapa: Nanda Vaccha, Kisa Saṅkicca and Makkhali Gosāla.
>
> Reverend sir, these are the six species made known by Pūraṇa Kassapa.[110]

This taxonomy appears to present a hierarchy of human beings in which *bhikkhus*—presumably referring, at least in part, to Buddhists—are near the bottom, just a step above the complete reprobates, and then are followed, in sequence, by Jains, lay disciples, ordinary Ājīvikas, and finally the fully realized Ājīvika saints. What is important for our purposes to note is that the *bhikkhus* are identified as *kammavādā* and *kriyavādā*, while the various other groups of people that can variously be identified as Jain or Ājīvika are not.

While *Vin.* I.71 is alone in identifying *jaṭilas* as *kammavādino* and *kiriyavādino*, and the *Aṅguttara* passage just cited does not specify who, other than *bhikkhus*, are *kammavādā* and *kriyavādā*, two other passages appear to link these doctrines to the Brahmans. In two encounter dialogs, the Brahman interlocutor praises the Buddha in a long formula that includes the following line: "The *samaṇa* Gotama is indeed a proponent of action, a proponent of causative action, devoted without sin to the Brahmanical people."[111] Here, then, we have Brahmans not only mirroring the attribution of *kammavāda* and *kiriyavāda* to *jaṭilas* found in the Vinaya, but *explicitly linking those doctrines to Brahmanhood.*

Now, it is not entirely clear why the authors of the early Buddhist texts see *kammavāda* and *kiriyavāda* as doctrines tying themselves to the *jaṭila*s and even householder Brahmans, and distinguishing them from Jains and Ājīvikas, but I think that we can hazard a guess. In Pūraṇa Kassapa's taxonomy cited above, *bhikkhus*, whom I take to refer to as Buddhists, are not only referred to as *kammavādā* and *kriyavādā* but also as *kaṇṭakavuttikā,* an obscure term I translate as "of the thorn-practice." Presumably this refers to a perception that Buddhists, and others like them who are left unspecified, are in some sense austere in their practices. This perception (or rather perception of a perception, since the words are put into Pūraṇa Kassapa's mouth by the Buddhist author of the text) is mirrored by depictions of Ājīvika teachings in the Pali *sutta*s, which typically depict them as rejecting the efficacy of *karma*. In the *Sāmaññaphala Sutta* (*DN* 2), for example, Pūraṇa Kassapa himself is said to proclaim a doctrine known simply as "non-causative action" (*akiriyaṃ*). Makkhali Gosala declares that "there is no condition for the defilement of beings; without cause, without condition are beings defiled."[112] Ajita Kesakambalī denies that there are any fruits of actions or any other world in which to enjoy them, and Pakudha Kaccāyana declares a doctrine of atomism whereby killing entails not killing, but a mere separation of the elements. Now, as Bronkhorst has convincingly shown, these doctrines, although they misrepresent the actual doctrines held by those being criticized, probably do nonetheless reflect an actual Ājīvika belief that one could not attain liberation through actions; one could only wait for one's karma to "burn off" over countless lifetimes before being liberated. In this respect, they differed from the Jains only insofar as the latter believed that one *could* undertake austerities to speed up the process of burning off karma and thus attain liberation more quickly.[113] In both cases, the ultimate *goal* was complete non-action. I argue that the Buddhists, who clearly valued the efficacy of good karma (i.e., merit, or *puṇya*) to, among other things, transform a person into a Buddha, perceived this as a rejection of karma, and as distinguishing both the Jains and the Ājīvikas from themselves, Vedic Brahmans, and *jaṭila*s.

In addition, although a full discussion of the issue is beyond the scope of this book, it is very likely that (1) the term *kriyāvāda* and its antithesis, *akriyāvāda,* were used more as polemical labels than as coherent philosophical positions in ancient India and that (2) even as a label of self-identity, it possessed a certain fluidity. We have already noted that there are Buddhist *sutta*s in which Brahman interlocutors praise the Buddha for embracing *kammavāda* and *kiriyavāda*, but in another *sutta* (*AN* 4.24.233), a Brahman accuses the Buddha of proclaiming a doctrine of the non-effectiveness of action.[114] On this occasion, the Buddha responds simply by denying that he denies the effectiveness of action, but on other occasions the Buddha responds to a similar accusation by responding that he affirms *both* the effectiveness of action (*kiriyavāda) and* the non-effectiveness of action (*akiriyavāda*). We see this, for example, in *AN* 2.4.3, in which the Buddha explains to a Brahman who makes the accusation that he is a proponent of the doing of good deeds and the non-doing of bad deeds.[115] It seems that a certain word-play is at work here: interpreting *kiriyavāda* and *akiriyavāda* not as mutually exclusive philosophical positions pertaining to the effectiveness or non-effectiveness of action, but somewhat more literally as "what is to be done" and "what is not to be done."[116]

Interestingly, however, the Buddha also gives such an explanation when accused of teaching *akiriyavāda by a Jain.* In *Vin.* I.233–238, a certain general named Sīha who is a lay follower of the Jains decides that he would like to visit the Buddha but is initially discouraged from doing so by the Nigaṇṭha Nātaputta (Mahāvīra) himself. The reason? According to Mahāvīra, it is inappropriate for someone who accepts *kiriyavāda* to visit a teacher who teaches *akiriyavāda*. Thus, we find here that the Jains *do* consider themselves to uphold the efficacy of actions—but this would seem to contradict other passages from the Pali Canon that we have already seen, in which it is implied that Jains *do not* uphold the efficacy of actions. One explanation for this is simple: As a polemical term, *kiriyavādī* is in the eye of the beholder, so just because the Jains regarded themselves to uphold the efficacy of action does not mean that the Buddhists did.[117] In addition, the Jain texts themselves do not seem to agree on whether *kriyāvāda* is or is not the proper Jain philosophical position. A single text, the *Sūyagaḍaṃga*, contains contradictory passages that on the one hand criticize *kriyāvāda* and on the other hand embrace it.[118] Thus, it is possible that the Jain position on the issue changed or solidified over time.

For our purposes, however, it is not important why exactly the early Buddhists saw themselves as linked uniquely to the *jaṭilas* as *kammavādino* and *kiriyavādino,* to the exclusion of the Jains, who might seem to fit that label as well. What is important is that that is how they understood themselves, irrespective of any imagined boundaries between Brahmanical and non-Brahmanical. The early Buddhists certainly have pointed critiques for householder Brahmans and *jaṭilas*, just as much as they do for Jains and Ājīvikas, but on the matter of karma they see themselves as more similar to the former than to the latter. Any dichotomization of early Indian religion into "Brahmanical" and "non-Brahmanical" obscures the way in which various groups made use of a common vocabulary—including *śramaṇa, brāhmaṇa, brahmacārin, parivrājaka, jaṭila,* and others—to taxonomize and situate themselves within the socio-religious world in which they lived.

## *The Unambiguous Other: Householders*

So far, we have seen three things. First, early Buddhists and Jains understood themselves to be Brahmans. Second, they had a credible case to make that they *were* Brahmans on the basis of *brahmacarya.* And third, in a world where many groups were claiming to be Brahmans, the sense of affinity between competing groups, as exemplified by the Buddhists and *jaṭilas* (*vānaprasthas*), does not appear to have respected the putative boundary between Brahmanical and non-Brahmanical. But this raises an important question: If "Brahmanical" versus "non-Brahmanical" was not an operative dichotomy in ancient India, what, if anything, was? Was there in fact some other binary that conditioned the way in which competing claimants to Brahmanhood in ancient India understood their own identity and their relationship to other groups? I will argue that there was: the binary between householder and renouncer. For those who claimed Brahmanhood on the basis of celibacy like the Buddhists and Jains, the total other to their sense of self-identity was not "the Brahmans," since this was not a meaningful category of otherness to them anyway. Rather, it was the householder per se that they saw as their complete other.

This statement may initially appear problematic. After all, in living Jain and Buddhist cultures, monks and nuns live in a symbiotic relationship with their laity. The former rely on the latter for material goods, in particular food, and the latter rely on the former to provide a source of "merit" that will provide them with a better rebirth. In what sense then can we say that householders, on whom they depended for material existence, were the complete "other" of the early Jains and Buddhists? I think part of the confusion here is a matter of terminology and translation. As it happens, the English word *householder* does not translate a single word found in the relevant Sanskrit, Pali, and Ardhamāgadhī texts, but several. Of these, two are most important for our purposes. The Sanskrit word *gṛhastha* literally means "situated" (*stha*) in a "house" (*gṛha*). It is of central importance in the Dharma Sūtras, where it is listed as one of the *āśramas*. It is also found as *gahaṭṭha* in the Buddhist Pali Canon, but with a less central role. There, the word more frequently translated as "householder" is *gahapati,* which is equivalent to Sanskrit *gṛhapati* and literally means "lord" (*pati*) of a "house" (*gaha/gṛha*). (The early Jain texts in Ardhamāgadhī use a variety of terms that Jacobi all translates as "householder," which we will discuss in due course.) What, if anything, is the distinction between the term *gahapati* preferred by the Buddhists and the term *gṛhastha* preferred by the Brahmanical Dharma Sūtra authors? In order to answer this question, we will first consider the significance of *gahapati* and then turn to *gṛhastha*, and we will find that it is the latter, rather than the former, that more properly embodies the "other" to the early Buddhist and Jain visions of celibate Brahmanhood.

Although the Pali word *gahapati* is not exactly the same as the Sanskrit word *gṛhastha*, at face value it would appear to convey a similar meaning, though with a greater emphasis on such a person's lordship or dominion over the house in which he lives. That the basic meaning of the word is simply a person who lives in a house—that is, a householder—is confirmed, however, by the way it is defined, repeatedly, in the *Suttavibhaṅga* of the *Vinaya*, which is a commentary on the *Pātimokkha*, the list of rules for Buddhist monks. For *Pātimokkha* rules in which the word *gahapati* appears, the following gloss is given: "A *gahapati* is whoever inhabits a house."[119] This is the same gloss that is given for other rules[120] that instead use the word *agārika* (a word that more literally refers to a person who lives in a house), implying that the two words are interchangeable.

Uma Chakravarti has argued, however, that there is more to the *gahapati* than simply living in a house. She writes, "While the term *gahapati* in the sense of householder or one who lives in a house or possesses a house is equivalent to other words implying the same—such as *gihi, gahaṭṭha* and *ajjhāvasati*—these terms do not imply the range of characteristics that *gahapati* carries with it."[121] The category *gahapati* is often found together with the categories *khattiya* and *brāhmaṇa,* and as such, Chakravarti argues that it represents the economy, as one of the "seven treasures" (*sattaratanāṇi*) of a *cakkavatti* ("wheel-turning") monarch,[122] as a controller of property, as a tax-payer, and as one who makes a living off of agriculture.[123] The category appears to imply some status and to refer specifically to the *paterfamilias* rather than simply to any human being who happens to live in a house.[124] Indeed, as Chakravarti notes, we have also the term *gahapatiputta,* which is glossed twice in the *Suttavibhaṅga* as "whoever are sons and brothers" (i.e., of the *gahapati,* who is mentioned just prior).[125] This would appear to refer to (male) dependents of the *gahapati,* who would in turn be the head of the household.

Chakravarti is, therefore, certainly correct that what *gahapati* generally referred to was not "merely" a householder in the sense of a person living in a house; it was a title of status, referring to a true "lord" of a household, a person of means and a controller of property.[126] In fact, we do find in a few instances in the Pali Canon when a more generic sense of "one living in a house" is intended, the word *gahaṭṭha* (which is the Pali equivalent of *gṛhastha*) itself. This word is found far less frequently than the word *gahapati,* and it is often paired together with *pabbajita* to refer, quite literally, to those who "stay" at home and those who "go forth."[127] The function here is clearly to refer to living in a house in general rather than anything more specific, as in the case of *gahapati*. Given that this more general term was known and available to the authors of the early Buddhist texts, then, we must ask ourselves why they generally preferred *gahapati* as a category to speak about householders. In addition, to what extent does the category of the *gahapati* as it is found in the early Buddhist texts differ from that of the *gṛhastha* as it is found in the Dharma Sūtras?

In response to the second question, I would argue not as much as it might seem at first. It is true that the category *gahapati* is often found together with the categories *khattiya* and *brāhmaṇa,* which could be taken to imply a sort of three-fold division of society,[128] perhaps even a colloquial equivalent to the Brahmans' *varṇa* system. Chakravarti adduces in support of this supposition another gloss in the *Suttavibhaṅga* that defines a *gahapatika* as follows: "Setting aside a king, a king's servant, (or) a Brahman, what remains is a called a *gahapatika*."[129] This gloss should not be taken too literally, however, as a comprehensive division of society into its components. If we look back at the original rule that it is commenting upon, we find that it is simply mimicking the categories found there: The rule begins, "In case a king or one in the service of a king or a brahmin or a householder should send a robe-fund for a monk by a messenger . . . ."[130] The gloss on *gahapatika,* in other words, simply indicates that *in this rule* the word *gahapatika* is being used as a catch-all term for anyone other than a king, a king's servant, or a Brahman who happens to send a robe-fund for a monk. No comprehensive division of society into *khattiyas, brāhmaṇas*, and *gahapatis* is implied. Moreover, although the category is often found throughout the Canon together with the categories *khattiya* and *brāhmaṇa,* they are never found together in compound, nor, for that matter, necessarily found in isolation as a group of three.[131] The more important lesson to be taken from the frequent use of *gahapati* together with *khattiya* and *brāhmaṇa* is not that they form a comprehensive division of society into three parts, but rather that, as Bronkhorst has noted, early Buddhist texts fail to use the *varṇa* system to divide society, even when categories shared in common with the *varṇa* system are present.[132]

Indeed, we know that the category *gahapati* cannot have been mutually exclusive of *khattiya* and *brāhmaṇa* because it is often used in the compound *brāhmaṇagahapatika* to refer to "Brahman householders."[133] This compound is often found in this sense in encounter dialogs in which the Buddha stays at a Brahman village (*brāhmaṇagāma*) and is visited by the inhabitants of the village, who are referred to as *brāhmaṇagahapatikā*.[134] As Chakravarti notes, this pairing of *brāhmaṇa* and *gahapati* in compound is unique; *khattiya* is not used in compound with *gahapati*, that is, to refer to "*khattiya* householders." She argues further that the use of the term *gahapati* to describe Brahmans, given that it is found in the context of "Brahman villages," appears to "[refer] to *brāhmaṇas* based on land in villages which were probably inhabited almost entirely by *brāhmaṇas*."[135] Bronkhorst has further suggested that these villages were characteristic of the migration of Brahmans into new regions: They "did not mix with the local population," but "created villages for their own exclusive use."[136] In addition, *brāhmaṇagahapatikā* are found frequently in what I call "encounter dialogs," in which the Buddha debates with "Brahmans" whose arguments clearly advance the tenets of Neo-Brahmanism. In fact, in one particular encounter dialog the debate in which the Buddha engages with his Brahman interlocutor is precisely over the relative value of the householder and the renunciate, with the Brahman asserting that only the way of the householder (*gahaṭṭha*) is the "skillful *dharma*" (*dhammaṃ kusalaṃ*).[137] It is then no surprise that we would find these people, whose own texts advance a householder ideal, clearly demarcated as "householders."

But why would the Buddhist texts prefer the term *gahapati*, with its more honorific implication of *dominion* over a household rather than mere residence therein, over *gahaṭṭha*? Bronkhorst argues that the exalted nature of the *gahapati* may reflect a "propagandistic tendency of the texts to depict the Buddha as being in interaction with important people rather than with the proletariat,"[138] and while there may be some truth to this, I think there is a simpler explanation. The early Buddhist texts refer to *gahapatis*—to *heads* of households, rather than to people who dwell in houses as such—most frequently for the very same reason that they refer to other prominent members of society, such as *khattiyas*, *brāhmaṇas*, *rājās*, and even courtesans (*gaṇikā*)—*because they were the only people who could act as free agents in ancient Indian society*. Although the early Buddhist texts clearly evince a rejection of the *varṇa* system, it is a mistake, as Oldenberg argued over a century ago, to see the Buddha (or, for that matter, those who constructed him as a literary character in the early Buddhist *sūtras*) as a great social reformer. There is in fact little evidence in the early Buddhist texts of any substantive critique of prevailing social structures with their concomitant inequalities, and in fact a great deal of evidence that social hierarchy and inequality were accepted as ordinary parts of life. It is true that *varṇa* was criticized, but this is a matter of rejecting a novel social schema being introduced by Neo-Brahmanism rather than overthrowing a preexisting system of social inequality. Social inequality at the time when the early Buddhist texts were written was encoded instead, it seems, in terms like *gahapati* that denoted a patriarchal household structure in which a single adult male controlled not only society's smallest units of land and wealth, but also most likely a fair number of other human beings.

Insofar as the early Buddhists accepted such social inequality as normal, it is unnecessary to appeal to a model of "propaganda" to explain the prevalence of socially important individuals such as *gahapatis* in the early texts. Only people who had the capacity to act as free agents in a society would be relevant in most social interactions that would take place with the Buddha or his *saṅgha*—no matter whether that interaction might involve joining the *saṅgha*, taking refuge and becoming an *upāsaka*, giving *dāna*, or engaging in debate or even a simple conversation. In addition, the Buddhist tradition has held consistently that the Buddha was born into a *khattiya* lineage—and although later tradition may have exaggerated or otherwise distorted what exactly that would have meant,[139] we can be confident that it was considered a high birth. Chakravarti has found through an exhaustive study of references to the social origins of the members of the *saṅgha* and lay followers in the Pali Canon that, at least as represented in the texts, the same was true of early Buddhism as a whole. The ordained are dominated by Brahmans, *khattiyas*, and other people of high birth,[140] while the laity are dominated by Brahmans, *gahapatis*, *khattiyas*, and other people of high birth.[141] Members of lower classes (barbers, potters, fishermen, etc.) are represented, but in far lower numbers.[142] Although it is difficult to know for certain, it is very well possible that early Buddhism, at least by the time the bulk of the early *sūtras* were written, was an elitist movement that established an economy of merit through the ritualized transfer of goods between members of well-to-do families who retained ownership over the resources they controlled and other members of the same families who formally "renounced" ownership over those resources but still continued to enjoy them.[143] In other words, the exchange relationship between monks and laypeople in the society represented by the early Buddhist texts may be even more restricted than is commonly thought. It would have consisted, I am suggesting, of a fairly narrow reciprocal relationship in which certain members of well-to-do families agreed to renounce their birthright to become lords over landed estates, so as to become a "field of merit," while in exchange for access to this "field of merit" other members of the same families supported them with the resources drawn from their own landed estates.[144]

In such a system, *gahapati*s would clearly represent a key social category, for two reasons. First, they are the most basic "free individuals" with whom the *saṅgha* could interact. Although any member of a household could technically interact with the *saṅgha* on some level, the ultimate disposal of a household's resources would have been determined by the *gahapati*.[145] Second, as the most basic free individual of lay society, the *gahapati* represents the mirror image of the *bhikkhu*. The Vinaya rules for entrance into the *saṅgha* prevent the ordination of people who lack the social authority to act on their own behalf—whether it be because they have not reached the age of majority, lack their parents' permission, are a slave, are under penalty of the law, are in debt, or are in service to the king.[146] A *bhikkhu* and a *gahapati* are flip sides of the same coin—both are free agents, one of which has used his agency to take control of a household, the other of which has used his agency to renounce that prerogative.

As such, the word *gahapati* in the early Buddhist texts represents the householder in his symbiotic, or at least potentially symbiotic, relationship with the Buddhist monk. A *gahapati* is a householder who has the capacity to donate material goods to the Buddhist *saṅgha* or even join it himself. It is for this reason that we find the word *gahapati* used frequently in the Pali Canon, in the context of dialogs in which the Buddha meets with actual or potential lay supporters. The word *gahaṭṭha* (=Skt. *gṛhastha*), on the other hand, is used, as we have noted, to refer to a householder as the *opposite* of one who has "gone forth" (*pabbajita*). We can note as well that a similar division of labor between different words for householder can be found in early Jain texts. The first book of the *Āyāraṅga* uses the word *gāhāvaī* (=P. *gahapati*) several times to refer to a householder (1.7.2.1–2, 1.7.3.3, 1.7.5.2); in each case, the word is used in the context of describing a meeting between a monk and a householder, and in two cases (1.7.2.1–2, 1.7.5.2), the householder wants to give the monk gifts. In the first book of the *Sūyagaḍaṃga*, on the other hand, we have a variety of words that more literally refer to "one who lives in a house," used in contexts emphasizing the *difference* between a monk and a householder.[147]

We can thus see that there is a certain tension between the renunciate and the householder in the early texts of the Jains and Buddhists—especially the latter, who appear to have dedicated a significant portion of their texts to appealing to those outside of the ordained *saṅgha* itself. On the one hand, the *gahapati* is a potential ally, a source of patronage or even recruits. On the other hand, the *gahaṭṭha* is precisely the opposite of the Brahmanical ideal propounded by these two traditions. Modern scholarship has noted the tension between the householder and the renouncer in Brahmanism/Hinduism as well. [148] It is a mistake, however, to simply frame this tension as an internal one within a particular tradition (i.e., Brahmanism/Hinduism), or even as an internal tension shared by all Indian traditions (Brahmanism, Buddhism, and Jainism). The tension between the householder and the renouncer was internal to each tradition *even while it fueled the external dialectic that was constitutive of those traditions in the first place.*

Each side of this debate, in other words, had to grapple with its opposite—not only as its other to be rejected, but as a necessary evil within itself. For the Buddhists and Jains, this tension consisted of a necessary dependence on goods and recruits derived from the absolute other—the householder. Although they understood Brahmanhood as consisting in the total rejection of the householder lifestyle, they nonetheless depended on householders for their very existence. In the next chapter, we will explore the mirror image of this tension, found in the Neo-Brahmanism first expounded by the authors of the Dharma Sūtras. These early Indian thinkers understood Brahmanhood as consisting of precisely what the Jains and Buddhists rejected—householdership, ritual, marriage, and the production of children. Yet because they purported to offer a totalistic vision of society, they had to account in some way for the existence of groups who did renounce householder life. I will argue that they did so through the *āśrama* system, a theoretical construct designed to categorize and exclude lifestyles based on celibate renunciation, but later converted to *include* them within a normative lifecycle.

Each group in ancient India necessarily subsumed *within itself* a tension and/or rapprochement between the householder and the renouncer. But we should not allow ourselves to forget that each group also took a stand on whether the householder or the renouncer was ideal. Thus, at the same time that there was a tension *within* each group between the householder and the renouncer, there was also a tension *among* the various groups on the question of which was ideal. For the early Buddhists and Jains, the renouncer, who (at least in theory) was homeless and celibate, was the ideal. Indeed, they specifically conceived of the Brahman as a celibate renouncer. In spite of the fact that they lived in a symbiotic relationship with a householding laity, householders were the direct antithesis of the ideal that they espoused—their absolute other.

## *Conclusion: What Makes a* Śramaṇa?

We are finally in a position to answer the question that we left unanswered at the end of the last chapter: How did the category *śramaṇa* arise? In this chapter we have seen that the early Buddhists and Jains considered themselves to be Brahmans, and that this was a coherent claim based on the practice of celibate studentship known as *brahmacarya*. In addition, the fact that the early Buddhists gave a special privilege to the *jaṭila*s that they did not grant to the Jains shows that the sense of affinity between different groups in ancient India did not respect a putative divide between Brahmans and *śramaṇa*s. In other words, the early Buddhists could feel a sense of affinity with *jaṭila*s irrespective of their association with a Brahman other, because the *jaṭila*s were, like them, celibate renunciates. Indeed, in spite of the fact that they lived in a symbiotic relationship with laity, early Buddhists and Jains took the celibate renouncer as their ideal, and thus the absolute other to that ideal was the householder, not the Brahman. All groups in ancient India had to deal with the tension between the householder and the renouncer, but all also took a stand one way or the other on which was ideal.

But this divide, between groups who saw the householder as ideal and those who saw the renouncer as ideal, is not coterminous with the categories *Brahman* and *śramaṇa*. Each group saw itself as Brahmans and therefore *all* other groups, either explicitly or implicitly, as non-Brahmans. In other words, *Brahman* was not primarily a category of otherness in ancient India, but of selfhood. This is not to say that we never see the category *Brahman* used to refer to other groups in the ancient texts—obviously we do, in texts of the Jains and Buddhists, where it is used to refer to the proponents of Neo-Brahmanism. But as I will argue in the chapters that follow, this was the result of a particular process whereby the proponents of Neo-Brahmanism successfully arrogated the category *Brahman* to themselves. The Jains' and Buddhists' use of the category *Brahman* to refer to them is therefore secondary to the primary use of *Brahman* to refer to one's own conception of the ideal, in which all groups participated.

Concomitant with the insight that *Brahman* was first and foremost a category of *selfhood* for the early Buddhists and Jains, we should also consider the use of the word *śramaṇa* as a category of *otherness* for these two groups. In their texts, the early Buddhists and Jains do indeed often use the category *śramaṇa* to refer to themselves, but they also use it to refer to other groups that they criticize. This is most frequently seen in the expression "some *śramaṇa*s and Brahmans," which we investigated thoroughly in the last chapter. But at times we find simply a blanket condemnation of "some" *śramaṇa*s who hold wrong views. An example can be found in the Jain texts at *Sūyag.* 1.1.2.10, which refers to "some *samaṇa*s" (*samaṇā ege*) who hold "wrong views" and are "un-Aryan" (*micchādiṭhī aṇāriyā*). An even better example can be found in the Buddhist *Aṭṭhaka Vagga*, which, as we have already discussed above, repeatedly refers to the Buddhist ideal person as a Brahman.

Tilmann Vetter has shown that, within the *Aṭṭhaka*, not only is the ideal person—by whatever name he is called—not contrasted with the "literal" Brahman by birth; he is actually contrasted with the *samaṇa*. Verse 828 of the *Pasūra Sutta* (8) warns,

> These disputes arise among *samaṇa*s. Among them there is victory and defeat.
> Having seen this too, one should abstain from disputes, for there is no other aim than the gain of praise.[149]

Likewise, in the *Cūḷabyūha Sutta* (12), an (unnamed) interlocutor says to the Buddha,

> What some say is true, real, others say is vain, false.
> And having thus gotten started, they dispute [with one another].
> Why do the *samaṇa*s not speak as one?[150]

To this, the Buddha answers enigmatically,

> There is only one truth; there is no second about which a wise man might dispute with a wise man.
> Variously they proclaim their own truths; therefore, the *samaṇa*s do not speak as one.[151]

As the Buddha continues to answer the interlocutor's questions, it becomes clear that what he is referring to is a non-dual, apophatic truth beyond the positions that people take in disputes. Therefore, the claims of all the various *samaṇas* to truth are invalid, since they all equally claim that they are right and the others are wrong:

> For if one is inferior by the word of another, the latter is of inferior intelligence along with him.
> And if he has himself attained to knowledge and is intelligent, there is no one who is a fool among the *samaṇas*.[152]

*Samaṇas* are therefore defined by their wont for disputes and concomitant lack of access to truth. To this is contrasted the ideal person, the Brahman, who does not enter into disputes and does not cling to views.

Thus, not only was *Brahman* first and foremost a category of self-identity in ancient India; in addition, *śramaṇa* could be and was used to refer to other groups that one wished to distinguish oneself from. But there is one key exception to this. The word *śramaṇa* is *never* used to refer to householder Brahmans—that is, the proponents of Neo-Brahmanism. This is a key point, because it shows that, by definition, *śramaṇas* are not householders, or at the very least not ordinary householders. Rather, *śramaṇas* are (as their name, being derived from the verbal root *śram*, suggests) those who "toil" or "strive" in some special way—generally speaking, through renunciation of the householder life and adherence to celibacy. Now, this might not at first seem like any great insight. After all, in modern scholarship and pedagogy, "renunciation" is part of the textbook definition of the *śramaṇa*, and the word itself is in fact often translated as "ascetic" or "renouncer." But what has too often been overlooked is that the *śramaṇas* were defined by special "toil"—asceticism, renunciation of the householder life, celibacy—*and that is all.* They were *not* defined by opposition to "the Brahmans," either as a specific social group or as an abstract category. *Śramaṇa* groups could not be defined by opposition to the Brahmans because they saw *themselves* as Brahmans. If they wanted to criticize other *śramaṇa* groups—that is, other groups of renunciates—they could and sometimes did do so by referring to them as *śramaṇas*. *Brahman* remained the more important category for referring to themselves as the ideal.

Confusion on this point has been caused by the fact that there was one group who, just like all the other groups, claimed to be the *true* Brahmans but, unlike the others, neither referred to themselves nor were referred to as *śramaṇa*s. The reason for this is that they were ordinary householders who married, procreated, performed rituals, and amassed wealth, and therefore were by definition not *śramaṇa*s. Indeed, it was central to their ideology that one *must* be a householder, and that Brahmanhood was defined by birth rather than any sort of "striving" that was on offer among the *śramaṇa* groups. It is likely because of the existence of this one group that the phrase "some *śramaṇa*s and Brahmans" became standard among *śramaṇa* groups like the early Buddhists and Jains for referring to various "other" groups whose views they disagreed with. That is, because the views of the householder Brahmans were among those being criticized, the category *śramaṇa* was not wide enough to include all "wrong views." At the same time, though, this phrase, as we saw in the last chapter, was never used to imply an opposition between Brahman and *śramaṇa* because these two categories were not mutually exclusive. All of the groups being criticized claimed to be Brahmans, but not all could claim to be *śramaṇa*s. It is to the one exceptional group—the householder Brahmans—that we turn in the next chapter.

# 5

# *The Brahman as the Head of a Household*

WE HAVE SEEN that by dropping the assumption of a preexisting distinction between Brahmanical and non-Brahmanical, early Buddhist and Jain texts read not as articulations of an opposition to Brahmanism or a co-opting of its categories; rather, they read as articulations of a renunciant and celibate understanding of what it means to be a Brahman, with real roots in the ancient North Indian tradition. Now we turn to their opponents, those people who held that Brahmanhood must be rooted in householdership and the production of children. We can refer to these people as the proponents of a *Neo-Brahmanism*, in recognition of the fact that while claiming to be the heirs of an ancient tradition, they were in fact reinventing that tradition in the fashion of any number of so-called conservative, but more aptly called reactionary, groups throughout history. They might equally be called "householder supremacists" in recognition of the central ideological pillar of their movement, or "householder Brahmans" to distinguish them both from the *jaṭila* Brahmans who embraced renunciation but retained Vedic learning and sacrifice and from more radical Brahman groups like the Buddhists and Jains.

The earliest and, in some sense, only systematic articulation of the ideology of the householder Brahmans is found in the Dharma Sūtras. These were texts written in the imperial period, at first as part of the appendices to the Veda (*vedāṅga*), in particular as part of the Kalpa Sūtra genre that focused on explication of ritual. Although the Dharma Sūtras grew out of this genre and were modeled on the earlier Śrauta and Gṛhya Sūtras that explicated the solemn and household rituals, respectively, they went beyond a narrow ritual focus to explain the much broader category of *dharma*, which is in many ways akin to the Western concept of "Law." As such, they served as a transition to the Indian legal tradition known as Dharmaśāstra that, beginning with the *Mānava Dharmaśāstra* around the turn of the era, broke free of the structure of Vedic schools completely.[1]

While the roots of the ideology of the householder Brahmans, just as much as those of their renunciatory opponents, can be found in the Vedic Saṃhitās, Brāhmaṇas, and Upaniṣads, as well as in the supplemental Śrauta and Gṛhya Sūtras, they are not fully explicated as a coherent ideology of "householder supremacy" until the Dharma Sūtras. Later texts, on the other hand, including the literary pillars of classical Hinduism, the *Mānava Dharmaśāstra* and the *Mahābhārata*, display substantial concessions to the opposing side insofar as they concede legitimacy to renunciatory lifestyles, at least within certain parameters. Indeed, we already see signs of concessions to the renunciatory ideal in the later Dharma Sūtras, especially Baudhāyana, half of which is an interpolation dubbed by Patrick Olivelle "Deutero-Baudhāyana"[2] that inexplicably explains, as if legitimate, various renunciatory lifestyles, in blatant contradiction to their rejection in the original part of the text.

The clearest, simplest, and most straightforward presentation of what I will argue is the ideology of the householder Brahmans is found in the *Āpastamba Dharma Sūtra*. Patrick Olivelle, who has made the most recent translation of the Dharma Sūtras into English and dealt with them extensively in his scholarly work, has noted that Āpastamba is the best-preserved of the four, in part because it attracted early commentaries.[3] He has also convincingly argued that it is, for these and other internal reasons, the earliest Dharma Sūtra.[4] Āpastamba is concise and well organized because its author, as the pioneer of what would become a very long tradition of Brahmanical Dharmaśāstra, had a very pointed argument to make, even if his successors made substantial concessions in their re-articulations of that argument. His text is flanked, like a well-crafted modern essay, by an introduction and conclusion that state and re-state the primary thesis: *Dharma* is allied with the Veda. The first line of the text makes this unambiguously clear: "Now (I will explain) conventional practices. The standard (for determining them) is the consensus of those who know *dharma*, and the Vedas."[5] Given that this text likely dates from the imperial period,[6] one can hardly avoid reading this argument as a response to the explosion of articulations of *dharma*—Jain and Buddhist to be sure, but also under the imperial sanction of Aśoka and likely other members of his dynasty—that did *not* associate it in any way with the Vedas.

The body of the text can for our purposes be divided into two distinct parts of unequal length. The second and shorter of these is focused on the laws pertaining to kingship. While this section draws on the important motif of the alliance between *brahman* and *kṣatra* found in the Vedas, and served as the basis for Brahmanical articulations of righteous kingship for centuries to come, our interest is more in the much larger section that precedes it. This section explains the normative life cycle of a twice-born (*dvija*) male. It begins with the customs associated with Vedic studentship, continues with rules to be followed by a student after returning home and the procedures for the ritual bath ending his studentship, and concludes with his duties and responsibilities as a householder, after marriage. Insofar as this description of the life cycle begins with the study of the Veda and ends with the production of children and performance of ritual as a householder, it clearly reflects the viewpoint of those committed to a non-renunciatory, householder lifestyle.

What makes this a polemic, however, and not simply a prescriptive account of the householder's life, is the brief discussions that serve as bookends to the section on the normative life cycle. At the beginning, immediately after the initial statement that *dharma* and Veda are linked but before the description of Vedic studentship, we find the following simple and unambiguous statement of what we now call the *varṇa* system: "There are four *varṇas*: Brahmans, *kṣatriyas*, *vaiśyas*, and *śūdras*. Of them, each preceding is superior by birth (to those that follow)."[7] This statement has three critical components: It names the four *varṇas*; it refers to them using the term *varṇa*; and it states explicitly that they are based on birth. Although these three components are found in isolation in earlier texts, as will be discussed below, this is, to my knowledge, the earliest text in which they are all found together. Āpastamba begins his description of the normative life of the householder, in other words, with the first explicit, complete, and unambiguous articulation of the *varṇa* system.

He also ends that description with a first: the first articulation of the *āśrama* system. This is, of course, the system of four lifestyles that would come to be paired with *varṇa* as *varṇāśramadharma*, one of the key ideological pillars of classical Hinduism: the *brahmacārin*, or celibate student; the *gṛhastha*, or householder; the *vānaprastha*, or forest-dwelling ascetic; and the *parivrājaka*, or wandering ascetic. In the classical formulation of the *āśrama* system, as found beginning in the *Mānava Dharmaśāstra*, the *āśramas* are a series of life stages to be entered into, in order, over the course of a single life. But as Olivelle has shown, this was not the original form that the system took. Instead, the *āśrama* system was originally, as described in the four early Dharma Sūtras, beginning with Āpastamba, a system of four "choices" of *lifelong* vocations one could make after completing one's Vedic studentship.[8]

Āpastamba therefore presents, under the controlling principle that *dharma* and Veda are linked, a two-part explication of *dharma* that addresses the normative life cycle of a householder and the duties of a king. The description of the normative life cycle of a householder, in turn, is flanked by two novel social theories, one addressing social classes and the other addressing individual lifestyles, that would, after considerable modification, come to be united in the principle of *varṇāśramadharma* in classical Hinduism. The later three Dharma Sūtras deviate from this structure in various ways, but for the most part they retain all of the constituent parts, albeit in different orders and with different emphases, and with considerable elaborations upon various parts. The most significant elaboration for our purposes, not found in Āpastamba but found in all three of his successors, is the concept of "mixed castes"—castes that result when parents from two different *varṇa*s have a child. As already mentioned above, Baudhāyana as it comes down to us includes a large interpolation that, contrary to Āpastamba, embraces renunciatory lifestyles, and Vasiṣṭha contains some developments in the same direction as well. Nevertheless, all four Dharma Sūtras contain a discussion of the *āśrama* system in its preclassical formulation, that is, as four *lifelong options*, rather than four *stages of life*. As we will see, this original formulation of the *āśrama* system is key to the Dharma Sūtras' articulation of the ideology of householder supremacy, which would then be compromised beginning with Manu.

The Dharma Sūtras, most clearly in the original formulation of Āpastamba but in the other three as well, should not be read simply as discussions of duties for kings and proper behavior for householders internal to a pre-defined Brahmanical identity. Rather, they should be read as polemical texts that articulated, within the context of early North Indian society as a whole, a particular vision of Brahmanical identity as based on a householder ideal. Modern scholars have understood the Dharma Sūtras as primarily internal "Brahmanical" documents, but this reading is based on a misunderstanding of the relationship between the normative and the descriptive, which are intertwined in these texts in a fashion quite foreign to modern sensibilities. Āpastamba's articulation of the *varṇa* system was, although it became ubiquitous in the Indian literature (including Buddhist and Jain texts), not simply a description of a long-standing social reality, but rather a polemical and rhetorical strategy that served a particular ideological agenda. Conversely, the *āśrama* system, while found for the first time in Āpastamba and never found outside of Brahmanical texts, was indeed based on colloquial categories with relevance beyond his or any particular Brahmanical tradition. The *āśrama* system must therefore be understood not as a "theological construct" authored by "liberal Brahmans," but rather a theoretical taxonomy composed by householder Brahmans to describe in detail actual social practice, and then reject all lifestyles that did not conform to their own. The *varṇa* and *āśrama* systems, as deployed by Āpastamba and the other Dharma Sūtra authors, worked in tandem to advance the householder supremacist agenda by describing society first as it should be, and then as it unfortunately actually was.

## *The Āśrama System as a "Brahmanical Theological Construct"*

Āpastamba's discussions of the *varṇa* and *āśrama* systems, which serve as bookends to his discussion of the life cycle of the householder, are the key to interpreting that discussion. Of these two systems, the *varṇa* system lived on, in the same form as articulated by Āpastamba, to serve as one of the ideological pillars of classical Hinduism. The *āśrama* system, conversely, underwent significant revision before taking its classical form. It therefore is useful to begin with the *āśrama* system in unraveling the interpretive dilemma posed by the Dharma Sūtras, since it apparently came to be seen as the "squeaky wheel" in the ideological system they articulated that required adjustment. The very success of the *varṇa* system, the "unsqueaky wheel" in the Dharma Sūtras' system, will then explain why the *āśrama* system had to be revised.

The eponymous book-length study of the *āśrama* system by Patrick Olivelle, the doyen of preclassical Brahmanical studies, has become the standard and definitive source for understanding the history of the system, so is important to begin by re-examining how he interprets it. Olivelle defines the *āśrama* system as a "theological construct"[9] and argues that as such, it should not be confused with any "social institutions." It is therefore "improper to claim as many scholars do, for example, that the first two *āśramas* are known from early vedic times; it is not these *āśramas* but the institutions of vedic studentship and marriage that are so known."[10] This important distinction allows Olivelle to dispense with debates over the "pre-history" of the *āśrama* system that often do more to obscure than to illuminate, and instead focus on the history of the very idea of an *āśrama* system. Olivelle's conclusion on this point is that the *āśrama* system was invented by "Brahmins living in urban centers [who] were influenced by and open to new ideas and institutions [more] than their village counterparts."[11] It was, in other words, an invention of "liberal" Brahmans who were open to new ways of life and sought to legitimate them within a Vedic framework. The *āśrama* system was then quoted, often disapprovingly, as the opinion of "some" by the more conservative authors of the Dharma Sūtras. This explanation is in contradistinction with the theory advanced by many earlier scholars, which was that conservative Brahmans invented the *āśrama* system "with the intention of resisting the new religious movements and of safeguarding the Brāhmaṇical religion by incorporating the renunciatory life style into a scheme that would lessen its impact and reduce or eliminate the conflict between it and the life of the householder."[12] This theory, Olivelle argues convincingly, is based on the erroneous use of the "classical" formulation of the *āśrama* system (which does seem to have been an orthodox attempt to incorporate asceticism safely into a Brahmanical framework) to speculate on the origins of the *āśrama* system.[13]

Although Olivelle rejects the theory that the *āśrama* system was created by conservative Brahmans such as the ones who describe it in the Dharma Sūtras,[14] he still places its creation firmly in the Brahmanical tradition. As he writes, "The authors of the *āśrama* system were without doubt Brahmins."[15] He concedes that the description of the *āśrama* system may be colored by the fact that the authors of the Dharma Sūtras in which it is first presented are Brahmans. At the same time, however, he argues that the viewpoint of the opponents who are cited by the Dharma Sūtra authors "shows all the marks of the Brāhmaṇical way of thinking and arguing."[16]

The most convincing evidence that Olivelle presents for a Brahmanical identity for the authors of the *āśrama* system is the fact that Baudhāyana quotes two verses in support of the *āśrama* system, both from the *Taittirīya Saṃhitā*, and then refutes them with his own appeals to Vedic authority. The first of these "pro-*āśrama*" citations appears to be the basis for the fourfold schema itself:

> Four paths leading to the gods cross between heaven and earth. Of them, entrust us, all (you) gods, to that which brings us to the state of non-injury. (*TS* 5.7.2.3, *BDhS* 2.11.11)[17]

Baudhāyana refutes this by saying that "for lack of a Vedic text" (*adṛṣṭatvāt*) in support of another interpretation, " 'Four paths . . . ' refers to rites of *iṣṭi* sacrifices, animal sacrifices, and *soma* sacrifices, and ladle-oblations."[18] He then introduces another verse in support of the *āśramas* using the words "Now this is cited" (*tad eṣābhy anūcyate*):

> This is the eternal greatness of a Brahman: he is not increased by karma, nor is he decreased. Having known the realization of its own footprint, the self is not smeared by sinful karma. (*TB* 2.12.7–8, *BDhS* 2.11.30)[19]

Baudhāyana immediately refutes this argument by presenting two other verses, one from the *Taittirīya Saṃhitā* and the other from the *Ṛg Veda*, that emphasize the importance of the Veda and the Vedic ritual.[20]

Now, this argument does provide fairly convincing evidence that Baudhāyana, at least, was responding in part to a "Brahmanical" argument in favor of the validity of the four *āśramas*. It is worthwhile, however, to pause for a moment and consider from a methodological standpoint what exactly this means. Olivelle himself has argued, in a critique of Bronkhorst's work, that a "pernicious effect of thinking about Indian history in terms of 'Vedic' and 'non-Vedic' is that these are often unconsciously assumed to be *reified* and *static* entities."[21] A similar argument can be made for the categories *Brahmanical* and *non-Brahmanical*. Olivelle notes that *Vedic* and *Brahmanical* are often used interchangeably, and that this is problematic because it is not necessarily the case that "all brahmins must have subscribed to everything Vedic."[22] But I would argue that the methodological problem runs even deeper than this. Not only are the terms *Vedic* and *non-Vedic* problematic, but the terms *Brahmanical* and *non-Brahmanical* are as well. As we saw in the last chapter, early Buddhists and Jains called themselves Brahmans and articulated a vision of Brahmanical identity, with roots in ancient Indian tradition that defined the Brahman as a celibate renunciant. But this raises a tantalizing possibility: If, methodologically speaking, we take Buddhists and Jains at their word that they were Brahmans, rather than privileging the claim of their householder opponents to exclusive Brahman identity, then wouldn't it make sense that they, and others like them, were the "liberal Brahmans" to whom Olivelle attributes the *āśrama* system?

## *The* Varṇa *System as a Rhetorical Bulwark against Alternative Brahmanisms*

Because the Dharma Sūtra authors attribute the *āśrama* system to the opinion of "some" and argue with them in "Brahmanical" terms, Olivelle has assumed that the debate over the *āśrama* system was an internal debate within "the" Brahmanical community. But given that early Jains and Buddhists called themselves Brahmans, spoke in Brahmanical terms, and lived the very lifestyles sanctioned by the *āśrama* system, I suggest that they were (among) the "liberal Brahmans" criticized by the Dharma Sūtra authors. The main obstacle to this interpretation is the *varṇa* system, since it, beginning with Āpastamba, unambiguously identifies Brahmanhood with membership in a closed, endogamous community defined by birth. Uncritical acceptance of the rhetoric of the *varṇa* system has prevented scholars such as Olivelle from arriving at the otherwise obvious interpretation of (1) the *āśrama* system specifically as a polemic against Buddhists, Jains, and other proponents of celibate Brahmanhood and (2) the Dharma Sūtras as a whole as outwardly looking articulations of an identity rather than inwardly looking products of an identity.

Now, one could argue that what makes "real" Brahmans really Brahmans, and Buddhists and Jains who call themselves Brahmans just rhetorical copycats, is the existence of lineages of Brahmans who transmitted the Vedas in the centuries prior the time of the Buddha. While such lineages certainly did exist, scholarship both on the Vedic texts themselves and on the relationship between the *śramaṇa* movements and Brahmanism has complicated the assumption that the *varṇa* system was simply a social fact of ancient India that long predated the rise of Buddhism and Jainism. To begin with, it has long been known that, aside from its late tenth book, the *Ṛg Veda* does not appear to be aware of the *varṇa* system in any form. This was shown as far back as the 1940s by the great scholar of Dharmaśāstra, Pandurang Vaman Kane, who argued convincingly that the system was not yet in place in Ṛg-Vedic times:

> Though the words brāhmaṇa and kṣatriya occur frequently in the Ṛgveda, the word varṇa is not used in connection with them. Even

> in the Puruṣasūkta (Ṛgveda X.90) where the words brāhmaṇa, rājanya, vaiśya, and śūdra occur the word varṇa is not used. . . . It is often argued that as the word brāhmaṇa denotes a caste in later literature, in the Ṛgveda also it must be presumed to have the same meaning. But this begs the whole question. . . . Besides we cannot forget that the final redaction of the Ṛgveda must been held to have been separated from the composition of the individual hymns by several hundred years (if not more) and that even if it be conceded that at the time when the Puruṣasūkta was composed, the four varṇas had been constituted and had become castes, yet the same cannot be affirmed for the time of the original composition of the other hymns.[23]

But if the lack of a rigid *varṇa* system in the early hymns of the *Ṛg Veda* is relatively clear and noncontroversial, the question of when the *varṇa* system did come into place is less so, complicated as it by the question of dating the various strata of Vedic texts, the only historical sources for the period before the rise of Buddhism and Jainism.

The work of Michael Witzel is seminal in this regard because it provides a chronological and theoretical framework for understanding the compilation, development, and dissemination of the Vedas. Witzel's method is to use internal evidence in the Vedic texts (geographical, climatic, and technological references, as well as linguistic features) to arrange them according to geographical and historical provenance. He finds that the earliest of the Vedic texts, that is, the oldest parts of the *Ṛg Veda,* appear to be focused on the Punjab, while later *saṃhitā* texts evince a shift to the Kuru-Pañcāla region, and still later texts appear to show a shift even further to the east.[24] Witzel divides the Vedic textual material into three chronological strata: Early Vedic (corresponding to the *Ṛg Veda*), Middle Vedic (corresponding to the *mantras*, Yajur-Vedic prose, and early Brāhmaṇas), and Late Vedic (corresponding to the late Brāhmaṇas, Āraṇyakas, Upaniṣads, and Sūtras). He argues that the early Vedic material corresponds to a time of competing tribes in the Punjab who had a little-developed tradition of sacrifice and little or no caste organization. Later, as the Vedic tribes moved east, the Kurus, whom Witzel calls the "first Indian state," consolidated their power by exacting tribute (*bali*), which they redistributed through a newly reorganized and expanded *śrauta* ritual system. This resulted in the formation of a highly specialized ritual priesthood, who in turn produced the literature of the middle Vedic period and developed the sophisticated institutional system of *śākhās* for preserving and transmitting the growing corpus of Vedic texts. These Vedic *śākhās* spread further east, where they produced the literature of the late Vedic period, under the patronage of kings there who sought their ritual services to legitimate their rule—a process that Witzel refers to as "early Sanskritization."[25]

The work of Witzel can be said to provide a chronological grounding to the earlier work of Jan Heesterman. Several decades ago in several articles including, most importantly, "Brahman, Ritual, and Renouncer," Heesterman provided strong evidence that the classical *śrauta* ritual was a relatively late ritualization of an original "agonistic" sacrifice in which competing clan leaders traded roles as *yajamāna* and officiating priests.[26] This would mean that although the term *brāhmaṇa,* for example, is found frequently even in the early Ṛg-Vedic texts, it need not be interpreted as a rigidly conceived *varṇa* determined by birth, as in the classical theory. Indeed, Heesterman argues that originally the concept of *varṇa* did not prescribe "strict separation," but rather "a system of connubial and other exchanges."[27] Unfortunately, Heesterman's theory has remained somewhat controversial due to the fact that the book in which he most fully fleshed out this theory, *The Broken World of Sacrifice,*[28] was widely criticized as relying too heavily on late evidence (primarily the Śrauta Sūtras) to the neglect of the early texts such as the *Ṛg Veda* that presumably would be more relevant to the time period Heesterman was addressing. Read in light of Witzel's more recent work, however, we can understand the transition from the earlier "agonistic" sacrifice to the codified *śrauta* ritual as having taken place in the Middle Vedic period under the auspices of the emerging Kuru-Pañcāla state.

Did the development of the *śrauta* ritual result in the development of a rigid *varṇa* system? Heesterman himself made this structurally a part of his theory, albeit without chronological grounding. He tied the development of the *varṇa* system to the development of the *śrauta* ritual, which "broke" the earlier agonistic sacrificial system under which *varṇa* roles were reciprocal and required a professional priestly caste for its proper execution. Witzel, likewise, in his more chronologically driven account, places the origins of the "caste system" in the Middle Vedic period, when the old hymns of the *Ṛg Veda* were collected and put to use in a codified ritual system, together with the newly composed *mantras* of the *Yajur Veda.*[29] Even Kane, skeptical as he was of the antiquity of the caste system, admits,

> It is clear that the Saṃhitās other than the Ṛgveda and Brāhmaṇa works show that the three classes of brāhmaṇas, kṣatriyas and vaiśyas had become differentiated and their privileges, duties and liabilities had become more or less fixed in those times.[30]

In the case of all three of these scholars, the conclusion that the *varṇa* system arose *after* the time of the earliest Ṛg-Vedic texts, but still well within the Vedic period, appears to rest primarily on the fact that the terms *brāhmaṇa, kṣatriya* (or *rājanya*), *vaiśya*, and *śūdra* appear first in the *Puruṣa Sūkta* and then increasingly in later texts.

The scholar who has argued most forcefully for the antiquity of the *varṇa* system is Brian K. Smith. In his *Classifying the Universe*, Smith argues that throughout the Vedic texts, Brahmins wrote their class superiority into the universe by using the *varṇa* system to classify the gods, space, time, flora, fauna, and even their own scriptures. In making this argument, he presupposes that "[a]lthough it has sometimes been argued that originally the social classes we encounter in the most ancient texts of India were fluid groups, . . . [i]t is far more demonstrable that the three or four social classes are in the Veda . . . regarded as separate and hereditary."[31] The evidence Smith adduces in his book, however, does not bear out this claim. Smith does demonstrate that *varṇa* and *varṇa*-related categories are equated with a variety of things throughout the universe, but as many scholars, including Smith himself, have shown, it was a characteristic of Brahmanical philosophical practice since at least the time of the Brāhmaṇas to seek *bandhus* ("connections") between seemingly unrelated objects. What remains to be demonstrated is that the early Brahmans considered *varṇa* to be primary and constructed *bandhus* between *varṇa* categories and various objects throughout the universe as an intellectual technology for social domination. In point of fact, however, most of the examples Smith presents do not involve *varṇa* categories directly, and they do not present the sort of one-to-one mapping of flora, fauna, and the like onto the four *varṇas* that one would expect if the latter were the dominant paradigm. Far more common than the actual four *varṇas* in Brahmanical classification schemes are the three "functions"—*brahman, kṣatra,* and *viś*—which are included in various combinations in schemes that include three, four, five, or even six categories.[32] As a result, in many cases the four *varṇas* or three functions cannot account in a straightforward way for all of the categories in the classification scheme.

Indeed, the four *varṇas* proper, and references to *brāhmaṇas* in particular, are not very common across the Vedic literature; far more often one finds reference to the three functions, especially *brahman* and *kṣatra*. When the word *brāhmaṇa* itself does appear in the Vedic texts, it is generally not used in a way that unambiguously indicates that it refers to a hereditary priesthood. What these references do make clear is that Brahmans performed sacrifices, were seen as possessing special powers, and were valued for their learning.[33] As Kane noted, the earliest and most famous elaboration of the "four *varṇas*" in toto, the *Puruṣa Sūkta* (*RV* X.90), does not even call them *varṇas*. The use of the term *varṇa* to refer to the four categories *brāhmaṇa, rājanya* (*sic*), *vaiśya*, and *śūdra* appears to date from the much later *Śatapatha Brāhmaṇa*.[34] In neither case, however, is there any statement that these four categories, whether called *varṇa* or not, are determined by birth.

Indeed, birth is not brought up frequently in the earliest Vedic texts, and in one case where it is, a Brahman named Kavaṣa Ailūṣa, who is spurned by the seers as "the son of a slave-woman, a cheat, not a Brahman," is ultimately welcomed by them when they realize that "the gods know him."[35] Likewise, as Lauren Bausch has shown, Yājñavalkya defines Brahmanhood in the *Bṛhadāraṇyaka Upaniṣad* in ethical terms similar to those found in the early Buddhist texts rather than in terms of birth.[36] Statements of the superiority of the Brahman are found, but again, in the earliest texts they are not connected to birth.[37] Even in the comparatively late *Jaiminīya* and *Śatapatha Brāhmaṇas*, Brahmanical supremacy is hardly unambiguous. The *ŚB* describes a ritual in which the Brahman makes his royal patron weaker than himself, but it also says that the Brahman is an object of respect *after* the king.[38] Likewise, the *JB* openly acknowledges that both the Brahman and the *vaiśya* are subject to the *kṣatriya*.[39] The earliest passage I have found that refers unambiguously to one being born into a *varṇa* is in the *Jaiminīya-Upaniṣad Brāhmaṇa*, which speaks of a person's desire to be reborn into a family of Brahmans (*brāhmaṇakula*)—but of course the very reference to rebirth itself makes it clear that this is an extremely late text.[40] Another late passage, from the second half of the *Aitareya Brāhmaṇa*, seems to imply fixed *varṇas*—but its ultimate import is that a *kṣatriya* to whom "evil" happens will have Brahman-like offspring, "a receiver [of gifts], a drinker [of Soma], a seeker of livelihood, one to be sent away at will."[41] This implies not only that a family lineage can undergo a *varṇa*-transformation, but that a transformation from *kṣatriya* to Brahman is considered an unlucky fate!

In any case, the work of Witzel has, at the very least, vindicated Heesterman's basic idea that there was a tradition of sacrifice, whose traces remain in the *Ṛg Veda,* that preceded the codification of *śrauta* ritual, and that that earlier tradition of sacrifice was not tied to a rigid *varṇa* system. Witzel places the codification of *śrauta* ritual in the Kuru-Pañcāla region, that is, slightly to the west of the Buddhist homeland, and somewhat before the time of the Buddha as well. He ties this "Kuru-Pañcāla orthodoxy" that emerged from the middle Vedic literature to a "successively stricter stratification into the 3 *ārya* (twice-born) and the additional *śūdra* (aboriginal) classes (*varṇa*)."[42] Nevertheless, Bronkhorst's theory of the dissemination of the "new Brahmanism" (what I call Neo-Brahmanism) shows that it is possible to construct a viable model of early Indian culture in which the ideological content of, and culture surrounding, the Vedic texts is irrelevant to most of India until Neo-Brahmanism spread a reformulated version of those ideas to the rest of India slowly over the course of many centuries. That is, even if a rigid *varṇa* system was developed and in some sense put into practice in conjunction with the composition of the middle Vedic literature prior to the time of the Buddha, this development would have been limited to the Kuru-Pañcāla region and would have had no immediate bearing on the rest of South Asia, including the Buddhist homeland just to the east.

Even within the cultural world that produced the Vedas, however, we should be wary of assuming the antiquity of a rigid *varṇa* system. Timothy Lubin has recently published interesting work on the Gṛhya Sūtras that shows that only in that fairly late, indeed post-Vedic, body of literature do we find the idea that all three *ārya-varṇas* should receive Vedic initiation and undergo *brahmacarya,* and concomitantly it is in that body of literature that the term *dvija* ("twice-born") is first applied to *kṣatriyas* and *vaiśyas*. In earlier literature, the term *dvija* is applied only to Brahmans, and it is assumed that anyone undergoing initiation and *brahmacarya* is a Brahman.[43] Interestingly, the shift in the use of the *dvija* to refer to *three varṇas* in the Gṛhya Sūtras, instead of just Brahmans, is found within the earliest systematic accounts of the procedures for the *upanayana,* the ceremony initiating one into *brahmacarya* and Vedic study. The Gṛhya Sūtras as a whole presuppose the slightly earlier Śrauta Sūtras and model their "household" rituals on solemn rituals found in the latter. Consistent with this practice, they model *upanayana* on the *dīkṣā* as described in the Śrauta Sūtras—that is, the ritual that prepares a ritual sponsor (*yajamāna*) for a Soma sacrifice.[44]

Lubin himself is reluctant to read too much into the sudden appearance of systematic descriptions of the *upanayana* ceremony with their concomitant attribution of the appellation "twice-born" to three distinct *varṇas*. Usually he refers to this change as one of an *expansion* of the term *dvija*, along with the study of the Vedas associated with the term, from Brahmans to *kṣatriyas* and *vaiśyas*. He does, however, mention cautiously that "if at one time Brahminhood was not considered a birth status, initiation and study would then have constituted a man as a Brahmin."[45] The implications of this observation should not be overlooked. As discussed in the previous chapter, *brahmacarya* is often discussed in quite expansive terms in the Vedic texts, in such a way in fact that they can be seen to support the practices of Buddhists and Jains just as much as of ritual-oriented Brahmans. Moreover, as we saw, *brahmacarya* is said in the Vedic literature to be a process that gives "birth" to a Brahman—hence the word "twice-born" (*dvija*). Passages such as these help to explain why groups such as the early Buddhists and Jains would have understood themselves as Brahmans—without recourse to concepts of "polemical borrowing" or "marketing"—since their practice of *brahmacarya* would have constituted them as such. Read in this light, then, the effort on the part of the authors of the Gṛhya Sūtras to redefine *dvija* as referring to three distinct *varṇas* appears to be not so much an expansion of the concept of "twice-born" as it was a restriction of the category *Brahman* to a specific group defined by birth rather than by *brahmacarya*. The introduction of the concept of three *dvija varṇas*, in other words, would represent a pivotal moment in the development of the ideology of *varṇa*, which culminated in its full, explicit articulation in the *Āpastamba Dharma Sūtra*.

Even when there definitely was a conception of Brahmanhood by birth, there is evidence that the conception was often more rhetorical than real. In the *Ambaṭṭha Sutta* (*DN* 3), the Buddha humiliates a young Brahman student (*mānava*) named Ambaṭṭha[46] by revealing that he is descended, not from a pure Brahmanical lineage as he claims, but from the black (*kaṇha*) baby of a slave-girl of King Okkāka (i.e., Ikṣvāku), whom the Sakyans regard as their ancestor. Now, this story could simply be dismissed as a polemical fiction, but the discussion that follows cannot be so easily dismissed. The Buddha asks Ambaṭṭha a series of questions about how children of mixed unions would be treated, respectively, by the Brahmans and by the *khattiyas* (=Skt. *kṣatriyas*). In each case, Ambaṭṭha admits that the Brahmans would accept the child of the mixed union, while the *khattiyas* would not—thus demonstrating that *khattiyas* are in fact more strict in preserving pure lineages than the Brahmans are.[47] Of course, this dialog is a Buddhist polemic as well, but given that it is presented as a reasoned argument, it is difficult to imagine that it would have been very convincing if it did not refer to actual social practice.

Another Buddhist text pokes fun at the pretensions of Brahmans with a similar appeal to a social reality of impure Brahman lineages. A *sutta* in the *Aṅguttara Nikāya* (5.191), which has been studied by Oliver Freiberger,[48] lists five *brāhmaṇadhammā* that are now found among dogs but no longer among Brahmans. The first of these is taking only females of one's own kind as a mate: while dogs only take female dogs as mates, Brahmans, according to this *sutta*, now frequently go to non-Brahman women. The polemic of this *sutta* depends on a concept of the purity of the Brahmans of old—a trope found in several other early Buddhist texts as well[49]—but it also depends on the observation, presumably derived from actual social practice, that Brahman lineages are not pure.

Interestingly, an example of the sort of acceptance of children of "impure" lineage as Brahmans discussed in the Buddhist texts can also be found in a Brahmanical text, the *Chāndogya Upaniṣad*. Here we find a short anecdote about how the Upaniṣadic teacher Satyakāma Jābāla first came to enter *brahmacarya*. Satyakāma, wanting to study with Hāridrumata Gautama, asks his mother what his *gotra* is.[50] She replies,

> I do not know what *gotra* you are, dear. I had you in my youth when I was a maid who got around a lot. So I do not know what *gotra* you are. But I am named Jabālā. You are named Satyakāma. So you should just call yourself Satyakāma Jābāla.[51]

Satyakāma goes to Hāridrumata, and when the latter asks him what his *gotra* is, he does not simply give his name as Satyakāma Jābāla, but honestly admits that he has asked his mother about it and discovered that he is a bastard. At this, Hāridrumata replies, "A non-Brahman would not declare that!" (*ChU* 4.4.5: *naitad abrāhmaṇo vivaktum arhati*) and accepts Satyakāma as a student. As Brian Black comments on this passage, whether or not Satyakāma is "actually" a Brahman is left "wonderfully ambiguous," but what is interesting is that he is accepted as a student in spite of not having any known paternal lineage whatsoever.[52]

Bronkhorst's recent work on the spread of Brahmanism provides a useful framework for understanding such examples of dubious Brahmanical lineages. As already discussed in the Introduction, Bronkhorst argues in *Buddhism in the Shadow of Brahmanism* that

> [t]he primary task of the new Brahmanism was to impose its vision of society. Imposing its vision of society meant speaking about society as hierarchically ordered into Brahmins, *kṣatriyas*, *vaiśyas*, and Śūdras. Our earliest non-brahmanical sources do no such thing. The Aśokan inscriptions do not use this terminology, even though they acknowledge the presence of Brahmins. The early Buddhist canon does not do so either, with the exception of some passages that normally discuss the brahmanical claims.[53]

Indeed, as Uma Chakravarti has noted,

> One important feature of the term *vaṇṇa* [in the Pali Canon] is that it appears only in the context of abstract divisions of society into various social categories. We have no evidence of it being used in any concrete situation. . . . It seems to have remained a theoretical concept without any parallel in actual practice.[54]

Furthermore, when *varṇa* (P. *vaṇṇa*) is referred to in the Pali Canon, it is generally in the context of debates between the Buddha and Brahman interlocutors,[55] what I am referring to here as encounter dialogs. Thus, it appears that at the time these encounter dialogs were composed, Vedic Brahmans were pushing their hierarchical *varṇa* theory of society; the encounter dialogs record pushback against that theory, involving, as we have just seen above, an apparently empirical appeal to a mismatch between the theory of *varṇa* and social reality.

Nevertheless, as Bronkhorst has argued, Brahmanism was so successful not because it converted people to its position by logical or other means, but because it changed the terms of social discourse throughout India. Bronkhorst calls such a strategy "framing the debate" and compares it to the way in which Republicans introduced the phrase "tax relief"—which implies that taxes are an affliction—into American political discourse. Over time the media picked up on the phrase, and eventually Democrats were forced to use it as well by default—thus putting them in the awkward position of implying by their own language that Republican hostility toward taxes was justified.[56] It is important to note that for such a strategy to work, it is not necessary to make a logically coherent argument, or, to put it differently, to make an argument that one's opponents would (or at least theoretically could) be logically convinced by. Indeed, as we have seen from the example of the *Ambaṭṭha Sutta,* early Buddhists were not convinced by the theory of *varṇa* and Brahmanical superiority thereby, based on the simple empirical observation that Brahmans do not have pure lineages. What is important, rather, for such a strategy to work is simply to "frame the debate" by popularizing terms that, when ingrained into the popular consciousness, force people to think about the world in a way that seems to lead naturally to one's own position.

One of the ways in which Brahmans did this for *varṇa,* I would argue (other than simply speaking about society in terms of the four *varṇa*s per se), was with the concept of "mixed castes." This concept is not found in Āpastamba,[57] but it is addressed systematically in the other three major Dharma Sūtras, as well as in later Dharmaśāstra literature such as Manu.[58] Although these systematizations purport to indicate how the particular child of a particular union of two persons of different *varṇa*s would be classified, both the fact that the different Dharmaśāstric authors often differ on which mixed class derives from which mixed union, and more importantly the names that are given to many of these mixed classes, indicate that there was a different purpose to these "mixed class" schemas. That is, many of the so-called mixed classes have names that appear to be those of either certain occupations or certain ethnic or tribal groups. Within the Dharma Sūtras we find the following occupation-like names for mixed classes: *dhīvara* (fisherman),[59] *karaṇa* (lit., "doer," a helper or companion),[60] *kṣattṛ* (attendant or doorkeeper),[61] *mūrdhāvasikta* (expert in *dhanurveda*),[62] *rathakāra* (chariot-maker),[63] *sūta* (charioteer),[64] *śvapāka* (dog-cooker),[65] and *vaiṇa* (maker of bamboo-work).[66] Even more interestingly, we find the following names that appear to refer to tribal groups or inhabitants of various countries: *ambaṣṭha* (the name of a country and its inhabitants),[67] *māgadha* (person from Magadha),[68] *niṣāda* (a non-Aryan tribe),[69] *pāraśava* (a people in the southwest),[70] *vaideha/vaidehaka* (person from Videha),[71] and even *yavana* (a Greek!).[72]

Now, it is of course possible that some of these names were used in different senses, one relating to an ethnic group or occupation and the other to a mixed class, and indeed the normative force of the Dharmaśāstric texts may have led to this becoming the case. The overall preponderance of such names in the schemes of mixed classes, however, is highly suggestive that their purpose was not so much to define the status of the progeny of various un-*dharmic* sexual unions[73] as to naturalize the *varṇa* system, which by itself likely bore no resemblance to social reality. It did so by mapping the *varṇas*, through the concept of mixture, onto preexisting social groups. Some of these groups were likely caste-like groups within (or on the margins of) Aryan society, such as *cāṇḍālas*,[74] but others may have simply been ethnic groups that were not recognized as fully Aryan and whose existence could be explained as resulting from intermarriage between hypothetically pure *varṇas* in the past.[75] Such an interpretation appears to be confirmed by the fact that Baudhāyana, in a section of his Dharma Sūtra apart from the enumeration of mixed classes, declares, "The people of Avantī; the people of Aṅga and Magadha; the people of Surāṣṭra; the people of the Southern Path; the people of Upāvṛt, the Sindh, and Suvīra—these come from mixed wombs."[76] In Manu we find even more references to ethnic groups as mixed classes: *ābhīra, andhra, avantya, draviḍa, khasa, licchivi, malla, sātvata, vāṭadhāna.*[77] In addition, a whole host of well-known non-Aryan peoples are said to be *kṣatriyas* who have become *vṛṣalas* "by neglecting rites and disregard[ing] Brahmans"[78]: *puṇḍraka, coḍa* (Coḻa), *draviḍa* (Dravidian), *kāmboja, yavana* (Greek), *śaka, pārada, pahlava, cīna* (Chinese), *kirāta, darada.*

Needless to say, it is impossible to take literally the assertion that entire ethnic groups, or the inhabitants of entire geographical areas, are people who were born from unions between parents of two different *varṇas*. "Mixed castes" are rather a rhetorical device intended to insinuate an ideological system into a descriptive taxonomy. On the one hand, this device is descriptive insofar as it provides a taxonomy of actual social groups. On the other hand, it is normative insofar as it places a value judgment on those groups by dismissing them as "mixed castes." Moreover, it normalizes the very idea of *varṇa* by explaining the entire social world, including those social groups that clearly do not accept it, in terms of *varṇa* categories.

To summarize, then, Āpastamba's articulation of the *varṇa* system should be understood not simply as a description of an uncontested social reality, but as an ideological statement with a particular polemical purpose. It had its roots, to be sure, in a relatively old schema of four types of people, said to be derived from four parts of the primordial person in the *Puruṣa Sūkta*. Later, these four types of people came to be known as *varṇas*, as reflected in the *Śatapatha Brāhmaṇa*. Although Āpastamba was likely the first to state explicitly that these four categories, subsumed under the genus *varṇa*, were determined by birth, there are scattered references in the earlier Vedic literature to the birth of Brahmans. These references are often ambiguous, however, and are complicated by the fact that *brahmacarya* appears to have been understood as giving "birth" to a Brahman—the origin of the term *dvija*, "twice-born." A pivotal moment in the emergence of clear distinction between Brahmans and other *varṇas* came in the Gṛhya Sūtras, which transformed the word *dvija* into a genus composed of three distinct *varṇas*, thus breaking the link between *brahmacarya* and Brahmanhood. This transformation was then made explicit in the Dharma Sūtras, which, beginning with Āpastamba, articulated the *varṇa* system as a system of four distinct classes of people determined by birth and detailed the distinct roles played by each of those classes. Āpastamba's successors went a step further and mapped this system of four classes onto the entire known social world, encompassing even the Greeks, with the concept of "mixed castes."

Even after the full classical articulation of the *varṇa* system had taken place, there is ample evidence that it was more an ideological system than an accurate description of social reality. Aśoka's edicts make no reference to it, and early Buddhist texts do so only in the context of debates with householder Brahmans. Buddhist texts also attest to a lack of actual purity in the lineages of householder Brahmans. Finally, the Dharma Sūtras themselves belie a literal interpretation of *varṇa* categories with their literally impossible enumeration of "mixed castes."

Why, then, did householder Brahmans feel the need to construct, articulate, and normalize the *varṇa* system? Simply put, it allowed them to restrict the category of *Brahman* to a closed group by distinguishing Brahmans from others of high birth (*kṣatriyas* and *vaiśyas*) and severing the link between *brahmacarya* and Brahmanhood. *Brahmacarya*, after all, posed a threat to an ideological system oriented toward householdership and the production of children, since its primary characteristic was celibacy. This threat was addressed more directly in the second novelty introduced by Āpastamba, the *āśrama* system.

## Āśrama *Categories in Colloquial Discourse*

Now that we have seen that the *varṇa* system was not simply a naïve description of social reality but rather an ideological tool intended to restrict Brahmanhood to a particular group of individuals, we can return to the question of the interpretation of the *āśrama* system, which serves as the closing bookend in Āpastamba's description of the normative life of the householder. As already discussed above, Olivelle quite rightly notes that the *āśrama* system as such appears for the first time in the Dharma Sūtras, and he criticizes attempts to project *āśrama* as a system onto older texts in which particular categories are found (such as *brahmacarya*) that came to be incorporated into the *āśrama* system. In a similar fashion, he notes that the concept of *āśrama* as a system of four lifestyles is found only in Brahmanical texts, and he uses this fact to argue that it was an element of a purely internal Brahmanical discourse. That is, it was created by "liberal Brahmans" to justify their accommodation to celibate lifestyles and then criticized for the same reason by the more conservative authors of the Dharma Sūtras.

Although it is true the *āśrama* system as a theoretical system is unique to Brahmanical texts, there is ample evidence that the individual *categories* incorporated into it were used colloquially within North Indian society writ large, rather than being restricted to a closed Brahmanical community. Let us begin with the evidence provided by Megasthenes, the Greek ambassador to the court of Candragupta Maurya. Megasthenes appears to superimpose the *brāhmaṇa-śramaṇa* distinction on a set of practitioners roughly coterminous with three of the *āśramas*. The following description, for example, is given of the *Brachmanai* (*Βραχμᾶναι*):

> The philosophers reside in a grove in front of the city within a moderate-sized enclosure. They live in a simple style and lie on pallets of straw and (deer) skins. They abstain from animal food and sexual pleasures; and occupy their time in listening to serious discourse and in imparting knowledge to willing ears . . . . After living in this manner for seven-and-thirty years, each individual retires to his own possessions, where he lives in security and under less restraint, wearing robes of muslin and a few gold ornaments on his fingers and in his ears . . . . They may marry as many wives as they please, with a view to having many children, for from many wives greater advantages are derived.[79]

To be clear, this does not describe the *brahmacārin āśrama,* but rather a site for practicing temporary *brahmacarya* and the normative life cycle, culminating in the householder *āśrama,* prescribed by the Dharma Sūtras. One remains celibate while dwelling in the "grove in front of the city," and the time spent there is limited (although the amount of time given is anomalous—the Dharma Sūtras prescribe a maximum of 48 years, or 12 for each Veda[80]). This is followed by what clearly is a householder's existence; notice not only the mention of possessions but also the emphasis on producing children. What we are seeing described here, then, are householder Brahmans faithfully carrying out temporary celibacy during a period of studentship and then becoming householders and producing children, as enjoined by the Dharma Sūtras.

The description of the *[S]armanai* (*[Σ]αρμᾶναι*) attributed by Strabo to Megasthenes, on the other hand, divides them into groups that clearly parallel the *vānaprastha* and the *parivrājaka* of the *āśrama* system. First, Strabo describes a group he calls *hylobioi* (*ὑλόβιοι*), which means "living in the woods" and thus is a credible translation of the Sanskrit *vānaprastha*. This is confirmed by the description of the *hylobioi* that he gives:

> Of the Sarmanes the most honourable, he [Megasthenes] says, are those called the Hylobioi. They live in the forests, subsist on leaves and wild fruits, wear garments made from the bark of trees, and abstain from wine and commerce with women. They communicate with the kings who consult them by messengers regarding the causes of things, and who through them worship and supplicate the deity.[81]

This closely parallels the description of the *vānaprastha* found in the Dharma Sūtras; for example, Āpastamba writes,

> From that very state [temporary Vedic studentship], remaining celibate, he goes forth . . . . Clothes of the wilderness are prescribed for him. Then he should wander subsisting on roots, fruits, leaves, and grass.[82]

The similarities are unmistakable: Both the *hylobioi* and the *vānaprastha* bear the name "forest dweller," remain celibate, wear natural clothes, and live off of food that they gather from the wild.

Megasthenes' second category of *[S]armanai*, the "physicians" (*ἰατρικοί*), while lacking any discernible relationship in nomenclature to the final remaining *āśrama* category, the *parivrājaka*, nonetheless clearly parallels them in the substance of its description. Strabo begins his description of them in the following terms:

> Next in honour to the Hylobioi are the physicians, for they apply philosophy to the study of the nature of man. They are frugal in their habits, but do not live in the fields. Their food consists of rice and

> barley-meal, which every one gives who is asked, as well as every one who receives them as a guest . . . . Women study philosophy with some of them, but they too abstain from sexual intercourse.[83]

This clearly refers, in addition of course to celibacy, to the practice of living off of alms given by ordinary householders, and most likely refers as well to the path of insight into the nature of the *ātman* that a *parivrājaka* is said to follow (*ĀDhS* 2.21.13–14; *VDhS* 10.14).

It appears, however, that much of Megasthenes' description of the "physicians" is based on their actual practices rather than any normative ideal. A clear distinction is made between them and the *hylobioi* through the observation that, though frugal, they "do not live in the fields." One cannot help but be reminded here of the tension in Buddhism between the ideal of wandering nine months of the year and the reality—which may likely have become the norm by Candragupta's time—of living year-round in settled monasteries. Actual practice, as opposed to normative ideals, may also explain the appellation "physician," which Strabo elaborates upon in some detail:

> By their knowledge of medicine they can make persons have a numerous offspring, and make also the children to be either male or female. They effect cures rather by regulating diet than by the use of medicines. The remedies in most repute are ointments and plasters. All others they suppose to partake largely of a noxious nature.[84]

Although such practices are not listed in the normative descriptions of the *parivrājaka*, nor, to my knowledge, in the normative accounts of Jain or Buddhist monks, we know that they must have been current among ascetic groups since they are listed among the various "bestial sciences" practiced by "some *samaṇa*s and Brahmans" that the Buddha can be praised for abstaining from in the *Brahmajāla Sutta* (*DN* 1):

> While some venerable *samaṇa*s and Brahmans, having eaten food given in faith, make a living by wrong livelihood, by such bestial sciences as . . . causing virility, causing impotence . . . an emetic, purgative, up-purge, down-purge, head-purge, anointing of the ear, cleansing of the eye, treatment of the nose, ointment, anointing, ophthalmology, surgery, pediatrics, the giving of a balm as remedy for a medicine previously given, and so forth, the *samaṇa* Gotama

> abstains from wrong livelihood, from such bestial sciences as these.[85]

We can feel confident that these medical arts—as well as the many other practices that are criticized in the *Brahmajāla Sutta,* most of which pertain to astrology and divination—were indeed practiced by ancient Indian ascetics not only because it would be pointless for the author of this Buddhist text to criticize them if they did not, but also because many of them, including folk medicine, are practiced even in modern times by Buddhist monks.[86]

Thus, in the testimony of Megasthenes we have evidence that categories similar to those found in the *āśrama* system—certainly, at least, those of the *vānaprastha* and *parivrājaka*—were indeed in colloquial use in India around the time of the writing of the Dharma Sūtras. Note too that, reflecting a time when *Brahman* and *śramaṇa* had become discrete and opposed categories, Megasthenes places the categories of "forest dweller" and "physician" specifically under the genus *śramaṇa.* The term *Brahman* is reserved for those who eschew these lifestyles and instead follow the normative life of a householder as outlined in the Dharma Sūtras. This suggests, as we discussed in Chapter 2, that a distinction between the categories *śramaṇa* and *Brahman* had already become operative by the time the Greeks came into contact with Indian culture. But it strongly suggests that the Dharma Sūtra authors, in discussing the *āśrama* system, were not simply engaging in an intra-Brahmanical debate; rather, they were engaging with categories that described the entire field of North Indian religious practice in their day.

This is confirmed by the fact that similar categories are also found in the early Buddhist texts, though again not in any way organized into a fourfold system. In fact, what is interesting about these categories as they are found in the Buddhist texts is that they do not at all follow the same pattern as the Brahmanical *āśrama* system, and in fact are never mentioned together in one place, yet when considered together demonstrate an early Buddhist articulation of self-identity that offers a striking parallel to the Neo-Brahmanical identity constructed by the early Dharmaśāstric presentation of the *āśrama* system.

In the last chapter, we already discussed at length three *āśrama*-like categories found in the early Buddhist texts, so it is unnecessary to go into much detail about these here. As we saw, the primary identity early Buddhists associated with themselves was *brahmacārī.* The sort of *brahmacarya* they advocated was identical to that described (and criticized) as the first *āśrama* in the Dharma Sūtras—a lifelong commitment to celibacy under the tutelage of a teacher. Not implausibly, they understood this *brahmacarya* as making them Brahmans. As a total other to this celibate identity was the *gahapati*, or "house-lord"—a man akin to the Roman *paterfamilias* who married, had children, and thus had the resources and social independence to support the Buddhist *saṅgha*. Finally, forest-dwellers, referred to in the Buddhist texts using the slang term *jaṭila*, were understood as in a sense "bizarro-Buddhists"—practitioners of a markedly different lifestyle whom the Buddhists nevertheless saw as akin to themselves because of a common commitment to *kriyāvāda* (the "doctrine of action").

This leaves one *āśrama* category, the *parivrājaka*. The category of the *paribbājaka*—which is simply the Pali form of *parivrājaka*, the term used by Baudhāyana and Vasiṣṭha to refer to the fourth *āśrama*[87]—occurs frequently in the Pali Canon and is constructed as a proximate other to the *bhikkhu*. By this, I mean that we can infer that Buddhist monks would have been considered, within colloquial discourse, as *paribbājakas*, but that the early Buddhist texts seek rhetorically to distance the category *bhikkhu* from the category *paribbājaka*; that is, they reserve the latter category almost exclusively for non-Buddhist *paribbājakas*, even though Buddhist monks clearly would have been considered *paribbājakas* as well.

That *bhikkhus* within the early Buddhist tradition would have been considered *paribbājakas/parivrājakas* is clear from the way in which the category *parivrājaka* is defined in the Dharma Sūtras. Gautama, who in fact refers to this *āśrama* with the term *bhikṣu* instead of *parivrājaka*, defines the category as follows:

> A beggar (*bhikṣu*) is without possessions, keeps his semen up (i.e., is celibate), (and) stays in one place during the rains. He should go to the village for the purpose of alms. He should go last, without turning back, without giving a blessing. He is controlled with respect to speech, eyes, and actions. He should wear a cloth to conceal the private parts. Some (say he should wear) a cast-off (cloth) after washing it. He should not take a limb from a plant or tree that has not fallen (on its own). He should not stay a second night in a village out of season. He (should be) shaven or wear a tuft of hair. He should avoid the destruction of seed. He (treats) beings equally, whether in violence or in kindness. He is not enterprising.[88]

Baudhāyana's description, which refers to this *āśrama* as that of the *parivrājaka,* is quite similar, making reference to wandering except for a "rains retreat" when the person in question should stay in one place, giving up all possessions, shaving the head, and subsisting off of alms.[89] Vasiṣṭha also uses the term *parivrājaka* and describes him as shaving his head, begging for food, and lacking a fixed residence.[90] Finally, Āpastamba, who uses the term *parivrāja,* says that the person who chooses this *āśrama* wanders, begs for food, and wears discarded clothes, although, like Vasiṣṭha, he makes no mention of a rains retreat.[91] Clearly, the Buddhist *bhikkhu,* at least as he was ideally constructed in the early Buddhist texts, falls into this category, especially as it is described by Gautama and Baudhāyana.[92]

Although, as I will show, the early Buddhist texts tend to distance the *bhikkhu* from the category of *paribbājaka,* it can nonetheless easily be inferred from the same texts that *bhikkhu*s would, in common parlance, have ordinarily been understood as belonging to that category. One of the most common ways in which these early texts refer to *paribbājaka*s is through the stock phrase *aññatitthiyā paribbājakā*—"wanderers of other sects."[93] This phrase is used, much as the compound *samaṇa-brāhmaṇā* often is, to refer to non-Buddhist vocational practitioners collectively as a group. Indeed, on occasion it is even grouped together with *samaṇa*s and *brāhmaṇa*s in a single compound used to refer collectively to non-Buddhists.[94] Most often, *aññatitthiyā paribbājakā* are referred to by the Buddha while teaching to distinguish their views and practices from his own, or even more specifically in the context of telling his monks how to respond when members of other sects ask them about his teaching. Thus, in *MN* 11, which can be taken as exemplary, the Buddha says to his monks,

> It is possible, monks, that wanderers of other sects might say thus: "But what is your confidence, what the strength, by which you speak thus? . . . Speaking in this way, monks, wanderers of other sects should be answered thus . . . .[95]

What follows is the Buddha's teaching, which the monks can then use to answer the questions of the wanderers of other sects. Presumably, texts such as this one were intended to train monks in how to represent themselves, as members of the *saṅgha* and followers of the Buddha, to members of other sects.

Clearly, much as in the case of references to *samaṇa-brāhmaṇā* that we examined in Chapter 3, these references to *aññatitthiyā paribbājakā* attempt to construct a Buddhist identity by clearly demarcating distinctions in doctrine and practice between the Buddhists themselves and the collective *paribbājaka* other. This demarcation is reinforced by the fact that the category *paribbājaka* is reserved in the early Buddhist texts for that other; to my knowledge, the Buddha and his monks are never referred to directly in the Pali Canon as *paribbājakas*. Nevertheless, by the very phrasing "wanderers of other sects," it is clearly implied that this sect, that of the followers of the Buddha, is itself a sect of wanderers. This conclusion is reinforced by the fact that, on a couple of occasions (*AN* 3.144, 11.10), the Buddha is said to have stayed at a *paribbājakārāma*—a "pleasure park" for wanderers. Insofar, then, as *paribbājaka* is a category to which the Buddhist *bhikkhu* should belong according to ordinary parlance, but against which it constructed itself, it can be understood as serving as a proximate other in the early Buddhist texts.

We have ample evidence that while the *āśrama* system as such was restricted to a particular Brahmanical discourse represented by the Dharma Sūtras, it drew from categories that were in common colloquial use at the time and applied to the full range of religious practitioners and not just a closed group of "Brahmans." Megasthenes refers quite clearly to two of the categories, *vānaprastha* (as *hylobioi*) and *parivrājaka* (less literally as "physicians"), and identifies them specifically as *śramaṇas*. Early Buddhist texts refer to all four of the categories found in the *āśrama* system, but deploy these categories in a very different way to articulate their own unique identity. If the *āśrama* system is only found in Brahmanical texts, but draws from categories that were (1) in general colloquial use and (2) used by Buddhists to articulate their own identity, it seems only logical that the *āśrama* system too was a tool to articulate a particular identity in terms of colloquial categories.

## *The* Āśrama *System as a Polemical Systematization of Actual Social Practice*

Returning now to the matter of the presentation of the *āśrama* system in the Dharma Sūtras, we can address the question of whom Gautama and Baudhāyana were arguing against when they rejected the *āśrama* system. Clearly, all of the Dharma Sūtras represent Neo-Brahmanism insofar as they advocate the *varṇa* system; declare Brahmans superior to the other three classes by birth; and, like the Buddha's Brahman interlocutors in the encounter dialogs, adhere to the householder lifestyle as the best or even the only *dharmic* way of life. What then of the opponents they allude to who support the *āśrama* system? It is true that, as already discussed, some of these opponents appear to have made arguments based on the Vedas, but all this definitely means is that there was someone whom Baudhāyana (the only Dharma Sūtra author who makes reference to such arguments) saw fit to refute, who was willing and able to make an argument based on Vedic scripture in support of lifelong celibate lifestyles. One can call such a person a "liberal" Brahman[96] if one wishes, but more apropos for our purposes is that he is not within the tradition represented by the Dharma Sūtras. He is not, in other words, an advocate of Neo-Brahmanism.

Indeed, the rhetoric used against the supporters of the *āśrama* system in the Dharma Sūtras suggests not so much a point of disagreement within a self-conscious tradition, but rather a boundary marker serving to distinguish the tradition out of which the Dharma Sūtras come from those outside that tradition. Baudhāyana, the only Dharma Sūtra author who presents Vedic quotes in support of the *āśrama* system,[97] also quotes the following saying in support of his position that there is only a single *āśrama,* the householder *āśrama*: "There was an *asura* named Kapila, the son of Prahlāda. He made this division, battling with the gods. A wise person should pay no attention to them."[98] So even if Baudhāyana's opponents are able to quote Vedic texts in support of their position, they are not merely other Brahmans from Baudhāyana's own tradition with whom he respectfully disagrees over their interpretation of the Vedas; they are in fact followers of a demonic enemy of the gods. Likewise, Āpastamba, after presenting the view of his opponents that the celibate *āśrama*s are superior to that of the householder, begins his rebuttal by stating simply, "The position of the elders of the Triple Veda, however, is that the Vedas are the standard."[99] Again, this does not seem like a statement directed toward a member of Āpastamba's own tradition; rather, it sounds like a concise definition of Āpastamba's own tradition, precisely in that aspect that most distinguishes it from that of his opponents. Āpastamba, like the other Dharma Sūtra authors and like all of the Brahman interlocutors with whom the Buddha speaks in the encounter dialogs of the Pali Canon, is a Brahman who defines himself in terms of his knowledge of and adherence to the three Vedas.

Is it possible, then, that the Dharma Sūtra authors cited opinions not just of fellow Vedic Brahmans who happened to have minor differences of opinion, but also of those whose opinions were fundamentally opposed to their own brand of Veda-centric Brahmanism? Telling clues that this is what is happening in the case of the *āśrama* system can be found in descriptions of the *parivrājaka*. For example, Āpastamba writes that "discarded clothing is prescribed for him," but then adds, "Some (say he should be) free of all" (i.e., he should go naked).[100] The option for a *parivrājaka* to go naked is presented, as with other options in the Dharma Sūtras, as the opinion of "some" (*eke*), but it seems unlikely that Āpastamba is simply citing here the opinion of certain other Vedic Brahmans—that is, other teachers in his own tradition, with whom he would identify in some way—that a *parivrājaka* should go naked. Rather, given what we know about Indian religious practice in this time period, it seems likely that he is simply describing one particular *parivrājaka* practice, the *acelaka* practice—which is known to have been practiced by Jains and Ājīvikas. Similarly, Gautama and Baudhāyana ascribe to the *parivrājaka* the practice of staying in one place during the rainy season (*GDhS* 3.13, *BDhS* 2.11.20), a known practice of the Buddhists and Jains. Baudhāyana also refers to the known Buddhist practice of wearing "ochre clothes" (*BDhS* 2.11.21: *kāṣāya-vāsāḥ*) and the known Jain practice of straining water (*BDhS* 2.11.24). He even puts into the mouth of his hypothetical *parivrājaka* a statement that sounds remarkably Buddhist: "Having rejected Vedic rites, cut off from both sides, we embrace the middle path."[101] Rather than hypothesizing "liberal Brahmans" who advocated such practices, but for whom we have no evidence, it seems much more prudent to conclude that the Dharma Sūtra authors were describing the actual practices of various *parivrājaka* groups for which we do have evidence, such as the Ājīvikas, Jains, and Buddhists.

Indeed, an often-overlooked aspect of the Dharma Sūtras is that they are simultaneously normative and descriptive texts; indeed, they blur the distinction between normative and descriptive in ways that can be quite disconcerting to modern readers. As Richard Lariviere has argued of *dharma* as it is conceived in the Dharma Sūtras, "There is much made of the Vedic source, but ultimately, the immediate source is custom. The legal texts themselves tell us this in very clear terms. All custom is binding."[102] Lariviere argues that the fact that "the *dharma* literature is a record of custom is obfuscated by the fact that the idiom of all the *dharma* literature is one of eternality and timelessness . . . . It is further obfuscated by the fact that the *dharma* literature clings to the claim that all of its provisions can be traced directly or indirectly to the Veda, the very root of *dharma*."[103] The Dharma Sūtras do, in fact, explicitly cite actual practice as a source of *dharma,* although they rank it below the Vedas (*ĀDhS* 1.1.1–3, *GDhS* 1.1–2, *BDhS* 1.1.1–4, *VDhS* 1.4–5). This privileging of the Veda, Lariviere argues, was rhetorical and had to be accommodated to actual custom:

> In general, however, the brāhmaṇa *dharmaśāstra* writers were constrained by the burden placed on them as recorders and synthesizers of customary practice. They were obliged by the interested constituencies, by the king, and by considerations of social and political harmony to record the practice as they found it. They were also obliged to explain how these customs fit with the tradition, and it is in these 'explanations' that we may find the most outré flights of brāhmaṇa imagination.[104]

The task of the Dharma Sūtra authors, in other words, was not simply to determine *dharma* through exegesis of the Vedic texts; it was also to justify established customary law as *dharma* on the basis of the Vedas.[105]

This is not to say that the Dharma Sūtra authors accepted all aspects of actual social practice and found ways to justify them on the basis of the Veda. It does appear, however, that they did attempt to address a wide variety of social practices in one way or another. The *āśrama* system serves as a prime example of this. *Āśrama* as it is presented in the Dharma Sūtras served as a means for advocates of Neo-Brahmanism to account for, taxonomize, and respond to much of the same "empirical" social data—that is, actual social practices—that were referred to more loosely in colloquial discourse by the concept of *śramaṇa-brāhmaṇā.* Now, this does not at all preclude the possibility that, as Olivelle has argued, the original idea of a schema of four *āśrama*s was formulated by someone else who favored and wanted to legitimate celibate, ascetic lifestyles—whether that may have been a "liberal Brahman," a person from an entirely different group willing to make an argument from a Vedic text, or someone else. What I would like to emphasize, however, is that there is no direct evidence for such a source. The only evidence we do have is for, on the one hand, a colloquial discourse on *śramaṇa-brāhmaṇā,* encompassing a variety of lifestyles, and on the other an elite, systematized discourse on roughly the same social phenomena but conceived of as four *āśrama*s, confined to the emerging orthodox Brahmanical tradition (i.e., Neo-Brahmanism). The adoption of the language of *āśrama* would also explain why there is a relative lack of reference to *śramaṇas* or *śramaṇa-brāhmaṇas* in the Brahmanical literature. There would be no need to refer to these colloquial categories when the tradition had at its disposal a set of categories that both were more systematic and thus more amenable to the taxonomizing tendency within Brahmanical discourse—and also, whatever the original purpose of the system may have been, ultimately proved amenable to advancing a particular Brahmanical agenda.

Seen in this light, the presentation of the *āśrama* system by the different Dharma Sūtras need not be viewed primarily as a matter of acceptance or rejection. All of the four Dharma Sūtras clearly fall within the aegis of a Neo-Brahmanical movement that privileged the householder lifestyle, and none of them show much sympathy toward the radical celibate lifestyles that the three non-householder *āśramas* were meant to refer to. Although Olivelle refers to Āpastamba and Vasiṣṭha as "accepting" the *āśrama* system,[106] Āpastamba delivers a lengthy argument against those who see the celibate *āśramas* as superior, and he maintains that "immortality is (having) offspring"[107]; likewise, Vasiṣṭha declares that "of the four *āśramas*, the householder is superior."[108] I would argue, therefore, that Āpastamba and Vasiṣṭha do not "accept" the *āśrama* system so much as Gautama and Baudhāyana go an extra rhetorical step in their critique of it by explicitly rejecting the non-householder *āśramas*. All four authors are clearly uncomfortable with celibate lifestyles—lifestyles that moreover had a tendency to promote teachings that obviated the need for study of the Vedas[109]; they simply differ in how exactly they respond to such lifestyles, which they clearly felt obligated to comment upon since they formed a significant part of actual social practice. Gautama and Baudhāyana may have actually been the more radical of the four insofar as they rejected the celibate *āśramas* outright, instead of adopting the more usual Dharmaśāstric rhetorical practice of justifying social customs within a Vedic framework.[110] They do not appear to represent a diachronic movement either toward or away from rejection of the celibate *āśramas*[111]; in fact, they appear to represent an idiosyncratic opinion that was superseded by the accomodationist rhetoric that became dominant in the later classical Dharmaśāstric texts, with the shift to understanding *āśramas* as stages. In spite of their differences, they are united with the other two Dharma Sūtras in using the *āśrama* system as a vehicle to grapple with the empirical existence of lifestyles other than their own preferred householder lifestyle.[112]

## *Conclusion: Householder Brahmanism and the Preclassical* Varṇāśramadharma

We are now in a position to interpret the unique structure of the *Āpastamba Dharma Sūtra* and the rhetorical tools it bequeathed to its successors in the Dharma Sūtra and broader Dharmaśāstra traditions. As already described at the beginning of this chapter, Āpastamba framed his text with a statement and restatement of his primary thesis that *dharma* and Veda are linked. The body of the text is then divided into two parts: one addressing the normative life cycle of a householder, the other addressing the duties of a king. The first of these is by far the larger of the two and can thus be understood as providing the dominant narrative of the text. It is in turn framed by two novel concepts introduced by Āpastamba: the first complete and explicit statement of the *varṇa* system and the first articulation of the *āśrama* system. These two systems can be understood as antipodes that serve to strictly define the parameters of the normative lifestyle described between them.

The *varṇa* system is an ideologically driven description of society. It draws upon, and puts together definitively for the first time, a variety of precedents from the Vedic tradition, assembled in such a way as to favor the exclusive claim of householder Brahmans like Āpastamba to Brahmanhood. It did this in part by taking a relatively old set of four social categories and linking them explicitly to birth. It also drew upon the innovation, first found in the Gṛhya Sūtras, of conferring both *dvija* status and the right to engage in Vedic study during a temporary period of *brahmacarya* on three distinct classes of people: the Brahmans, *kṣatriyas*, and *vaiśyas*. This had the effect of severing the link, attested in old Vedic texts, between the practice of *brahmacarya* and Brahmanhood. This innovation had the distinct advantage of limiting Brahmanhood to those who were born into recognized Vedic lineages—or at least giving the rhetorical appearance of such. Given evidence from both Buddhist and Brahmanical texts, it seems likely that in practice, householder Brahmans were loose in their standards of birth in accepting Brahman students; the rhetoric of birth simply allowed them to claim exclusive rights to the title of *Brahman*.

The *āśrama* system, on the other hand, is in a sense the antithesis of the *varṇa* system. It describes the actual social situation in late first-millennium North India, one in which Brahmanhood was not restricted to a particular group determined by birth but was claimed by a number of different groups, many of which based their claims to Brahmanhood on a lifelong commitment to *brahmacarya* and therefore posed a direct threat to the householder Brahmans. The purpose of the *āśrama* system in the Dharma Sūtras was to provide a full taxonomy of the range of practices found in early North India, so as to reject as "un-Vedic" all but the one lifestyle favored by the authors of these texts: the lifestyle of the householder.

What Āpastamba is saying, therefore, in what we might dub his preclassical formulation of *varṇāśramadharma*, is that Brahmanhood is the exclusive domain of his own group of householder Brahmans. As such, it is intimately tied up with reproduction. On the one hand it can only be inherited, at birth, from one's father. On the other hand it brings with it the responsibility to produce children of one's own. In the process, Brahmanhood is definitively divorced from the practice of *brahmacarya*, which, when properly practiced (as opposed to its incorrect practice as the first of the four *āśramas*) is a temporary period of Vedic studentship open even to certain classes of non-Brahmans. The affirmation of hereditary Brahmanhood, along with the rejection of lifelong celibacy, thus provides a clear frame for Āpastamba's description of the normative life cycle. This life cycle fulfills all three of the debts prescribed by the *Taittirīya Saṃhitā*: It includes a period of *brahmacarya*, which in turn trains one to perform sacrifices, and which culminates in the taking of a wife and establishment of a household so as to produce progeny. In addition, by being at least nominally available to all three *ārya varṇas*, this life cycle severed the (dangerous, from the householders' perspective) link between *brahmacarya* and Brahmanhood.

As already suggested at the beginning of this chapter, Āpastamba's uncompromising assertion of householder supremacy did not last long. While the other three Dharma Sūtra authors reproduced Āpastamba's articulation of the *āśrama* system as a taxonomical tool for rejecting celibate lifestyles, Manu completely revamped the system so as to produce an accommodation with renunciation. That is, he transformed the four *āśramas* from one legitimate and three illegitimate lifelong vocations into four normative stages of life. This transformation allowed for the accommodation of renunciatory lifestyles, but only after the obligation to produce children had been fulfilled. It was this new formulation of *varṇāśramadharma* that became the ideological pillar of classical Hinduism, and that laid the foundation for the tension between world-affirming and world-denying practices that has defined Hinduism throughout its history.

# 6

# *The Emergence of the Snake and the Mongoose*

NOW THAT WE have articulated a credible model of the Indian religious field in the late 1st millennium BCE as one of competing Brahmanisms, I would like to return to the diachronic project begun at the beginning of Chapter 4. There I showed that in the earliest Buddhist texts, the *Aṭṭhaka Vagga* and the core verses of the *Pārāyaṇa Vagga*, the word *Brahman* is used straightforwardly to refer to the Buddhist ideal, without any apparent contrast to another group of "real" Brahmans. Moreover, I showed that the category *Brahman* is used similarly in early Jain texts to refer to the Jain ideal, again without any contrast to "actual" (i.e., Vedic) Brahmans. I argued that we should take these claims to Brahmanhood seriously on their own terms, and concomitantly understand them as part of a period of contestation over the category *Brahman* rather than prejudicing the issue by assuming that the winners of that period of contestation were the real Brahmans, and all others mere copycats.

Thus we have evidence that early Buddhists and Jains did, with some justification, claim to be Brahmans. We also have decentered Neo-Brahmanism by showing it to be, not *the* Brahmanism but rather a particular articulation of Brahmanism that, unlike those of the Buddhists and Jains, was rooted in householdership. But we also saw, in Chapter 2, that the relevant evidence *as it comes down to us* reflects a milieu in which a bifurcation between the categories *śramaṇa* and *Brahman*, rooted in the rhetoric of Neo-Brahmanism, had already arisen. This is reflected in particular in passages in the early Buddhist *sūtras* that do not simply refer to the Buddhist ideal as a "Brahman," but reframe this language as a polemic against the proponents of Neo-Brahmanism. Can we adduce any evidence for an actual *process* by which the "snake and mongoose" emerged in early Buddhist literature—that is, by which the credible claims of Buddhists[1] to śramaṇic Brahmanhood were transformed into mere polemics against the established claim of the householder Brahmans to Brahmanhood? What I would like to show, in other words, is that I am not simply using the oral nature of the Buddhist texts as an excuse to explain away passages that have been interpreted by previous scholars as polemics against or "marketing" that coopts the prestige of a preexisting Brahmanism. Through a close examination of the textual traditions of the Buddhist *Aṭṭhaka* and *Pārāyaṇa*, I will demonstrate that the rhetoric of Brahmanhood in the early Buddhist oral literature was treated differently over time by examining commentaries on older root texts and the framing of older texts within a newer narrative framework.[2]

In taking this approach, I am inspired by the method used by Grace Burford in her study of the *Aṭṭhaka*—that is, comparing the root text to the early commentary in the *Mahāniddesa* and later commentary in the *Paramatthajotikā II*. This method allows one not only to compare a term or concept in *different* literary contexts and in texts that were *likely* written at different times; it allows one to compare a term or concept in the *same* literary context and in texts that were *definitely* written at different times. In other words, we get to see directly how a later author grappled directly with the problematic terms and concepts in an earlier text. While Burford looked at the way the later commentators dealt with the problematic doctrinal aspects of the root text, however, I will be looking at the way in which later authors dealt with the problematic treatment of the word *Brahman*.

I will begin by applying this method to the *Aṭṭhaka*, which may be a bit older than the *Pārāyaṇa* and in any case appears to be more uniformly at odds with mainstream canonical doctrine. There are two significant texts that allow us to see how later authors grappled with the original[3] verses of the *Aṭṭhaka* and the problematic ideas found therein. The first is the *Mahāniddesa*, a canonical text which provides the earliest formal commentary on the *Aṭṭhaka* and clearly seeks to interpret it within an orthodox doctrinal framework. The second is another version of the *Aṭṭhaka* itself—namely, a version now only fully extant in Chinese translation that embeds the verses of the **Arthavargīya* within prose frame narratives. These two texts, I will show, represent two different approaches to dealing with the figure of the Brahman in the *Aṭṭhaka*/**Arthavargīya*. Next, I will turn to the *Pārāyaṇa*, which presents a somewhat more complicated case than the *Aṭṭhaka* because of the heterogeneous way in which it treats the category

*Brahman*. There the focus will be on the extant text of the *Pārāyaṇa* itself and the way in which its internal composition served to frame and thus make meaningful references to the ideal person as a Brahman within something more akin to the mainstream canonical narratives on Brahmans and Brahmanhood.

## *The* Mahāniddesa *Commentary on the* Aṭṭhaka Vagga

As a word-by-word commentary, the *Mahāniddesa* is mostly focused on the explication of problematic terms or, as Burford has argued, on transforming the poetic language of the *Aṭṭhaka* into a system of technical terminology consistent with broader canonical usage. Needless to say, this does not leave much room for extended narrative frameworks, such as we find elsewhere in the Canon, that would display a clear conception of Buddhist identity vis-à-vis the category *Brahman*. Nevertheless, there are some clues scattered throughout the commentary that do point to a somewhat different conception of the category than we find in the *Aṭṭhaka* itself. To begin with, we find repeated reference—more than in the *suttas* of the four main Nikāyas, in fact—to the four *varṇas* (*brāhmaṇa, khattiya, vessa*, and *sudda*).[4] This would imply that the *Niddesa* author was well aware—perhaps even accepting—of the *varṇa* system. Moreover, on the commentary on v. 859, the one place in the *Aṭṭhaka* (as we have seen) that refers to *samaṇabrāhmaṇāse*, the *Niddesa* glosses the compound by splitting it into its constituents (i.e., as a *dvandva*) and glossing *brāhmaṇā* as "whoever says '*Bho*'" (*ye keci bhovādikā*). Thus, although the context of the compound *samaṇabrāhmaṇā* in the original *sutta* renders the distinction between *samaṇa* and *brāhmaṇa* irrelevant (both being contrasted with the ideal *muni*), the commentator imposes a distinction between them and makes clear that a particular social class is being referred to by *brāhmaṇa* (*bho* being the term of address they used with their perceived social inferiors).

The *Mahāniddesa* also supplies some Brahman interlocutors for the Buddha where none exist, explicitly at least, in the original *Aṭṭhaka*. On a couple of occasions, this takes the form of short quotations from the Buddha himself that include the vocative *brāhmaṇa* to refer to the person whom the Buddha is addressing.[5] The most significant case, however, is the *Māgandiya Sutta* (9), one of only a few *suttas* in the *Aṭṭhaka* that has a named interlocutor.[6] This *sutta* is included within the "core" identified by Vetter because, with the exception of its first two verses, it consists of a dialog between the Buddha and a certain Māgandiya in which the Buddha takes the strong position, typical of the core *suttas* of the *Aṭṭhaka*, that purity does not come from holding a particular view, which can only lead to disputes.[7] The *Aṭṭhaka* does not identify the Buddha's interlocutor except by name, although, at least in the context of his debate with the Buddha in v. 837–847, he could easily be the Māgandiya of *MN* 75—a *paribbājaka* who debates with the Buddha and in the end is converted—or else someone like him. Tradition, however, appears to have identified the Māgandiya of the *Aṭṭhaka* with another Māgandiya entirely—one rather ill-suited for the heady philosophical debate that takes up the bulk of the *Māgandiya Sutta*—namely, a certain rich Brahman who is impressed by the Buddha and offers his daughter's hand to him in marriage.

The connection is already indicated by the first verse of the canonical *Māgandiya Sutta*, a verse that can be quoted as a prime example of Buddhist misogyny,[8] in which the Buddha rather contemptuously rejects Māgandiya's daughter:

> Having seen Taṇhā, Arati, and Ragā [the daughters of Māra], there
> was not even the desire for sexual intercourse.
> What indeed is this, full of urine and excrement? I wouldn't want
> to touch it even with my foot.[9]

This verse appears to be rather clearly an addition to the *Māgandiya Sutta* (albeit a relatively early one) intended to identify the Māgandiya of the *sutta* with the Brahman Māgandiya who offered the Buddha his daughter. There are two reasons to suspect this. First, the verse itself makes little sense as a lead-in to a philosophical debate on abandoning all views. It makes perfect sense, however, in the story of the Brahman Māgandiya offering his daughter to the Buddha, which is recounted in the Pali tradition in the *Aṭṭhakathā* commentary on the *Dhammapada* (2.1.5), where the Buddha does indeed respond to Māgandiya's offer with this contemptuous response but does not follow up with a teaching on abandoning all views. (Instead, the girl becomes rather understandably angry at the Buddha's insult and marries King Udena of Kosambī.)

The second reason to suspect that the first verse of the canonical *Māgandiya Sutta* was added is that the second canonical verse is even more suspect than the first. The second verse, intended as Māgandiya's response to the Buddha's rejection, rather clumsily attempts to tie the Buddha's response to a marital offer to the debate on views that follows:

> If you do not want such a jewel, a woman desired by many kings,
> What sort of view, morality, vows, way of life, and rebirth into existence, then, do you profess?[10]

This verse is almost certainly not original because, as already noted, it is the only canonical verse of the *Aṭṭhaka* not commented upon by the *Mahāniddesa*, and moreover it has no parallel in the Chinese translation of the **Arthavargīya*. The latter has in its place the following two verses, which serve to provide an even clumsier transition to the philosophical debate that follows:

> I have said that I do not desire sexual intercourse. I do not observe within any un-*dharmic* action.
> Even though I hear something ugly, I do not bear hatred. As long as it does not stop within, there are innumerable sufferings.
> One sees the outside as beautiful; muscle is covered by skin. Why should the sage accept this?
> Be aware of and look at inner and outer actions. As for craftiness, I say it is a foolish action.[11]

The version preserved in Chinese also includes a prose narrative prior to the verses that recounts the story of how Māgandiya offered his daughter to the Buddha; it is similar to the account preserved in the Pali *Dhammapada-aṭṭhakathā*, but by no means identical. The story is also recounted, again with its own idiosyncratic details, by Buddhaghosa in his commentary on the *Māgandiya Sutta* in the *Paramatthajotikā II*.

It appears, then, that an original series of verses outlining a debate over the abandonment of all views between the Buddha and an otherwise unidentified Māgandiya, when it was incorporated into the *Aṭṭhaka/ *Arthavargīya*, had the "urine and excrement" verse added at the beginning to associate it with the story of the Brahman Māgandiya offering the Buddha his daughter. Different traditions sought to incorporate this verse into the original *sutta* in different ways, as evidenced by the lack of agreement between the intervening verses in the Pali and Chinese versions. Finally, frame stories were added on in slightly different ways by different traditions—inserted directly into the **Arthavargīya* that is preserved in Chinese, but delivered as a commentary by Buddhaghosa in the *Paramatthajotikā II*—to place the *sutta* in the context of the story of Māgandiya offering the Buddha his daughter.

The *Mahāniddesa,* for its part, appears to represent an intermediate stage in this development. On the one hand it accepts the initial "urine and excrement" verse as part of the *sutta* and comments upon it, and it appears to be aware of the story of the Brahman Māgandiya that it alludes to insofar as it glosses the word *māgandiya* when it appears throughout the *sutta* as "that Brahman" (*taṃ brāhmaṇaṃ*) whom the Buddha "addresses by name" (*nāmena ālapati*). On the other hand, the *Mahāniddesa* does not comment upon (and thus presumably is not aware of) v. 836, which is the only attempt within the canonical version to create a plot link between the story of Māgandiya's daughter and Māgandiya's debate with the Buddha over views. Moreover, it makes no attempt to flesh out that story through a prose narrative, as the version preserved in Chinese does, and the later commentary by Buddhaghosa will do. But even though it fails to provide a complete narrative, the *Mahāniddesa* accomplishes quite a lot just by identifying Māgandiya as a Brahman. Originally the debate in the *Māgandiya Sutta* was consistent with the other core *suttas* of the *Aṭṭhaka* insofar as it advanced a non-dualist position that rejected all views and referred to the ideal person in this respect as a Brahman. By identifying Māgandiya, however, who clearly is antagonistic to the Buddha's non-dualist teaching in this debate, as a Brahman—that is, one can only presume, a Brahman by birth—the *Mahāniddesa* set up a dichotomy between the literal Brahman represented by Māgandiya and the metaphorical or "true" Brahman represented by the ideal presented in the Buddha's teaching.

The final and most basic way that the *Mahāniddesa* transforms the use of the word *Brahman* in the *Aṭṭhaka* is the gloss that it gives for the word itself. The word *Brahman* appears eight times in the *Aṭṭhaka* (excepting its single appearance in the compound *samaṇabrāhmaṇa*), and each time the *Mahāniddesa* glosses the word as follows:

> [One is] a Brahman due to the warding off of seven *dhammas:* the heresy of individuality is warded off, uncertainty is warded off, attachment to ceremonies is warded off, passion is warded off, aversion is warded off, delusion is warded off, pride is warded off. He has warded off evil, unskillful *dhammas,* which are corrupting, lead to further becoming, are troublesome, cause suffering, and lead in the future to birth, old age, and death.

Having removed all evils (said the Blessed one to Sabhiya),
He abides without stain, well-concentrated.
Having overcome *saṃsāra,* he is alone—thus unattached he is
called Brahmā.[12]

Although in some ways it follows the spirit of the *Aṭṭhaka,* such as in mentioning freedom from attachment to ceremonies, this gloss clearly is attempting to fit the *Aṭṭhaka*'s use of the word *Brahman* into the mainstream trope of the "true Brahman" by making the word an explicit metaphor for a set of virtues that can be taken as representative of a mainstream Buddhist saint. More importantly, however, in doing so it sets up a dichotomy between purity and impurity, skillful and unskillful, that contradicts many of the very verses it is commenting upon.

In addition, the verse quotation found at the end of the gloss—which is taken from the *Sabhiya Sutta* (*Sn.* 3.6, v. 519)—introduces an element of figurative language where none existed in the original *Aṭṭhaka.* The verse in question, in its original context in the *Sabhiya Sutta,* is the beginning of a 4-verse response by the Buddha to a question asked by his interlocutor Sabhiya, a *paribbājaka:*

Attaining what do they call him a Brahman? (asked Sabhiya)
Due to what [do they call him] a *samaṇa,* and why [is he] a "bath-
graduate" (*nhātaka*=Skt. *snātaka*)?
Why is he called a "*nāga*"?
Asked by me, may the Blessed One explain.[13]

In the four verses that follow, the Buddha explains why a person is called each of four epithets named by Sabhiya, in each case using a pun: One is a *brāhmaṇa* because of "having removed" (*bāhitvā*) all evils; one is a *samaṇa* by "quieting oneself" (*samitāvi*); one is a *nhātaka* by "having washed away" (*ninhāya*) all evils; and one is a *nāga* because one "does not commit offense" (*āguṃ na karoti*).[14] Contrast with this the situation in the *Aṭṭhaka.* The epithets *brāhmaṇa* and *nāga*[15] are used straightforwardly, without any punning or other figurative language, as honorifics to refer to the ideal person who is beyond views. The word *samaṇa,* as we have seen, is used in a negative sense to refer to those decidedly non-ideal persons who engage in endless disputes. Finally, *nhātaka,* which literally must clearly refer to the "bath-graduate" (Skt. *snātaka*) of the Dharmaśāstric tradition, is not found at all. By quoting from *Sabhiya Sutta,* the author of the

*Mahāniddesa* is placing the word *brāhmaṇa* into a different context—one in which *samaṇa* is recognized as positive, technical terminology from the Dharmaśāstric (i.e., Neo-Brahmanical) tradition are known and referred to, and problematic terms are dealt with by using punning.

Overall, then, the *Mahāniddesa*'s treatment of the problematic category *Brahman* bears an interesting parallel to its treatment of the problematic teachings found in the *Aṭṭhaka*. As Gómez and Vetter have shown, the *Aṭṭhaka*, or at least certain key parts of it, advances a non-dualistic teaching that rejects all views and other markers of purity as inherently one-sided and incomplete, leading only to conflict. And as Gómez and Burford have shown, the *Mahāniddesa* breaks the non-dualism of the *Aṭṭhaka* to make it conform to the dualistic teaching of the rest of the Canon. I would argue that it does much the same with the category *Brahman*: It introduces a dichotomy where none existed before. On the one hand it refers to the *varṇa* system and to individual Brahmans such as Māgandiya, thus introducing a polemic against Neo-Brahmanism where none existed in the root text. On the other hand it transforms the actual usage of the category *Brahman* found in the *Aṭṭhaka* into a metaphor by introducing punning and defining it in terms of orthodox Buddhist ideals that are foreign to the *Aṭṭhaka* itself.

## *The Chinese Translation of the* *Arthavargīya *and Narrative Framing*

A useful complement to the *Mahāniddesa* is provided by another version of the *Aṭṭhaka* entirely, namely the *Yìzújīng* (義足經).[16] The *Yìzújīng* is a Chinese translation of an Indian text, which for the sake of convention I will refer to as the **Arthavargīya*,[17] that clearly is related to the *Aṭṭhaka-vagga* of the Pali *Sutta Nipāta* in spite of some important differences that we will discuss shortly. The translation is attributed—reliably, according to modern scholars—to Zhī Qiān (支謙), a non-ordained translator living during the first half of the 3rd century CE,[18] and it is named in the 6th-century catalog of Sēngyòu (僧祐, 出三藏記集, T. 2145)[19] as one of 36 works "translated by Zhī Qiān during the time of Emperor Wén 文帝 of the Wei, from the beginning of the Huángwǔ 黃武 period [=222-229 CE] of the Wǔ king Sūn Quán 孫權 through the middle of the Jiànxīng 建興 period [253 CE] of Sūn Liàng 孫亮."[20] In Zhī Qiān's translation, the verses are separated into 16 divisions referred to as *sūtras* (經); each *sūtra* contains a group of verses that has a direct parallel in one of the 16 *suttas* of the *Aṭṭhaka Vagga*.

Although there are certain discrepancies between the Chinese version and the Pali version (including, in some cases, entire verses in one that are not found in the other), in each case the *number* of verses in a Chinese *sūtra*[21] is the same as that found in the corresponding Pali *sutta*. The two versions also largely agree on the *order* of the *sūtras*, with the exception of two (nos. 10 and 15 in the Pali) that appear to have been misplaced and simply tacked on the end in the Chinese version (see Table 1).[22]

Generally speaking, however, the titles of the *sūtras* in the *Yìzújīng* do not correspond to those of the *suttas* in *Aṭṭhaka Vagga*. This is related to the most important difference between the two versions: While the *Aṭṭhaka* contains only verses, the *sūtras* of the *Yìzújīng* embed these verses within a narrative frame that is written in prose. As is often the case with Buddhist texts in which verses are embedded into prose narratives—including, as we will see later, in the Pali tradition—the verses often have little other than a tenuous connection to the plot of the prose narrative in which they are embedded. This explains the discrepancy between the *sūtra* titles in the two versions; while the titles in the Pali version can of necessity refer only to the content of the verses themselves, the titles in the Chinese version often refer to characters in the prose narrative that are not found in the verses. While the exact nature of the Indian text from which the *Yìzújīng* was translated (language, sectarian affiliation, etc.) is unknown, we can feel confident that there was an Indian version (or versions) of the **Arthavargīya* that included prose frame narratives with the verses, and that they were not simply added by Zhī Qiān. Fragments of a Sanskrit text from Eastern Turkestan were published near the beginning of the 20th century that contain verses corresponding to the Pali *Aṭṭhaka* together with prose similar to that found in the *Yìzújīng*, but not found in the Pali text.[23]

The *Yìzújīng* therefore can be taken to represent a scriptural transmission of the **Arthavargīya* that, unlike the Pali transmission, embedded its verses within prose narratives. The exact relationship between the "prose-encrusted" transmission(s) and the Pali transmission is not entirely clear, but it seems that they were largely, if not one-hundred percent, independent. We have already seen that the *Mahāniddesa* seems to be aware of a story behind the verses in the *Māgandiya Sutta* insofar as it refers to Māgandiya as a Brahman, just as he is identified in the Chinese version. This is somewhat understandable, however, given that the first verse, in which the Buddha rejects a woman as "full of urine and excrement," was apparently added to an otherwise erudite discussion about abandoning all

Table 1 Contents of the Chinese *Arthavargīya and Pali Aṭṭhaka

| Chinese *sūtra* | Corresponding Pali *sutta* |
|---|---|
| 1. 桀貪王經 (*King Jiétān Sūtra*) | 1. *kāmasuttaṃ* (*Sensual Desire Sutta*) |
| 2. 優填王經 (*King Udayana Sūtra*) | 2. *guhaṭṭhakasuttaṃ* (*Cave Sutta*) |
| 3. 須陀利經 (*Sundarī Sūtra*) | 3. *duṭṭhaṭṭhakasuttaṃ* (*Wicked Sutta*) |
| 4. 摩竭梵志經 (*Makara the Brahman Sūtra*) | 4. *suddhaṭṭhakasuttaṃ* (*Pure Sutta*) |
| 5. 鏡面王經 (*King Mirror-Face Sūtra*) | 5. *paramaṭṭhakasuttaṃ* (*Highest Sutta*) |
| 6. 老少俱死經 (*Old and Young All Die Sūtra*) | 6. *jarāsuttaṃ* (*Old Age Sutta*) |
| 7. 彌勒難經 (*Question of Maitreya Sūtra*) | 7. *tissametteyyasuttaṃ* (*Tissa Metteyya Sutta*) |
| 8. 勇辭梵志經 (*Yǒngcí the Brahman Sūtra*) | 8. *pasūrasuttaṃ* (*Pasūra Sutta*) |
| 9. 摩因提女經 (*Daughter of Māgandika Sūtra*) | 9. *māgandiyasuttaṃ* (*Māgandiya Sutta*) |
| 10. 異學角飛經 (*Flying Quarrels of Other Teachings Sūtra*) | 11. *kalahavivādasuttaṃ* (*Quarrels and Disputes Sutta*) |
| 11. 猛觀梵志經 (*Suddenly-Sees the Brahman Sūtra*) | 12. *cūḷabyūhasuttaṃ* (*Minor Arrangement Sutta*) |
| 12. 法觀梵志經 (*Sees-Dharma the Brahman Sūtra*) | 13. *mahābyūhasuttaṃ* (*Great Arrangement Sutta*) |
| 13. 兜勒梵志經 (*Dōulè the Brahman Sūtra*) | 14. *tuvaṭakasuttaṃ* (*Speedy Sutta*) |
| 14. 蓮花色比丘尼經 (*Bhikṣuṇī Lotus-Blossom-Color Sūtra*) | 16. *sāriputtasuttaṃ* (*Sāriputta Sutta*) |
| 15. 子父共會經 (*Meeting of Son and Father Sūtra*) | 10. *purābhedasuttaṃ* (*Before Dissolution Sutta*) |
| 16. 維樓勒王經 (*King Wéilóulè Sūtra*) | 15. *attadaṇḍasuttaṃ* (*Stick Taken Up Sutta*) |

Note that the order of the *sūtras* in the Chinese version appears to have come about by extracting *suttas* 10 and 15 from the Pali version and placing them at the end. Note also the general discrepancy between titles of corresponding *sūtras*. (For names in Chinese *sūtra* titles, I have given a Sanskrit equivalent when the Chinese is a transcription whose Sanskrit equivalent is clear, a direct English translation when the Chinese is itself a meaningful translation of the name rather than a transcription, or simply *pinyin* when I am uncertain of the translation or transcription.)

views, at a very early date, to suggest a connection to the story of Māgandiya offering his daughter to the Buddha. The *Mahāniddesa* makes no attempt, regardless, to elaborate upon this story, nor does it construct a narrative for any other *sutta* in the *Aṭṭhaka*.

We *do* find an attempt to "narrativize" the *Aṭṭhaka* in Buddhaghosa's *Paramatthajotikā II*, but aside from being quite late, this narrativization neither is complete nor does it correspond in any exact way to the narrativization found in the *Yìzújīng*. It is incomplete insofar as it does not provide individual background stories for six of the *suttas* in the *Aṭṭhaka* (nos. 10–15); instead, it gives a perfunctory introduction to these *suttas* saying that they were spoken on the same occasion as already described earlier in the same commentary for the *Sammāparibbājanīya Sutta* (*Sn.* 2.13), when the Buddha was asked by a *nimmitabuddha* to preach for the benefit of a group of deities "of lustful behavior" (*rāgacaritadevatānaṃ*).[24] Buddhaghosa does provide individual background stories for the other 10 *suttas* of the *Aṭṭhaka* (nos. 1–9 and 16), but at least some of these are completely different from those provided in the *Yìzújīng*. Others bear a greater or lesser similarity to their counterparts in the *Yìzújīng*, but none of them can be said to be exactly the same.

The most similar perhaps is the story Buddhaghosa provides for the *Māgandiya Sutta* (9), which, as we would expect, fleshes out the details of how Māgandiya offered his daughter to the Buddha only to have her rejected as "full of urine and excrement." Also quite similar is the commentary on *sutta* 5, which, like the corresponding *sūtra* in the *Yìzújīng*, includes the famous parable of the blind men and the elephant. The details are different, however. The Chinese version begins with Brahmans arguing over their various viewpoints and has the Buddha tell a story about how a king in the past had a group of blind men describe an elephant to him. Buddhaghosa's version, on the other hand, identifies the people who are arguing simply as *nānātitthiyā*, rather than as Brahmans, and has a king in their own time order the demonstration of blind men describing an elephant rather than having the Buddha recount it. Buddhaghosa also associates the same story with *sutta* 3, as does the Chinese version—namely, in which a group of jealous non-Buddhists sent a woman named Sundarī to the *saṅgha* and then killed her, so as to discredit the Buddhist monks by making it look as though they had been consorting with this woman and then killed her to cover it up. Buddhaghosa only recounts this story in brief, however, and refers readers to the full account that is preserved in the Pali tradition at *Udāna* 6.4. The story that Buddhaghosa provides for the *Kāma Sutta* (1) is similar to the story found in the *Yìzújīng*, insofar as it involves the Buddha teaching a certain Brahman after the latter loses his entire crop, but again there are great variations in the details. In the Chinese version, the Brahman loses the crops to hail, while in Buddhaghosa's he loses it to a flood. The content of the Buddha's subsequent teaching is different in the two versions, and overall the Chinese version is considerably longer.[25] Likewise, Buddhaghosa's story for *sutta* 2 is similar to the Chinese version in that it involves a king named Udena (=Skt. Udayana)—but, as Bapat notes, "the stories differ considerably in details."[26]

Taken together, then, it appears that Buddhaghosa had access to a tradition or traditions that had some relationship to the traditions that went into the composition of the version of the **Arthavargīya* from which the Chinese *Yìzújīng* was translated, namely to the extent that certain stories, most likely well known in general outline but not fixed in details, were associated with specific sets of verses—such as the story of Māgandiya/Māgandika offering his daughter with *sutta/sūtra* 9, or the story of the blind men and the elephant with *sutta/sūtra* 5. There is no evidence, however, that Buddhaghosa had access to the **Arthavargīya* from which the *Yìzújīng* was translated itself—and, indeed, much evidence to suggest that he did not, since in most cases he does *not* provide a story paralleling that found in the *Yìzújīng*.

Regardless of this evidence, however, it is unnecessary to assume that Buddhaghosa would have had access to a prose-encrusted **Arthavargīya* to be able to provide the backstories for his commentary. There is abundant evidence from the early Buddhist tradition that certain well-known stories were circulated in early Buddhist communities—and in many cases may originally not have had any sectarian affiliation at all—and were "solidified" at various times, in various sectarian communities, and at various stages of the processes of canonical and commentarial formation by rendering them into prose and associating them with verses.[27] Even though the Pali tradition does not preserve prose narratives together with the verses of the *Aṭṭhaka*, many of the stories found in the *Yìzújīng* are found in other contexts within the Pali tradition—in the *Jātaka* commentary, the *Dhammapada* commentary, the *Udāna*, and the *Sutta Nipāta* commentary.[28] Thus, it appears that different traditions had access to a common set of stories with which to flesh out the Buddha's life, and they did so by anchoring those stories to verses that were already established *buddhavacana*; each tradition, however, made its own, at least semi-independent choices as to which verses to anchor those stories to. What is interesting about the *Yìzújīng*, therefore, is not so much the stories per se, but rather the way in which they were used by the author(s) of the **Arthavargīya* from which it was translated to frame the verses, and thus implicitly interpret them.

Given that we do not possess the **Arthavargīya* in an original Indian language, our effort to interpret the use of a particular word is complicated by the vicissitudes of translation. Generally speaking, Zhī Qiān translates the word *Brahman* (*brāhmaṇa*) as *fànzhì* (梵志).[29] Although, as we will see, this word appears frequently in his translation of the prose portions of the text, it appears only once in his translation of the verses. This is in stark contrast to the Pali *Aṭṭhaka* where it appears eight times (not including the compound *samaṇabrāhmaṇā* in v. 859 of *sutta* 10[30]). Now, it is *possible* that the reason for this is that the word *Brahman* only appeared once in verses of the text Zhī Qiān was translating. I think this is unlikely, however; a more plausible explanation is that Zhī Qiān simply omitted the word *Brahman* for two reasons: at two characters, it takes up precious space within the constraints of the six-character *pāda*, and it is not necessary to produce a meaningful translation in Chinese, which routinely omits the subject when it is understood from context.[31] Indeed, given these factors, the fact that *fànzhì* shows up even once in Zhī Qiān's translation makes it likely, I would argue, that it was present in the original text in other cases as well. Moreover, an examination of the Chinese text shows that most of the verses in which *Brahman* occurs in the Pali *Aṭṭhaka* are preserved recognizably intact in the Chinese, and that the omission of the word *Brahman* in those cases is understandable because it does not appreciably affect the meaning of the verse.[32] Therefore, in what follows, I will be operating under the assumption that the word *Brahman* did appear in the **Arthavargīya* in the verses of the same *sūtras* as it appears in the *Aṭṭhaka*.

The *Suddhaṭṭhaka Sutta* (4) is the first of the four *suttas* in the *Aṭṭhaka* that have the word *Brahman* in them. The word appears twice in this *sutta* (v. 790 and 795), and the second of these instances happens to be the one case in which it is translated explicitly as *fànzhì*. The corresponding *sūtra* in the *Yìzújīng*, the *Makara*[33] *the Brahman Sūtra*, is therefore an excellent place to start with our investigation of the way framing has been used to implicitly interpret the word *Brahman* in the **Arthavargīya*, since it is the one *sūtra* for which there is absolutely no doubt that the word *Brahman* appeared in the verses of the Indian original. The prose narrative for the *Makara the Brahman Sūtra* is fairly short compared to other prose narratives in the *Yìzújīng*. It begins by introducing the character for whom the *sūtra* is named—Makara, a Brahman living in Śrāvasti who died while the Buddha happened to be staying in town at Jetavanārāma. His "fellow-students" (同學) put his body on display and make the following announcement around town: "Those who saw Makara [when he was alive] all attained liberation; if you now see his corpse, you will also be liberated; later on, those who hear his name will also be liberated."[34] The Buddhist monks hear this while they are on their alms-round, and they report it to the Buddha. In response, the Buddha utters verses corresponding to *sutta* 4 in the *Aṭṭhaka*. The connection between the story and the verses appears to be based on the first verse (v. 788), which in the Pali criticizes the idea that "*diṭṭhena saṃsuddhi narassa hoti*"—"A man has purification by means of *what is seen.*" With the addition of the prose narrative, therefore, the sophisticated and doctrinally problematic teaching on the independence of purity from anything at all (what is seen, heard, or felt, as well as morality and vows) is reduced to a criticism of the more specific claim that one can attain purity simply by looking at a holy man's corpse or hearing his name.

The framing provided by the prose narrative not only serves to smooth over doctrinal difficulties; it also serves to contextualize the use of the word *Brahman*. In the original verses, *Brahman* is simply used as an honorific term to refer to the ideal person, who is "beyond boundaries" (v. 795) and who therefore "does not say that purity is from something else, in what is seen, in what is heard, in morality and vows, or in what is thought" (790). There is no contrast, explicit or implied, between this Brahman and some other sort of Brahman; the only contrast is between the Brahman who is "beyond boundaries" and the non-Brahman, who is not. The prose narrative of the **Arthavargīya* provides the former sort of contrast and conflates it with the latter. We now have "literal" Brahmans—that is, members of the social group that call themselves Brahmans—being contrasted with the Buddhist or "true" Brahman of the verses—precisely on the basis that they, unlike the Brahman of the verses, think that purity comes from seeing something, namely their dead comrade.

Other *suttas* of the *Aṭṭhaka* that have the word *Brahman* in their verses are paralleled by *sūtras* in the *Yìzújīng* that contain prose sections that contextualize the term in much the same way—by introducing Neo-Brahmanical agents to be contrasted with the ideal Brahman of the verses. The fifth *sutta* of the *Aṭṭhaka*, the *Paramaṭṭhaka Sutta*, contains the word *Brahman* in its final two verses (v. 786–787), and it is paralleled by the fifth *sūtra* of the *Yìzújīng*, the *King Mirror-Face Sūtra*. We have already discussed the prose section of the latter version briefly in the context of the comparison to the prose narratives in Buddhaghosa's commentary—both the story in the *Yìzújīng* and the story provided by Buddhaghosa incorporate the well-known tale of the blind men and the elephant. This story is indeed well suited to the corresponding verses, which criticize people who cling to their own view and think that it is better than anyone else's. There are several differences, as already mentioned, between the *Yìzújīng* version of the story and Buddhaghosa's, but one in particular is important for our purposes: the identity of the people fighting over who has the highest view, whom the parable of the blind men and the elephant is intended to criticize. In Buddhaghosa's version, they are simply called "various sectarians" (*nānātitthiyā*), and the king summons a bunch of blind men to describe an elephant so as to demonstrate to them the ridiculousness of their sectarian squabbles. In the *Yìzújīng*, however, they are specifically identified as Brahmans. Not only this, but they are used by the Buddha to introduce the story of the blind men in the following way: "The Buddha said, 'These Brahmans are not stupid in [only this] one lifetime. Long in the past . . . .' "[35] Then he recounts the story of the blind men and the elephant, ending by saying, "At that time I myself was King Mirror-Face, and these Brahmans of the debate hall were the blind men."[36] Once again, then, the author of the **Arthavargīya* prose has gone out of his way to introduce literal Brahmans as characters into his story to exemplify what is criticized by the verses, and thus serve as a counterpoint to the ideal Brahman of the verses.

The *Māgandiya Sutta*, number 9 in the *Aṭṭhaka*, also features a Brahman—namely, Māgandiya himself—in the prose narrative found in the parallel version (*sūtra* 9) in the *Yìzújīng*. Since we have already discussed this *sutta* and the story associated with it more than once, it is unnecessary to discuss it in any great detail here. I would only like to once again point out that Māgandika is presented as a Brahman in the Chinese version, and that even the author of the *Mahāniddesa* seems to be aware of a story involving a Māgandiya who is a Brahman, since he identifies him as such in his glosses of the name. As I have already argued, moreover, it is likely that the story of the Brahman Māgandiya was implicitly attached to this set of *Aṭṭhaka*/**Arthavargīya* verses quite early in the compilation of the text, through the addition of a verse at the beginning in which the Buddha rejects a woman as "full of urine and excrement." There is little that can be said about the framing effect that the story has on the verses, however, since the connection of the story to the verses is quite tenuous and in fact seems to be based on little more than the fact that the interlocutor in the verses is named Māgandiya. What we have here is less an attempt to frame, contextualize, or interpret the verses than simply an attempt to explain who Māgandiya is, by connecting it to a story that also includes a character named Māgandiya.

*Sutta* 13 in the *Aṭṭhaka*, which is paralleled by *sūtra* 12 in the *Yìzújīng*, contains two verses (907 and 911) that use the word *brāhmaṇa*, although the first of these verses appears to be completely different in the Chinese translation. The prose narrative that precedes the verses in the Chinese version serves primarily to introduce a certain Brahman named Sees-Dharma (法觀),[37] after whom the *sūtra* is entitled. Unlike in other stories, this Brahman does not appear to be a hostile or even non-Buddhist interlocutor; on the contrary, he appears within a large crowd of human and divine beings who have come to pay their respects to the Buddha. This Brahman is nonetheless singled out, however, because he holds a pernicious view:

> At that time, among the seated there was a Brahman named Sees-Dharma who was also among the large crowd. Because of his karma, he held the view that one who is liberated in *nirvāṇa* has a body; therefore, he gave rise to doubt on account of his karma. The Buddha knew the doubt that the Brahman Sees-Dharma had given rise to, so at that time he created a Buddha, well-built and incomparable in form. All who saw him were pleased. He had the 32 marks of a Great Man; he had a golden color and also shined; he wore the great garment of *dharma*; and so forth as said above.[38]

The purpose of this second, mind-made Buddha that the Buddha creates is to pronounce the verses that are parallel to *sutta* 13 of the *Aṭṭhaka*, presumably in an effort to free Sees-Dharma of his pernicious view that liberation is a purely corporeal phenomenon.

Unfortunately, the effort to discern the connection between the frame narrative and the verses is complicated somewhat by the fact that the Chinese version of the verses is more substantially different from the Pali than in other *sūtras*, differing both in order and in some cases in content.[39] In spite of this difficulty, generally speaking both the Chinese version and the Pali version of the verses can be described as being, as with many other *suttas* in the *Aṭṭhaka*, a criticism of those who cling to their own view and enter into disputes over views, and concomitantly a praise of those who do not cling to views and thus are beyond disputes. It is not entirely clear to me how this theme speaks to Sees-Dharma's pernicious view that the person who is liberated has a body, although a criticism of those who see only name-and-form (v. 909) may serve as a tenuous connection in this regard.

Regardless of the precise logical connection between the story and the verses, however, the frame story clearly does introduce, once again, a proponent of Neo-Brahmanism who can serve as a counterpoint to the ideal Brahman spoken of in the verses. The doubt of Sees-Dharma, and the pernicious view on which it is based, serves as a counterpoint to the ideal that is represented by the Brahman in the verses. His view evinces a materialistic understanding of the Buddhist teaching that does not recognize that the liberation that it points to transcends material form. Even more so than by the verses, in fact, this view is successfully refuted by the Buddha's initial act of creating another Buddha out of thin air.[40] This Buddha's ethereal body is marked by auspicious signs, including the 32 marks of a Great Man, but these signs, as well as the body as a whole, are ultimately not real. If the Brahman of the verses represents the ideal, then the literal Brahman represents the opposite of that ideal—a person who thinks in terms of material form and is impressed, like other members of his *varṇa*, by the outward signs thereof.

With the exception of *sutta* 15,[41] then, the parallel versions of all the *Aṭṭhaka suttas* that use *Brahman* to refer to the ideal person introduce, through the prose narrative frame, a proponent of Neo-Brahmanism who serves as a counterpoint to the ideal Brahman described in the verses. Insofar as the Brahman in the prose narrative embodies the claims of Neo-Brahmanism—namely, that society is to be divided into four *varṇas*, and that certain people are the highest of these four *varṇas*, namely Brahmans, by virtue of their birth—it transforms the word *Brahman* in the verses from a straightforward honorific for the ideal person into a polemical rejoinder to the conception of the Brahman embodied by the character in the frame narrative. This does not necessarily mean that when a frame narrative was added to a set of verses, the person who did so accepted that the proponents of Neo-Brahmanism are really Brahmans—indeed, the whole point of counterposing the ideal Brahman represented in the verses seems to be that they are not—but it does demonstrate a degree of acceptance that there are real social agents in the world who arrogate the category *Brahman* to themselves.

Moreover, even though the *Yìzújīng* represents an effort to frame only a small collection of verses out of the many that circulated in the early

Buddhist tradition, and even though it in and of itself was apparently unknown to the Pali tradition, its technique of introducing proponents of Neo-Brahmanism to serve as counterpoints to ideal Brahmans in verses is not unique, nor is it foreign to the Pali tradition. I have already mentioned that there are many collections in the Pali tradition that encapsulate verses in prose frame narratives in the same way that the *Yìzújīng* does. Within these, the *Brāhmaṇa-saṃyutta* of the *Sagāthā-vagga* of the *Saṃyutta Nikāya*, the commentary on the *Brāhmaṇa-vagga* of the *Dhammapada*, and to a lesser extent the *Bodhi-vagga* of the *Udāna* all contain verses that refer to the ideal person as a Brahman, which are then framed by prose narratives that introduce Neo-Brahmanical characters—often given funny names to emphasize their buffoonish quality—who serve as a counterpoint to the ideal Brahman described in the verses. At times the verses already contain a contrast between the ideal Brahman and the proponent of Neo-Brahmanism, but often they do not, and thus the prose narratives serve to either introduce for the first time or at the very least accentuate the sense of dichotomy between the meaning of Brahman as a normative Buddhist ideal, and the meaning of Brahman as, increasingly, a social reality. The use of the Neo-Brahmanical character as a framing device was therefore a commonplace in the early Buddhist tradition, clearly transcending sectarian boundaries.

## *Framing in the* Pārāyaṇa

The *Pārāyaṇa* is probably a bit less old than the *Aṭṭhaka*, and it places less emphasis on such radical ideas as the rejection of all views. Nevertheless, there are certain uses of the word *Brahman*—particularly in the dialogs with Mettagū (4, v. 1059), Dhotaka (5, v. 1063, 1065), and Posāla (14, v. 1115)—that are quite similar to the usage found in the *Aṭṭhaka*. In the case of the dialog with Dhotaka, the use of the word *brāhmaṇa* actually goes *further* than the *Aṭṭhaka*, not only as an honorific for the ideal person in the abstract but for the Buddha himself. And as we saw in Chapter 4, nothing in the immediate context of these three dialogs suggests, any more than in the case of the *Aṭṭhaka*, that the use of *Brahman* as an honorific is any more unique or "metaphorical" than that of other honorifics such as *muni*. Therefore, it will be useful to explore how framing has contextualized and thus given an implicit interpretation to these otherwise straightforward uses of the word *Brahman* to refer to the ideal person.

Unlike in the case of the *Aṭṭhaka*, the most significant examples of framing are not to be found in commentaries or other extracanonical texts; rather, they are to be found in the canonical Pali text of the *Pārāyaṇa* itself. The oldest commentary on the *Pārāyaṇa*, the *Cūḷaniddesa*, does provide a certain amount of framing, but not in such a way as to really add anything not already found in the root text. When the word *Brahman* does appear in the latter in reference to the ideal person, the *Cūḷaniddesa* provides the exact same gloss as does the *Mahāniddesa*, defining the Brahman in terms of an ideal more consonant with orthodox canonical doctrine than the immediate context of the *Pārāyaṇa* or *Aṭṭhaka*.[42] The *Cūḷaniddesa* also provides a small amount of information, not included in the verses on which it comments, about a figure named Bāvarī, but, as we will see, this additional information is for the most part already present in the canonical text of the *Pārāyaṇa* in the introductory verses known as the *vatthu-gāthā*. The extracanonical *Paramatthajotikā II* commentary also provides little additional framing; although it does contain some prose narrative, this serves merely to elaborate upon the narrative already found in the *vatthu-gāthā* that serves as the introduction to the canonical text. If we are to understand how the dialogs of the *Pārāyaṇa* have been framed, then, we must look within the canonical text of the *Pārāyaṇa* itself, and in particular to the *vatthu-gāthā*.

In order to understand how this framing process took place, it will be useful to begin by looking at the finished product—the text of the *Pārāyaṇa* as it stands in the Canon, *with* the *vatthu-gāthā* and all its other constituent parts. In this canonical form, the *Pārāyaṇa* has a total of 19 parts: the introduction (*vatthu-gāthā*), 16 dialogs with interlocutors identified as Brahmans, and two epilogues (*atthuti-gāthā* and *anugīti-gāthā*). The text begins in the *vatthu-gāthā* with an extended narrative explaining how a certain Brahman named Bāvarī came to send his 16 disciples to the Buddha. Although he is not explicitly described as such, this Bāvarī clearly fits the type of a *jaṭila*: "Desiring the absence of possessions" (v. 975: *ākiñcaññaṃ patthayāno*), he "lived on the bank of the Godhāvarī, off of gleanings and fruit" (v. 977: *vasi godhāvarīkūle uñchena ca phalena ca*), where he "performed a great sacrifice" (v. 978: *mahāyaññam akappayi*) and dwelt in an *āśrama* (v. 979). After performing the great sacrifice, he is visited by another Brahman who is dirty, thirsty, and hungry, and demands five hundred pieces of money (v. 979–980). When Bāvarī explains that he does not have any money to give him, the other Brahman gets angry and declares that Bāvarī's head will split open if he does not give him the money within seven days (v. 982–983). Bāvarī is understandably distressed by this threat, but he is put at ease by a deity (*devatā*) who tells him that the other Brahman is just a "cheat . . . desiring money" (v. 987: *kuhako . . . dhanatthiko*) who knows nothing about head-splitting. Bāvarī therefore asks the deity what he knows about head-splitting, and the latter tells him he has to speak to the Buddha if he wants to know more (v. 988–993). Bāvarī is excited to hear that there is a Buddha in the world, and so he sends his 16 disciples to go find him (997–998). They ask him how they will know the Buddha when they meet him, and Bāvarī replies that there are two ways of knowing: First, the Buddha will have the thirty-two "marks of a Great Man" (v. 1001: *mahāpurisalakkhaṇā*), and second, he will be able to read their minds (v. 1004–1005). The Brahman students ultimately find the Buddha at the Pāsāṇaka *cetiya* in Magadha, where they find that he indeed has the full set of marks and is able to read their minds (v. 1013–1024). Excited that they have actually found the Buddha, they ask him about head-splitting, and the Buddha replies with a metaphorical explanation in which the "head" stands for ignorance, which is in turn "split" by knowledge, faith, mindfulness, concentration, resolution, and effort.[43]

The 16 sections of the text that follow are short dialogs in which each of the 16 Brahmans asks the Buddha his own individual questions. The dialogs cover a variety of topics that are generally united by the common theme of going to the "far shore" (*pāraṃ*) of birth and old age—that is, escaping rebirth. They are followed by two epilogues, the first of which contains a mixture of prose and verse, and the second of which contains only verse. The first epilogue is, in a sense, the most internally coherent of the two; it repeats the names of the 16 Brahmans who spoke to the Buddha, explains why the Buddha's teaching to them is called the *Pārāyaṇa* (because it leads to the "far shore"), and records that after hearing this teaching, the 16 Brahmans "practiced *brahmacariya* in the presence of the one of excellent wisdom" (v. 1128: *brahmacariyaṃ acariṃsu varapaññassa santike*).

The second epilogue, on the other hand, is less internally coherent, but in a sense provides ultimate closure to the text. In this second epilogue, Piṅgiya, the last of the 16 Brahmans who spoke to the Buddha, announces, "I will sing *Going to the Far Shore*" (v. 1131: *pārāyanam anugāyissaṃ*), and then engages in an extended conversation with an unnamed interlocutor, whom he addresses as "Brahman," in which he heaps praises on the Buddha, whom he just met, and says that he cannot go back to see him because of his old age and therefore visits him in his mind (v. 1142–1144). According to the *Cūḷaniddesa*, the Brahman with whom Piṅgiya is speaking in this second epilogue is his teacher Bāvarī[44]; this is confirmed by Buddhaghosa in his commentary on the *anugīti-gāthā* in the *Paramatthajotikā II*. Indeed, this would appear to be the logical interpretation of the second epilogue, given the context of the canonical version of the *Pārāyaṇa* in which it appears, including the introductory story about how the 16 Brahmans were sent by Bāvarī. The second epilogue brings closure to this story by having one of Bāvarī's students return (presumably) to him and report to him the greatness of the Buddha.

While the canonical version of the *Pārāyaṇa* does appear to present a fairly coherent narrative overall—from Bāvarī dispatching his disciples to the Buddha at the beginning to Piṅgiya's recounting of the greatness of the Buddha at the end—there are nevertheless several inconsistencies that prevent a straightforward interpretation of the text as a forming a cohesive narrative. To begin with, in the *vatthu-gāthā*, when Bāvarī asks the deity who appears to him where he can find the Buddha, the deity answers, "The conqueror is in Sāvatthī, palace of the Kosalas" (v. 996: *sāvatthiyaṃ kosalamandire jino*).[45] When Bāvarī's 16 students actually go to find the Buddha, however, they pass through many cities, including Sāvatthī, but they ultimately end up at the Pāsāṇaka *cetiya* in Magadha (v. 1011–1013), which is a completely different *janapada* to the east of Kosala. Although Buddhaghosa's commentary explains that the Buddha left Sāvatthī after the Brahmans began their journey, and therefore the latter had to continue their journey past Sāvatthī to find him,[46] the text itself contains no such explanation; v. 1011–1013 are simply consistent with the prose section in the first epilogue, which reports that "the Blessed One said this while he was dwelling among the Magadhans at the Pāsāṇaka *cetiya*,"[47] and inconsistent with the deity's earlier statement in v. 996.

Second, in spite of the rather lengthy introduction at the beginning of the text, in which Bāvarī figures prominently as the main character, Bāvarī's name is never mentioned again in the entire *Pārāyaṇa*. This is the case in all of the 16 dialogs that form the core of the *Pārāyaṇa*; when the 16 Brahmans approach the Buddha, none of them make any mention of their teacher, the mission they have been sent on, or indeed any of the themes dealt with in the *vatthu-gāthā*. It is also the case in the first epilogue; although the names of the 16 Brahmans are listed, no mention is made of them having been sent by Bāvarī. Most surprisingly, perhaps, Bāvarī is not even mentioned in the second epilogue, which appears from context to be (and indeed is interpreted by the commentaries as) a dialog between Piṅgiya and his teacher Bāvarī. When read by itself, without the benefit of the context provided by the *vatthu-gāthā*, the *Cūḷaniddesa*, or the *Paramatthajotikā II*, the *anugīti-gāthā* is simply a dialog between Piṅgiya and an unnamed "Brahman."

This brings us to the third inconsistency, which relates to the character of Piṅgiya himself. As already mentioned, Piṅgiya is the last Brahman to speak to the Buddha, and as such his dialog with the Buddha is the last of the 16 dialogs that form the core of the *Pārāyaṇa* (v. 1120–1123). When Piṅgiya speaks to the Buddha, the first thing he says is, "I am old, weak, my complexion gone" (v. 1120: *jiṇṇo'ham asmi abalo vītavaṇṇo*). This is confirmed by the second epilogue, in which Piṅgiya says that he cannot return physically to the Buddha because "I am old and of feeble strength" (v. 1144: *jiṇṇassa me dubbalathāmakassa*). Yet the introductory story is to have us believe that he, along with the other 15, is a student (*sissa*) of Bāvarī—a narrative element reinforced by the use of the word *māṇava* in the titles of each of the 16 core dialogs.[48] At the same time, there is also an inconsistency in what Piṅgiya did after meeting with the Buddha. As already mentioned, in the second epilogue Piṅgiya tells whomever he is talking to—whether Bāvarī or someone else—that he cannot return to the Buddha in person because he is too old. But in the first epilogue, it had already been said that all 16 Brahmans practiced *brahmacariya* "in the presence" (v. 1128: *santike*) of the Buddha. The canonical text of the *Pārāyaṇa*, therefore, cannot decide whether Piṅgiya is an old man or a young student, whether he eagerly practiced *brahmacariya* in the presence of the Buddha or left and could only return to him in his mind due to the feebleness of his body.

Finally, there is a small but troublesome inconsistency introduced into the text by v. 1146 of the second epilogue. In this verse, whomever Piṅgiya is speaking to, after listening to Piṅgiya's effusive praises of the Buddha, says to him,

> As Vakkali has declared his faith, and Bhadrāvudha and Āḷavi
> Gotama,
> Even so should you too declare your faith.
> You will go, Piṅgiya, to the far shore of the realm of death.[49]

Unfortunately, nowhere in the text of the *Pārāyaṇa* are the declarations of faith of these three people mentioned. Not only this, but of the three, only Bhadrāvudha's name is mentioned elsewhere in the *Pārāyaṇa*, as one of the 16 students of Bāvarī. The other two have no apparent place in the narrative of the *Pārāyaṇa*, and one of them—Āḷavi Gotama—is not attested anywhere else other than this verse in the entire Pali Canon![50]

These inconsistencies are not entirely surprising, however, if we assume that the *Pārāyaṇa* is a composite text. As already discussed above, Vetter has come out in favor of this position, and many scholars have assumed that at the very least the *vatthu-gāthā* must be later than the rest of the *Pārāyaṇa* since it is not commented upon by the *Cūḷaniddesa*. N. A. Jayawickrama, in his classic study of the *Sutta Nipāta*, has also adduced convincing arguments for the lateness of the *vatthu-gāthā* on the basis of internal evidence, including the use of late terminology such as *visaya* (v. 977) and *mandira* (v. 996), the inclusion of the developed legend of the Buddha as a Great Man possessing 32 marks, and a reference to the fairly late doctrine of *vāsanā* (1009).[51] This does not mean that the story of Bāvarī was not known to the author of the *Niddesa*—indeed, the references to Bāvarī in the *Niddesa*, however oblique, make it certain that its author was aware of the story in some form[52]—but it does make it unlikely that he was aware of the *vatthu-gāthā* as we have them today, or at the very least considered them to be authoritative.[53] The supposition that there was a "Bāvarī legend" associated with the *Pārāyaṇa* prior to the composition of the Pali *vatthu-gāthā* is strongly supported by fragments of a Sanskrit version of the *Pārāyaṇa*, which refer to Bāvarī by name but in a context that cannot be directly correlated to the Pali text of the *vatthu-gāthā*.[54] Thus, it is likely that the author of the *Niddesa* had access to a text of the *Pārāyaṇa* that did not include the *vatthu-gāthā*, but was aware of some sort of frame story according to which the 16 Brahmans who visited the Buddha were students of a Brahman named Bāvarī. This story came to be recorded at different times in different ways—through occasional comments in the *Cūḷaniddesa*, through a more extended narrative in the *Paramatthajotikā II*, through the *vatthu-gāthā* of the canonical Pali version, and through the story, now mostly lost, that was apparently included in a Sanskrit version of the *Pārāyaṇa*. All of these, of course, are quite late and represent attempts to frame the *Pārāyaṇa* within a particular narrative.

What does the *Pārāyaṇa* look like without this particular frame narrative? Quite different, as it turns out. To begin with, the first 92 verses of the *Pārāyaṇa* as it was commented upon by the *Cūḷaniddesa*—that is, the core 16 dialogs of the text—introduce a series of interlocutors who discuss with the Buddha a range of topics concerning meditation, morality, and the path to deliverance from rebirth, without any mention of Bāvarī; head-splitting; the Buddha's 32 marks; or indeed even, for the most part, anything about their own identity or why they are there.[55] Only in the first epilogue do we finally get some information about the context of the 16 dialogs—where they happened and who the interlocutors were. The information provided here does not strictly speaking contradict what is found in the *vatthu-gāthā*, but it does little to confirm it; on the one hand it serves as an ill-fitting conclusion to the story begun by the *vatthu-gāthā*, insofar as it makes no mention of Bāvarī or the concerns that supposedly led him to send his 16 students to the Buddha in the first place, and on the other hand, it reads much as if it is explaining the circumstances of the 16 dialogs *for the first time* rather than concluding a story that had mostly been told already.

The first epilogue begins with the following statement, in prose, giving the setting of the 92 verses that had preceded it: "The Blessed One said this while dwelling among the Magadhans at the Pāsāṇaka *cetiya*."[56] No mention is made of Sāvatthī, where the deity in the *vatthu-gāthā* told Bāvarī the Buddha would be dwelling, nor of any movement that led to him being found in Magadha. The prose section then continues, "Requested and asked in turn by the 16 attendant Brahmans, he answered their questions."[57] This is the first time that we hear that the 16 interlocutors, as a group, are Brahmans. Nothing else is said about their identity as Brahmans, however. They are not described as *jaṭilas*; they are not said to be students of another Brahman, named Bāvarī or otherwise; indeed, they are not said to be related to one another in any particular way. Indeed, the way their names are listed in the first three verses of this epilogue seems to suggest that they are not:

> Ajita, Tissametteyya, Puṇṇaka and Mettagū,
> Dhotaka and Upasīva, Nanda and also Hemaka, (v. 1124)
> Both Todeyya and Kappa, and Jatukaṇṇī the wise,
> Bhadrāvudha and Udaya, as well as Posāla the Brahman,
> Mogharāja the intelligent, and Piṅgiya the great seer, (v. 1125)
> These approached the Buddha, the seer of perfect conduct.
> Asking subtle questions, they approached the best of Buddhas.
> (v. 1126)[58]

As Vetter notes, the grand epithets used for the people in this list, such as *mahāisi* for Piṅgiya, suggests that they are prominent figures in their own right rather than students sent to do their master's bidding.[59] The same list, it must be noted, is given in the *vatthu-gāthā* (v. 1006–1008), but it is likely that it was simply copied from the first epilogue, where it makes more sense in context, to produce a sense of consistency in the resultant text when the *vatthu-gāthā* was added.[60]

The second epilogue, when bereft of the context provided by the *vatthu-gāthā*, is difficult to interpret. It is, to begin with, unexpected, since it serves to continue the text after the first epilogue seemingly already brought it to a close.[61] In it, Piṅgiya praises the Buddha to an interlocutor whom he refers to as "Brahman," and that interlocutor responds in a few verses (v. 1138–1139, 1146), but it is not clear who that interlocutor is. Insofar as it acknowledges that Piṅgiya is an old man (v. 1144), in fact, it agrees better with the core dialog between Piṅgiya and the Buddha (where the former is also said to be an old man) than with the *vatthu-gāthā*, in which he is said to be Bāvarī's student. On the other hand, as already noted, it does not agree with the first epilogue insofar as it says that the Piṅgiya is too old to return physically to the Buddha, while the first epilogue says that he practiced *brahmacariya* in the Buddha's presence. Even worse, as we have also noted, it makes a totally inexplicable reference to declarations of faith made by Vakkali, Bhadrāvudha, and Āḷavi Gotama (v. 1146), even though no such declarations of faith are recounted anywhere in the *Pārāyaṇa*. Moreover, two of the three people are not even mentioned in the *Pārāyaṇa* either—in spite of the fact that an author familiar with the contents of the *vatthu-gāthā*, the first epilogue, or even just the 16 core dialogs would have 16 (17 if we count Bāvarī) names to choose from! It is hard to avoid the conclusion, then, that the second epilogue was either taken as a whole, or else cobbled together from pieces[62] that were taken, from a context or contexts now lost. In any case, given its redundancy after the closure provided by the first epilogue, as well as its lack of consistency with it, it seems likely that the second epilogue was, as Vetter suggests, "an earlier addition."[63]

If we look at just the 16 core dialogs and the first epilogue by themselves, what we see is a *Pārāyaṇa* with a very simple frame narrative—what I will call for convenience the inner-frame *Pārāyaṇa*. Sixteen Brahmans approach the Buddha at the Pāsāṇaka *cetiya* in Magadha with various questions about meditation, morality, and the attainment of liberation. The Buddha answers their questions and in the process teaches them how to go to the "far shore" of birth and old age. They decide to practice *brahmacariya* under him, and, as a result, they attain liberation. Finally, the reader or listener is told that he too shall attain liberation if he practices in accordance with the teaching of the *Pārāyaṇa*.

But what of the category *Brahman* in this *Pārāyaṇa*? At first glance, the *Pārāyaṇa* may appear much like an encounter dialog, in which the Buddha encounters interlocutors clearly identified as Brahmans and debates with them. In the inner-frame *Pārāyaṇa*, however, the Buddha does not really "debate" with the Brahmans who approach him; rather, they approach him as a knowledgeable teacher and he instructs them. Moreover, in an encounter dialog not only are the interlocutors clearly identified as Brahmans, but the Buddha is clearly identified as belonging to a separate category, *samaṇa*. In the inner-frame *Pārāyaṇa*, this is not the case; in fact, we can even say the opposite is true: The Buddha is portrayed as categorically *similar* to his interlocutors, and he is even, in one case, referred to explicitly as a Brahman by his interlocutor (v. 1063 and 1065 in the *Dhotaka-māṇava-pucchā*). More commonly the Buddha is referred to as a "Great Seer" (*mahesi=mahāisi*),[64] an epithet shared by one of his interlocutors, Piṅgiya (v. 1125).

Finally, as we have seen, the 16 Brahmans who approach the Buddha are referred to in the prose section of the first epilogue as "16 attendant Brahmans" (*paricārakasoḷasānaṃ brāhmaṇānaṃ*). Given the context provided by the *vatthu-gāthā*, this can be interpreted as referring to the fact that they are students and thus "attendants" of Bāvarī; indeed, this is one interpretation that the *Cūḷaniddesa* provides for the phrase.[65] The *Cūḷaniddesa* also provides another interpretation for the phrase, however, one that better fits the immediate context of the first epilogue and the "inner frame" it provides for the *Pārāyaṇa*: "Or, alternatively, those sixteen Brahmans are attendants (*paddhā, paddhacarā, paricārakā*) [and] students of the Buddha—and thus [it says] '16 attendant Brahmans.' "[66] The inner-frame *Pārāyaṇa*, therefore, portrays the Buddha as a Brahman among Brahmans. Their Brahmanhood is neither portrayed in terms of the Neo-Brahmanical criteria of birth and knowledge of the Vedas, nor is it contrasted to such an understanding of Brahmanhood[67]; instead, it is used as an honorific, equally of the Buddha, his interlocutors, and the ideal person in the abstract, much as in the *Aṭṭhaka*.

The addition of what we can call the "outer frame"—the story of Bāvarī sending his 16 disciples to meet the Buddha, in whatever form, whether commentarial or in the *vatthu-gāthā*—changes the role of the category *Brahman* completely. At the very least, it decenters the Buddha as a Brahman teacher among Brahmans and sets up a dichotomy between the Buddha, who "converts" the Brahmans, and the Brahmans' original Brahman teacher, Bāvarī. In the fully developed narrative form of the *vatthu-gāthā*, the dichotomy between the Buddha as "Brahman" and Bāvarī as a proponent of Neo-Brahmanism is made complete through the detailed description of Bāvarī's knowledge of the *mantras* (v. 976), practice of sacrifice (v. 978), and dwelling in an *āśrama* (v. 979). Moreover, the *vatthu-gāthā* clearly imitates encounter dialogs by incorporating a key formulaic element: the reference to the Buddha's possession of 32 marks that are supposedly predicted by the Vedas as signs of a "Great Man" (*mahāpurisa*), as well as the chief Brahman interlocutor's desire to discover whether the Buddha actually possesses all of them, much as we saw in the *Ambaṭṭha Sutta* earlier in this chapter. In addition, the *vatthu-gāthā* refers to the concept of head-splitting, which is found elsewhere in Buddhist encounter dialogs but also has parallels in the Brahmanical literature. Although there are limitations to the extent to which the *vatthu-gāthā* can transform the *Pārāyaṇa* into a true encounter dialog—it only serves as a frame, and thus the core 16 dialogs are left intact and do not display the formulaic forms of address that distinguish the interlocutor *qua* Brahman from the Buddha *qua samaṇa*—it does serve quite effectively to place references to the ideal person, including the Buddha as exemplar, in a context of comparison to Bāvarī, a proponent of Neo-Brahmanism, and thus make the "Buddhist" use of the word *Brahman* appear non-literal and polemical.

## *Conclusion*

As I explained in Chapter 2, the early Buddhist *sūtras* are an important piece of evidence for understanding the period just prior to the imperial unification of India at the end of the 4th century BCE, but their use as such is complicated by the fact that they were passed down orally and thus were not fixed in writing until well into the imperial period. I argued, however, that the verses *Aṭṭhaka* and *Pārāyaṇa* attained a fixed form at a relatively early date in comparison with the rest of the Canon. In Chapter 4, I then showed that these verses evince a straightforward articulation of the Buddhist ideal as "Brahman," unlike later canonical texts that reduce this trope to a polemic against the proponents of Neo-Brahmanism. In this chapter, we have now seen that the transition from a straightforward articulation of Brahmanical identity to a defensive polemic against Neo-Brahmanism need not simply be inferred; it can actually be demonstrated by examining the way in which the early Buddhist tradition dealt with the *Aṭṭhaka* and *Pārāyaṇa* over time. Early Buddhist texts evolved through narrative framing—that is, the framing of older texts, often verses, within larger narratives and commentaries. The verses of the *Aṭṭhaka* and *Pārāyaṇa* were both implicitly framed by two layers of commentary, one canonical and the other extracanonical; in addition, both were given frame narratives in various traditions (the prose frame narratives of the *Yìzújīng* and the verse frame narrative of the *Pārāyaṇa*). We saw that, while the original verses used the word *Brahman* straightforwardly as an epithet to refer to the Buddha or other Awakened Buddhist, various frame narratives and commentaries transformed this epithet into a polemic against those who claimed Brahmanhood on the basis of birth.

This chapter thus concludes the diachronic analysis of the early Buddhist literature, which has demonstrated that the polemical trope of the Buddhist as "Brahman" was preceded by and was itself a transformation of an earlier straightforward Buddhist articulation of Brahmanhood. We have, in other words, been able to trace the emergence of the "snake and mongoose" in early Buddhist literature. But this still leaves the question of how. How did it come about that the early Buddhists—and by extension the Jains—were reduced to reframing their earliest articulations of a celibate Brahmanhood as a mere polemic against householder Brahmanism? How, in other words, did the householder Brahmans succeed in arrogating the category *Brahman* to themselves? It is to answering this question that we turn in the next chapter. As we shall see, "framing" itself proved pivotal to the success of Neo-Brahmanism in this regard.

# 7

# *Losing an Argument by Focusing on Being Right*

THROUGH A DIACHRONIC analysis of the textual traditions for the *Aṭṭhaka* and *Pārāyaṇa*, we have now seen that the treatment of the category *Brahman* in the Buddhist tradition changed over time, reflecting the emergence of a bifurcation between the categories *śramaṇa* and *Brahman*. But how did the opposition between the snake and the mongoose, the *śramaṇa* and the Brahman, arise? We can see the emergence of the opposition in the Buddhist tradition, but it hardly seems likely that the early Buddhists willingly abrogated their claims to Brahmanhood. Indeed, the record shows that they continued to claim to be Brahmans, albeit increasingly defensively. The question is thus equivalent to asking how one particular group, the proponents of Neo-Brahmanism, succeeded in arrogating to themselves the category *Brahman*. Indeed, it is precisely the success the proponents of Neo-Brahmanism had in arrogating the category *Brahman* to themselves that has obscured for so long the period of contestation over the category that once existed. But *how* did they succeed in doing so? How did one group succeed in defining Brahmanhood in terms of birth rather than celibate renunciation when there were so many who opposed them?

In the last chapter, we saw how the Buddhist treatment of the category *Brahman* (as with many other concepts) was transformed over time through narrative and commentarial framing. This framing is internal to the early Buddhist oral tradition. Taking up a suggestion made by Bronkhorst, I will now argue that the concept of framing, when applied to intra-sectarian relations, also helps us to understand how the Buddhists (and Jains) were coerced into abrogating the category *Brahman*. The proponents of Neo-Brahmanism succeeded in arrogating the category *Brahman* to themselves because they were able to "frame the debate" by setting the terms through the *varṇa* system. Instead of attacking the positions of their opponents directly, they stayed relentlessly on message, allowing opponents to come to them and debate on their terms. When this debate took place, it took the form of what I call encounter dialogs—narratives found in abundance in Buddhist literature (but with some clear Jain parallels) in which a Buddhist figure (most often the Buddha) encounters a Vedic Brahman and debates with him over the tenets of Neo-Brahmanism. Although the critiques of Neo-Brahmanism found in these encounter dialogs are often quite damning, the narratives themselves had the unwanted side-effect of reproducing the very Neo-Brahmanical framework they sought to refute. While intended to criticize, refute, or simply mock the pretensions of the Neo-Brahmanical movement, such an approach instead had the effect of thoroughly naturalizing Neo-Brahmanical ideology and thus implicitly ceding the category *Brahman* to the householder Brahmans.

## *The* Varṇa *System as a Framing Device*

The basic hermeneutical principle of understanding the success of "the Brahmans" in terms of framing has already been articulated by Johannes Bronkhorst. He explains this principle by making a comparison to modern American politics, which is sufficiently illustrative to be worth quoting at length:

> At this point it may be interesting to make a reference to a political debate that took place a few years ago in the United States. Opponents of President Bush claimed that his Conservative Party won the elections by "framing the debate." It succeeded in conducting discussions with Liberals in terms that were favourable to its own worldview. The philosopher George Lakoff analysed this practice in his booklet *Don't Think of an Elephant* (2004) and gave as example the expression *tax relief.* "For there to be relief", he points out (p. 3), "there must be an affliction, an afflicted party, and a reliever who removes the affliction and is therefore a hero. And if people try to stop the hero, those people are villains for trying to prevent relief. When the word *tax* is added to *relief,* the result is a metaphor: Taxation is an affliction. And the person who takes it away is a hero, and anyone who tries to stop him is a bad guy. This is the frame." Lakoff points out that this expression came to be adopted by

> the news media, and concludes (p. 4): "And soon the Democrats are using *tax relief*—and shooting themselves in the foot."[1]

In parallel to this near-contemporary case of political framing, Bronkhorst argues that

> the discussion about society in ancient India was framed by the Brahmins. The Brahmins had a sophisticated terminology for the increasingly stratified structure of society, and those who disagreed with them had to use that same terminology, presumably because there was nothing else around.[2]

Now, I do not necessarily agree with Bronkhorst that the key to the success of Neo-Brahmanical social theory was its "sophistication"; on the contrary, I think the simplicity of the *varṇa* system may have been a contributing factor to its success—as is simplicity often a strength in contemporary political discourse as well. Nor do I think that the opponents of "the Brahmans" had to use their terminology because there was "nothing else around." There is *always* an alternative way of saying things. "Tax relief," for instance, could just as easily be called "bailouts for billionaires." Nevertheless, I think we can agree with Bronkhorst on the *mechanism* by which Neo-Brahmanical social theory propagated itself: "Opponents, even while arguing against the Brahmins' language, would in this way reinforce the frame. By framing the debate, the Brahmins had a clear advantage which contributed to their ultimate victory."[3]

The key here is not sophistication or lack of an alternative, but rather *relentlessness*. In modern political terms, we can refer to this as "staying on message." The proponents of Neo-Brahmanism were relentless in articulating a vision of society based on the *varṇa* system, in referring to themselves and themselves alone as Brahmans, and in (mostly) ignoring alternative conceptions of Brahmanhood. Throughout the vast Brahmanical literature generated around the turn of the Common Era, we do not generally find direct debates with or refutations of the opponents of Neo-Brahmanism, such as the Buddhists and the Jains. Indeed, we hardly find any reference to these real-world opponents at all. Instead, we find texts like the *Mahābhārata*, which, although (or in a sense because) it claims to contain "everything" within it,[4] describes an imaginary world governed by the *varṇa* system and totally bereft of Buddhists, Jains, and kings such as Aśoka who were supportive of these opponents. In recent years, several scholars have convincingly argued that beneath the literal surface of the *Mahābhārata*'s narrative, the challenge posed by these opponents and their royal patrons such as Aśoka is a recurring, beneath-the-radar theme.[5] Nevertheless, what is significant is that the *Mahābhārata* and the bulk of Brahmanical literature produced around the turn of the Common Era deals with these opponents only indirectly. It does not refute Buddhist or Jain doctrines by name. It does not introduce the Buddha, Mahāvīra, or Buddhist or Jain monks as characters to be mocked or criticized. *The genius of the Brahmanical literature of this period is that it denies any existence to the opponents of Neo-Brahmanism simply by writing a world in which they do not exist.*

There is one notable exception to this general rule, however: the *āśrama* system. As I argued in the last chapter, the *āśrama* system was a theoretical construct used to categorize all of the *actual* lifestyles found in ancient India. In its earliest form, found in the Dharma Sūtras, the purpose of this categorization tool was ultimately to subordinate all lifestyles based on celibacy to the householder ideal. Nevertheless, the mere act of naming and refuting opposing viewpoints ultimately appears to have left the door open just enough for those opposing viewpoints to have an important and increasing influence on the emerging Brahmanical orthodoxy/praxy that would become central to Classical Hinduism. We will return to the exception posed by the *āśrama* system at the end of this chapter.

## *The "Encounter Dialog" Genre*

The strategy used by the advocates of a celibate, renunciatory conception of Brahmanhood in confronting their opponents was quite different from that used by the proponents of Neo-Brahmanism. While the latter were relentless in pushing their vision of society encapsulated in the *varṇa* system, making hardly any concession to even the mere existence of opponents of that system, the former criticized their Neo-Brahmanical opponents directly and by name. This was particularly true of the early Buddhists. As already mentioned in Chapter 3, there exists an entire genre of *sūtras* among the early Buddhist texts in which the Buddha encounters and engages in a discussion with a proponent of Neo-Brahmanism. I refer to all such *sūtras*, which present the Buddha as *śramaṇa* entering into dialog with an interlocutor identified as a Brahman, as *encounter dialogs*.[6] In using this particular term, I am inspired by the language used by Brian Black in an article in which he studies what I would consider some important examples of this genre.[7] Buddhist encounter dialogs, as well as some similar texts found in the Jain tradition, were quite potent in providing a both logical and at times mocking critique of the claims of Neo-Brahmanism. At the same time, however, their very narrative format ensured the reproduction and eventual success of the Neo-Brahmanical *varṇa* system and the concomitant arrogation of the category *Brahman* by a (theoretically) closed hereditary lineage.

In Chapter 3, I distinguished encounter dialogs as a genre of early Buddhist texts from another genre that I called "teachings on wrong views." The key distinction between these two genres of texts is that encounter dialogs involve non-Buddhist interlocutors specifically identified as Brahmans, while "teachings on wrong views" treat "*śramaṇa*s and Brahmans" as a single category of others against which to construct Buddhist identity. My differentiation between these two genres of texts is based in part on the observation by Bronkhorst and Chakravarti that, generally speaking, the early Buddhist *sūtra*s refer to the *varṇa* system only in contexts where the Buddha is engaged in conversation with a (Vedic) Brahman, that is, in what I call encounter dialogs. This implies that the *varṇa* system was not, at the time the early Buddhist *sūtra*s were written, universally accepted but rather was accepted only by "the Brahmans."[8] We can go a step further than this, however. "Teachings on wrong views" are texts in which the early Buddhists construct their own identity vis-à-vis all other groups. The categories *Brahman* and *śramaṇa* are not differentiated or opposed in these texts because all relevant groups claimed to be Brahmans, and nearly all were also *śramaṇa*s. Encounter dialogs, on the other hand, are texts that confront one particular non-Buddhist group: the proponents of Neo-Brahmanism whom we studied in Chapter 5. The relationship between the categories *Brahman* and *śramaṇa* is called into question in these texts because the proponents of Neo-Brahmanism were unique among all groups in ancient India in claiming to be Brahmans in spite of (or in their minds, because of) not following a *śramaṇa* lifestyle.

In order to see that the proponents of Neo-Brahmanism are indeed the focus of the encounter dialogs, it behooves us to survey the key exemplars of this genre across the early Buddhist *sūtra* literature. For convenience and ease of reference, I will refer primarily to the early Buddhist *sūtra*s in their Pali form in the Theravāda tradition, although it should be noted that most of these *sūtra*s have parallels in other sectarian traditions, preserved in other languages such as Chinese, which I will refer to when relevant. Two groups of encounter dialogs appear to have been transmitted as units, at least in the Theravāda and Sarvāstivāda traditions: the entire *Brāhmaṇa Saṃyutta* of the *Saṃyutta Nikāya* and several of the *suttas* of the *Sīlakkhandha Vagga* in the *Dīgha Nikāya*. There are also several key examples of the encounter dialog genre found in the *Majjhima Nikāya*, the *Aṅguttara Nikāya*, and the *Sutta Nipāta*, but they are grouped far less systematically across the sectarian traditions.

## *The* Brāhmaṇa Saṃyutta *Paradigm*

The *Brāhmaṇa Saṃyutta* of the *Saṃyutta Nikāya* can in many ways be considered the prototype of the encounter dialog genre; although the *suttas* in this collection are short and fairly simple in structure, the 22 *suttas* in the collection contain the basic elements. Each *sutta* consists of a brief encounter between the Buddha and an interlocutor identified as a Brahman. In many cases, the encounter is, initially at least, tense or even downright hostile. The first four *suttas*, for example, begin with a Bhāradvāja Brahman angrily confronting the Buddha. The first confronts the Buddha because he is angry that his own wife has been speaking in praise of the Buddha. When the Buddha teaches him to still his anger, however, he ordains as a Buddhist monk and becomes an *arahant*. In the second *sutta* of the collection, another Bhāradvāja Brahman angrily confronts the Buddha over the fact that the first Bhāradvāja Brahman has ordained as a monk, but he is in the end converted and becomes a monk himself. This same pattern is followed in the third and the fourth *suttas* of the collection, as a third and fourth Bhāradvāja Brahman angrily confront the Buddha only to be converted and ordain in the end. These first four *suttas* set the tone for the collection, a tone of confrontation between the Buddha's teaching and "Brahmans" who are fundamentally hostile to the renunciate lifestyle it advocates.

The *suttas* that follow in this collection vary in the degree of hostility shown by the Brahman interlocutor, but all involve the Brahman being taught by the Buddha and eventually brought into the Buddhist fold, either as a monk (up through *sutta* number 10) or as a lay follower (*suttas* 11–22). The tone of these *suttas* is generally one of gentle mocking toward the Brahman. This is seen most explicitly in the choice of a "funny" or punning name given to some of the Brahman interlocutors. For example, the Brahman in the fifth *sutta* is named Ahiṃsaka ("non-violent"), but the Buddha points out that he is not non-violent as his name implies. In the sixth *sutta*, the Brahman is named Jaṭā ("tangle"), and his conversation with the Buddha centers on how to disentangle the "tangle" the world is in. The Brahman of the eighth *sutta*, the Brahman Aggika (a name signifying he is a fire-worshiper), tries to deny alms to the Buddha because the latter does not possess the "triple knowledge" (the three Vedas), but the Buddha convinces him that he does possess the three knowledges of (1) his own past lives, (2) the destinies of others, and (3) the end of rebirth.[9] Likewise, in the eleventh *sutta*, the Brahman Kasi ("plowing") criticizes the Buddha for not growing his own food, but the Buddha turns the accusation on its head and makes the case that he engages in his own sort of "farming" through his cultivation of morality and wisdom.

The *suttas* of the *Brāhmaṇa Saṃyutta* in the *Saṃyutta Nikāya* set the basic parameters for an encounter dialog[10]: The Buddha encounters a Brahman, who is in many cases outright hostile toward him, but in any case an explicit or implied tension between the Buddha and the Brahman is resolved when the Buddha teaches the Brahman and the latter becomes either a Buddhist monk or a lay follower. Although it is not always made fully explicit, the tension that is resolved in these *suttas* can be understood to be based in the conflict between the Buddha's teaching and the Neo-Brahmanical ideology represented by the Brahman interlocutor. That this is the basis of the tension is made much clearer in encounter dialogs found outside the *Saṃyutta Nikāya*, which are longer and have a more complex narrative structure, allowing for a more robust exchange of ideas between the Buddha and his Brahman interlocutor in which the ideological conflict is laid bare.

## *The Height of the Encounter Dialog Genre in the* Dīgha Nikāya

Nowhere is this ideological conflict more evident than in the *Dīgha Nikāya*, which as its name implies (*dīgha*="long"), contains the longest *suttas* in the Canon. There are several *suttas* in the *Dīgha Nikāya* that can be considered to belong to the encounter dialog genre,[11] but I will focus on three, which are perhaps the most widely known of all encounter dialogs[12]: the *Soṇadaṇḍa Sutta*, the *Kūṭadanta Sutta*, and the *Ambaṭṭha Sutta*. These three *suttas* all belong to the *Sīlakkhandha Vagga*, one of the three major divisions of the *Dīgha Nikāya*, and as such they are, like all *suttas* in the *Sīlakkhandha Vagga*, built around a long stock passage that I call the "Tathāgata Arises" formula, in which the Buddha explains at length the process by which a person attains Awakening.[13] A very similar collection of *suttas* built around this stock passage, including the three *suttas* we are interested in here, is found in all three sectarian versions of the *Dīrghāgama* (Skt. for *Dīgha Nikāya*) that we have extant,[14] suggesting that it is a collection of *suttas* of some antiquity and/or popularity in the early Buddhist oral tradition.[15]

The three encounter dialogs we are examining here all begin according to a formulaic pattern that is identical in the *Soṇadaṇḍa Sutta* and the *Kūṭadanta Sutta*, but shows a certain variation in the *Ambaṭṭha Sutta*. All three *suttas* begin by introducing a Brahman interlocutor—Soṇadaṇḍa and Kūṭadanta respectively in the *suttas* of the same names, and Pokkharasāti in the case of the *Ambaṭṭha Sutta*. The opening passage of each *sutta* states that the Brahman in question lives in a particular town that was given to him as a *brahmadeyya* land grant.[16] The Brahman then hears that the Buddha is in town, which is expressed through a stock formula that I call the "Fame of Gotama" formula. This formula is found in several encounter dialogs in the Pali Canon,[17] and given that it states succinctly the accomplishments of the Buddha, it is used to this day as a prayer in Theravāda Buddhist countries.[18]

At this point, the *Ambaṭṭha Sutta* diverges somewhat from the *Soṇadaṇḍa* and *Kūṭadanta Suttas*. In the *Soṇadaṇḍa* and *Kūṭadanta Suttas*, the named Brahman interlocutor actually hears about the "Fame of Gotama" from the other Brahmans in town,[19] who have already decided to go see the Buddha. Seeing a large group of them going somewhere, the Brahman interlocutor sends a servant to find out where, and sends word for them to wait so he can join them. This then prompts yet another group of Brahmans to protest that he should not go to see the Buddha, as the Buddha is of lower status and therefore should be the one to go visit *him*. This results in a formulaic exchange in which the contrary Brahmans first praise the primary Brahman interlocutor using what I call the "Well-Born on Both Sides" formula,[20] and then the primary Brahman interlocutor uses a modified version of the same formula to in turn praise the Buddha. This convinces the other Brahmans, who then decide that they would like to visit the Buddha as well.

The *Ambaṭṭha Sutta* introduces its narrative somewhat differently than the other two *suttas*. As before, the Buddha's presence becomes known to the prominent Brahman in question (in this case, Pokkharasāti) through the "Fame of Gotama" formula but, unlike in the other two *suttas*, there is no mass movement of people to go to see the Buddha that this Brahman decides to join; in fact, Pokkharasāti does not initially go to see the Buddha at all. Instead, he sends his student Ambaṭṭha, and he sends him with the specific instruction to see if the Buddha really does have all 32 marks of a Great Man (*mahāpurisa*). Although these 32 marks are mentioned in the "Fame of Gotama" formula that (as we already saw) plays a prominent role in the *Soṇadaṇḍa* and *Kūṭadanta Sutta*s, this particular interest in checking to see if the Buddha actually has the marks represents a new narrative element. Thus, in the introductory section of the *Ambaṭṭha Sutta* we do not find an argument over whether the Brahman interlocutor should go to see the Buddha or the Buddha should come to see him; instead, we find Pokkharasāti explaining to his student Ambaṭṭha what to look for when he meets the Buddha. This consists, in part, of what I refer to as the "Two Courses of a Great Man" formula,[21] which recapitulates the prediction, well known from the classic story of the Buddha's birth, that a person born with the 32 marks will become either a Buddha or a *cakravartin*, a "wheel-turning" monarch.

In spite of the variations between the *Ambaṭṭha Sutta* and the other two *sutta*s, the formulaic introductions to these three *sutta*s all introduce the basic framing elements of the encounter dialog genre that we saw in the *sutta*s of the *Brāhmaṇa Saṃyutta* in the *Saṃyutta Nikāya*. First, like several of the *Saṃyutta Nikāya sutta*s, the eponymous Brahman interlocutors of these three *Dīgha Nikāya sutta*s appear to have been given humorous or satirical names. *Soṇadaṇḍa* means "dog-stick," and *Kūṭadanta* means either "false tooth," "sharp tooth," or "ox tooth," depending on how the word *kūṭa* is taken.[22] Likewise, Bronkhorst has convincingly argued that if we Sanskritize *Ambaṭṭha* as *Ambaṣṭa*, then this name is a satirical reference to Ambaṭṭha's low birth (about which below), because Ambaṣṭa is one of the mixed castes listed in the Dharma Sūtras.[23] In addition, the introductions to the three *sutta*s set up a narrative tension between the authority of the Buddha and the authority of the Brahman interlocutors. In the *Soṇadaṇḍa* and *Kūṭadanta Sutta*s, the Brahman interlocutor's decision to visit the Buddha is temporarily blocked by a group of Brahmans who argue that it is beneath his dignity to pay the Buddha a visit. The Well-Born on Both Sides formula, through which this objection is expressed, appeals explicitly to a cardinal tenet of Neo-Brahmanism: supremacy based on birth. The *Ambaṭṭha Sutta* introduces a similar narrative tension, albeit more subtly. Pokkharasāti is not initially inclined to visit the Buddha himself, but rather sends his student Ambaṭṭha to see if the Buddha does indeed possess the 32 marks of a "Great Man" as he is reputed to. This opening sets up a narrative trap whereby the Brahman interlocutor's willingness to subordinate himself to the Buddha is predicated on another one of the primary Neo-Brahmanical claims to superiority, namely knowledge of the Vedas.[24] Thus, with the introduction of Brahmans with satirical names and the laying of a key element of Neo-Brahmanical ideology (birth or the Vedas) on the line, the tone is set for a confrontation between the claims of Neo-Brahmanism and the teaching of the Buddha.

This confrontation becomes explicit in the debates that take place between the Buddha and his Brahman interlocutor in these three *suttas*. Functionally, in other words, each of the three *suttas* can be understood as a narrative refutation of the claims of Neo-Brahmanism. I will begin with the *Soṇadaṇḍa Sutta*, which deals with the breadth of the claims of Neo-Brahmanism through a succinct narrative between the Buddha and his Brahman interlocutor.

When Soṇadaṇḍa meets the Buddha, he secretly wishes that the Buddha will ask him a question that he, as a scholar of the Vedas, will be able to answer. The Buddha obliges by asking him what characteristics a person must have to be a Brahman. Soṇadaṇḍa lists five characteristics: He must be of the proper birth, going back seven generations; he must be learned in the Vedas; he must be handsome; he must be virtuous; and he must be wise. The Buddha asks him repeatedly if any of these characteristics can be omitted as not *necessary* for being called a Brahman, and Soṇadaṇḍa admits, in turn, that the first three—that is, the three most connected with the claims of Neo-Brahmanism—are not necessary. This creates an uproar among the Brahmans present, who accuse Soṇadaṇḍa (rightly) of abandoning the ideological position of Neo-Brahmanism and taking up the position of the Buddha himself. When the Buddha asks if the remaining two characteristics—virtue and wisdom—can be omitted, Soṇadaṇḍa says that they cannot. Not surprisingly, the Buddha agrees with this assessment, and then proceeds to give an extended sermon on what virtue and wisdom consist of. This sermon is based on the Tathāgata Arises formula found common to all of the *suttas* found in the *Sīlakkhandha Vagga* (and its parallels in the other traditions). Virtue consists of all of the training up to the acquisition of *jhāna*, and wisdom consists of the rest of the training, from the *jhānas* to final realization.

The *Kūṭadanta Sutta* also addresses the claims of Neo-Brahmanism but focuses more narrowly on one aspect thereof—namely, the Vedic sacrifice. Kūṭadanta is planning on holding a great sacrifice, and when he hears that the Buddha is in town, he decides to ask the Buddha how to hold a sacrifice, because he has supposedly heard that the Buddha is an expert in this.[25] The Buddha answers his question by telling a Jātaka, in which a king holds a grand sacrifice in which no animals are killed. This story is a Jātaka because, as Kūṭadanta guesses, the Buddha was one of the characters within it. The ultimate point of the story, of course, is that a truly meritorious sacrifice should not involve killing. But after telling the story, the Buddha makes it clear that such a Vedic-style sacrifice, even when completely vegetarian, is of relatively little benefit. When Kūṭadanta asks if there are any more beneficial sacrifices, the Buddha successively enumerates various actions, such as giving *dāna* and taking refuge (the list varies somewhat between the two sectarian traditions), that are consistent with being an *upāsaka* of the Buddha. This list culminates with the Tathāgata Arises formula, tracing the training of a monk from his going forth to his attainment of Awakening—and this, of course, the Buddha deems the most beneficial "sacrifice" of all.

Of all the encounter dialogs found in the early Buddhist literature, the *Ambaṭṭha Sutta* probably represents the longest, most damning, and most derisive condemnation of the claims of Neo-Brahmanism. We have already seen that the introduction to this *sutta* differs from that of the *Soṇadaṇḍa* and *Kūṭadanta Sutta*s in introducing two Brahman interlocutors: Pokkharasāti and his student Ambaṭṭha. The primary narrative begins when the student Ambaṭṭha goes to visit the Buddha. Here again we find a key difference from the *Soṇadaṇḍa* and *Kūṭadanta Sutta*s: Whereas Soṇadaṇḍa and Kūṭadanta were eager to see the Buddha and treat him respectfully, Ambaṭṭha is clearly not eager to make the visit and acts quite rudely toward the Buddha—he refuses to sit down while the Buddha is himself seated, a serious breach of etiquette since it results in his head being higher than the Buddha's. Interestingly, while this narrative element represents a break from the more common narrative structure of encounter dialogs within the early Buddhist tradition, as exemplified by the *Soṇadaṇḍa* and *Kūṭadanta Sutta*s, Brian Black has argued convincingly that it draws upon a broader Indian trope of the humble teacher and his arrogant student, which is also found outside the Buddhist tradition in the Upaniṣadic story of Uddālaka Āruṇi and his student Śvetaketu.[26] The Buddha asks the reason for Ambaṭṭha's rude behavior, and the latter replies that he felt that he had been shown disrespect by the Śākyas when he was visiting Kapilavastu with his teacher Pokkharasāti. The Buddha dismisses this as a trifle and says that the Śākyas can act as they wish in their own home, using the specific comparison to birds in their own nest. The upshot of Ambaṭṭha's complaint, however, is that he and his teacher are Brahmans, and the Śākyas, being mere *kṣatriyas*, should show them respect on that basis alone.

Ambaṭṭha's explanation of the reason for his anger toward *kṣatriyas*, and Śākyas in particular, reveals the main theme of this text, which strikes right at the heart of the claims made by the proponents of Neo-Brahmanism. Whereas the previous two texts we have examined address various sources of Brahman pride—birth, Vedic learning, and appearance in the *Soṇadaṇḍa Sutta* and the Vedic sacrifice in the *Kūṭadanta Sutta*—this text confronts head-on the most radical claim that was made by Neo-Brahmanism—namely, that society is divided into four *varṇas*, and by virtue of their birth, Brahmans are superior to the other three. The remainder of the narrative in this *sutta* cannot but be read as a scathing, systematic, and comprehensive attack on this claim.

This attack begins with an *ad hominem* attack on Ambaṭṭha's personal ancestry. Since Ambaṭṭha claims to be superior *qua* Brahman on the basis of birth, we would expect him to indeed come from a high lineage of Brahmans going back many generations. This, however, is not true: As the Buddha reveals, Ambaṭṭha is in fact descended from the black (*kaṇha*=Skt. *kṛṣṇa*) baby of a slave-girl of the Śākyas, and this is the reason that his clan name today is Kaṇhāyan. The Śākyas themselves, however, are descended from King Ikṣvāku (P. Okkāka), founder of the great Solar Dynasty (*sūryavaṃśa*). The Buddha demands that Ambaṭṭha confirm that he knows this story is true, and although he is reluctant to do so at first, Ambaṭṭha finally admits to it when Vajrapāṇi—in likely the first reference to him in Buddhist literature—appears and threatens to split his head into seven pieces if he does not answer.[27]

This revelation creates an uproar among the other Brahmans who have come with Ambaṭṭha and is clearly intended as a dramatic turning point in the narrative, akin to the point in a soap opera when a man and a woman who are involved in a romantic relationship discover that they are long-lost siblings, or the moment in *Star Wars* when Luke Skywalker discovers that Darth Vader is his father. The particular details of this dramatic revelation, however, serve two purposes. First, they render ridiculous Ambaṭṭha's claim to any sort of superiority on the basis of birth. Ambaṭṭha is not only not descended from the Vedic *ṛṣis*; he is descended from the lowest sort of person imaginable—a slave. Second, by making this slave-ancestor of Ambaṭṭha's not just any slave, but a slave *of the Śākyas*, the narrative produces a dramatic reversal of Ambaṭṭha's earlier claim to superiority over the Śākyas by making him clearly—and humiliatingly—subordinate to them. The Buddha does then soften his attack on Ambaṭṭha's ancestry by noting that, in spite of his birth, the "black" baby Kaṇha/Kṛṣṇa grew up to become a great sage in his own right. But even in making this concession the narrative is preparing the audience for the ultimate point of the text, which is that excellence depends on conduct and not on birth.

The Buddha does not, however, come to this conclusion directly. Contrary to the modern perception that the Buddha taught the equality of *varṇa*s, the Buddha actually drives home the point that not only are Brahmans not superior to *kṣatriya*s, but *kṣatriya*s are in fact superior to Brahmans. I have already made reference to the arguments here in Chapter 5, where I noted that they would only make sense if Brahmans were in fact known to not be fastidious in maintaining pure lineages. The Buddha gets Ambaṭṭha to concede that, while *kṣatriya*s will not accept as a *kṣatriya* a person of mixed birth, Brahmans will. In particular, the "mixed births" in question are between Brahmans and *kṣatriya*s. That is, according to the argument made here, while a *kṣatriya* will not accept as a *kṣatriya* someone who has a Brahman for a parent, Brahmans *will* accept as a Brahman someone who has a *kṣatriya* as a parent.[28] The point being made here, then, is not only that Brahmans come from impure lineages but that they implicitly acknowledge the superiority of *kṣatriya* lineages by accepting Brahmans who have one *kṣatriya* parent. As noted above, Bronkhorst has argued that, although Ambaṭṭha was Sanskritized in the later Buddhist tradition as Ambāṣṭa, another equally valid Sanskritization is Ambaṣṭha—which happens to be the term used in much of the DHARMAŚĀSTRA literature for the product of a union between a Brahman man and a non-Brahman woman.[29] It is possible, then, that Ambaṭṭha's name was chosen to make humorous reference to the propensity, noted here, of Brahmans to take non-Brahman wives.

The narrative continues by making further points that establish the superiority of *kṣatriya*s to Brahmans. These revolve around the apparent fact, conceded by Ambaṭṭha, that *kṣatriya*s will not welcome a disgraced and exiled Brahman but that Brahmans will welcome any *kṣatriya*, even one who is disgraced and exiled. The Buddha concludes his argument by quoting a verse said to have been uttered by a Brahmā. The Pali version of the verse is as follows:

> The *kṣatriya* is best among those people who rely on *gotra*.
> He who is endowed with knowledge and [good] conduct is best
> among gods and men.[30]

Playing off of the reference to "knowledge and conduct" in this verse, the Buddha then teaches the path to Awakening using the Tathāgata Arises formula. The quotation of the verse of Brahmā therefore represents a turning point in the Buddha's debate with Ambaṭṭha—from a direct assault on the new Brahmanical claim to *varṇa* superiority based on birth, to the formulaic teaching on the Buddhist training that characterizes the entire *Sīlakkhandha Vagga*.

After giving this teaching, the Buddha solidifies Abaṭṭha's defeat in the debate by listing four "entrances to ruin" (*apāyamukhāni*) and asking if Ambaṭṭha and his teaching fulfill even these. These "entrances to ruin" appear to describe the *vānaprastha-āśrama*, which we examined in Chapter 4, and which, I argued there, appears to correspond to the lifestyle of the *jaṭilas* that are held with a certain amount of esteem in the early Buddhist tradition. The Buddha then continues by ridiculing the Brahmans' claim to speak for the Vedic *ṛṣis*, saying that they do not speak for them simply by saying so any more than a person would speak for King Pasenadi just by saying so. He then compares Brahmans such as Ambaṭṭha and Pokkharasāti—that is, proponents of Neo-Brahmanism who are householders and argue, as in the Dharma Sūtras, that non-householder lifestyles were invalid—unfavorably to the *ṛṣis*, noting that the latter did not live with all the luxuries of a householder,[31] while the former do.

The point of this line of argument is to establish a hierarchy of lifestyles and demonstrate that Ambaṭṭha is, precisely the opposite of his original claim, at the dead bottom of that hierarchy. At the top are those people who go forth as *paribbājakas*, train in the Buddha's *dharma*, and attain Awakening. Next in line are *jaṭilas* (or *vānaprasthas*, in the language of the Dharma Sūtras), who do not ultimately accomplish Awakening through their lifestyle, but at the very least lead lives in conformity with the Vedic *ṛṣis* of old. Finally, at the bottom are the proponents of the new Brahmanism, who justify their "luxurious" lives by rejecting all lifestyles other than that of the householder, and in so doing not only fail to make any progress toward Awakening, but fail even to live up to the example of the *ṛṣis* they claim falsely to speak for.

With this, we come to the end of the debate between the Buddha and Ambaṭṭha, which, as we might expect, entails the utter and abject defeat of the latter. Ambaṭṭha finally does what he came to do—he looks for the 32 marks of a Great Man on the Buddha's body. This is treated in formulaic fashion: As with every other Brahman who looks for the 32 marks on the Buddha's body, Ambaṭṭha is able to see only 30, and the Buddha reveals the other two—his long tongue and "sheathed penis." Ambaṭṭha then returns to his teacher, who is enraged at him for embarrassing him in front of the Buddha. Finally, Pokkharasāti visits the Buddha personally. Thus, although the introduction of a Brahman student to the narrative—and one who is incredibly rude to boot!—entails a significant deviation from the pattern followed by the *Soṇadaṇḍa* and *Kūṭadanta Suttas*, the *Ambaṭṭha Sutta* returns to that pattern in the end by having Pokkharasāti—the Brahman initially introduced as interlocutor who dwells in a *brahmadeyya* land grant given to him by the king—respond positively to the Buddha's teaching.

The actual narrative content of these three *suttas* in the *Dīgha Nikāya* thus clearly marks them as examples of encounter dialogs. Each in some way tackles, the claims being made by proponents of Neo-Brahmanism. The *Soṇadaṇḍa Sutta* attacks the Neo-Brahmanical conception of Brahmanhood as being based on birth, Vedic learning, and appearance. The *Kūṭadanta Sutta* undermines the importance of the Vedic sacrifice. And, most damningly, the *Ambaṭṭha Sutta* attacks the primary claim of the new Brahmanism, which is that society is divided into four *varṇas* with the Brahmans at the top. Thus, with their narrative elements, extended use of oral formulae, and incisive critiques of new Brahmanical ideology, these three texts represent highly developed examples of the encounter dialog genre, especially when viewed in comparison with the *suttas* of the *Brāhmaṇa Saṃyutta*. While the *suttas* of the latter served to convert verses into short and most likely humorous jabs at Brahmanical pretensions, these long dialogs of the *Dīgha* tradition make use of well-established formulaic patterns to mount extended and detailed rhetorical attacks on Neo-Brahmanical ideology. In so doing, they represent the epitome of the encounter dialog genre, and most likely as a result have had the greatest influence on later perceptions of antagonism between early Buddhism and Brahmanism.

## *Other Buddhist Encounter Dialogs and Jain Parallels*

Other significant encounter dialogs are found elsewhere in the early Buddhist literature, which reflect the same purpose of narratively refuting the tenets of Neo-Brahmanism but in a somewhat shorter format. In the Pali tradition,[32] several of these encounter dialogs are found together in the *Brāhmaṇa Vagga* of the *Majjhima Nikāya*. In the *Assalāyana Sutta* (93), the student Assalāyana is sent by his teachers to debate with the Buddha over the superiority of Brahmans to other *varṇas*. Similarly, in the *Caṅkī Sutta* (95) the Brahman student Kāpaṭhika defends the Brahmans' claim to superiority to the Buddha. In both the *Ghoṭamukha Sutta* (94) and the *Subha Sutta* (99), the topic addressed is the Neo-Brahmanical claim, championed by the Dharma Sūtras, that only the householder lifestyle is valid. In the *Esukārī Sutta* (96), a Brahman of the same name debates with the Buddha over the claim that each *varṇa*, beginning with the Brahmans, is to be served by lower *varṇas*, and that there are occupations proper to each *varṇa*. And in the *Vāseṭṭha Sutta* (98), the Brahmans Vāseṭṭha and Bhāradvāja go to the Buddha to settle their dispute over whether Brahmanhood is determined by birth or conduct.

We also find encounter dialogs addressing Neo-Brahmanical themes in the *Aṅguttara Nikāya* and the *Sutta Nipāta*, albeit not collected in any particular way. Themes addressed by encounter dialogs in the *Aṅguttara Nikāya* include the Vedic sacrifice (*AN* 4.39–40, 7.44), other Brahmanical rites (10.119, 10.167, 10.169, 10.177), the meaning of *tevijja* or "triple knowledge" (*AN* 3.58–59), and the Buddha's lack of respect for elderly Brahmans (*AN* 3.51–52, 4.22, 5.192, 8.11). There are also seven encounter dialogs in the *Sutta Nipāta*, although two of them are exact duplicates of encounter dialogs found in the *Majjhima Nikāya* (*Sn*. 3.7=*MN* 92 and *Sn*. 3.9=*MN* 98). Of the remaining five, four (*Sn*. 1.4, 1.7, 3.4, 3.5) are similar in style to the *suttas* of the *Brāhmaṇa Saṃyutta*. Two of these, in fact, are partially parallel to two *suttas* in the Pali *Brāhmaṇa Saṃyutta* (*Sn*. 1.4 and 3.4), while the two others (*Sn*. 1.7 and 3.5) have parallels in the *Brāhmaṇa Saṃyukta* of the Sarvāstivādin *Saṃyuktāgama* preserved in Chinese (*SĀ* 102=*SĀ*2 268 and *SĀ* 1159=*SĀ*2 82, respectively).

The one remaining encounter dialog in the *Sutta Nipāta*—the *Brāhmaṇadhammika Sutta* (*Sn*. 2.7), which has no known parallel in Pali or elsewhere—is a significant contributor to the anti-Neo-Brahmanical message of the encounter dialog genre. In this *sutta*, a group of aged *mahāsālā*[33] Brahmans approach the Buddha and ask him if Brahmans in their own day meet the standards of the Brahmans in the past. The Buddha's response, entirely in verse, is quite interesting, and although it has no parallel elsewhere in and of itself, it clearly expresses ideas that are found in the other, more widely known encounter dialogs of the main Nikāya/Āgama traditions that we have already examined above. The Buddha's response, in short, is no; contemporary Brahmans are not like the Brahmans of old. According to the Buddha, the Brahmans of old did not accumulate wealth, did not indulge themselves in sensual pleasures, did not kill living beings for their sacrifices,[34] and took wives properly (through mutual consent) and had sex with them only at the proper time (not during the period). These themes are touched upon, as we have already seen, in the *Ambaṭṭha Sutta*, in which the Buddha gets Ambaṭṭha to admit that he and his teacher, with their wealth and indulgence in sensual pleasures, are nothing like the ancient *ṛṣis*, and in the *Kūṭadanta Sutta*, in which the Buddha describes in a Jātaka an ancient sacrifice that did not involve the slaughter of any animals. They are also touched upon in the *Doṇa Sutta* (*AN* 5.192), in which the Buddha criticizes Brahmans for the improper acquisition of and relations with their wives. What the *Brāhmaṇadhammika Sutta* adds to these themes, however, is an explanation of how contemporary Brahmans came to be so degenerate, with their wealth, indulgence in sensual pleasures, and violent sacrifices. According to the Buddha, Brahmans became jealous of the wealth and women possessed by kings and wanted to possess such things for themselves. They therefore made an arrangement with King Okkāka (Skt. Ikṣvāku), such that they would perform animal sacrifices for the king and compose hymns for that purpose, and in return they would receive the wealth sacrificed by the king.[35]

Although encounter dialogs are for the most part a feature of the early Buddhist oral literary tradition, it is worth noting that similar narratives are also found in the Jain tradition. Two examples are found in the *Uttarajjhāyā*, one of the four "root" (*mūla*) *sūtras* that deal with the practice of a Jain ascetic.[36] Both of these narratives are different from Buddhist encounter dialogs in that they do not involve an encounter between a proponent of Neo-Brahmanism and the founder of the order, in this case Mahāvīra, but rather between a proponent of Neo-Brahmanism and an ordinary Jain monk. Otherwise, these two Jain narratives are quite similar to Buddhist encounter dialogs. Both stories introduce a narrative tension between the Jain and his Brahman interlocutor and then resolve it through a discussion that directly addresses a tenet of Neo-Brahmanism. The narrative frameworks for these two stories also happen to be quite similar to one another. In both cases, a Jain monk approaches a Brahman or Brahmans engaged in a Vedic sacrifice in search of alms. In one case, however, the Jain monk is identified as coming from a very low status Śvapāka lineage (*Utt.* 12.1: *sovāgakulasaṃbhūo*), while in the other, the Jain protagonist is identified as being himself a Brahman by birth (*Utt.* 25.1: *māhaṇakulasaṃbhūo*). In the former case, the Brahmans performing the sacrifice are predictably offended that a person of such low birth would even approach them. When he asks them for alms, they refuse, saying that their food has been prepared for Brahmans, and only Brahmans are worthy of such gifts (*Utt.* 12.11, 13). The Jain monk responds that their birth and learning mean nothing given their pride and possessions, and that only renunciates such as he are worthy of such gifts (*Utt.* 12.14–15). This enrages the Brahmans, who encourage some young men nearby to beat the ascetic, and he is only saved by the impassioned plea of a woman to whom he had once been betrothed (*Utt.* 12.18–24).

In the narrative in which the Jain protagonist is himself a Brahman by birth, the non-Jain Brahman he approaches also refuses to grant him alms, pointing to his own knowledge of the Vedas as making him rather than the renunciate worthy of gifts (*Utt.* 25.6–8). The Brahman-turned-Jain-monk then gives an extended teaching in which he says that Vedic Brahmans are not true Brahmans; the true Brahmans are instead renunciates (*Utt.* 25.11–26). This teaching is very similar to the trope of the "true Brahman" found in the Buddhist tradition that we examined in Chapter 2. Indeed, stylistically, the teaching in this Jain text is quite similar to that found in the verses of the *Brāhmaṇa Vagga* of the Buddhist *Dhammapada*, which all verses end with the refrain, "Him *I* call a Brahman" (*tam ahaṃ brūmi brāhmaṇaṃ*). Here too, the Jain monk's teaching includes several verses ending with the almost identical refrain, "Him *we* call a Brahman" (*Utt.* 25.20–29: *taṃ vayaṃ būma māhaṇaṃ*).

## *Losing an Argument by Focusing on Being Right*

Overall, Buddhist *suttas* of the encounter dialog genre, along with similar Jain narratives, offer a powerful rhetorical punch against the claims of Neo-Brahmanism. These texts target several of those claims specifically, including the importance of Vedic sacrifice, the value of Vedic knowledge, and supremacy on the basis of birth. In response, they make arguments that either show the inconsistency of the "Brahmans'" claims (e.g., claiming superiority on the basis of birth while lacking pure lineages) or offer an alternative conception of Brahmanhood based on celibate, renunciatory values. Encounter dialogs also often subtly or not-so-subtly mock the proponents of Neo-Brahmanism. Sometimes, as is common the *Brāhmaṇa Saṃyukta*, this consists of little more than giving the Brahman a funny or punning name and/or portraying him as lacking control over his emotions (through anger at the Buddha), thus proving through his own actions that he is not worthy of the title "Brahman." In the *Ambaṭṭha Sutta*, on the other hand, the Brahman interlocutor is not simply lightly mocked; he is thoroughly humiliated through the public exposure of his descent from the slave-girl of an ancestor of the Buddha. Finally, encounter dialogs frequently end with the Brahman interlocutor either joining the *saṅgha* as a monk or else becoming a lay follower. The message of encounter dialogs is clear: These so-called Brahmans are ridiculous; the claims to Brahmanhood they make are ridiculous; and when confronted with the ridiculousness of their claims, they acknowledge that true Brahmanhood lies in the celibate, renunciatory ideal espoused by the Buddhist (or Jain) teaching.

While serving as a powerful rhetorical tool against Neo-Brahmanism in the short term, however, the encounter dialog genre ultimately undermined its own purpose, in two ways. First, by arguing against and lampooning the absurdities of Neo-Brahmanism, it replicated and amplified the very ideas it was arguing against. This is especially true in the Buddhist tradition, which includes dozens of encounter dialogs and countless other references to Brahmans, making the early Buddhist literature one of the richest sources of evidence for modern Indologists and scholars of religion in reconstructing the history of Brahmanism in ancient India other than the Brahmanical literature itself. Encounter dialogs were, in effect, free advertising for Neo-Brahmanism, at least insofar as there is "no such thing as bad publicity." The Buddhists (and Jains) may have had powerful arguments against the *varṇa* system, the householder ideal, and Vedic knowledge and ritual, but every time they made those arguments, they broadcast the opposing viewpoint that Brahmanhood was indeed the privilege of a closed, hereditary group of ritual-performing householders.

The second way in which the encounter dialog genre undermined its own purpose was through its basic narrative structure. By definition, an encounter dialog consists, at the very least, of an encounter between the Buddha and an interlocutor who identifies as a Brahman. But this Brahman is a proponent of Neo-Brahmanism; he conceives of Brahmanhood according to a householder ideal, based on birth and Vedic knowledge and ritual, rather than the renunciatory practice of a celibate ascetic. In arguing against this conception of Brahmanhood, the Buddha becomes a placeholder for the *śramaṇa*, insofar as he argues in favor of renunciatory values against a non-*śramaṇ*ic conception of Brahmanhood. We thus end up with a narrative tension between two characters: a Brahman and a *śramaṇa*. The simplicity of the Neo-Brahmanical position was an advantage here. By focusing on one category of self-identity, *Brahman*, there was little room for opponents to force them into another category; they literally had nothing else to call them. The proponents of Neo-Brahmanism were not and did not claim to be *śramaṇas*. Although the Buddhists saw this position as absurd, as they, like many other groups, understood Brahmanhood as lying in a *śramaṇic* lifestyle, juggling the two categories *Brahman* and *śramaṇa* proved cumbersome in fighting an opponent that only sought to claim one. The Buddhists, through their encounter dialogs, had to play the role of *śramaṇas* because the proponents of Neo-Brahmanism wanted to be Brahmans without being *śramaṇas*. In doing so, however, they fell into a narrative trap that forced them to implicitly cede the category *Brahman* to their opponents.

*Suttas* that I include within the encounter dialog genre have been studied by previous scholars,[37] but these scholars have tended to interpret these dialogs in the context of a dichotomous understanding of Brahmanism versus non-Brahmanism, as exemplifying the attempt of the early Buddhists to situate themselves vis-à-vis a preexisting "Brahmanism." I, on the other hand, have abandoned the assumption of a fundamental dichotomy between the categories *Brahman* and *śramaṇa*; moreover, I interpret Buddhist encounter dialogs in light of the framing strategy of the proponents of Neo-Brahmanism. With this approach, we can see clearly how these Buddhist narratives played a pivotal role not in negotiating the relationship between Buddhists and Brahmans, *but in constituting these identities in the first place*. By opposing a non-*śramaṇic* Brahman to the Buddha, who by that very fact was forced to play the role of the *śramaṇa*, encounter dialogs helped to foster a sense of opposition between the categories *Brahman* and *śramaṇa*. While making the explicit claim that the Buddha and his Awakened disciples are the true Brahmans, encounter dialogs implicitly ceded the category *Brahman* to the very people it was arguing against. Encounter dialogs do not simply reflect the opposition between the snake and the mongoose; they are not simply narratives of encounter between a *śramaṇa* and a Brahman. Rather, through the dialectical structure of the encounter, they helped to bring the *śramaṇa* and the Brahman into being as opposed identities.

## *Conclusion: The Perils of Rhetoric*

The result of the process we have been studying in this chapter was no less than the emergence of "the snake and the mongoose" as a characteristic of Indian history. The success of the householder Brahmans in arrogating the category *Brahman* to themselves, in other words, led to a bifurcation between the categories *Brahman* and *śramaṇa*. This bifurcation, which as I have argued was by no means inherent to these two categories, made it possible for Patañjali in the 2nd century BCE to list *śramaṇabrāhmaṇa* ("*śramaṇa*s and Brahmans") as an example of an "oppositional compound." This snake and mongoose binary is not a metahistorical principle at work in the history of Indian religions. It is, rather, the product of a particular history of contestation over what it means to be a Brahman.

We are now in a position to address the question of why the Buddhist treatment of the category *Brahman*, traced in the last chapter, changed over time. In short, the development of the Buddhist literary tradition can be understood as reflecting the progressive success of the Neo-Brahmanical strategy of framing. Early Buddhist texts themselves evolved through another sort of framing—that is, the framing of older texts, often verses, within larger narratives and commentaries. These intra-Buddhist narrative frames, it turns out, replicated the framing that was being performed on the early Buddhists by the proponents of Neo-Brahmanism, which the early Buddhists unwittingly invited upon itself through its counterproductive encounter dialog genre. Like a modern political party that is subtly forced over the course of time toward its opponent's position when its opponent successfully sets the terms of debate, the Buddhists were increasingly forced to acknowledge the *varṇa* system as a social reality, not only in spite of but because of its repeated attempts to refute that same Neo-Brahmanical ideology.

There is, however, a certain irony to the success of the proponents of Neo-Brahmanism in arrogating that title to themselves. Throughout this chapter I have been focusing on the process by which the Buddhists and the Jains, but particularly the former, adduced powerful arguments for why householder-supremicist Vedic specialists were wrong to call themselves Brahmans, but nonetheless ended up losing the category *Brahman* to them because the latter were most successful in framing the debate. This by no means, however, means that Buddhists and Jains were total losers in this process of contestation. For even though they ended up effectively ceding the appellation *Brahman* to a closed hereditary group (theoretically) committed to Vedic knowledge and sacrifice, they were indeed quite successful in at least gaining a prominent place for celibate, renunciatory values in the discourse on Brahmanhood from that time forward.

The proponents of Neo-Brahmanism, in other words, were successful in restricting Brahmanhood *as a category* to themselves on the basis of birth, but in the process they ended up to various degrees tolerating, accepting, or even embracing the very values of celibacy and renunciation they had originally been striving against in the Dharma Sūtras.

To see why this is so, we must return to an aspect of Neo-Brahmanical ideology that I alluded to at the beginning of this chapter but have held off addressing until now: the *āśrama* system. At the beginning of this chapter, I made the case that the proponents of Neo-Brahmanism were successful in framing the debate on Brahmanhood because they were relentless in pushing their ideological system, encapsulated in the *varṇa* system, while almost completely ignoring alternative claims to Brahmanhood. The *āśrama* system is the one key exception to this rule. As I argued in Chapter 5, the *āśrama* system was not simply the formulation of a dispute within a pre-defined "Brahmanical" community; rather, it was an attempt by the proponents of a particular vision of Brahmanism, rooted in householdership and the production of children, to categorize all forms of religious practice in their day so as to subordinate all deviant practices to the householder ideal. In so doing, the Dharma Sūtra authors necessarily made reference to their ideological opponents, albeit somewhat obliquely. Buddhists, Jains, Ājīvakas, and for that matter *jaṭilas*[38] are not mentioned by name, nor are their views examined and refuted in any detail, a practice that would not arise in Brahmanical texts for many centuries.[39] Nevertheless, their practices of celibacy and renunciation are clearly referred to in the *āśrama* system, and the *āśrama* system makes use of certain generic rather than sectarian-specific terms—*brahmacārin, vānaprastha,* and *parivrājaka*—to categorize various non-householder lifestyles.

It is important to keep in mind that the purpose of the *āśrama* system within the Dharma Sūtras was *not* to define fields of acceptable Brahmanical renunciatory practice. As I demonstrated in Chapter 5, all four Dharma Sūtra authors assert the superiority of the householder *āśrama*. For them, the *āśrama* system was simply a tool to taxonomize actual social practice, with the end goal of privileging a particular type of social practice as normative. It was not a system of four acceptable Brahmanical lifestyles, whether temporary or permanent. Nevertheless, that is what it became in the Brahmanical tradition. This transformation took several forms. First, the *āśrama* system created space for celibate and renunciatory practices within the scope of Brahmanism as defined by the *varṇa* system. The *vānaprastha* lifestyle became not only acceptable for hereditary Brahmans but also, perhaps even more so if we accept Bronkhorst's argument,[40] a key Neo-Brahmanical propaganda tool in the competition for royal patronage. Likewise, while the egalitarian *parivrājaka* movements that had risen to prominence in the imperial period, such as Buddhism and Jainism, were excluded from Brahmanhood by the successful promulgation of the *varṇa* system, new renunciatory movements arose *within* the *varṇa*-defined Brahmanical community itself, imitating the practices of the original *parivrājaka* movements and producing in time their own literature to contribute to the Brahmanical tradition.[41]

The second transformation wrought by the *āśrama* system emerged in the Dharmaśāstric formulation of the *āśrama* system itself. Manu completely reformulated the *āśrama* system, transforming it from a system of four *lifelong vocations* from which to choose after one's Vedic studentship to a system of four *stages of life*, one of which was itself Vedic studentship. Given that Olivelle has already provided an in-depth study of this transformation,[42] it is unnecessary to go into great detail here. Suffice it to say that this transformation of the *āśrama* system represented a major accommodation to the celibate, renunciatory lifestyles that two of the Dharma Sūtra authors explicitly rejected and the other two clearly disfavored. This accommodation was made without compromising the Vedic injunction to produce children by cleverly redefining the three celibate *āśramas*. *Brahmacarya* was redefined as Vedic studentship, undertaken temporarily prior to marriage, while the *vānaprastha* and *parivrājaka* stages were relegated to old age, after one had already married and produced children. Although it is not clear that following these four life-stages in the manner described in the Dharmaśāstras was ever widely practiced, the very fact that Dharmaśāstra authors beginning with Manu felt the need to redefine the *āśrama* system in this way demonstrates that there was an increasing prestige associated with renunciation that made it impossible to dismiss out of hand.

The third and most important transformation wrought by the *āśrama* system is that, even while playing a role in defining a Brahmanism as separate from the *śramaṇa* movements, it created an ideological "leak" through which most of the actual *content* of *śramaṇic* teachings made its way into Brahmanism and became an integral part of classical Hinduism. Although the process by which this happened was long and complicated, and therefore beyond the scope of this book, the actual transformation is quite striking and has been noticed by scholars for a long time. Classical Hinduism looks quite different from the religion of the Vedas, even though it demonstrates important continuities with Vedic thought and practices. Aside from the fact that renunciatory practices similar to those of the *śramaṇa* movements became an important part of classical Hinduism, the basic worldview of the Buddhists, Jains, and Ājīvakas, consisting of a beginningless cycle of rebirths driven by karma from which one eventually hopes to escape, was also adopted. Bronkhorst has explained this transformation in terms of an encounter between an originally western Brahmanism and the indigenous religious worldview of Greater Magadha.[43] While there may be something to Bronkhorst's hypothesis of a geographical factor in the differences between Vedic and *śramaṇ*ic religion, what I am arguing here is that the *āśrama* system was, in a sense, the weak point in Neo-Brahmanism that doomed to failure the efforts of the Dharma Sūtra authors to head off the growing popularity of celibate, renunciatory lifestyles.

Simply by referring to these lifestyles, the Dharma Sūtra authors gave them an implicit legitimacy, even when, as did Gautama and Baudhāyana, they explicitly rejected them. The *āśrama* system was free advertising for renunciatory lifestyles. In addition, once formulated it was open to interpretation by *varṇa*-determined Brahmans in ways that went against the original intent of the Dharma Sūtra authors. This took the form both of those Brahmans who engaged in renunciatory practices in accordance with the descriptions given in the *āśrama* system and of the total reformulation of the *āśrama* system by Manu to formally accommodate renunciatory lifestyles. In this respect, the *āśrama* system was the mirror image of the encounter dialogs of the Buddhists. Encounter dialogs were intended to refute the claims of householders to Brahmanhood, but the result instead was that the category *Brahman*" was lost to them. Likewise, the *āśrama* system was intended to assert the supremacy of the householder lifestyle, but the result instead was that celibate renunciation became an accepted and important part of Brahmanical religion. The celibate Brahmans and householder Brahmans that we explored in Chapters 4 and 5 actually outframed each other. The householder Brahmans may have won exclusive rights to the category *Brahman*, but they lost the debate on celibacy and renunciation. The celibate Brahmans may have lost the category *Brahman*, but their values of celibacy and renunciation became an important part of Brahmanhood nonetheless.

# 8

# *Conclusion*

IN THIS BOOK, I have made the case for adopting a new methodology in the study of ancient Indian religion. As fruitful as comparative studies of Brahmanism, Buddhism, and Jainism have been in contextualizing them in terms of one another, such studies have tended to retain an assumption of a fundamental dichotomy between Brahmanism on the one hand and the non-Brahmanical (*śramaṇ*ic) traditions on the other. Concomitant with this assumption has been a privileging of Brahmanism as metahistorically prior to the *śramaṇ*ic traditions. This privileging is problematic, as recent scholarship has shown, because Brahmanism itself was very much a work in progress; its identity was as much a reaction to the *śramaṇ*ic traditions as the latter were to it. While it is important to contextualize the data bequeathed to us by the Brahmanical, Buddhist, and Jain traditions in terms of one another, Brahmanism does not provide *the* context for the other two, since Brahmanism lacks an essence that can provide that context.

I have argued that by dropping the assumption of a fundamental dichotomy between Brahmanism and the *śramaṇ*ic tradition, and of the metahistorical priority of the former, we see more clearly how Brahmanical and *śramaṇ*ic identities, their relationship symbolized in modern scholarship by the snake and the mongoose, arose in ancient India. When we decenter Brahmanism in this way, we cannot understand *śramaṇ*ism as an offshoot of Brahmanism or as arising in opposition to it. The conflict in ancient India was not between Brahmans and *śramaṇas*. It was, rather, over Brahmanhood itself. Several groups, of which the Buddhists and Jains survive to this day, embraced aspects of the Indian tradition that sought power through celibacy and askesis. Their reaction to increasing urbanization was (in principle) to reject the householder lifestyle that entailed ownership, procreation, and enmeshment in social relations. This was the *śramaṇa* lifestyle engaged in by the early Buddhists, Jains, Ājīvakas, *jaṭilas/vānaprasthas*, and likely other groups who have been lost to history. They, I have argued, understood Brahmanhood itself to derive from this *śramaṇic* lifestyle, A particular group, however, defined Brahmanhood in the opposite way. The proponents of Neo-Brahmanism, as I have called their ideology, embraced the householder lifestyle made possible by India's increasing urbanization. They not only argued that the procreative householder lifestyle was consistent with *dharma*; they insisted that *only* such a lifestyle was consistent with *dharma*. They effectively rejected the ascetic (*śramaṇa*) lifestyle by arguing that the only true askesis (*āśrama*) is that of the householder. In order to make this audacious claim, the proponents of Neo-Brahmanism linked Brahmanhood to birth instead of celibate asceticism.

A couple of historical circumstances that followed have made it difficult to see, in retrospect, the fact that *Brahman* was in antiquity a contested rather than an essential category. First, the proponents of Neo-Brahmanism were very effective at arrogating the category *Brahman* to themselves, to the point that the category came to appear an essential one derived from the earliest times. They did so by not focusing on direct rational debate with their opponents, but instead constructing an *imaginaire* in which Brahmanhood was and had always been an essential characteristic derived from birth. Second, although the proponents of Neo-Brahmanism were ultimately successful in asserting exclusive claim to Brahmanhood, they were not successful in their arguably more fundamental desire to reject celibate lifestyles. Given the inclusivistic logic by which all Indian traditions operated, they were forced to modify the *āśrama* system from a rejection of celibate lifestyles into a partial accommodation of them, paving the way for celibate and ascetic lifestyles under a Brahmanical rubric for the next 2000 years. This has given, in retrospect, the impression that the "inner conflict of tradition" was a characteristic of Brahmanism/Hinduism quite apart from the "non-Brahmanical" religions (Buddhism and Jainism). In fact, the Brahmanism upon which classical Hinduism was based was itself a product of a broader, trans-sectarian tension between renunciant and householder lifestyles, in which it itself originally (i.e., at the time of the Dharma Sūtras) was firmly on the *householder* side of the debate. Brahmanical identity emerged on the householder side of a dialectic between householder and renunciant lifestyles, but then promptly reproduced the same dialectic within itself.

This, in summary, is the argument I have offered in this book. While the argument is thoroughly historical, I have not focused on constructing a positivistic account of what precisely happened in the hundred or so years prior to Alexander's invasion that led to the emergence of discrete Brahmanical and *śramaṇ*ic identities in Indian discourse. Instead, I have focused primarily on the methodological issues surrounding the relationship between the categories *śramaṇa* and *Brahman*. The reason for this is simple: Given the nature of the evidence at our disposal, a positivistic account would necessarily be rather speculative. In the spirit of speculation, however, I can offer a brief outline of what I imagine the historical process might have looked like. To begin with, there likely were a great number of groups of teachers and disciples throughout the *janapada*s of North India, with a great deal of fluidity between these groups as various teachers staked out reputations and disciples shopped around in search of a suitable teacher. Such would be the situation implied by an early Jain text, the *Isibhāsiyāiṃ*, which purports to give the teachings of a variety of "seers," the names of several which (e.g., Yājñavalkya, Śāriputra, Mahākāśyapa, Maskarin Gośāla, Vardhamāna, Pārśva, Uddālaka) came to be associated specifically with the Buddhist, Jain, or Brahmanical tradition. All of these seers are made in this text to proclaim more-or-less Jain doctrines, but they are presented as independent teachers in a diverse field, rather than as representatives of rigidly defined sects.[1] The *Isibhāsiyāiṃ*, in other words, would appear to reflect the diverse field of religious teachers present in ancient India, most of whom were either forgotten or else subordinated to a particular sectarian agenda.

There is no way to know for certain, but given that Brahmanhood was claimed by both the early Buddhists and the early Jains—as well as, of course, the proponents of Neo-Brahmanism—it seems reasonable to assume that these various teachers generally claimed to be Brahmans and to provide a path to Brahmanhood for their disciples. The *content* of their teaching, moreover, should be understood as broadly speaking continuous with the intellectual tradition preserved in the Vedas. Obviously these teachers would have differed from one another and actively sought to differentiate themselves from one another, and thus there would have been varying degrees to which various teachers innovated upon the older Vedic teachings. We can think of the field in terms of more traditional teachings and an avant-garde. The early Jains and Buddhists, as *parivrājaka* groups, certainly represent this avant-garde. They embraced the most innovative ideas, which took earlier speculations on karma and rebirth (such as are found in the Upaniṣads,[2] the latest Vedic texts) to an extreme conclusion: the worldview of *saṃsāra*, a beginningless cycle of suffering through rebirth that should be transcended. As an avant-garde, however, these teachings should be seen as continuous with more traditional teachings,[3] deriving from a process of progressive innovation rather than from an outside source.

The evidence simply does not exist to trace this process in step-by-step detail, but we can arguably catch glimpses of it. The Buddhist tradition, for example, records that before his Awakening, the Buddha studied meditation under two teachers: Āḷāra Kālāma and Uddaka Rāmaputta. These teachers taught him *jhāna* (meditative absorption) up to two consecutive levels, but the Buddha found each of them in turn lacking. At least one strand of the early Buddhist tradition preserves these meditative absorptions as the two highest of the so-called *arūpa-jhānas* (formless absorptions) and, in an early act of Indian inclusivism, places the Buddha's Awakening one step above them in what is called *saññāvedayitanirodha* ("cessation of perception and sensation"). Alexander Wynne has convincingly argued that the formless meditative absorptions of Buddhism can be understood as reflecting ideas preserved in the Brahmanical tradition; thus, he argues that the Buddha studied "Brahmanical meditation" under Āḷāra Kālāma and Uddaka Rāmaputta before attaining Awakening on his own.[4]

Several scholars have questioned the historicity of the account of the Bodhisattva (the Buddha prior to his Awakening) studying under these two teachers,[5] but for our purposes it does not really matter whether it "really happened." The account, which was in any case partially superseded in the later tradition by the account of the Bodhisattva's extreme asceticism with the group of five, gives a plausible glimpse of the sorts of progressive innovations that would have taken place in the avant-garde of the ancient Indian intellectual world. The teachings of Āḷāra Kālāma and Uddaka Rāmaputta would themselves already represent an avant-garde, not simply reflecting a solidified Vedic practice but nevertheless clearly traceable, as Wynne has shown, within a Brahmanical thought-world. The Buddha, according to the account, found their teachings insufficient, but discovered an adequate teaching that went just beyond theirs. As the *saṅgha* (monastic community) and *śāsana* (training) founded by the Buddha developed an institutional identity, the links to older Brahmanical thought were lost, and Buddhism developed an autonomous intellectual tradition of its own. As we have seen, however, this process of identity formation took time. Working within a paradigm that posits a dichotomy between Brahmanical and non-Brahmanical, Wynne argues that the Buddha studied "Brahmanical meditation" with his teachers and then went on to develop his own technique. Using the methodology I have presented in this book, however, we should be very clear that the Buddha was not a "non-Brahman" who studied "Brahmanical" meditation. He was, instead, an active participant in the development of Brahmanical thought in ancient India.

Although coming from a strain of the avant-garde that may have diverged from more traditional intellectual thought and practice even earlier than did Buddhism, the Jain tradition also preserves glimpses of the sort of progressive innovations within an ever-shifting network of teacher–student relationships that would have driven the increasing diversity of ancient Indian thought. As already mentioned, an early Jain text, the *Isibhāsiyāiṃ*, projects Jain teachings onto a variety of ancient Indian teachers. One of the teachers mentioned in that text, Pārśva, was recognized by later Jain tradition as the 23rd Tīrthaṅkara ("ford-maker"), and certain Jain evidence seems to imply that the 24th Tīrthaṅkara, Mahāvīra, may have been born to parents devoted to the teaching of Pārśva, and that Mahāvīra may have built his own teaching upon that of the earlier teacher.[6] Likewise, evidence from the Jain tradition would seem to imply that the most revered teacher of the Ājīvakas, Makkhali Gosāla, was originally a follower of Mahāvīra before becoming a teacher claiming omniscience in his own right.[7] As Bronkhorst has shown, the Ājīvakas likely had teachings very similar to the Jains, agreeing with the latter that the goal was to end all physical action (karma), but denying that there was any possibility of hastening the process whereby previously accrued karma could be eliminated.[8] Again, although the exact nature of the links between the teachings, practices, and major figures of early Jainism and Ājīvakism are difficult to establish in any positive sense, the evidence available suggests that they were involved, like the Buddha, in a rapidly progressing avant-garde around the 5th century BCE.

Locating the more traditional teachings within the field of ancient Indian thought is more difficult than locating the avant-garde. In large part, this is because "tradition" is always a construct, an assertion of identity rather than an essence. In some ways, the *jaṭila/vānaprastha* groups, although certainly innovative in their own way, represent a fairly traditional continuation of practices and ideas found in the Vedic texts. They continued the practice of Vedic sacrifice in an intensive way that also placed value on the ascetic aspects of the Vedic tradition. On the other hand, as I hope to have shown in this book, there is great value in *not* locating "traditional" practice in the householder Brahmanism represented by the Dharma Sūtras. These Neo-Brahmanical householder Brahmans were in key ways not traditional, but reactionary: They sought to construct a Brahmanical "tradition" that validated the householder lifestyle and excised or marginalized aspects of the tradition, accepted by the *jaṭila/vānaprastha* groups and positively seized upon by the more avant-garde Jains and Buddhists, that encouraged celibacy or renunciation. As I have suggested, the formalization of the *varṇa* system played a key role in the construction of this Neo-Brahmanical "tradition," rooting Brahmanhood in birth rather than the practice of *brahmacarya* and thus circumventing the plurality of Brahmanisms that had proliferated under that practice.

Ultimately, for scholars of early South Asia, I hope that this book will open the door for seeing Buddhism and Jainism not just as reactions to but as participants in 5th-century BCE Brahmanical culture, and thus having much more to say about the history of Brahmanism than has been hitherto realized. The project I envision is analogous to the one that has been staked out by Daniel Boyarin for Christianity vis-à-vis Judaism. Boyarin has argued that, far from representing radical aberrations from 1st-century Judaism, many of the key teachings of Christianity, including the divinity of the Messiah, represent aspects of Hellenistic Jewish thought that were, along with Hellenism in general, later consciously suppressed by the rabbinic tradition in reaction to Christianity.[9] I would argue that we need to view the roles of Buddhist, Jain, and Brahmanical evidence for Indian religion in antiquity in the same way. A comparative approach that simply seeks to situate Buddhism and Jainism against a Brahmanical context and catalog the interactions between the three traditions is insufficient. Recognizing that these traditions *brought each other into existence*, we need to use Buddhist and Jain evidence as *evidence for the history of Brahmanism* and develop a deeper understanding of what from the past was rejected and what was simply fabricated as Neo-Brahmanism constructed a "Brahmanical" tradition in reaction to its *śramaṇ*ic rivals.

With respect to the academic study of religion more broadly, the emergence of distinct Brahmanical and *śramaṇ*ic identities in ancient India provides an interesting comparison to the emergence of distinct religious identities in other parts of the world. As I discussed in the Introduction, I see my work in this book as contributing to an increasing interest in the emergence of religious identity, which has also been studied with respect to Christianity and Judaism, Protestantism and Catholicism, Islam and

Judeo-Christianity, and the Sunni–Shi'ite split. But the Indian case provides interesting contrasts to parallel cases in the world of Abrahamic religions. In particular, the preponderance of inclusivistic strategies of boundary policing in India make for a vivid contrast to the more exclusivistic strategies found in the Abrahamic traditions. Boyarin has shown that the boundary between Judaism and Christianity was constructed by elites on both sides who used heresiology to define "orthodoxy" as excluding the external other.[10] In other words, an external boundary was created by constructing and excluding internal others, ultimately driving the mainstream doctrines and practices of Christianity and Judaism further apart.

In India, the process appears to have been somewhat different—in some ways opposite to this one. Yes, exclusivistic strategies akin to Western heresiology were attempted; the genre of "teachings on wrong views" in the Buddhist tradition and the earliest formulation of the *āśrama* system in the Neo-Brahmanical tradition come to mind. But inclusivistic strategies provided a powerful countervailing force; most importantly, the switch from an exclusivistic to an inclusivistic *āśrama* system in Manu's reformulation ironically led to a proliferation of *śramaṇa*-like practices under the rubric of a Brahmanism that was constructed as specifically non-*śramaṇ*ic. As a result, classical Hinduism came to look in many ways like Buddhism and Jainism, with karma, rebirth, and a prominent place for renunciatory practices. Indeed, as the Indian religious traditions informed by the Neo-Brahmanical *imaginaire* continued to develop into a variety of different "sects," the centripetal force lent by the inclusivistic strategies they all shared arguably allowed for the construction of a diverse but unitary "Hinduism" in early modern India independently of the discourse of Western modernity, as has recently been argued by Elaine Fisher.[11]

The contrast I have just outlined between the exclusivism of the West and the inclusivism of India is of course simplistic and intended only as suggestive of what can be learned in the comparative study of religious identity formation. All religious traditions employ both exclusivistic and inclusivistic strategies of boundary policing, and future study of the emergence of religious identity must take into account the complex ways in which these different strategies interacted. Exploring both the similarities and the differences between the way in which such strategies were used in different parts of the world will open up opportunities to gain a deeper understanding of religious identity formation than when individual cases are studied in isolation.

I conclude with a brief word on the wider relevance of the emergence of the "snake and mongoose," and the study of the emergence of religious identity, beyond academia. Although this book is a work of scholarship, focused on the ancient past, I write it with the humble recognition that the past is very much alive in the world today. As I discussed in the Introduction, the conception of the Brahman as a monolithic figure in Indian history, coupled with a "snake and mongoose" model of the relationship between Brahmanism and (in particular) Buddhism, has played a role in modern Indian social discourse. The debates that have taken place and continue to take place in this discourse, as well as the discourse of world religions writ large in which it is embedded, turn on issues going far beyond the academic, historical, and theoretical concerns addressed primarily on this book. But given that the present and the past can never be truly extricated from one another, I hope that this study makes a small contribution to seeing, thinking about, and constructing the past more clearly, not only for its own sake but also for ours in the present.

# *Notes*

## CHAPTER 1

1. This chapter includes extracts (*c.* 2000 words) from Ch. 2, "The Buddha: Historicizing Myth, Mythologizing History," by Nathan McGovern, in Patrick Gray, ed., *Varieties of Religious Invention: Founders and Their Functions in History* (2015). By permission of Oxford University Press.
2. Romila Thapar, *Interpreting Early India*, in *History and Beyond* (Oxford: Oxford University Press, 2000), 63.
3. Gavin Flood, *An Introduction to Hinduism* (Cambridge, England: Cambridge University Press, 1996), 82; Thomas R. Trautman, *India: Brief History of a Civilization*, 2nd ed. (New York: Oxford University Press, 2016), 54; G. C. Pande, *Foundations of Indian Culture: Vol. 1, Spiritual Vision and Symbolic Forms in Ancient India*, 2nd ed. (Delhi: Motilal Banarsidass, 1990), 61; Padmanabh S. Jaini, *Collected Papers on Buddhist Studies* (Delhi: Motilal Banarsidass, 1990), 49; Gerald James Larson, *India's Agony Over Religion* (Albany: SUNY Press, 1995), 67; Bruce Rich, *To Uphold the World: The Message of Ashoka and Kautilya for the 21st Century* (New Delhi: Penguin Viking, 2008), 45.
4. The compound *ahi-nakula* (as *ahinakulikā*) is found only once in Patañjali's *Mahābhāṣya*, in a completely different context, commenting on Pāṇini 4.2.104. The compound *śramaṇa-brāhmaṇa* is not found in this context.
5. Johannes Bronkhorst, *The Two Sources of Indian Asceticism* (Bern: Peter Lang, 1993), 76; Patrick Olivelle, *The Āśrama System: The History and Hermeneutics of a Religious Institution* (New Delhi: Munshiram Manoharlal Publishers, 2004 [1993]), 11; Steven Collins, *Selfless Persons: Imagery and Thought in* Theravāda *Buddhism* (Cambridge, England: Cambridge University Press, 1982), 270 n. 7.
6. There is of course a long-standing dispute over whether "Hinduism" is an applicable category at all prior to British colonialism, when the word *Hindu*, taken from the Persian word for the indigenous inhabitants of India, came to be used to refer to the "religion" (itself a Western category) of those in India who could

not otherwise be categorized as Muslim, Buddhist, Christian, Jain, Sikh, etc. Representative of this debate are Stietencron, who argues that "Hinduism" is a creation of the British, and Lorenzen, who is critical of this constructivist argument. See Heinrich von Stietencron, "Religious Configurations in Pre-Muslim India and the Modern Concept of Hinduism," in Vasudha Dalmia and Heinrich von Stietencron, eds., *Representing Hinduism: The Construction of Religious Traditions and National Identity* (SAGE Publications, 1995), 51–81; David N. Lorenzen, "Who Invented Hinduism?" *Comparative Studies in Society and History* 41, no. 4 (1999): 630–659. Here I use "Hinduism" to refer loosely to the texts, practices, and ideologies that were in place in the "classical" period of the Guptas and came to be associated with Hinduism as a modernly constructed world religion.

7. See the section "Broader Implications" below.
8. Donald S. Lopez, Jr., "Buddha," in Donald S. Lopez, Jr., ed., *Critical Terms for the Study of Buddhism* (Chicago: University of Chicago Press, 2005), 16–17.
9. Philip C. Almond, *The British Discovery of Buddhism* (Cambridge, England: Cambridge University Press, 1988), 29–31.
10. Katia Buffetrille and Donald S. Lopez, Jr., "Introduction to the Translation," in Eugène Burnouf, *Introduction to the History of Indian Buddhism,* trans. Katia Buffetrille and Donald S. Lopez, Jr. (Chicago: University of Chicago Press, 2010), 14.
11. Burnouf, *Introduction,* 162.
12. Ibid.
13. Ibid., 156.
14. These are, I might add, all tropes that would lay the groundwork for later Orientalist constructions of "pristine" Buddhism.
15. Andy Rotman dates the *Divyāvadāna* to the early centuries of the Common Era—Andy Rotman, trans., *Divine Stories: Divyāvadāna,* Part 1 (Boston: Wisdom Publications, 2008), 1.
16. For example, while the texts of the Pali Canon certainly refer to Brahmanical gods (Sakka, Brahmā) and personages (Brahmans themselves), they do not refer, generally speaking, to as wide a variety of gods as Burnouf mentions finding in his texts—"Nārāyaṇa, Śiva, Varuṇa, Kuvera, Brahmā or Pitāmahā, Śakra or Vāsava, Hari or Janārdana, Śaṃkara, which is only another name for Śiva, and Viśvakarman" (Burnouf, *Introduction,* 163)—some of whom are clearly of a more "classical" provenance. Recently Bronkhorst has made a convincing argument that, far from Buddhism and Brahmanism becoming increasingly "separated" with time, the spread of Brahmanical ideology throughout India led to an *increasing* incorporation of Brahmanical themes into Buddhist texts—Johannes Bronkhorst, *Buddhism in the Shadow of Brahmanism* (Leiden: Brill, 2011), 153–170.
17. Buffetrille and Lopez, "Introduction," 1.

18. I believe that this statement holds in spite of the recent critique by Johannes Bronkhorst in *Greater Magadha: Studies in the Culture of Early India* (Leiden: Brill, 2007). Nevertheless, Bronkhorst provides several insights that must nuance our understanding of the "priority" of Brahmanism, which I will explore below.
19. Almond, *British Discovery of Buddhism*, 73.
20. Ibid.
21. Buffetrille and Lopez, "Introduction," 17.
22. Within popular discourse, on the other hand, the narrative of the Buddha as "reformer" is of course alive and well. In India, it takes a particular political valence; Richard Gombrich laments that in lecturing at Indian universities he has "found the view that the Buddha was 'born a Hindu' and was a Hindu reformer to be virtually universal"—Richard Gombrich, *How Buddhism Began: The Conditioned Genesis of the Early Teachings* (New Delhi: Munshiram Manoharlal Publishers, 2007), 15. I would argue that the "reformer" narrative continues to haunt Western scholarly discourse as well; it remains an "obvious" comparison because Protestantism's myth of origins is so inextricably tied up in the Western conception of *religion* on which the modern study of Buddhism is based. This is one key reason that I think establishing a sophisticated theoretical understanding of the relationship between Buddhism and Brahmanism is so important.
23. Hermann Oldenberg, *Buddha: His Life, His Doctrine, His Order*, trans. William Hoey (London: Williams and Norgate, 1892), 170–172.
24. Almond, *British Discovery of Buddhism*, 75.
25. Most importantly Hermann Oldenberg, *Die Religion des Veda* (Berlin: Verlag von Wilhelm Herz, 1894).
26. T. W. Rhys Davids, *Buddhist India* (New York: G.P. Putnam's Sons, 1903), 2. These themes have been returned to quite recently by Johannes Bronkhorst, as I will discuss below.
27. This includes everything from coins, weights and measures, etc., to cults of tree spirits, *nāgas*, and the like. The obvious objection to Rhys Davids' argument would be that even if Brahmanical texts give a skewed picture of early India insofar as they are normative, Buddhist texts are no better because they are normative as well. At the very least we can excuse Rhys Davids because he was providing a corrective at the time he wrote his book, but I think we can go further and say that Rhys Davids' argument continues to have salience and relevance today. That is, I would agree with Rhys Davids that the Brahmanical texts obscure the situation in early India in a way that the Buddhist texts do not; that is, while the Buddhist texts are content to simply subordinate rival cults to the Buddha (e.g., by having *nāga* kings take refuge in the Buddha, having Brahmā urge the Buddha to preach, etc.), the Brahmanical texts weave a totalizing ideology that penetrates all aspects of (its depiction of) Indian social life and thus gives a false impression that early India was, as Burnouf thought, thoroughly Brahmanical. Although, as I will discuss in Chapter 5, I disagree with his

main conclusion, Brian K. Smith amply demonstrates the mechanism by which Vedic texts write Brahmanical ideology into the fabric of the universe itself in his *Classifying the Universe: The Ancient Indian* Varṇa *System and the Origins of Caste* (New York: Oxford University Press, 1994). More recently, Johannes Bronkhorst has argued convincingly that the centerpiece of the Brahmanical movement's strategy was insinuating itself into the Indian social and historical discourse, in *Buddhism in the Shadow of Brahmanism*.

28. Rhys Davids, *Buddhist India*, 61.
29. Ibid., 159, emphasis mine.
30. The recent publication of Bronkhorst's *Buddhism in the Shadow of Brahmanism*—which as I have already noted in significant ways recapitulates (although obviously with more sophistication and the benefit of a hundred years of additional scholarship) Rhys Davids' argument about the misleading picture of early Indian society provided by Brahmanical texts—demonstrates that Rhys Davids' insight is still as relevant today as it was in 1903.
31. Étienne Lamotte, *History of Indian Buddhism: From the Origins to the Śaka Era*, trans. Sara Webb-Boin (Louvain-la-Neuve: Université Catholique de Louvain, 1988 [1958]), 7.
32. For a further discussion of such trends in the contemporary study of Buddhism, see Nathan McGovern, "The Contemporary Study of Buddhism," in Michael Jerryson, ed., *The Oxford Handbook of Contemporary Buddhism* (New York: Oxford University Press, 2017), 701–714.
33. Gregory Schopen, "Archaeology and Protestant Presuppositions in the Study of Indian Buddhism," *History of Religions* 31 (1991): 1–23.
34. For a discussion of "orthogenetic" and "heterogenetic" approaches, see Geoffrey Samuel, *The Origins of Yoga and Tantra: Indic Religions to the Thirteenth Century* (Cambridge, England: Cambridge University Press, 2008), 18–22.
35. For a more detailed overview of the early 20th-century scholarship on the philosophical relationships between Buddhist and Brahmanical schools, including references to important bibliographies, see de Jong, "Buddhist Studies in the West," 84–87.
36. The work of Michael Witzel, building on a century of scholarship beginning with Herman Oldenberg, has given us a detailed understanding of the development of the Vedic texts and associated eastward spread of Vedic *śākhās* from the Punjab region to the Gangetic plain from the late 2nd millennium to the mid-1st millennium BCE. See Michael Witzel, "On the Localization of Vedic Texts and Schools (Material on Vedic *śākhās*, 7)," in G. Pollet, ed., *India and the Ancient World. History, Trade and Culture before A.D. 650. P.H.L. Eggermont Jubilee Volume*, Orientalia Lovaniensia Analecta, vol. 25 (Leuven, 1987), 173–213; Michael Witzel, "Early Sanskritization: Origins and Development of the Kuru State," *Electronic Journal of Vedic Studies* 1, no. 4 (Dec. 1995); Michael Witzel, "Tracing the Vedic Dialects," in Collette Caillat, ed., *Dialects dans les littératures indo-aryennes. Actes*

*du Colloque International organisé par UA 1058 sous les auspices du C.N.R.S avec le soutien du College de France, de la Fondation Hugot du College de France, de l'Université de Paris III, du Ministre des Affaires Etrangères, Paris (Fondation Hugot) 16–18 Septembre 1986* (Paris: College de France, Institut de Civilisation Indienne, 1989), 97–264; Michael Witzel, "The Development of the Vedic Canon and its Schools: The Social and Political Milieu (Material on Vedic *śākhās*, 8)," in Michael Witzel, ed., *Inside the Texts, Beyond the Texts: New Approaches to the Study of the Vedas*, Opera Minora, vol. 2 (Cambridge, MA: Harvard University Department of Sanskrit and Indian Studies, 1997), 257–345.

37. The work of Jan Heesterman on the "agonistic sacrifice," if chronologically problematic, has drawn attention to evidence of pre-classical sacrifice in the Vedas. See J. C. Heesterman, "Brahmin, Ritual, and Renouncer," in *The Inner Conflict of Tradition: Essays in Indian Ritual, Kingship, and Society* (Chicago: University of Chicago Press, 1985), 26–44; J. C. Heesterman, *The Broken World of Sacrifice: An Essay in Ancient Indian Ritual* (Chicago: University of Chicago Press, 1993).
38. Thapar has developed a useful model of the broad social changes that took place in India in the 1st millennium BCE as the transition was made from lineage-based societies to more complex states; see Romila Thapar, *From Lineage to State: Social Formations in the Mid-First Millennium B.C. in the Ganga Valley*, in *History & Beyond* (New Delhi: Oxford University Press, 2000).
39. Black has situated the Upaniṣadic literature in a milieu of eastward expansion by Brahmanical culture; see Brian Black, *The Character of the Self in Ancient India: Priests, Kings, and Women in the Early Upaniṣads* (Albany, NY: SUNY Press, 2007).
40. Olivelle's seminal work on the *āśrama* system, which he has shown was first developed in the Dharma Sūtras from the 3rd century BCE, but did not take its classical form until Manu in the 2nd century CE, is Olivelle, *Āśrama System*. Olivelle's complete work on the Dharmaśāstra literature is too extensive to cite here, but his most recent volume on *dharma* provides a useful summary based on his career of research, as well as an extensive bibliography of his own work: Patrick Olivelle, trans. and ed., *A Dharma Reader: Classical Indian Law* (New York: Columbia University Press, 2017).
41. Timothy Lubin, "The Transmission, Patronage, and Prestige of Brahmanical Piety from the Mauryas to the Guptas," in Federico Squarcini, ed., *Boundaries, Dynamics and Construction of Traditions in South Asia* (Florence: Firenze University Press, 2005), 77–103; Timothy Lubin, "Vráta Divine and Human in the Early Veda," *Journal of the American Oriental Society* 121, no. 4 (Oct.–Dec. 2001): 565–579.
42. Alf Hiltebeitel, "Buddhism and the Mahābhārata. Boundary Dynamics in Textual Practice," in Federico Squarcini, ed., *Boundaries, Dynamics, and Construction of Traditions in South Asia* (London: Anthem Press, 2011), 107–131; Alf Hiltebeitel, *Dharma: Its Early History in Law, Religion, and Narrative* (Oxford: Oxford

University Press, 2001); James L. Fitzgerald, "Making Yudhiṣṭhira the King: the Dialectics and the Politics of Violence in the *Mahābhārata*," *Rocznik Orientalistyczny* 54, no. 1 (2001): 63–92; James L. Fitzgerald, *The Mahābhārata, Volume 7* (Chicago: University of Chicago Press, 2004); Madeleine Biardeau, *Le Mahābhārata: Un récit fondateur du brahmanisme et son interpretation*, 2 vols. (Paris: Editions de Seuil, 2002).

43. Sheldon Pollock, *The Language of the Gods in the World of Men: Sanskrit, Culture, and Power in Premodern India* (Berkeley: University of California Press, 2006).
44. Patrick Olivelle, ed., *Between the Empires: Society in India 300 BCE to 400 CE* (Oxford: Oxford University Press, 2006).
45. Johannes Bronkhorst, *Greater Magadha: Studies in the Culture of Early India* (Leiden: Brill, 2007); Johannes Bronkhorst, *Buddhism in the Shadow of Brahmanism* (Leiden: Brill, 2011); Johannes Bronkhorst, *How the Brahmins Won: From Alexander to the Guptas* (Leiden: Brill, 2016).
46. For a more comprehensive overview of the scholarship on this topic, see Stuart Ray Sarbacker, "The Debate over Dialogue: Classical Yoga and Buddhism in Comparison," ch. 4 in *Samādhi: The Numinous and Cessative in Indo-Tibetan Yoga* (Albany, NY: SUNY Press, 2005), 75–109.
47. In this genre, we should first make mention of a very useful article by K. R. Norman that provides a concise catalog of Brahmanical terms that are referred to in the Pali Canon, which he argues were given "new senses" by the Buddha: K. R. Norman, "Theravāda Buddhism and Brahmanical Hinduism: Brahmanical Terms in a Buddhist Guise," *The Buddhist Forum* 51 (1991): 193–200. Oliver Freiberger has done work on the Buddhist reinterpretation of the word *yajña* (Vedic sacrifice) and the comparison of Brahmans to dogs in some early Buddhist *sutras*: Oliver Freiberger, "The ideal sacrifice. Patterns of reinterpreting brahmin sacrifice in early Buddhism," *Bulletin d'Etudes Indiennes* 16 (1998): 39–49; Oliver Freiberger, "Negative Campaigning: Polemics Against Brahmins in a Buddhist *Sutta*," *Religions of South Asia* 3, 1 (2009): 61–76. The work of Matthew Sayers on rituals of ancestor worship, while focusing mostly on Brahmanical sources, also includes Buddhist ancestral rites within the broader Indian history of such practices: Matthew R. Sayers, *Feeding the Dead: Ancestor Worship in Ancient India* (Oxford: Oxford University Press, 2013). Joanna Jurewicz has argued that the Buddhist doctrine of *pratītya-samutpāda* has antecedents in Vedic cosmogonic concepts: Joanna Jurewicz, "Playing with Fire: The *pratītyasamutpāda* from the Perspective of Vedic Thought," *Journal of the Pali Text Society* 26 (2000): 77–103. Brian Black has argued that there are interesting parallels between the accounts of the Brahman students Śvetaketu in the Upaniṣads and Ambaṭṭha in the Pali Canon: Brian Black, "Ambaṭṭha and Śvetaketu: Literary Connections Between the Upaniṣads and Early Buddhist Narratives," *Journal of the American Academy of Religion* 79, no. 1 (March 2011): 136–161. Some of the most comprehensive work on parallel narrative motifs has been undertaken by Naomi Appleton, who has

recently published a book-length study of characters shared between Buddhist, Jain, and Hindu narratives: Naomi Appleton, *Shared Characters in Jain, Buddhist and Hindu Narrative: Gods, Kings and Other Heroes* (London: Routledge, 2017). In my own work, I have argued that polemics found in the early Buddhist *sūtras* against the Brahmanical god Brahmā led to his abandonment as supreme deity in favor of Viṣṇu and Śiva: Nathan McGovern, "Brahmā: An Early and Ultimately Doomed Attempt at a Brahmanical Synthesis," *Journal of Indian Philosophy* 40, no. 1 (Feb. 2012): 1–23.

48. Narendra Wagle, *Society at the Time of the Buddha* (New York: Humanities Press, 1967).
49. Uma Chakravarti, *The Social Dimensions of Early Buddhism* (Delhi: Oxford University Press, 1987), 145–146.
50. Tsuchida Ryutaro, "Two categories of Brahmins in the early Buddhist period," *The Memoirs of the Toyo Bunko* 49 (1991): 51–95.
51. Greg Bailey and Ian Mabbett, *The Sociology of Early Buddhism* (Cambridge, England: Cambridge University Press, 2003), 109.
52. That Gombrich is the exemplar of this particular methodological approach to the study of early Buddhism is perhaps somewhat ironic, given that Gombrich rejects "methodology" altogether: Richard Gombrich, *What the Buddha Thought* (London: Oxford Center for Buddhist Studies, 2009), 92–93.
53. Richard Gombrich, *How Buddhism Began: The Conditioned Genesis of the Early Teachings* (New Delhi: Munshiram Manoharlal Publishers, 2007), 15–16.
54. Ibid., 51.
55. Ibid., 48.
56. Ibid., 65–72.
57. Richard Gombrich, "The Buddha's Book of Genesis?" *Indo-Iranian Journal* 35 (1992): 159–178.
58. Bronkhorst, *Greater Magadha*, 75–174.
59. Bronkhorst, *How the Brahmins Won*, 7–240.
60. Bronkhorst, *Buddhism in the Shadow of Brahmanism*, 1.
61. Ibid., 27–42.
62. Ibid., 65.
63. Ibid., 65–74.
64. Ibid., 74–97.
65. Ibid., 153–170. Bronkhorst notes (p. 168, n. 232) that this phenomenon makes it unsurprising that Burnouf, who was confined to late Sanskritic sources, would come to the conclusion that the Buddha lived in a thoroughly Brahmanical world.
66. As has been pointed out to me, this nomenclature has the potential to cause confusion given that "Neo-Brahmanism" also has a modern referent in contemporary Indian discourse. I can think of no better term to use, however, and in any case, such terminological duplication can be seen as symptomatic of the fact

that, throughout its history, Brahmanism can always be understood as having a "Neo-" aspect.

67. Geoffrey Samuel, *The Origins of Yoga and Tantra: Indic Religions to the Thirteenth Century* (Cambridge, England: Cambridge University Press, 2008), 48–51.
68. Richard Fynes, "Review of *Greater Magadha* by Johannes Bronkhorst," *Journal of the Oxford Centre for Buddhist Studies* 1 (Oct. 2011): 212–215; Jason Neelis, "Review of *Greater Magadha* by Johannes Bronkhorst," *Journal of the Royal Asiatic Society (Third Series)* 18, no. 3 (2008): 381–383.
69. Johannes Bronkhorst, personal communication, Dec. 16, 2013. The idea of a distinction between a "Brahmanic system" with Western origins and the "single Brahmins" who had lived for a longer time in Greater Magadha has been explored more formally in Jens Schlieter, "Did the Buddha Emerge from a Brahmanic Environment? The Early Buddhist Evaluation of 'Noble Brahmins' and the 'Ideological System' of Brahmanism," in Volkhard Krech and Marion Steinicke, eds., *Dynamics in the History of Religions between Asia and Europe: Encounters, Notions, and Comparative Perspectives* (Leiden: Brill, 2012), 137–148.
70. Jean-François Bayart, *The Illusion of Cultural Identity*, translated by Steven Rendall, Janet Roitman, Cynthia Schoch, and Jonathan Derrick (Chicago: University of Chicago Press, 2005).
71. On the role of Orientalist scholarship in privileging Brahmans in the construction of "Hinduism," as well as the appropriation of this construct by nationalist discourse, especially through the thought of Subramanian Iyer, see M. S. S. Pandian, *Brahmin and Non-Brahmin: Genealogies of the Tamil Political Present* (Ranikhet, India: Permanent Black, 2007), 45–59.
72. Stephen Hay, ed., *Sources of Indian Tradition*, 2nd ed., vol. 2 (New York: Columbia University Press, 1988), 21.
73. C. S. Adcock, *The Limits of Tolerance: Indian Secularism and the Politics of Religious Freedom* (Oxford: Oxford University Press, 2014).
74. Rosalind O'Hanlon, *Caste, Conflict, and Ideology: Mahatma Jotirao Phule and Low-Caste Protest in Nineteenth-Century Western India* (Cambridge, England: Cambridge University Press, 1985).
75. Aditya Nigam, *The Insurrection of Little Selves: The Crisis of Secular-Nationalism in India* (New Delhi: Oxford University Press, 2006), 200–201; Pandian, *Brahmin and Non-Brahmin*, 104.
76. Nigam, *Insurrection of Little Selves*, 201.
77. Pandian, *Brahmin and Non-Brahmin*, 120–141.
78. Ibid., 188–193.
79. Ibid., 144–186; 193.
80. Ramesh Bairy T. S., *Being Brahmin, Being Modern: Exploring the Lives of Caste Today* (London: Routledge, 2010); Nigam, *Insurrection of Little Selves*; Pandian, *Brahmin and Non-Brahmin*.

81. Tomoko Masuzawa, *The Invention of World Religions* (Chicago: University of Chicago Press, 2005); Talal Asad, *Genealogies of Religion: Discipline and Reasons of Power in Christianity and Islam* (Baltimore: Johns Hopkins University Press, 1993).
82. Richard King, *Orientalism and Religion: Postcolonial Theory, India and 'The Mythic East'* (London: Routledge, 1999), 35–41.
83. Almond, *British Discovery of Buddhism*; Lopez, "Buddha"; Richard King, "Orientalism and the discovery of 'Buddhism,'" in *Orientalism and Religion*, 143–160.
84. Tomoko Masuzawa, "Buddhism, a World Religion," in *Invention of World Religions*, 121–146.
85. Paul Hacker, *Inklusivismus: Eine Indische Denkform*, ed. Gerhardt Oberhammer (Vienna: De Nobili Research Library, 1983).
86. To be fair, Christianity can be considered inclusivistic in a sense, insofar as it demoted polytheistic gods to demons; on this process in the late Roman Empire, see Ramsay MacMullen, *Christianizing the Roman Empire: A.D. 100–400* (New Haven: Yale University Press, 1984). The category *magic* in the Middle Ages then played an important role in negotiating the boundary between permissible and non-permissible pagan practices within a newly Christianized Europe, with the non-permissible understood as involving demons; see Valerie I. J. Flint, *The Rise of Magic in Early Medieval Europe* (Princeton: Princeton University Press, 1991). Christianity's exclusivistic tendency in a sense only came into full force with respect to alternative supernatural beings with the Reformation, and especially the Enlightenment skepticism that followed thereupon; on this process of disenchantment, see Euan Cameron, *Enchanted Europe: Superstition, Reason, and Religion, 1250–1750* (Oxford: Oxford University Press, 2010).
87. McGovern, "Brahmā."
88. Daniel Boyarin, *Border Lines: The Partition of Judeo-Christianity* (Philadelphia: University of Pennsylvania Press, 2004).
89. Fred M. Donner, "From Believers to Muslims: Confessional Self-Identity in the Early Islamic Community," *Al-Abḥāth* 50–51 (2002–2003): 9–53; Fred M. Donner, *Muhammad and the Believers at the Origins of Islam* (Cambridge, MA: Belknap Harvard University Press, 2010).
90. Maria Massi Dakake, *The Charismatic Community: Shi'ite Identity in Early Islam* (Albany, NY: SUNY Press, 2007).
91. For an example of an approach to the Reformation as process in Western Christendom, rather than rupturing event, see Diarmaid MacCullogh, *The Reformation* (New York: Penguin, 2003).

## CHAPTER 2

1. For a list of various proposed dates, see Lamotte, *History of Indian Buddhism*, 216 n. 1.

2. There have been, it should be noted, many proposals for evidence of writing in India prior to Aśoka, both in the form of references apparently made to writing in texts that are presumed to be older than Aśoka and in the form of inscriptions that have been suggested to be themselves pre-Mauryan. To date, there is still no consensus on the issue of pre-Aśokan writing. For a useful summary of scholarship, see Richard Salomon, *Indian Epigraphy* (New York: Oxford University Press, 1998), 10–14.
3. See E. Hultzsch, *Inscriptions of Aśoka*, Corpus Inscriptionum Indicarum, vol. 1 (Tokyo: Meicho-Fukyū-kai, 1977), xxxi.
4. Hultzsch, *Inscriptions of Aśoka*, 45, 47: *n[a]thi cā ṣe jan[a]pade yatā nathi ime nikāyā ānatā Y[o]neṣ[u] baṃhmane c[ā] ṣamane cā.*
5. For an overview of Alexander's invasion of India, see Klaus Karttunen, *India and the Hellenistic World* (Helsinki: Finnish Oriental Society, 1997), 19–54.
6. Patrick Olivelle, *The Origin and Early Development of Buddhist Monachism* (Colombo: Gunasena, 1974), 25 n. 1. For an overview of what is known of Megasthenes' life and work, see Karttunen, *India and the Hellenistic World*, 69–93.
7. Strabo, *Geography*, 15.39; cf. Arrian, *Indika*, 11.1. Much ink has been spilled over the fact that Megasthenes speaks of seven "castes" (γένοι) instead of the expected four. Bronkhorst has recently argued that Megasthenes is not aware of the four *varṇas* because he visited Magadha at a time when it had not yet been Brahmanized—Bronkhorst, *Buddhism in the Shadow of Brahmanism*, 73.
8. Strabo, *Geography*, 15.59; on the form *Γαρμᾶναι*, see John W. McCrindle, *Ancient India as Described in Classical Literature* (St. Leonards: Ad Orientem, 1971[1901]), 65 n. 1.
9. McCrindle, *Ancient India in Classical Literature*, 75 n. 5.
10. Strabo, *Geography*, 15.70: McCrindle, *Ancient India in Classical Literature*, 76.
11. Olivelle, *Āśrama System*, 12, 14.
12. George Turnour, *The Mahávanso*, vol. 1 (Ceylon: Cotta Church Mission Press, 1837), xlviii; on the key role played by Turnour in the history of modern research on the date of the Buddha, see Lance S. Cousins, "The Dating of the Historical Buddha: A Review Article," *Journal of the Royal Asiatic Society* 6, no. 1 (1996), 58.
13. Heinz Bechert, *The Dating of the Historical Buddha*, 2 vols. (Göttingen: Vandenhoeck and Ruprecht, 1991–1992).
14. For a useful summary of the history of research on the date of the Buddha's death and a review of the volume that resulted from Bechert's 1988 conference, see Cousins, "The Dating of the Historical Buddha."
15. On this transition, see Thapar, *From Lineage to State.*
16. Although fully exploring the issue goes beyond the scope of this book, I agree with Lance Cousin's hypothesis that the Oral Theory of Milman Parry and Albert Lord can be fruitfully applied to the early Buddhist oral literature, implying that this literature was originally passed down in a conservative but nevertheless fundamentally improvisatory manner: Lance S. Cousins, "Pali Oral Literature,"

in P. Denwood and A. Piatigorsky, eds., *Buddhist Studies Ancient and Modern* (London: Curzon Press, 1983), 1–11. Some scholars, however, have questioned Cousins's improvisatory model for the early oral transmission of Buddhist literature: Richard Gombrich, "How the Mahāyāna Began," *Journal of Pali and Buddhist Studies* 1 (March 1988), 22; Mark Allon, "The Oral Composition and Transmission of Early Buddhist Texts," in Sue Hamilton and Peter Connolly, eds., *Indian Insights: Buddhism, Brahmanism and Bhakti. Papers from the Annual Spalding Symposium on Indian Religion* (London: Luzac Oriental, 1997), 52; Anālayo, *A Comparative Study of the* Majjhima-nikāya, vol. 1 (Taipei: Dharma Drum Publishing, 2011), 17. All scholars agree, however, that the various texts of the *Tripiṭaka* were composed over some period of time.

17. By far the greatest number of texts parallel to those found in the Pali Canon are preserved in the Chinese Canon, which includes at least one version of each of the four main Āgamas (equivalent to the Nikāyas of the Pali *Sutta Piṭaka*), as well as several sectarian versions of the Vinaya and Abhidharma texts. A useful resource that identifies parallels between texts preserved in Pali, Chinese, Sanskrit, Tibetan, and other languages can be found at www.suttacentral.net. For a more detailed discussion of the parallels between the Pali Nikāyas and their counterparts in Chinese and other languages, see Nathan McGovern, "Buddhists, Brahmans, and Buddhist Brahmans: Negotiating Identities in Indian Antiquity" (PhD dissertation, University of California, Santa Barbara, 2013), 402–462.
18. The continuous manuscript tradition for the Pali Canon dates only to the late 15th century: Oskar von Hinüber, *A Handbook of Pāli Literature* (Berlin: Walter de Gruyter, 2000), 4. The oldest isolated Pali manuscript was found in Nepal and dates to the 9th century: Oskar von Hinüber, *The Oldest Pali Manuscript: Four Folios of the Vinaya-Piṭaka from the National Archives, Kathmandu* (Mainz: Akademie der Wissenschaften und der Literatur, 1991).
19. Gregory Schopen, "Two Problems in the History of Indian Buddhism: The Layman/Monk Distinction and the Doctrines of the Transference of Merit," in *Bones, Stones, and Buddhist Monks: Collected Papers on the Archaeology, Epigraphy, and Texts of Monastic Buddhism in India* (Honolulu: University of Hawai'i Press, 1997), 24.
20. E. W. Adikaram, *Early History of Buddhism in Ceylon, or "State of Buddhism in Ceylon as Revealed by the Pāli Commentaries of the 5th Century A.D."* (Colombo: M. D. Gunasena and Co., 1946), 3.
21. von Hinüber, *A Handbook of Pāli Literature*, 22.
22. It should be acknowledged that the relevant passage in the *Dīpavaṃsa* is problematic, and therefore its reliability has been questioned. For a detailed treatment of the issue, see Lance S. Cousins, "The Early Development of Buddhist Literature and Language in India," *Journal of the Oxford Centre for Buddhist Studies* 5 (2013), 108–111. Cousins actually comes to the conclusion that the *Tipiṭaka* may have

been written down even earlier, in India, and that the *Dīpavaṃsa* reference is to these written texts being brought to Sri Lanka in the 1st century BCE.

23. While the divisions of the *Sutta Piṭaka* in the Pali tradition are referred to as Nikāyas, it appears that in other traditions these divisions were referred to as Āgamas. The Chinese translations of these *sūtra* collections use this nomenclature, transcribed into Chinese as *Āhán* (阿含). Thus it is conventional to the "Pali Nikāyas" and "Chinese Āgamas," which are in fact different sectarian versions of corresponding collections of *sūtras* preserved in two different languages.
24. The most important translation of the *Saṃyuktāgama* into Chinese, T. 99 (*Zá Āhán Jīng* 雜阿含經), was made from 435–436 CE by Guṇabhadra (Qiúnàbátuóluó 求那跋陀羅): Andrew Glass, *Four Gāndhārī Saṃyuktāgama Sūtras: Senior Kharoṣṭhī Fragment* 5, Gandhāran Buddhist Texts 4 (Seattle: University of Washington Press, 2007), 28, 38–39. The *Dīrghāgama* was translated into Chinese as T. 1 (*Cháng Āhán Jīng* 長阿含經) in 413 CE by Buddhayaśas (Fótuóyéshè 佛陀耶舍) and Zhú Fóniàn (竺佛念): Mayeda Egaku, "Japanese Studies on the Schools of the Chinese Āgamas," in *Genshi bukkyō seiten no seiritsushi kenkyū* [A History of the Formation of Original Buddhist Texts] (Tokyo: Sankibō Busshorin, 1964), 97. The *Madhyamāgama* was translated into Chinese as T. 26 (*Zhōng Āhán Jīng* 中阿含經) from 396–397 CE by a team led by Gautama Saṅghadeva (Qútán Sēngjiàtípó 瞿曇僧伽提婆): Anālayo, "Comparative Notes on the Madhyama-Āgama," *Fuyan Buddhist Studies* 2 (2007), 33. The *Ekottarikāgama* was translated into Chinese as T. 125 (*Zēngyī Āhán Jīng* 增壹阿含經) from 384–385 by Zhú Fóniàn (竺佛念) or, according to other sources, by Gautama Saṅghadeva: Mayeda, "Japanese Studies on the Schools of the Chinese Āgamas," 102.
25. Lamotte, *History of Indian Buddhism*, 150.
26. Vidya Dehejia, "On Modes of Visual Narration in Early Buddhist Art," *The Art Bulletin* 72, no. 3 (Sept. 1990): 374–392.
27. For a list of the texts named by Aśoka and possible identifications of them in the extant Buddhist literature, as well as references to other work that has been done on identifying the texts named by Aśoka, see Lamotte, *History of Indian Buddhism*, 234–237.
28. Rhys Davids is referring here to himself: T. W. Rhys Davids, *The Questions of King Milinda*, vol. 1 (New York: Dover Publications, 1963[1890]), xxxvii–xxxix.
29. T. W. Rhys Davids, "The Early History of the Buddhists," in E. J. Rapson, ed., *The Cambridge History of India*, vol. 1 (Cambridge, England: Cambridge University Press, 1922), 193.
30. Lamotte, *History of Indian Buddhism*, 235–236.
31. Even here, though, I think that Rhys Davids' thought experiment comparing Aśoka's inscription to a hypothetical Christian inscription listing edifying passages in the New Testament runs into a problem. The texts of the New Testament were written in the 1st century, but so were other early Christian texts; it was only after some time that a decision was made within the orthodox Christian

community as to which texts to include in the canon and which not. Rhys Davids' imaginary inscription would tell us nothing about what stage the early Christian community was at in this process of canon-formation, any more than Aśoka's inscription, I am arguing, tells us about the stage at which the early Buddhist community was in its process of developing the early Buddhist oral literature as a whole.

32. We can add to this that there must have existed some sort of Vinaya in Aśoka's day, since the first passage he refers to is *vinaya-samukkase*, or "Praise of the Vinaya." This is hardly surprising, and it says nothing about the extent of Vinaya literature during Aśoka's reign. Indeed Lamotte identifies the *vinaya-samukkase* with a passage found in the *Aṅguttara Nikāya* that is a praise of the *prātimokṣa*, the list of monastic rules, which by itself is just the barest skeleton of the fully developed Vinaya literature: Lamotte, *History of Indian Buddhism*, 235.
33. Bronkhorst, *Greater Magadha*, 353.
34. Stanley Tambiah, *World Conqueror & World Renouncer: A Study of Buddhism and Polity in Thailand Against a Historical Background* (Cambridge: Cambridge University Press, 1976), 39–53.
35. Nathan McGovern, "On the Origin of the 32 Marks of a Great Man," *Journal of the International Association of Buddhist Studies* 39 (2016): 207–247.
36. Nearly all of Aśoka's inscriptions address the subject of *dhamma*, and therefore need not be cited individually. Aśoka specifically expresses regret over his bloody campaign to conquer Kaliṅga, and his desire to instead rule by means of *dhamma*, in his 13th rock edict: Hultzsch, *Inscriptions of Aśoka*, 47–49. The famous Sarnath pillar incorporates wheels into its capital: Hultzsch, *Inscriptions of Aśoka*, xxi.
37. An alternative possibility is that Aśoka drew from a preexisting Buddhist conception of the *cakravartin* in formulating his own ideology of kingship. However, I think that this is distinctly less likely. First, Aśoka does not refer to the Buddhist concept of the *cakravartin*, which we would expect if it existed; rather, his discussions about *dhamma* seem to be the expression of an emerging ideology based on his own deeply personal experience of conversion to non-violence. Second, I consider it a priori unlikely that the Buddhists would have developed the *cakravartin* concept prior to the *actual* existence of imperial kingship stretching from ocean to ocean. Legitimizing imperial kingship would have been called for once the *saṅgha* had profited from the patronage such kingship could bring, but what possible reason would world-renouncing ascetics have had to speculate about a world-conquering monarch in a world in which no such world-conquering monarch had yet arisen? Finally, the entire tenor of the *Cakkavatti-sīhanāda Sutta* suggests a nostalgia for righteous kingship *in the past*. This would imply composition in the wake of the collapse of the Mauryan dynasty.
38. *DN* 16: *yāvatā, ānanda, ariyaṃ āyatanaṃ yāvatā vaṇippatho idaṃ agganagaraṃ bhavissati pāṭaliputtaṃ puṭabhedanaṃ.*

39. *DN* 16: *iti aṭṭha sarīrathūpā navamo tumbathūpo dasamo aṅgārathūpo.*
40. *evam etaṃ bhūtapubban ti.*
41. John S. Strong, *The Legend of King Aśoka: A Study and Translation of the* Aśokāvadāna (Delhi: Motilal Banarsidass, 1983), 109–119.
42. Gombrich, *How Buddhism Began*, 20.
43. Bailey and Mabbett, *Sociology of Early Buddhism*, 123.
44. Ibid., 121.
45. *tatreva, muṇḍaka; tatreva, samaṇaka; tatreva, vasalaka tiṭṭhāhī ti.*
46. Norman, *Group of Discourses*, 14.
47. *Sn.* 136: *na jaccā vasalo hoti, na jaccā hoti brāhmaṇo / kammunā vasalo hoti, kammunā hoti brāhmaṇo //.*
48. A parallel to this story of Mātaṅga can be found at *MBh.* 13.27–29, which is cited in David Gordon White, *Myths of the Dog-Man* (Chicago: University of Chicago Press, 1991), 250 n. 34. In this version of the story, a person named Mātaṅga learns that he is a *caṇḍāla* because he was born from the union of a *brāhmaṇī* and a *śūdra* barber. Indra appears to him and offers him a boon, so Mātaṅga asks him to make him a Brahman. Indra says that this is impossible, but Mātaṅga persists in his desire to become a Brahman and performs great austerities in the hopes that this will allow him to become one. In the end, Mātaṅga gives up his quest to become a Brahman and instead asks for the ability to assume any form, fly, and enjoy whatever pleasure he wishes. Indra grants his request by making him a god. The ultimate point of this story is that Brahmanhood—which Mātaṅga never does attain—is *even higher* than this high state that Mātaṅga attains through his perseverance in austerity.
49. As will be discussed further in Chapter 7, Brahmans in "encounter dialogs" often have humorous names.
50. Before the actual conversation between Soṇadaṇḍa and the Buddha begins, there is a long narrative recounting how Soṇadaṇḍa came to hear of the Buddha and his fame, decided to go visit him, and looked for and saw the 32 marks of a "Great Man" (*mahāpurisa*), all of which are formulaic features of a large subset of the encounter dialogs.
51. *ubhato sujāto hoti mātito ca pitito ca, saṃsuddhagahaṇiko yāva sattamā pitāmahayugā akkhitto anupakkuṭṭho jātivādena.*
52. *ajjhāyako hoti mantadharo tiṇṇaṃ vedānaṃ pāragū sanighaṇḍukeṭubhānaṃ sākkharappabhedānaṃ itihāsapañcamānaṃ padako veyyākaraṇo lokāyatamahāpurisalakkhaṇesu anavayo.*
53. *abhirūpo hoti dassanīyo pāsādiko paramāya vaṇṇapokkharatāya samannāgato brahmavaṇṇī brahmavacchasī akhuddāvakāso dassanāya.*
54. *sīlavā hoti vuddhasīlī vuddhasīlena samannāgato.*
55. *paṇḍito ca hoti medhāvī paṭhamo vā dutiyo vā sujaṃ paggaṇhantānaṃ.*
56. *sīlaparidhotā hi . . . paññā; paññāparidhotaṃ sīlaṃ.*
57. *yato kho, bho, ubhato sujāto hoti mātito ca pitito ca saṃsuddhagahaṇiko yāva sattamā pitāmahayugā akkhitto anupakkuṭṭho jātivādena, ettāvatā kho bho brāhmaṇo hotī ti.*

58. *yato kho, bho, sīlavā ca hoti vatasampanno ca, ettāvatā kho, bho, brāhmaṇo hotī ti.*
59. Verse 650 in the *Sn.* version of the *Vāseṭṭha Sutta*, in fact, states so in exactly the same words as v. 136 in *Sn.* 1.7 quoted above.
60. This would include *Dhp.* 396–423, which are identical or nearly identical to v. 620–647 of the *Sn.* version of the *Vāseṭṭha Sutta*. These are the verses, already discussed above, that end with the refrain *tam ahaṃ brūmi brāhmaṇaṃ* ("Him *I* call a Brahman"). There is good reason to believe that these verses were incorporated into the *Dhammapada* tradition first, and only later borrowed from there for use in the *Vāseṭṭha Sutta*, and then only by the Theravāda tradition. If this is true, then the verses that do not explicitly contrast the Brahman as ideal with the Brahman as someone born that way were imputed with such a contrastive meaning by the narrative framework of the *Vāseṭṭha Sutta*, in the same manner as I will discuss in Chapter 7.
61. *Dhp.* 393: *na jaṭāhi na gottena, na jaccā hoti brāhmaṇo / yamhi saccañ ca dhammo ca, so sucī so ca brāhmaṇo //.*
62. This is apparently a reference, perhaps somewhat snide, to the practice of reciting Vedic *mantras*.
63. *yo brāhmaṇo bāhitapāpadhammo / nihuṃhuṅko nikkasāvo yatatto / vedantagū vūsitabrahmacariyo / dhammena so brahmavādaṃ vadeyya / yassussadā natthi kuhiñci loke //.*
64. *na udakena sucī hotī, bahvettha nhāyatī jano / yamhi saccañca dhammo ca, so sucī so ca brāhmaṇo.*
65. This includes, ironically, *Dhp.* 396–423, which, in addition to their likely narrative framing through incorporation into the *Vāseṭṭha Sutta* (see Chapter 7), are also given humorous (and unrelated) frame stories involving silly Brahmans in the commentary on the *Dhammapada* itself.
66. Warder notes that the question is complicated by the fact that there are likely two strata in the *Aṭṭhaka* and *Pārāyaṇa* (about which more below) that need to be distinguished for the purposes of metrical analysis, but he argues that the *vatta* (Skt. *vaktra*, equivalent to the Sanskrit *anuṣṭubh* and precursor to the classical *śloka*) meter found in the *Aṭṭhaka* and *Pārāyaṇa* is more archaic than the *vatta* found in other texts such as the *Dhammapada*, *Thera/Therīgāthā*, and *Jātaka*—A. K. Warder, *Pali Meter* (London: Luzac, 1967), 199, 172–173. Warder bases his argument for the relative antiquity of the *vatta* in the *Aṭṭhaka* and *Pārāyaṇa* on the frequency with which the *pathyā* form of the prior *pāda* is used. The use of the *pathyā* form shows a clear increasing progression from 20% in Book 10 of the *RV* to 93% in the *Raghuvaṃśa*. Others have been critical of the metrical analysis approach to dating, such as K. R. Norman, who states bluntly, "Dating by metre is not particularly helpful." Nevertheless, Norman accepts the relative antiquity of the *Aṭṭhaka* and *Pārāyaṇa* on other grounds and acknowledges that this antiquity is supported at least in part by the fact that "the original core of verses in the Aṭṭhaka-v, is in the Triṣṭubh [Pali *tuṭṭhubha*] metre,

which is generally a sign of an early composition in Pāli"—Norman, *Group of Discourses*, xxix, xxvii, xxix.

67. This was pointed out to me at the American Academy of Religion Conference in Atlanta, GA, 2010, by Bhikkhu Sujāto, who is suspicious of arguments for the particular antiquity of the *Aṭṭhaka* and *Pārāyaṇa*. He cited as other examples of canonical commentaries the *Saccavibhaṅga Sutta* (*MN* 141), in which the Buddha gives a sermon expounding upon his first sermon that he had given in the Deer Park at Isipatana after his Awakening (i.e., the *Dhammacakkappavattana Sutta*), and the *Suttavibhaṅga* of the Vinaya, which is a commentary on the *Pāṭimokkha Sutta* (which latter, ironically, is not in and of itself canonical). See also Sujāto, "History of Mindfulness," 19, where he criticizes Schopen on this point.
68. Actually, two texts: The *Mahāniddesa* contains the commentary on the *Aṭṭhaka Vagga*, and the *Cūḷaniddesa* contains the commentaries on the *Pārāyaṇa Vagga* and the *Khaggavisāṇa Sutta*.
69. That the *Niddesa* is an early commentary on even older texts is confirmed by the fact that the *Aṭṭhaka* and *Pārāyaṇa*, as parts of the *Sutta Nipāta*, are also commented upon by the ordinary post-canonical commentary *Paramatthajotikā II*, which presupposes the existence of the *Niddesa* and even quotes directly from the *Mahāniddesa*—see Norman, *Group of Discourses*, xxxvii. The particular antiquity of the *Aṭṭhaka* and *Pārāyaṇa*—together with the *Khaggavisāṇa Sutta* (*Sn.* 1.3)—is moreover confirmed by the fact that the *Niddesa* only comments upon those three texts, rather than the *Sutta Nipāta* as a whole. This would suggest that the *Khaggavisāṇa Sutta*, *Aṭṭhaka*, and *Pārāyaṇa* were circulating as independent texts at the time that the *Niddesa* was written, prior to their incorporation into the *Sutta Nipāta*. In the case of the *Pārāyaṇa*, however, the form that it took at that time was most likely somewhat shorter than the form that it takes now in the *Sutta Nipāta*, since the introductory *vatthugāthās* found in the latter (*Sn.* 976–1031) are not commented upon by the *Cūḷaniddesa*
70. Within the Pali Canon there are six independent references that all treat the collections as unified, titled works with recognized divisions within them. According to *Ud.* 5.6, a certain "Ven. Soṇa . . . recited with melody all sixteen divisions of the *Aṭṭhaka Vagga*" (*āyasmā soṇo . . . soḷasa aṭṭhakavaggikāni sabbāneva sarena abhaṇi*). This reference is reproduced at Vin. I.196 with the number 16 (*soḷasa*) omitted. Five other references cite specific verses from specific sections of one of the collections: v. 844 in the *Māgandiyapañha* of the *Aṭṭhaka Vagga* (*SN* 3.1.22.3), v. 1038 in the *Ajitapañha* of the *Pārāyaṇa* (*SN* 2.1.12.31), v. 1048 in the *Puṇṇakapañha* of the *Pārāyaṇa* (*AN* 3.32, 4.41), v. 1106–1107 in the *Udayapañha* of the *Pārāyaṇa* (*AN* 3.32), and v. 1042 in the *Metteyapañha* of the *Pārāyaṇa* (*AN* 6.61)—cited in Norman, *Group of Discourses*, xxxiv–xxxv. The recognition of the existence of the *Aṭṭhaka* and *Pārāyaṇa* as independent collections is not limited to the Pali tradition, however; aside from the canonical references in Pali

just cited, we also find references to an *Arthavargīya* and *Pārāyaṇa* twice in the Sanskrit *Divyāvadāna*—cited in Norman, *Group of Discourses*, xxviii.

71. Ibid., xxxi–xxxii.
72. Luis O. Gómez, "Proto-Mādhyamika in the Pāli Canon," *Philosophy East and West* 26, no. 2 (Apr. 1976): 137–165. (According to Gómez, it was his intention for there to be a question mark at the end of the article title, but it was omitted inadvertently in the course of publishing.) In this article, Gómez argues that the ideas found in the *Aṭṭhaka*, and to a certain extent the *Pārāyaṇa*, bear more in common with Madhyamaka philosophy than anything found in the rest of the Pali Canon. In particular, Gómez argues, the *Aṭṭhaka* does not proclaim a path based on "right view," but rather a much more radical path based on abandoning attachment to any view whatsoever.
73. Vetter, "Older Parts of the Suttanipāta," 45–46, 50. While accepting Gómez's general conclusions regarding the incompatibility of certain passages in the collections with mainstream canonical doctrine, Vetter criticizes him for coming to broad conclusions about the collections based on those passages. He notes that "there remain six out of the sixteen suttas of the Aṭṭhaka that are not used by Gómez for his argument, and could not be used" because they do not advise overcoming apperception or abandoning views and the like. Vetter hypothesizes that the core *suttas* of the *Aṭṭhaka* were composed by a non-Buddhist "mystical movement" that was later incorporated into the Buddhist *saṅgha*. He argues further that the *Pārāyaṇa* was one of the first attempts to "include" the themes taught by the "mystical movement" behind the core *suttas* of the *Aṭṭhaka*, insofar as it refers to release from apperception and overcoming all views, but relates them to the goal of escaping birth and old age, as well as such other "Buddhist" themes as mindfulness and thirst.
74. Wynne, *Origin of Buddhist Meditation*, 75. Wynne argues that Vetter is too quick to identify incompatibilities between passages in different sections of the *Pārāyaṇa* that allow him to reduce the text as a whole to an "inclusivistic" exercise in compilation. Wynne argues that the *Pārāyaṇa* is, at least in part, a very old text, and that as such it can be used to show that "the Buddha taught a form of meditation similar to what Vetter calls 'Dhyāna-meditation', a meditative practice based on the goal of Āḷāra Kālāma that was thought to lead to a non-intellectual sort of insight." The "Dhyāna-meditation" referred to here is the full classical system of four *rūpa-* and four *arūpa-jhānas*
75. Grace G. Burford, *Desire, Death and Goodness: The Conflict of Ultimate Values in Theravāda Buddhism* (New York: Peter Lang, 1991).
76. Gombrich, *What the Buddha Thought*, 194.
77. The Pali Nikāyas and Chinese Āgamas, with the possible exception of the *Ekottarikāgama* preserved in Chinese, all came from Sthavira schools. On the sectarian attributions of the Chinese Āgamas, see Mayeda Egaku, "Japanese Studies on the Schools of the Chinese Āgamas," in *Genshi bukkyō seiten no seiritsushi*

*kenkyū* [A History of the Formation of Original Buddhist Texts] (Tokyo: Sankibō Busshorin, 1964), 94–103.

78. Burford, *Desire, Death and Goodness*, 71, 82–93, 125–131. Burford follows Gómez's lead in criticizing the *Niddesa*'s interpretation of an *Aṭṭhaka* passage by analyzing comprehensively the way that the two commentaries on the *Aṭṭhaka*—the *Mahāniddesa* and the *Paramatthajotikā II*—interpret it in different ways so as to fit its unique doctrines into "Theravādin" orthodoxy. These two commentaries use similar strategies for dealing with the "unorthodox" aspects of the *Aṭṭhaka*, but they bear subtle differences because they are written in different formats—the *Mahāniddesa* is strictly a word-by-word commentary, while Buddhaghosa's *Paramatthajotikā* employs a more discursive style. In her analysis of the *Mahāniddesa* commentary, Burford finds that while it retains the *Aṭṭhaka*'s preference for defining the problem at the root of the human condition in terms of desire, it complexifies the ideas presented in the *Aṭṭhaka* by defining words that are used interchangeably therein in distinct, hierarchical terms. In addition, it adds to the ideas present in the *Aṭṭhaka* by making it clear that the goal lies beyond death and rebirth; in other words, it inserts the orthodox concept of *nibbāna* as escape from rebirth into a text in which it is otherwise notably absent. According to Burford's reading, Buddhaghosa's commentary on the *Aṭṭhaka* in the *Paramatthajotikā II* serves much the same purpose as that in the *Mahāniddesa*—to interpret the *Aṭṭhaka* as a text that is both inwardly coherent and consistent with the main tenets of Theravāda orthodoxy—although it is able to do so somewhat more comprehensively because of its narrative format, which allows Buddhaghosa to simply skip over words in the root text that are problematic.
79. The study of these three chronological layers—the root texts, the *Niddesa* commentaries upon them, and the post-canonical commentary—is now greatly facilitated by the translation of these texts into English: Bhikkhu Bodhi, trans., *The* Suttanipāta: *An Ancient Collection of the Buddha's Discourses together with its Commentaries* (Somerville, MA: Wisdom Publications, 2017). Unfortunately, Bhikkhu Bodhi's translation and study was released too late for me to consult it in preparation of this book manuscript.
80. The first books of the *Āyāraṅga* and *Sūyagaḍaṃga* probably date to the 3rd or 2nd century BCE, perhaps a bit earlier for the former and a bit later for the latter: Paul Dundas, *The Jains*, 2nd ed. (London: Routledge, 2002), 23. For a more full discussion of the chronological stratification of the earliest Jain texts, see Suzuko Ohira, *A Study of the Bhagavatīsūtra: A Chronological Analysis* (Ahmedabad: Prakrit Text Society, 1994), 1–13. Ohira, however, places this earliest stratum of the Jain texts a bit earlier, from the 6th/5th–4th centuries BCE.
81. In his latest publication, Olivelle dates *Āpastamba* to the late 3rd century BCE, *Gautama* to the late 2nd century BCE, *Baudhāyana* to the early 1st century BCE, and *Vasiṣṭha* to the late 1st century BCE: Patrick Olivelle, *A Dharma Reader: Classical Indian Law* (New York: Columbia University Press, 2017), 51, 59, 61, 65.

## CHAPTER 3

1. As Stefan Baums pointed out to me, these are animals of a similar type to one another, in stark contrast to the example of "the snake and the mongoose" given later by Jayāditya and Vāmana. This suggests that (1) Patañjali saw the *śramaṇa* and Brahman as being fundamentally quite similar to one another, and (2) he may have given them, together with various animals, as an example of "eternal strife" as a tongue-in-cheek aside.
2. Greg Bailey and Ian Mabbett, *The Sociology of Early Buddhism* (Cambridge, England: Cambridge University Press, 2003), 112.
3. As was pointed out to me by an anonymous reviewer, it is still possible to interpret *brāhmaṇa-śramaṇa* as a *karmadhāraya* compound if we take *brāhmaṇa* as being in apposition to *śramaṇa*: thus, it would mean, "a *śramaṇa* who is a *brāhmaṇa*." While technically possible (and certainly supporting my thesis that *śramaṇa* and *brāhmaṇa* were not intrinsically separate categories), I think this interpretation is made grammatically unlikely by the fact that, as we saw in the last chapter, Aśoka at one point does refer to the categories *śramaṇa* and *brāhmaṇa* separately as two *nikāyas*.
4. See, for example, Bailey and Mabbett, *Sociology of Early Buddhism*; Gombrich, *How Buddhism Began*; Gombrich, *What the Buddha Thought*; Freiberger, "Negative Campaigning"; Freiberger, "Ideal Sacrifice"; Norman, "Theravāda Buddhism and Brahmanical Hinduism."
5. K. R. Norman, "A note on *Attā* in the *Alagaddūpama Sutta*," *Studies in Indian Philosophy: A Memorial Volume in Honour of Pandit Sukhlaji Sanghvi, LD series* 84 (Ahmedabad, 1981), 19–29; Gombrich, *How Buddhism Began*, 31–34.
6. Bronkhorst, *Greater Magadha*.
7. See, for example, Brian Black, "Review of *Buddhism in the Shadow of Brahmanism*," *The Journal of Hindu Studies*, vol. 5, no. 2 (2012): 232–233; Richard Fynes, "Review of *Greater Magadha: Studies in the Culture of Early India*," *Journal of the Oxford Centre for Buddhist* Studies, vol. 1 (Oct. 2011): 212–215; Jason Neelis, "Review of *Greater Magadha: Studies in the Culture of Early India*," *Journal of the Royal Asiatic Society*, third series, vol. 18, no. 3 (Jul. 2008): 381–383.
8. Recently, Joseph Walser has published an article based on a statistical analysis of the correlation between Brahmans and doctrines such as *anattā* in Pali *suttas*. His statistical analysis supports Bronkhorst's earlier observation (which surprisingly Walser does not mention) that the teaching of *anattā* is not correlated with Brahman interlocutors. Walser, however, uses this fact to come to the somewhat different conclusion that there were different functional canons for Brahman Buddhists and non-Brahman Buddhists: Joseph Walser, "When did Buddhism Become Anti-Brahmanical? The Case of the Missing Soul," *Journal of the American Academy of Religion* 86, no. 1 (March 2018): 94–125.

9. There are some exceptions, such as *MN* 4, in which the Buddha speaks about various types of ascetics and Brahmans with the Brahman Jānussoṇi (a sort of "stock" Brahman found in many early Buddhist *sūtras*), and *MN* 150, in which the Buddha speaks on a similar topic with a group of "Brahman householders" (*brāhmaṇa-gahapatikā*) in the "Brahman village" (*brāhmaṇānaṃ gāmo*) of Nagaravinda in Kosala. One should also note that the fact that an interlocutor is identified as a *paribbājaka* does not preclude his being a Brahman (about which more below); I merely mean to point out that the more common way in which an interlocutor is identified in *suttas* involving discussions of *samaṇas* and *brāhmaṇas* is as a *paribbājaka*, rather than as a Brahman.
10. In this respect, the compound *samaṇa-brāhmaṇa* appears to replace the category of *samaṇa* alone as the foil against which to construct a Buddhist identity, as found in the *Aṭṭhaka Vagga* of the *Sutta Nipāta*.
11. This is another exception to the tendency for "teachings on wrong views" not to involve an interlocutor who is identified as a Brahman. In many ways, though, this *sutta* can be categorized as an encounter dialog that happens to make use of the compound *samaṇa-brāhmaṇa*. This is particularly interesting because the distinction between *samaṇa* and *brāhmaṇa* is practically inoperative in the use of this compound, even in the context of an encounter with a Brahman.
12. *santi kho, bho gotama, eke samaṇabrāhmaṇā diṭṭhadhammābhiññāvosānapārami ppattā, ādibrahmacariyaṃ paṭijānanti. tatra, bho gotama, ye te samaṇabrāhmaṇā diṭṭhadhammābhiññāvosānapāramippattā, ādibrahmacariyaṃ paṭijānanti, tesaṃ bhavaṃ gotamo katamo ti?*
13. *santi, bhāradvāja, eke samaṇabrāhmaṇā anussavikā. te anussavena diṭṭhadhammā bhiññāvosānapāramippattā, ādibrahmacariyaṃ paṭijānanti; seyyathāpi brāhmaṇā tevijjā.*
14. *santi pana, bhāradvāja, eke samaṇabrāhmaṇā kevalaṃ saddhāmattakena diṭṭhadh ammābhiññāvosānapāramippattā, ādibrahmacariyaṃ paṭijānanti; seyyathāpi takkī vīmaṃsī.*
15. *santi, bhāradvāja, eke samaṇabrāhmaṇā pubbe ananussutesu dhammesu sāmaṃyeva dhammaṃ abhiññāya diṭṭhadhammābhiññāvosānapāramippattā, ādibrahmacariyaṃ paṭijānanti.*
16. This expression most likely refers to Brahmans who are identified as such in encounter dialogs. The expression *tevijjā brāhmaṇā* is, in fact, used repeatedly in one such encounter dialog, the aptly named *Tevijja Sutta* (*DN* 13). In this *sutta*, the Buddha encounters two Brahmans, Vāseṭṭha and Bhāradvāja, and discusses with them the merits (or rather lack thereof) of the teachings of Brahmans of the Triple Veda. Although the expression is not used with such regularity in other encounter dialogs that address the teachings of Brahmans or the definition of Brahmanhood, such dialogs, including the *Saṅgārava Sutta* that we are discussing here, do often begin with a formula that identifies the Brahman interlocutor as "perfected in the Three Vedas" (*tiṇṇaṃ vedānaṃ pāragū*).

17. *tatra, bhāradvāja, ye te samaṇabrāhmaṇā pubbe ananussutesu dhammesu sāmaṃyeva dhammaṃ abhiññāya diṭṭhadhammābhiññāvosānapāramippattā, ādibrahmacariyaṃ paṭijānanti, tesāhamasmi.*
18. This account of the Bodhisatta leaving home and attaining enlightenment is also found, with only slight differences, in *MN* 36 and *MN* 85. The account begins with the Bodhisatta leaving home against his parents' wishes (they are described as weeping as he cuts off his black hair and puts on the ochre robe) and going to study first under Āḷāra Kālāma and then under Uddaka Rāmaputta. (This first part of the story is also found in the *Ariyapariyesana Sutta, MN* 26.) Then, he tries several different types of physical austerity, such as holding his breath and starving himself, but he ultimately decides that austerity will get him nowhere, giving four similes to illustrate why it is impossible to attain enlightenment when the body is weakened in such a way. Finally, he remembers a pleasant experience he had as a child meditating under a tree in his father's garden; he decides to replicate that experience; and ultimately he attains enlightenment (which is expressed here as attainment of the three knowledges, *tevijjā*) after attaining each of the four *rūpa-jhānas* in sequence.
19. A. L. Basham, *History and Doctrines of the Ājīvikas: A Vanished Indian Religion* (Delhi: Motilal Banarsidass, 2002[1951]), 17. An excellent, and to my mind definitive, explanation of the hitherto unclear *niyativāda* ascribed to Gosāla Maṅkhaliputta as the point over which he and Mahāvīra parted ways can be found in Bronkhorst, *Greater Magadha,* 38–51. Bronkhorst argues, in short, that the difference between Jains and the Ājīvikas on this point had to do with past karma: Mahāvīra and the Jains taught that non-action had the power to both prevent new karma from accumulating and burn off old karma, while Gosāla and the Ājīvikas held that it could only prevent new karma from accumulating; old karma must come to fruition on its own over the course of thousands of lifetimes until it finally burns off.
20. Cited in Bronkhorst, *Greater Magadha,* 48 n. 86. The teachings attributed to Pūraṇa Kāśyapa in this text, however, correspond to those of Ajita Kesakambalī in the *Sāmaññaphala Sutta*—although this latter teaching is, as we will see, quite similar.
21. Basham, *History and Doctrines of the Ājīvikas,* 17, 80–81. The text is the Tamil poem *Nīlakēci,* in which "Lord Pūraṇaṉ, without comparison in intelligence" (*pūraṇaṉ eṉpāṉ puruvara-k-kaṟṟavaṉ*: v. 668) is presented as the head of a monastery of Ājīvika monks at Kukkuṭanagara at the time of the Buddha.
22. Basham argues that Ajita, therefore, may be "a forerunner of the later Cārvākas"—Basham, *History and Doctrines of the Ājīvikas,* 17. Bronkhorst has a much different theory of the Cārvākas, one that identifies them not with a non-Vedic group (of which Ajita must be one, since his doctrine explicitly rejects the efficacy of sacrifice), but with the Brahmans themselves, who he argues largely

rejected the doctrines of karma and rebirth—Bronkhorst, *Greater Magadha*, 309–328.

23. Basham, *History and Doctrines of the Ājīvikas*, 17, 236–239, 262–266. The texts in which atomism is attributed to the Ājīvikas are the *Maṇimēkalai*, the *Nīlakēci*, and the *Civañāṉa-cittiyār*. In addition to atomism, the *Nīlakēci* attributes to the Ājīvikas a doctrine, similar to that of Pakudha, that the universe is static, referred to by the commentator on the text as *avicalita-nityatvam*.
24. Ironically, the much-reviled evasiveness of the "eel-wrigglers" is virtually indistinguishable from the rhetorical tactics taken in certain Buddhist texts, including Nāgārjuna and his Mādhyamika followers, but also the *Aṭṭhaka Vagga* of the *Sutta Nipāta*, which is likely one of the earliest Buddhist texts still extant.
25. *abhijānāsi no tvaṃ, mahārāja, imaṃ pañhaṃ aññe samaṇabrāhmaṇe pucchitā ti?*
26. A passage in the *Milindapañha* (1.5) uses similar words to introduce the six heretics, but omits the word *samaṇa-brāhmaṇā: evaṃ vutte pañcasatā yonakā rājānaṃ milindaṃ etadavocuṃ: atthi, mahārāja, cha satthāro pūraṇo kassapo makkhaligosālo nigaṇṭho nāṭaputto sañjayo belaṭṭhaputto ajito kesakambalo pakudho kaccāyano, te saṅghino gaṇino gaṇācariyakā ñātā yasassino titthakarā sādhusammatā bahujanassa, gaccha tvaṃ mahārāja, te pañhaṃ pucchassu, kaṅkhaṃ paṭivinayassū ti.* Two suttas (*MN* 77, *SN* 4.10.9) also use similar words to introduce the six heretics, but introduce them individually and therefore omit the collective term *samaṇa-brāhmaṇā*. Another two *suttas* (*MN* 36, *SN* 1.2.3.10) refers to the six heretics in ways (including, in the case of the latter, through verse) that break from the formula entirely.
27. *yeme, bho gotama, samaṇabrāhmaṇā saṅghino gaṇino gaṇācariyā ñātā yasassino titthakarā sādhusammatā bahujanassa, seyyathidaṃ — pūraṇo kassapo, makkhali gosālo, ajito kesakambalo, pakudho kaccāyano, sañcayo belaṭṭhaputto, nigaṇṭho nāṭaputto.*
28. Note that in these cases, one could interpret the meaning as being "some striving Brahmans," as discussed above. There is nothing in this particular lecture of the *Sūyagaḍaṃga* that forces an interpretation of *samaṇā* and *māhaṇā* as two categories linked by "and," although other lectures later in the *Sūyagaḍaṃga* do suggest the latter interpretation.
29. *Sn.* 1079: *ye kecime samaṇabrāhmaṇāse, (iccāyasmā nando) / diṭṭhassutenāpi vadanti suddhiṃ / sīlabbatenāpi vadanti suddhiṃ, anekarūpena vadanti suddhiṃ.*
30. The nominative plural in *–āse* is found frequently in the *Sutta Nipāta*; it is an eastern form ("Māgadhism") derived from the Vedic *–āsas*—K. R. Norman, trans., *The Group of Discourses (Sutta Nipāta)*, vol. 2 (Oxford: Pali Text Society, 1992), 134.
31. *nāriṃsu jātijaran ti.* I follow Norman in emending *nāriṃsu to nātāriṃsu*—Norman, *Group of Discourses*, vol. 2, 377n.1080.
32. *Sn.* 1082: *nāhaṃ sabbe samaṇabrāhmaṇāse, (nandāti bhagavā) / jātijarāya nivutāti brūmi / ye sīdha diṭṭhaṃva sutaṃ mutaṃ vā, sīlabbataṃ vāpi pahāya*

*sabbaṃ / anekarūpampi pahāya sabbaṃ, taṇhaṃ pariññāya anāsavāse / te ve narā oghatiṇṇāti brūmi.*

33. *MN* 41, 76, 110, 114, 117; *SN* 3.3.1.5, 4.8.13; *AN* 8.1.3.9, 10.4.2.10, 10.5.1.1.

34. *atthi dinnaṃ atthi yiṭṭhaṃ atthi hutaṃ, atthi sukatadukkaṭānaṃ kammānaṃ phalaṃ vipāko, atthi ayaṃ loko atthi paro loko, atthi mātā atthi pitā, atthi sattā opapātikā, atthi loke samaṇabrāhmaṇā sammaggatā sammāpaṭipannā ye imañca lokaṃ parañca lokaṃ sayaṃ abhiññā sacchikatvā pavedentī ti.*

35. *natthi dinnaṃ natthi yiṭṭhaṃ natthi hutaṃ, natthi sukatadukkaṭānaṃ kammānaṃ phalaṃ vipāko, natthi ayaṃ loko natthi paro loko, natthi mātā natthi pitā, natthi sattā opapātikā, natthi loke samaṇabrāhmaṇā sammaggatā sammāpaṭipannā ye imañca lokaṃ parañca lokaṃ sayaṃ abhiññā sacchikatvā pavedentī ti.*

36. Fourth Kālsī Rock-Edict, Fourth Jaugada and Dhauli Rock-Edicts. From the Kālsī version, which is the most complete: *atika[ṃ]taṃ a[ṃ]ta[la]ṃ bahuni vasa-satāni v[adh]it[e] vā pā[nā]laṃbhe vi[h]isā cā bhutānaṃ nātinā asaṃ[pa]ṭip[a]ti samana-b[aṃ]bhanānaṃ asampaṭipati. s[e] ajā devānaṃpiyasā piyadasine lājine dhaṃm[a]-cal[an]enā bheli-ghose aho dhaṃma-ghose* (Hultzsch, *Inscriptions of Aśoka*, 30; trans. by Hultzsch on p. 31).

37. Ninth Kālsī Rock-Edict, Eleventh Kālsī Rock-Edict, Ninth Dhauli and Jaugada Rock-Edicts. The translation is taken from the Kālsī version: *he[tā] iyaṃ dāsa-bhaṭakasi s[a]myāpaṭip[a]ti gulunā apaciti [p]ā[n]ān[aṃ] saṃyame s[a]man[a]-baṃbhanānaṃ dāne ese aṃne cā heḍise dhaṃma-magale nāmā* (Hultzsch, *Inscriptions of Aśoka*, 38; trans. by Hultzsch on p. 38).

38. Third Kāḷsī Rock-Edict, Third Dhauli and Jaugada Rock-Edicts. From the Kālsī version: *sādhu māta-pitisu sususā mita-saṃthuta-nātikyān[aṃ] cā baṃbhana-sama[nā]naṃ [cā] sādhu d[ā]ne pānānaṃ anālaṃbh[e] sādhu [a]pa-v[i]yātā [a]pa-[bha]ṃ[ḍa]t[ā] sādhu* (Hultzsch, *Inscriptions of Aśoka*, 29).

39. Eighth Kālsī Rock-Edict, Eighth Jaugada and Dhauli Rock-Edicts. From the Kālsī version: *[h]etā iyaṃ hoti samana-baṃbhanānaṃ dasane cā dāne ca vudh[ā] naṃ dasa[n]e c[a] hilaṃna[paṭi[v]idhāne cā [jā]napadasā [ja]n[a]sā das[a]ne dhaṃmanusathi cā dhama-palipuchā cā tatopa[yā]* (Hultzsch, *Inscriptions of Aśoka*, 36–37; trans. by Hultzsch on p. 37). In his Seventh Delhi-Tōprā Pillar-Edict, Aśoka boasts that through imitation of him, his people "have been made to progress and will (be made to) progress in obedience to mother and father, in obedience to elders, in courtesy to the aged, in courtesy to Brāhmaṇas and Śramaṇas, to the poor and distressed, (and) even to slaves and servants": *tena vaḍhitā ca vaḍhisaṃti ca mātā-pit[i]su sususāyā gulusu sususāyā vayo-mahālakānaṃ anupaṭīpatiyā bābhana-samanesu kapana-valākesu āva dāsa-bhaṭakesu saṃpaṭīpatiyā* (Hultzsch, *Inscriptions of Aśoka*, 133; trans. by Hultzsch on p. 136).

40. The Seventh Delhi-Tōprā Pillar edict refers to an order for *mahāmātras* to look over the affairs of *saṅgha* (referring to the Buddhists), the Brahmans, the Ājīvikas, and the Nigaṇṭhas (Jains): *saṃghaṭhasi pi me kaṭe ime viyāpaṭā hohaṃti ti hemeva bābhanesu ā[j]īvikesu pi me kaṭe ime viyāpaṭā hohaṃti ti nagaṃṭhesu pi me kaṭe ime*

*viyāpaṭā hohaṃti nānā-pāsaṃḍesu pi me [ka]ṭe ime viyāpaṭā hohaṃti ti paṭivisiṭhaṃ paṭīvisiṭhaṃ tesu tesu [te te mahā]mātā* (Hultzsch, *Inscriptions of Aśoka*, 132).

41. Bronkhorst, *Buddhism in the Shadow of Brahmanism*, 12–17.
42. This formula is found at *SN* 2.1.2.3, 2.1.2.4, 2.1.3.9, 2.1.8.1, 2.3.4.8, 2.3.4.10, 2.6.3.5, 3.1.5.8, 3.2.1.5, 4.2.3.7, 5.4.1.6, 5.4.1.7, 5.4.3.9, 5.4.3.10, 5.4.4.4, 5.4.4.5, 5.12.3.2: *ye ca kho keci, bhikkhave, samaṇā vā brāhmaṇā vā . . . pajānanti, . . ., te kho me, bhikkhave, samaṇā vā brāhmaṇā vā samaṇesu ceva samaṇasammatā brāhmaṇesu ca brāhmaṇasammatā; te ca panāyasmanto sāmaññatthañca brahmaññatthañca diṭṭheva dhamme sayaṃ abhiññā sacchikatvā upasampajja viharantī ti.* This usually follows a negative formula: *ye hi keci, bhikkhave, samaṇā vā brāhmaṇā vā . . . nappajānanti, . . ., na me te, bhikkhave, samaṇā vā brāhmaṇā vā samaṇesu vā samaṇasammatā brāhmaṇesu vā brāhmaṇasammatā; na ca pana te āyasmanto sāmaññatthaṃ vā brahmaññatthaṃ vā diṭṭheva dhamme sayaṃ abhiññā sacchikatvā upasampajja viharanti.* The same formula, including both the negative and the positive versions, is also found at *Iti.* 4.4.
43. *yato kho, kassapa, bhikkhu averaṃ abyāpajjaṃ mettacittaṃ bhāveti, āsavānañca khayā anāsavaṃ cetovimuttiṃ paññāvimuttiṃ diṭṭheva dhamme sayaṃ abhiññā sacchikatvā upasampajja viharati. ayaṃ vuccati, kassapa, bhikkhu samaṇo itipi brāhmaṇo itipi.*
44. *sakkā ca panetaṃ abhavissa kātuṃ gahapatinā vā gahapatiputtena vā antamaso kumbhadāsiyāpi.*
45. *pakati kho esā . . . lokasmiṃ dukkaraṃ sāmaññaṃ dukkaraṃ brahmaññan ti.*
46. This name, which literally means "*śramaṇas* who are sons of the Śākyan," was apparently adopted at some point to refer to Buddhist renunciants. It refers to Buddhist monks as metaphorical "sons" of the Buddha, the "Śākyan." A sort of institution of this designation is given in the *Aggañña Sutta* (*DN* 27), in which the Buddha says, "Vāseṭṭha, coming from various births, from various names, from various clans, from various families, you have gone forth from home into homelessness. When asked, 'Who are you?' answer, 'We are Sakyan ascetics (*samaṇā sakyaputtiyā*).'" In spite of this illustrious story of institution by the Buddha himself, the phrase *samaṇā sakyaputtiyā* is not common in the early *sūtra* literature; in the Pali Canon, it is found in fewer than a dozen places in the *Sutta Piṭaka* (*DN* 27, *DN* 29, *MN* 86, *SN* 3.7.10, *SN* 4.8.10, *AN* 5.209, *AN* 8.19, *Ud.* 4.8, *Ud.* 5.5). The situation is completely different in the Vinaya, however, where there is an explosion in the use of the phrase. This expression may also be a precursor to the expression *śākyabhikṣu* that has been studied by Schopen—Gregory Schopen, "Mahāyāna in Indian Inscriptions," in *Figments and Fragments of Mahāyāna Buddhism in India* (Honolulu: The University of Hawai'i Press, 2005[1979]), 223–244. In this article, Schopen argues that the term *śākyabhikṣu* (for monks) and the term *paramopāsaka* (for laypeople) are closely associated in the epigraphic record with the Mahāyāna.

47. *alajjino ime samaṇā sakyaputtiyā dussīlā pāpadhammā musāvādino abrahmacārino. ime hi nāma dhammacārino samacārino brahmacārino saccavādino sīlavanto kalyāṇadhammā paṭijānissanti. natthi imesaṃ sāmaññaṃ, natthi imesaṃ brahmaññaṃ. naṭṭhaṃ imesaṃ sāmaññaṃ, naṭṭhaṃ imesaṃ brahmaññaṃ. kuto imesaṃ sāmaññaṃ, kuto imesaṃ brahmaññaṃ? apagatā ime sāmaññā, apagatā ime brahmaññā. kathañhi nāma puriso purisakiccaṃ karitvā itthiṃ jīvitā voropessatī ti.*
48. Olivelle, *Āśrama System*, 9–11.
49. *TĀ* 2.7: *vātaraśanā ha vā ṛṣayaḥ śramaṇā ūrdhvamanthino.* Cited in Olivelle, *Āśrama System*, 12 n. 20.
50. Olivelle, *Āśrama System*, 14.
51. *BĀU* 4.3.22; cited in Olivelle, *Āśrama System*, 14.
52. *atra pitāpitā bhavati mātāmātā lokā alokā devā adevā vedā avedāḥ. atra steno'steno bhavati bhrūṇahābhrūṇahā cāṇḍālo'cāṇḍālaḥ paulkaso'paulkasaḥ śramaṇo'śramaṇas tāpaso'tāpasaḥ.*
53. Olivelle, *Āśrama System*, 15 n. 31.
54. Ibid., 16.
55. Ibid., 17.
56. Ibid., 19.

## CHAPTER 4

1. Since most early Jain and Buddhist texts are written with an assumed audience of male monastics, the word *Brahman* is usually used in the masculine gender when referring to the ideal person in those texts. I have found one example, however, where an enlightened Buddhist nun appears to use the word *Brahman* (still in the masculine) to refer to herself: *Therī*. 290.
2. Bronkhorst, *Buddhism in the Shadow of Brahmanism*, 65–74.
3. Gómez, "Proto-Mādhyamika," 146.
4. Ibid., 140, 141, 142, 147.
5. The correlation is close, but not exact. Of the seven *suttas* in Vetter's "core," four (*Suddhaṭṭhaka, Paramaṭṭhaka, Māgandiya, Mahābyūha*) refer to the ideal person as a Brahman. Only one other *sutta* outside the core (*Attadaṇḍa*) does so.
6. Vetter, "Older Parts of the Suttanipāta," 46.
7. Vetter, however, uses this observation to further his theory that the core of the *Aṭṭhaka* was written by a non-Buddhist group that was later incorporated into the Buddhist *saṅgha*. I do not see any need for such a hypothesis to explain the difference between the anti-*diṭṭhi* views of the *Aṭṭhaka* and the *sammā-diṭṭhi* views of the bulk of the Canon.
8. *Sn*. 790: *na brāhmaṇo aññato suddhimāha, diṭṭhe sute sīlavate mute vā / puññe ca pāpe ca anūpalitto, attañjaho nayidha pakubbamāno //.*
9. Gómez, "Proto-Mādhyamika," 141.

10. *Sn.* 795: *sīmātigo brāhmaṇo tassa natthi, ñatvā va disvā va samuggahītaṃ / na rāgarāgī na virāgaratto, tassīdha natthī paramuggahītanti //.*
11. *Sn.* 802–803: *tassīdha diṭṭhe va sute mute vā, pakappitā natthi aṇūpi saññā / taṃ brāhmaṇaṃ diṭṭhim anādiyānaṃ, kenīdha lokasmiṃ vikappayeyya // na kappayanti na purekkharonti, dhammāpi tesaṃ na paṭicchitāse / na brāhmaṇo sīlavatena neyyo, pāraṅgato na pacceti tādīti //.*
12. *Sn.* 907: *na brāhmaṇassa paraneyyam atthi, dhammesu niccheyya samuggahītaṃ / tasmā vivādāni upātivatto, na hi seṭṭhato passati dhammam aññaṃ //.*
13. *Sn.* 911: *na brāhmaṇo kappam upeti saṅkhaṃ, na diṭṭhisārī napi ñāṇabandhu / ñatvā ca so sammutiyo puthujjā, upekkhatī uggahaṇanti maññe //.* I am accepting the variant *saṅkhaṃ* here rather than *saṅkhā*, as found in some manuscripts.
14. *Sn.* 843: *saccan ti so brāhmaṇo kiṃ vadeyya, musā ti vā so vivadetha kena / yasmiṃ samaṃ visamaṃ vāpi natthi, sa kena vādaṃ paṭisaṃyujeyya //.*
15. *Sn.* 946: *saccā avokkamma muni, thale tiṭṭhati brāhmaṇo / sabbaṃ so paṭinissajja, sa ve santoti vuccati //.*
16. *Sn.* 947: *sa ve vidvā sa vedagū, ñatvā dhammaṃ anissito / sammā so loke iriyāno, na pihetīdha kassaci //.*
17. *ĀS* 1.3.2.3: *aṇannaṃ cara māhaṇe // se na chaṇe na chaṇāvae chaṇantaṃ nāṇujāṇae //*; trans. by Hermann Jacobi, *Gaina Sûtras*, vol. 1, *Sacred Books of the East*, vol. 22 (Oxford: Clarendon Press, 1884), 31.
18. Paul Dundas, *The Jains*, 2nd ed. (London: Routledge, 2002), 180.
19. *ĀS* 1.7.8.20: *aciraṃ paḍilehittā vihare ciṭṭha māhaṇe //*; trans. by Jacobi, *Gaina Sûtras*, vol. 1, 77.
20. *ĀS* 1.7.1.4: *māhaṇeṇa maīmayā // jāmā tiṇṇi udāhiyā*; trans. by Jacobi, *Gaina Sûtras*, vol. 1, 63.
21. *ĀS* 1.7.2.5: *dhammam āyāṇaha paveiyaṃ māhaṇeṇa maīmayā samaṇunne // samaṇunnassa asaṇaṃ vā . . . paraṃ // āḍhāyamīṇe tti bemi //*; trans. by Jacobi, *Gaina Sûtras*, vol. 1, 66.
22. *ĀS* 1.8.1.23, 1.8.2.16, 1.8.3.14, 1.8.4.17: *esa vihī aṇukkanto māhaṇeṇa maīmayā / bahuso apaḍinneṇaṃ bhagavayā evaṃ rīyante // tti bemi //*; trans. by Jacobi, *Gaina Sûtras*, vol. 1, 82, 84.
23. *ĀS* 1.8.2.10, 1.8.4.3: *rīyaī māhaṇe abahuvāī*; trans. by Jacobi, *Gaina Sûtras*, vol. 1, 83, 86.
24. *Sn.* 859: *yena naṃ vajjuṃ puthujjanā, atho samaṇabrāhmaṇā / taṃ tassa apurakkhataṃ, tasmā vādesu n'ejati //.*
25. *ĀS* 1.4.2.3: *āvantī key' āvantī logaṃsi samaṇā ya māhaṇā ya puḍho // vivāyaṃ vayanti: se diṭhaṃ ca ṇe, suyaṃ ca ṇe, mayaṃ ca ṇe, // vinnāyaṃ ca ṇe, // uḍḍhaṃ ahe yā tiriyaṃ disāsu // savvao supaḍilehiyaṃ ca ṇe: savve pāṇā savve bhūyā savve jīvā // savve sattā hantavvā ajjāveyavvā pariyāveyavvā parighettavvā uddaveyavvā //*; trans. by Jacobi, *Gaina Sûtras*, vol. 1, 38.
26. *ĀS* 1.8.4.11–12: *adu māhaṇaṃ va samaṇaṃ vā gāma-piṇḍolagaṃ va aihiṃ vā / sovāgamūsiyāriṃ vā kukkuraṃ vā vivihaṃ ṭhiyaṃ purao, // vitti-ccheyaṃ vajjanto*

*tes' appattiyaṃ pariharanto / mandaṃ parakkame bhagavaṃ, ahiṃsamāṇo ghāsam esitthā. //*; trans. by Jacobi, *Gaina Sûtras*, vol. 1, 87.

27. *Sn.* 1079–1081: *ye kecime samaṇabrāhmaṇāse / diṭṭhassutenāpi vadanti suddhiṃ / sīlabbatenāpi vadanti suddhiṃ, anekarūpena vadanti suddhiṃ.*
28. In most Pali texts, the nominative plural form of this compound is the standard *samaṇabrāhmaṇā*, but in the *Sutta Nipāta*, the non-standard form *samaṇabrāhmaṇāse* is used. See ch. 3 n. 27.
29. *Sn.* 1082: *nāhaṃ sabbe samaṇabrāhmaṇāse / jātijarāya nivutāti brūmi / ye sīdha diṭṭhaṃva sutaṃ mutaṃ vā, sīlabbataṃ vāpi pahāya sabbaṃ / anekarūpampi pahāya sabbaṃ, taṇhaṃ pariññāya anāsavāse / te ve narā oghatiṇṇāti brūmi //.*
30. *Sn.* 1043–1045: *khattiyā brāhmaṇā devatānaṃ yaññam akappayiṃsu puthūdha loke.*
31. Another example of sorts would be *Pārāyaṇa* 11, which uses the word *brāhmaṇa* only once (v. 1100), in the vocative, to refer to the Buddha's interlocutor. This vocative is a nod to the narrative frame of the *Pārāyaṇa*, at least as we have it today, in which the *sutta*s of the text are said to be short dialogs between the Buddha and each of 16 Brahmans who approached him to ask him questions about how to go to the "far shore of old age and death" (*jarāmaraṇassa pāraṃ*) from which the *Pārāyaṇa* ("Going to the Far Shore") gets its name. This narrative frame is supplied both by the introductory *vatthugāthās* (v. 976–1031) and by the first epilogue (v. 1124–1130 and the short prose section preceding them), which both identify the Buddha's 16 interlocutors as Brahmans, but are otherwise somewhat contradictory. The first of these—the introductory *vatthugāthās*—are not commented upon in the *Cūḷaniddesa* and therefore are likely a late addition. This, however, still leaves the first epilogue, as well as the vocative in the 11th dialog, which are commented upon therein. The issue of the narrative frame of the *Pārāyaṇa* is somewhat complex, so we will return to it later when we discuss the use of framing and commentary to (re)interpret older material. Suffice it for now to note that *brāhmaṇa* as a vocative to refer to the Buddha's interlocutor occurs only once in the dialogs of the *Pārāyaṇa* and is only made intelligible by the narrative framework, which we have good reason to believe is a late addition.
32. *Suyāg* 1.2.1.5: *ṭhāṇā te vi cayanti dukkhiyā*; trans. by Jacobi, *Gaina Sûtras*, vol. 2, 250.
33. *Sn.* 1063: *passāmahaṃ devamanussaloke, akiñcanaṃ brāhmaṇamiriyamānaṃ / taṃ taṃ namassāmi samantacakkhu, pamuñca maṃ sakka kathaṃkathāhi //.*
34. *Sn.* 1065: *anusāsa brahme karuṇāyamāno, vivekadhammaṃ yam ahaṃ vijaññaṃ / yathāhaṃ ākāsova abyāpajjamāno, idheva santo asito careyyaṃ //.*
35. *Sn.* 1059: *yaṃ brāhmaṇaṃ vedagum ābhijaññā, akiñcanaṃ kāmabhave asattaṃ / addhā hi so ogham imaṃ atāri, tiṇṇo ca pāraṃ akhilo akaṅkho //.*
36. Norman lists the word *veda* as one of the "terms taken over by the Buddha but used with new senses," and under that entry, he writes, "The word *vedagu* [*sic*], which in its Brahmanical sense meant one who had gained competence in the *Vedas*, was interpreted as one who had gained knowledge of release from *saṃsāra*"—"Theravāda Buddhism and Brahmanical Hinduism," 198. It is not

clear, however, what exactly Norman means by "its Brahmanical sense," since there is little evidence that people learned in the Vedas were ever referred to as *vedagū*. This form, in fact, with the nominative singular in *–ū*, is not even found in Sanskrit. The *Paramatthajotikā II* (330.27; cited by Norman, *Group of Discourses,* 208 n. 322) takes the suffix as coming from the root *gam*, but Norman argues that the Pali form actually comes from an original Sanskrit *vedaka*, where the *k* in the suffix changed to *g* and then the word as a whole transferred from the *–a* to the *–ū* declension, both of which changes are otherwise attested—Norman, *Group of Discourses,* 208 n. 322, 208 n. 319, 181 n. 167. To my knowledge, however, neither putative Sanskrit original—*vedaga* or *vedaka*—was ever used to refer to someone versed in the Vedas. (*Vedaka* is attested, but instead with the meaning of "announcing" or "proclaiming"—Böhtlingk and Roth, *Sanskrit-Wörterbuch,* v. 6, 1358.) Since *veda* is a perfectly ordinary Indo-Aryan word, derived from the root *vid*, for "knowledge," I see no a priori reason to assume that is was "taken over" from "Brahmanism" and given a "new sense." The sense with which it is used in the *Aṭṭhaka* and *Pārāyaṇa* is, in fact, its most literal and therefore presumably original sense—"knowledge."

37. *Sn.* 1115: *ākiñcaññasambhavaṃ ñatvā, nandī saṃyojanaṃ iti / evam etaṃ abhiññāya, tato tattha vipassati / etaṃ ñāṇaṃ tathaṃ tassa, brāhmaṇassa vusīmato //.*
38. Wynne, *Origin of Buddhist Meditation*, 103–106.
39. *Sūyag.* 1.9.1: *kayare dhamma akkhāe māhaṇeṇa maīmayā /*; trans. by Jacobi, *Gaina Sûtras*, vol. 2, 301. The first hemistich of *Sūyag.* 1.11.1 is nearly identical except for replacing *dhamma* with *magga: kayare magga akkhāe māhaṇeṇaṃ maīmayā /.*
40. *Sūyag.* 1.2.1.15: *sauṇī jaha paṃsuguṇḍiyā vihuṇiya dhaṃsayaī siyaṃ rayaṃ / evaṃ daviovahāṇavaṃ kammaṃ khavai tavassi māhaṇe //*; trans. by Jacobi, *Gaina Sûtras*, vol. 2, 252.
41. Jacobi, *Gaina Sûtras*, vol. 2, 252 n.1.
42. Norman, "Theravāda Buddhism and Brahmanical Hinduism," 194–195.
43. *yāvajīvaṃ brahmacārī assaṃ, na methunaṃ dhammaṃ paṭiseveyyaṃ.*
44. *DN* 2: *abrahmacariyaṃ pahāya brahmacārī hoti ārācārī virato methunā gāmadhammā.* The same formula, or some variation thereof, is also found at *DN* 1; *MN* 27, 38, 51, 94, 101, 112; *AN* 3.71, 4.198, 5.180, 6.44, 8.41, 10.75, 10.99.
45. *SN* 4.1.19.4; *AN* 3.13, 3.27, 3.114, 4.243, 8.19, 8.20; *Ud.* 5.5; *It.* 2.2.11: *abrahmacārī brahmacāripaṭiñño.*
46. *DN* 21; *MN* 37; *SN* 3.1.1.4; *AN* 3.144–6, 7.61, 11.10.
47. *DN* 29; *MN* 8, 73, 81, 84, 99; *SN* 4.1.19.4; *AN* 3.13, 3.27, 3.62, 3.114, 4.243, 5.286, 5.293; *Ud.* 4.8.
48. Jacobi, *Gaina Sûtras*, vol. 2, 73.
49. Jacobi, *Gaina Sûtras*, vol. 2, 74–75.
50. *ĀS* 1.4.4.2, 1.5.2.4, 1.6.2.1, 1.6.4.1; *Sūyag.* 1.1.3.13, 1.3.1.13, 1.6.23, 1.14.1.

51. *ĀS* 1.6.2.1: *āuraṃ logam āyāe caittā puvva-saṃjogaṃ hiccā uvasamaṃ vasittā bambhaceraṃsi vasu vā aṇuvasu vā jāṇittu dhammaṃ ahā-tahā ah' ege tam accāī kusīlā vatthaṃ paḍiggahaṃ kambalaṃ pāya-puñchaṇaṃ viosijjā aṇupuvveṇa aṇahiyāsemāṇā parīsahe durahiyāsae*; trans. by Jacobi, *Gaina Sûtras*, vol. 1, 55. In his translation, Jacobi translates *bambhacera* with "chastity," as he does in almost all cases; I have replaced this with the original word here to let the context inform our interpretation of it.
52. *Sūyag.* 1.14.1: *ganthaṃ vihāya iha sikkhamāṇo uṭhāya subambhaceraṃ vasejjā / ovāyakārī viṇayaṃ susikkhe je cheya se vippamāyaṃ na kujjā //.*
53. *DN* 16, 29, 33, 34; *MN* 2, 5, 6, 15, 16, 18, 24, 26, 31, 36, 48, 61, 65, 67, 69, 77, 85–86, 88, 90, 100, 104, 124, 128, 133, 138, 141; *SN* 1.4.3.2, 2.5.8, 3.1.9.3, 3.1.9.8, 4.1.12.3, 4.1.12.4, 5.3.2.3–4; *AN* 2.33–42, 3.40, 4.87, 4.97, 4.111, 4.122, 5.21–22, 5.26, 5.31, 5.53, 5.65–6, 5.76, 5.81–7, 5.104–105, 5.135, 5.163–4, 5.166, 5.167, 5.205, 5.211, 5.232, 5.249, 6.11–12, 6.44–5, 6.54, 6.58, 6.60, 7.1–2, 7.23, 7.73, 8.2–4, 8.13, 8.62, 8.78, 9.4, 9.11, 9.71, 10.11, 10.14, 10.17–18, 10.23, 10.44, 10.48, 10.50, 10.71, 10.83, 10.87–88, 10.96, 10.115–116, 10.172, 11.6, 11.14; *Ud.* 1.10, 4.9; *Sn.* 4.16; *Ther.* 4.3, 6.3, 18.
54. Cited by Alexander Wynne, *The Origin of Buddhist Meditation* (London: Routledge, 2007), 13. For an account of the Bodhisattva's discipleship under first Āḷāra Kālāma and then Uddaka Rāmaputta, see, e.g., the *Ariyapariyesana Sutta* (*MN* 26).
55. *DN* 6: *etehi cepi, cunda, aṅgehi samannāgataṃ brahmacariyaṃ hoti, no ca kho satthā hoti thero rattaññū cirapabbajito addhagato vayoanuppatto. evaṃ taṃ brahmacariyaṃ aparipūraṃ hoti tenaṅgena. yato ca kho, cunda, etehi ceva aṅgehi samannāgataṃ brahmacariyaṃ hoti, satthā ca hoti thero rattaññū cirapabbajito addhagato vayoanuppatto. evaṃ taṃ brahmacariyaṃ paripūraṃ hoti tenaṅgena.*
56. Interestingly, the permutations for listing various types of lay disciples includes both those who are *brahmacārī* and those who are *abrahmacārī*—which terms must in this case refer to celibacy or non-celibacy.
57. *iddhañceva phītañca vitthārikaṃ bāhujaññaṃ puthubhūtaṃ yāva devamanussehi suppakāsitaṃ, . . . lābhaggayasaggappattaṃ.*
58. *Vin.* I.45, I.60.
59. Dundas, *The Jains*, 181.
60. In the first book each of the *Āyāraṅga* and *Sūyagaḍaṃga*, we find the specific word *satthāra* used three times: *ĀS* 1.6.4.1; *Sūyag.* 1.13.2, 1.14.26.
61. Olivelle, *Āśrama System.*
62. Buddhist ordination consists of (in Pali) *pabbajjā*, which makes one a novice or *sāmaṇera*, and *upasampadā*, which makes one a fully ordained *bhikkhu*. While Jain ordination is ordinarily referred to as *dīkṣā*, "the classical texts use the expressions 'going forth' (*pravrajyā*) and 'ordination' (*upasthāpanā*) to describe the separate stages involved"—Dundas, *The Jains*, 156.
63. Ibid.

64. Olivelle, *Āśrama System*, 28–29.
65. *RV* 10.109.5: *brahmacārī carati veviṣad viṣaḥ sa devānām bhavaty ekam aṅgam / tena jāyām anv avindad bṛhaspatiḥ somena nītāṃ juhvaṃ na devāḥ //.*
66. Wendy Doniger O'Flaherty, trans., *The Rig Veda* (London: Penguin Books, 1981), 275.
67. This somewhat unusual form is a participle of the root *viṣ*, which is a reduplicating verb of the third *gaṇa*—Arthur Anthony Macdonell, *A Vedic Grammar for Students* (Delhi: Motilal Banarsidass, 1993), 419.
68. *TS* 3.1.9.4: *mánuḥ putrébhyo dāyáṃ vy àbhajat sá nā́bhānédiṣṭham brahmacáryaṃ vásantaṃ nír abhajat.* The same story is also related at *AB* 22.9—cited by Pandurang Vaman Kane, *History of Dharmaśāstra*, vol. 2, part 1 (Poona: Bhandarkar Oriental Research Institute, 1974), 271 n. 624.
69. *TS* 6.3.10.5: *jā́yamāno vái brāhmaṇás tribhír ṛṇavā́ jāyate brahmacáryeṇā́rṣibhyo yajñéna devébhyaḥ prajáyā pitṛ́bhya eṣá vā́ anṛṇó yáḥ putrī́ yájvā brahmacārivāsī́.*
70. For a discussion of the history of the "theology of debts" in Brahmanical thought, see Olivelle, *Āśrama System*, 46–53. See also Charles Malamoud, "Théologie de la dette dans les Brāhmaṇa," *Puruṣārtha: Science Sociales en Asie du Sud* 4 (1980): 39–62; cited in Olivelle, *Āśrama System*, 47 n. 53.
71. This passage does seem to imply that Brahmans are born as such, but even this is unclear, since the "birth" referred to could be the second birth of initiation that makes one a Brahman.
72. *AVŚ* 7.109.7: *devā́n yán nāthitó huvé brahmacáryaṃ yád ūṣimá / akṣā́n yád babhrū́n ālábhe té no mṛḍantv īdṛ́śe //.*
73. *AVŚ* 6.108.2: *medhā́m aháṃ prathamā́ṃ bráhmaṇvatīṃ bráhmajūtām ṛ́ṣiṣṭutām / prápītāṃ brahmacāríbhir devā́nām ávase huve //.* (Whitney translates *prapītāṃ* as "drunk of," thus having the *brahmacārins* "drink" *brahman*, but he notes that the form is doubtful, and that the *Paippalāda* version has instead *praṇihitāṃ*, which would mean something more like "applied.") *AVŚ* 19.19.8: *bráhma brahmacāríbhir úd akrāmat tā́ṃ púraṃ prá ṇayāmi vaḥ / tā́m ā́ viśata tā́ṃ prá viśata sā́ vaḥ śárma ca várma ca yachatu //.*
74. *AVŚ* 6.133.3: *mṛtyór aháṃ brahmacārī́ yád ásmi niryā́can bhūtā́t púruṣaṃ yamā́ya / tám aháṃ bráhmaṇā tápasā śrámeṇānáyainaṃ mékhalayā sināmi.*
75. *AVŚ* 11.5:

*brahmacārī́ṣṇáṃś carati ródasī ubhé tásmin devā́ḥ sáṃmanaso bhavanti /*
*sá dādhāra pṛthivī́ṃ dívaṃ ca sá ācāryàṃ tápasā piparti //* (1)
*brahmacāríṇaṃ pitáro devajanā́ḥ pṛ́thag devā́ anusáṃyanti sárve /*
*gandharvā́ enam ánv āyan tráyastriṃśat triśatā́ḥ ṣaṭsahasrā́ḥ sárvānt sá devā́ṃs tápasā piparti //* (2)
*ācāryà upanáyamāno brahmacāríṇaṃ kṛṇute gárbham antáḥ /*
*táṃ rā́trīs tisrá udáre bibharti táṃ jātáṃ drá́ṣṭum abhisáṃyanti devā́ḥ //* (3)
*iyáṃ samít pṛthivī́ dyáur dvitī́yotā́ntárikṣaṃ samídhā pṛṇāti /*

*brahmacārī́ samídhā mékhalayā śrámeṇa lokā́ṃs tápasā piparti* // (4)
*pū́rvo jātó bráhmaṇo brahmacārī́ gharmáṃ vásānas tápasód atiṣṭhat* /
*tásmāj jātáṃ brā́hmaṇaṃ bráhma jyeṣṭháṃ devā́ś ca sárve amŕ̥tena sākám* // (5)
*brahmacāry èti samídhā sámiddhaḥ kā́rṣṇaṃ vásāno dīkṣitó dīrgháśmaśruḥ* /
*sá sadyá eti pū́rvasmād úttaraṃ samudráṃ lokā́nt saṃgŕ̥bhya múhur ācárikrat* // (6)
*brahmacārī́ janáyan bráhmāpó lokáṃ prajā́patiṃ parameṣṭhínaṃ virā́jam* /
*gárbho bhūtvā́mŕ̥tasya yónāv índro ha bhūtvā́surāṃs tatarha* // (7)
*ācāryàs tatakṣa nábhasī ubhé imé urvī́ gambhīré pr̥thivī́ṃ dívaṃ ca* /
*té rakṣati tápasā brahmacārī́ tásmin devā́ḥ sáṃmanaso bhavanti* // (8)
*imā́ṃ bhū́miṃ pr̥thivī́ṃ brahmacārī́ bhikṣā́m ā́ jabhāra prathamó dívaṃ ca* /
*té kr̥tvā́ samídhāv úpāste táyor ā́rpitā bhúvanāni víśvā* // (9)
*arvā́g anyáḥ paró anyó divás pr̥ṣṭhā́d gúhā nidhī́ níhitau brā́hmaṇasya* /
*táu rakṣati tápasā brahmacārī́ tát kévalaṃ kr̥ṇute bráhma vidvā́n* // (10)
*arvā́g anyá itó anyáḥ pr̥thivyā́ agnī́ saméto nábhasī antarémé* /
*táyoḥ śrayante raśmáyó 'dhi dr̥ḍhā́s tā́n ā́ tiṣṭhati tápasā brahmacārī́* // (11)
*abhikrándan stanáyann aruṇáḥ śitiṅgó br̥hác chépó 'nu bhū́mau jabhā́ra* /
*brahmacārī́ siñcati sā́nau rétaḥ pr̥thivyā́ṃ téna jīvanti pradíśaś cátasraḥ* // (12)
*agnáu sū́rye candrámasi mātaríśvan brahmacāry àpsú samídham ā́ dadhāti* /
*tā́sām arcī́ṃṣi pŕ̥thag abhré caranti tā́sām ā́jyaṃ púruṣo varṣám ā́paḥ* // (13)
*ācāryò mr̥tyúr váruṇaḥ sóma óṣadhayaḥ páyaḥ* /
*jīmū́tā āsant sátvānas táir idáṃ svàr ā́bhr̥tam* // (14)
*amā́ ghr̥táṃ kr̥ṇute kévalam ācāryò bhūtvā́ váruṇaḥ* /
*yádyad áichat prajā́patau tád brahmacārī́ prā́yachat svā́n mitró ádhy ātmánaḥ* // (15)
*ācāryò brahmacārī́ brahmacārī́ prajā́patiḥ* /
*prajā́patir ví rājati virā́ḍ índro 'bhavad vaśī́* // (16)
*brahmacáryeṇa tápasā rā́jā rāṣṭráṃ ví rakṣati* /
*ācāryò brahmacáryeṇa brahmacāríṇam ichate* // (17)
*brahmacáryeṇa kanyā̀ yúvānaṃ vindate pátim* /
*anaḍvā́n brahmacáryeṇā́śvo ghāsáṃ jigīṣati* // (18)
*brahmacáryeṇa tápasā devā́ mr̥tyúm ápāghnata* /
*índro ha brahmacáryeṇa devébhyaḥ svàr ā́bharat* // (19)
*óṣadhayo bhūtabhavyám ahorātré vánaspátiḥ* /
*saṃvatsaráḥ sahá r̥túbhis té jātā́ brahmacāríṇaḥ* // (20)
*pā́rthivā divyā́ḥ paśáva āraṇyā́ grāmyā́ś ca yé* /
*apakṣā́ḥ pakṣíṇaś ca yé té jātā́ brahmacāríṇaḥ* // (21)
*pŕ̥thak sárve prājāpatyā́ḥ prāṇā́n ātmásu bibhrati* /
*tā́nt sárvān bráhma rakṣati brahmacāríṇy ā́bhr̥tam* // (22)
*devā́nām etát pariṣūtám ánabhyārūḍhaṃ carati rócamānam* /
*tásmāj jātáṃ brā́hmaṇaṃ bráhma jyeṣṭháṃ devā́ś ca sárve amŕ̥tena sākám* // (23)
*bráhma bhrā́jad bibharti tásmin devā́ ádhi víśve samótāḥ* /
*prāṇāpānáu janáyann ā́d vyānáṃ vā́caṃ máno hŕ̥dayaṃ bráhma medhā́m* // (24)

*cákṣuḥ śrótraṃ yáśo asmā́su dhehy ánnaṃ réto lóhitam udáram* // (25)
*tā́ni kálpan brahmacārī́ salilásya pṛṣṭhé tápo 'tiṣṭhat tapyámānaḥ samudré* /
*sá snātó babhrúḥ piṅgaláḥ pṛthivyā́ṃ bahú rocate* // (26)

76. I am taking *brāhmaṇa* here as an adjective meaning "relating to the *brāhmaṇa* (noun)."
77. *Vin.* I.44–50 and I.60–61 describe, with great detail and in identical terms, the many ways that a new monk (i.e., ordained for less than 10 years) should behave toward his *upajjhāya* and *ācariya.* His duties essentially entail serving as a personal assistant, even a servant, for the more senior monk. On the use of these terms in the Brahmanical and Buddhist traditions, see Gishō Nakano and N.A. Jayawickrama, "Ācārya," in *Encyclopedia of Buddhism*, ed. G.P. Malalasekera, vol. 1 (Government of Ceylon, 1961), 163–168.
78. Lubin, "Boundaries," 85.
79. *ŚB* 11.5.4.6: *saṃvatsarasammitā vai garbhāḥ prajāyante.*
80. *ŚB* 11.5.4.12: *tadapi ślokaṃ gāyanti ācāryo garbhī bhavati hastam ādhāya dakṣiṇam / tṛtīyasyāṃ sa jāyate sāvitryā saha brāhmaṇa // iti.* The verse continues by saying that a Brahman should nevertheless be taught the *sāvitrī* at once because the Brahman is "related to Agni" and Agni is born at once: *sadyo ha tvāva brāhmaṇāyānubrūyād āgneyo vai brāhmaṇaḥ sadyo vā agnir jāyate tasmāt sadya eva brāhmaṇāyānubrūyāt.* The import of this admonition, which clearly contradicts the *śloka,* is unclear. Perhaps it reflects a later time when Brahmanhood is conceived of as deriving from (natural) birth, and thus the gestational period after *upanayana* was considered unnecessary.
81. Lubin, "Boundaries," 84–88.
82. *ŚB* 11.3.3.7: *na ha vai snātvā bhikṣeta apa ha vai snātvā bhikṣāṃ jayaty apa.*
83. Citations found in Kane, *History of Dharmaśāstra,* vol. 2., part 1, 271–274.
84. *ChU* 2.23.1: *atyantam ātmānam ācāryakule 'vasādayan.*
85. From an emic perspective, on the other hand, one can of course define "Brahmanism" however one wants. We will see in the next chapter that the Dharma Sūtra authors articulated a "Brahmanism" that did exclude lifestyles of lifelong celibacy.
86. It appears that some forest dwellers were celibate, while others were former householders who brought their families with them when they moved into the forest. This is seen most clearly in Āpastambha, who begins his description of the *vānaprastha* by explicitly saying that he should remain celibate (2.21.19). Later, however, he says that some teach that a person wanting to become a *vānapratha* should first get married and live a normal householder life, and only then move into the forest, with his family if he so wishes (2.22.6–9). The other three Dharma Sūtra authors do not give these two separate options, nor do they explicitly state whether the *vānaprastha* should be celibate or not. Nevertheless, as we will see in the next chapter, celibacy is implied by the hostility they all show to all of the *āśramas* other than that of the householder (*gṛhastha*). On the two options for the *vānaprastha* given by Āpastambha, cf. Johannes Bronkhorst, *The Two Sources*

*of Indian Asceticism*, 2nd ed. (Delhi: Motilal Banarsidass, 1998). I do not think it is necessary, as Bronkhorst argues, to see the two options Āpastambha gives for the *vānaprastha* as anything other than that—two options—but rather as two different types of ascetics, one Vedic and the other non-Vedic.

87. This is the term used by Āpastamba, Baudhāyana, and Vasiṣṭha. Gautama, however, uses the term *vaikhānasa*.
88. A key contribution to our understanding of the formation of Buddhist identity vis-à-vis other renunciant groups has been made by Claire Maes, "Dialogues With(in) the Pāli Vinaya: A Research into the Dynamics and Dialectics of the Pāli Vinaya's Ascetic Others, with a Special Focus on the Jain Other," (unpublished PhD diss., Universiteit Ghent, 2015). Unfortunately, I gained access to this dissertation too late to engage with it substantively in this book. Its publication as a book is much to be anticipated.
89. Bronkhorst, *Greater Magadha*, 91.
90. As we have already seen, Megasthenes refers to one of the two types of *Σαρμᾶνης* as *ὑλόβιοι*, "forest dwellers," which is an exact translation of *vānaprastha*. Megasthenes says that the *ὑλόβιοι* are the "most honourable" of the *Σαρμᾶνης* (Strabo, *Geography*, 15.60; trans. McCrindle, *Ancient India as Described in Classical Literature*, 67), which would imply that his local informants were in some way partial to the *vānaprastha* over and against the *parivrājakas* (which is what Megasthenes refers to as "physicians": see Ch. 5). It is interesting to note that Megasthenes also reports that "[t]he Brachmânes are held in the higher estimation [over the Garmânes—i.e., *śramaṇas*], for they agree more exactly in their opinions" (Strabo, *Geography*, 15.59; trans. McCrindle, *Ancient India as Described in Classical Literature*, 65). This would indicate that his informants were Brahmans. Taken together, these data support the conclusion that the *vānaprastha* had a special link to the (Vedic) Brahmanical tradition, which is paralleled by the link that the *jaṭila*s have to the Brahmans in the Pali Canon.
91. The actual "Jātaka tales" written in prose are found in the commentary and are not, strictly speaking, canonical. The canonical text of the *Jātaka* consists solely of the verses that are embedded in these stories.
92. *Jāt.* 89, 138, 277, 283, 313, 325, 344, 438, 454, 492, 505, 522, 532.
93. *ĀDhS* 2.22.1–3; *GDhS* 3.26, 34; *BDhS* 2.11.15; *VDhS* 9.1, 3.
94. *BDhS* 2.11.15: *baiṣkam apy upayuñjīta*.
95. *Jāt.* 505: *ayaṃ kūṭajaṭilo attano samaṇadhammaṃ akatvā paṇṇikakammaṃ karotī ti*.
96. *GDhS* 3.32, *BDhS* 2.11.15, *VDhS* 9.3.
97. Note that all four of the Dharma Sūtras state specifically that the *vānaprastha* should welcome guests: *ĀDhS* 2.22.17, *GDhS* 3.30, *BDhS* 2.11.15, *VDhS* 9.7. Vasiṣṭha even says specifically that he should "honor a guest who has come to his *āśrama* with almsfood of roots and fruits": *mūlaphalabhaikṣeṇāśramāgatam atithim abhyarcayet*.
98. *are duṭṭhajaṭila, tvaṃ rattiṃ corikaṃ katvā divā tāpasarūpena carasī ti*.

99. *Vin.* I.71.

100. The performance of ritual bathing is corroborated by Baudhāyana and Vasiṣṭha, both of whom describe the *vānaprastha* as performing ablutions at dawn, noon, and dusk (*BDhS* 2.11.15: *savaneṣūdakam upaspṛśañ; VDhS* 9.9: *triṣavaṇam udakopasparśī*). Likewise, Āpastamba says that the *vānaprastha* should bathe before offering oblations to his sacred fire (*ĀDhS* 2.22.12–14).

101. *Ud.* 1.9: *gayāyaṃ ummujjantipi nimujjantipi, ummujjanimujjampi karonti osiñcantipi, aggimpi juhanti*; emphasis mine.

102. *ĀDhS* 2.21.21, *GDhS* 3.27, *BDhS* 2.11.15, *VDhS* 9.10.

103. Gombrich has provided an insightful analysis of this sermon in the context of other metaphorical references to fire in the Pali Canon in *How Buddhism Began*, 65–72. Gombrich argues that the number of fires mentioned in this sermon is three (*rāga, dosa, moha*) because "the Buddha" is alluding to the three sacred fires of a Brahmanical householder. In support of this statement, Gombrich refers to *AN* 6.44, in which these three fires (which are to be avoided) are juxtaposed with the three fires of the householder (which are reinterpreted as referring to parents, dependents, and *samaṇabrāhmaṇā* and therefore worthy of veneration)—on which see also Gombrich, "Recovering the Buddha's Message," 17–20. I would argue that Gombrich's hermeneutic of polemic does work well for interpreting an isolated narrative such as the story of the conversion of the three Kassapas discussed here. As I have argued, this story appears to polemicize against the *jaṭila* practice of fire worship both by demonstrating the Buddha's superiority with respect to fire and by devaluing fire itself. I am less convinced by Gombrich's attempt to tie together numerous apparently fire-related metaphors scattered throughout the early Buddhist texts and attribute them to a singular polemic against "Brahmanism" conceived of by "the Buddha." The polemic found in the story of the conversion of the Kassapas is directed against *jaṭilas*, not Brahmanism broadly construed, and as such, it plays with the concept of "fire" in general, not the *āhavanīya, gārhapatya,* and *dakṣiṇāgni* specifically, as does *AN* 6.44 in the context of an encounter with a Brahman who is preparing a Vedic sacrifice. Absolutely nothing is made of the fact that *rāga, dosa,* and *moha* are three in number in the Fire Sermon, only of the fact that they are fires; indeed, it would make little sense to compare *rāga, dosa,* and *moha* to the three fires of the householder in the context of a polemic against *jaṭilas*/*vānaprasthas*, given that *vānaprasthas* were *not* householders and, according to the Dharma Sūtras, tended to only a single fire. Likewise, while Gombrich draws a connection between the negative portrayal of fire in the Fire Sermon and the concept of *nibbāna* (Skt. *nirvāṇa*), which literally means "blowing out," no such connection is made by the text itself. In fact, the word *nibbāna* is not used at all in the sermon, even though the 1,000 former *jaṭilas* attain Awakening at the

end. Virtually every metaphor for Awakening *except* "blowing out" (*nibbāna*) is used—knowledge (*ñāṇaṃ*), liberation (*vimutti*), dispassion (*virāga*), freedom from the "effluents" (*āsava*)—but not *nibbāna* itself.

104. *Vin.* I.25.

105. The other version, found at *Vin.* I.245–246, is essentially the same as the "frame story" for the *Sela Sutta*, in which Keṇiya meets the Buddha and feeds him and his entourage of monks, but without the embedded account about the Brahman Sela. Even though Sela makes no appearance in this version, however, the Buddha still initially objects to Keṇiya feeding him on the grounds that he is "devoted to the Brahmans."

106. A particular formula is used here to describe the "good reputation" (*kalyāṇo kittisaddo*) of Gotama that is characteristic of encounter dialogs with Brahmans, of which the *Sela Sutta* is a somewhat idiosyncratic example.

107. This is, again, a characteristic formula found in encounter dialogs, to be discussed in more detail in Chapter 6.

108. *tena kho pana samayena keṇiyo jaṭilo sele brāhmaṇe abhippasanno hoti.*

109. *ete kiriyaṃ na paṭibāhanti, atthi kammaṃ, atthi kammavipāko ti evaṃdiṭṭhikā.* The word *paṭibāhanti* here is somewhat ambigious. Does it mean "ward off," in the sense of avoiding engaging in causative action, or does it mean "reject," as in a philosophical position? The latter makes more sense in the immediate context of this sentence—it would imply that the people in question reject the theory of karma—but the former makes more sense as a description of what we know of Jain and Ājīvika soteriological theory. Perhaps this ambiguity is intentional—intended, that is, to blur the distinction between the Jains' and Ājīvikas' actual position and the accusation that they do not believe in karma at all.

110. *pūraṇena, bhante, kassapena chaḷabhijātiyo paññattā — kaṇhābhijāti paññattā, nīlābhijāti paññattā, lohitābhijāti paññattā, haliddābhijāti paññattā, sukkābhijāti paññattā, paramasukkābhijāti paññattā.*

*tatridaṃ, bhante, pūraṇena kassapena kaṇhābhijāti paññattā, orabbhikā sūkarikā sākuṇikā māgavikā luddā macchaghātakā corā coraghātakā bandhanāgārikā ye vā panaññepi keci kurūrakammantā.*

*tatridaṃ, bhante, pūraṇena kassapena nīlābhijāti paññattā, bhikkhū kaṇṭakavuttikā ye vā panaññepi keci kammavādā kriyavādā.*

*tatridaṃ, bhante, pūraṇena kassapena lohitābhijāti paññattā, nigaṇṭhā ekasāṭakā.*

*tatridaṃ, bhante, pūraṇena kassapena haliddābhijāti paññattā, gihī odātavasanā acelakasāvakā.*

*tatridaṃ, bhante, pūraṇena kassapena sukkābhijāti paññattā, ājīvakā ājīvakiniyo.*

*tatridaṃ, bhante, pūraṇena kassapena paramasukkābhijāti paññattā, nando vaccho kiso saṃkicco makkhali gosālo.*

*pūraṇena, bhante, kassapena imā chaḷabhijātiyo paññattā ti.*

111. *DN* 4, 5: *samaṇo khalu, bho, gotamo kammavādī kiriyavādī apāpapurekkhāro brahmaññāya pajāya.*
112. *natthi mahārāja hetu natthi paccayo sattānaṃ saṃkilesāya, ahetū apaccayā sattā saṃkilissanti.*
113. Bronkhorst, *Greater Magadha*, 38–51.
114. *purimāni, bho gotama, divasāni purimatarāni soṇakāyano māṇavo yenāhaṃ tenupasaṅkami; upasaṅkamitvā maṃ etadavoca — 'samaṇo gotamo sabbakammānaṃ akiriyaṃ paññapeti, sabbakammānaṃ kho pana akiriyaṃ paññapento ucchedaṃ āha lokassa — kammasaccāyaṃ, bho, loko kammasamāra mbhaṭṭhāyī' ti.*
115. *akiriyaṃ kho ahaṃ, brāhmaṇa, vadāmi kāyaduccaritassa vacīduccaritassa manoduccaritassa, anekavihitānaṃ pāpakānaṃ akusalānaṃ dhammānaṃ akiriyaṃ vadāmi. kiriyañca kho ahaṃ, brāhmaṇa, vadāmi kāyasucaritassa vacīsucaritassa manosucaritassa, anekavihitānaṃ kusalānaṃ dhammānaṃ kiriyaṃ vadāmi. evaṃ kho ahaṃ, brāhmaṇa, kiriyavādī ca akiriyavādī cā ti.*
116. For a useful discussion of the different ways in which *akiriyavāda* is used in the Pali Canon, see Ananda K. Coomaraswamy, "Some Pāli Words," *Harvard Journal of Asiatic Studies* 4, no. 2 (Jul. 1939), 119–122.
117. The position that categories such as *kriyavāda* were more polemical than substantive is shared by Claire Maes (personal communication).
118. *Sūyag.* 1.1.2.24 criticizes the *kriyāvāda* view; *Sūyag.* 1.10.17 appears to equally criticize *kriyāvāda* and *akriyāvāda*; conversely, *Sūyag.* 1.12.21 appears to embrace the label *kriyāvāda*. This seems to have been a source of great confusion to Jacobi in his translation. In a footnote on p. 83, he explains that *kriyāvāda* and *akriyāvāda* are two of the "four great heresies" criticized by Jains. In another footnote on p. 319, however, the page on which *Sūyag.* 1.12.21 appears, he is forced to admit, "It is evident that the Gainas considered themselves Kriyâvâdins. I had overlooked this passage when penning the note on p. 83"—Jacobi, *Gaina Sûtras*, vol. 2.
119. *Vin.* III.212, III.214, III.216, III.259, IV.224, IV.294: *gahapati nāma yo koci agāraṃ ajjhāvasati.*
120. *Vin.* IV.285, IV.302.
121. Chakravarti, *Social Dimensions*, 66.
122. *DN* 26: *bhūtapubbaṃ, bhikkhave, rājā daḷhanemi nāma ahosi cakkavattī dhammiko dhammarājā cāturanto vijitāvī janapadatthāvariyappatto sattaratanasamannāgato. tassimāni satta ratanāni ahesuṃ seyyathidaṃ cakkaratanaṃu hatthiratanaṃ assaratanaṃ maṇiratanaṃ itthiratanaṃ gahapatiratanaṃ pariṇāyakaratanameva sattamaṃ.*
123. Chakravarti, *Social Dimensions*, 67–71.
124. Ibid., 80.
125. *Vin.* IV.224, IV.294: *gahapatiputto nāma ye keci puttabhātaro.*

126. This conclusion is also supported by the fact that in modern Thai, the word คหบดี—a perfect phonetic transcription of the Pali *gahapati*—refers to a rich person. Other words such as ฆราวาส (*gharāvāsa*) and คฤหัสถ์ (*gṛhastha*) refer to "householders" as opposed to monks.
127. *Vin.* III.88–89, III.92, III.149, III.156, III.234, IV.31; *MN* 11; *AN* 5.57, 5.88, 5.90, 5.223, 7.61.
128. Chakravarti calls it a "triumvirate": *Social Dimensions*, 67.
129. *Vin.* III.222: *ṭhapetvā rājaṃ rājabhoggaṃ brāhmaṇaṃ avaseso gahapatiko nāma.*
130. Ibid.: *bhikkhuṃ paneva uddissa rājā vā rājabhoggo vā brāhmaṇo vā gahapatiko vā dūtena cīvaracetāpannaṃ pahiṇeyya . . . .*
131. See, e.g., *DN* 1: *yathā vā paneke bhonto samaṇabrāhmaṇā saddhādeyyāni bhojanāni bhuñjitvā te evarūpaṃ dūteyyapahiṇagamanānuyogaṃ anuyuttā viharanti, seyyathidaṃ — raññaṃ, rājamahāmattānaṃ, khattiyānaṃ, brāhmaṇānaṃ, gahapatikānaṃ, kumārānaṃ idha gaccha, amutrāgaccha, idaṃ hara, amutra idaṃ āharā"ti iti vā iti evarūpā dūteyyapahiṇagamanānuyogā paṭivirato samaṇo gotamo ti — iti vā hi, bhikkhave, puthujjano tathāgatassa vaṇṇaṃ vadamāno vadeyya.*
132. Bronkhorst, *Buddhism in the Shadow of Brahmanism*, 34–35. Chakravarti notes that the "division of *brāhmaṇa*, *khattiya*, *vessa*, and *sudda*, is associated most often with situations in which the Buddha converses with a *brāhmaṇa*"—*Social Dimensions*, 98; cited by Bronkhorst, *Buddhism in the Shadow of Brahmanism*, 35.
133. Bronkhorst cites Widmer as saying that this compound does not *always* mean Brahmans and householders, but is sometimes simply a *dvandva*—*Buddhism in the Shadow of Brahmanism*, 34 n. 16.
134. *DN* 4, 5; *MN* 41, 42, 60, 95; *SN* 1.4.2.8, 5.11.1.7; *AN* 3.64, 5.30, 6.42, 8.86; *Ud.* 7.9.
135. Chakravarti, *Social Dimensions*, 72–73.
136. Bronkhorst, *How the Brahmins Won*, 406.
137. *MN* 99. Interestingly, the word used here for householder is *gahaṭṭha*, but this is to be expected, since it is put into the mouth of the Buddha's Brahman interlocutor, a student (*mānava*) named Subha. This *sutta* does not refer to *brāhmaṇagahapatikā*, but it is not set in a *brāhmaṇagāma* and does not involve large numbers of Brahmans visiting the Buddha, only Subha.
138. Bronkhorst, *Buddhism in the Shadow of Brahmanism*, 35.
139. Compare, for example, the simple account of the Buddha's departure from home in the *Ariyapariyesana Sutta* (*MN* 26) with the elaborate account of the Bodhisattva's resplendent life before leaving "the palace" in the *Buddhacarita* (esp. ch. 2).
140. Chakravarti, *Social Dimensions*, 124.
141. Ibid., 132.
142. Ibid., 125.

143. An interesting parallel is offered by the early Franciscan movement in Italy. Kenneth Wolf has argued that the poverty advocated and strived after by St. Francis of Assisi was a "rich man's poverty" that both was qualitatively different from the poverty of the involuntarily poor, insofar as it was created by a formerly rich person as an intentional *disavowal* of riches, and diminished the value of involuntary poverty by valorizing a poverty that could effectively only be attained by the rich. As Wolf writes, "one could argue that it was his success in taking poverty as a virtue away from the involuntary poor and giving it, in a newly spiritualized form, to the rich that secured for Francis the respect and veneration of guilty burghers who had the resources and the influence to transform him overnight into an *alter Christus* and his followers into a powerful order"—Kenneth Wolf, *The Poverty of Riches: St. Francis of Assisi Reconsidered* (Oxford: Oxford University Press, 2003), 89.

144. Richard Cohen has provided an insightful analysis of exchange relationships at Ajaṇṭā using the categories *restricted exchange* and *generalized exchange* that were coined by Ivan Strenski—Richard S. Cohen, "Nāga, Yakṣiṇī, Buddha: Local Deities and Local Buddhism at Ajanta," *History of Religions* 37, no. 4 (May 1998): 360–400. Cohen too emphasizes the importance of "restricted exchange" in localizing Buddhism at Ajaṇṭā—in part by declining to view merit as somehow less real than material goods, which would imply that ordinary gifts of *dāna* to the *saṅgha* involve a deferral of reward and thus fall under the category of generalized exchange. None of this is to deny that generalized exchange is also involved here—clearly it is, insofar as monks renounce ownership of their inheritance in exchange for the deferred repayment in the form of goods from (possibly) another well-to-do family, and as such, this system of exchange would have "buil[t] up social solidarity" (p. 366) among the well-to-do families of a particular local community. But at the same time, insofar as the exchange is primarily between a finite group of well-to-do families and their own sons who agree to renounce their right to ownership, it is a "restricted exchange" that localizes Buddhism in a particular place by allowing the elite families of that place to gain access to the merit generated through the institution of the *saṅgha* while still effectively retaining control of the resources at their disposal, and thus retaining dominance in the broader economy. This would represent a form of localization that is in fact quite similar to that involved with the placation of *nāgas* at Ajaṇṭā: Just as Buddhists tend to *nāga* shrines in exchange for the *nāgas*' benevolence and protection, and *nāgas* allow the existence of the monastery in exchange for Buddhists giving them offerings, so too do elite families subsidize the *saṅgha* in exchange for effectively constituting the *saṅgha* (because they populate it with their own sons), and the sons of elite families agree to join the *saṅgha* in exchange for access to the property they "renounce" in the process, in the form of *dāna*.

145. Needless to say, even in a strongly patriarchal society, women, children, and other dependents are not magically deprived of their agency; they can and often do exert agency in various under-the-radar ways, some of which act to subvert the patriarchal power structure. While that certainly was the case in ancient India, most (though not all) early Buddhist texts do not seem interested in recording such acts of subversion, much less encouraging them.
146. *Vin.* I.73–78, I.82–83.
147. 1.2.2.20: a monk should not eat from the dish of a householder (*gihimatte*); 1.3.3.15–16: a debate on whether Jain ascetics properly distinguish themselves from householders (*gihiṇo*); 1.9.16: a monk should not talk to or eat the food of a householder (*sāgāriyaṃ*); 1.9.29: a monk should not stay in the house of a householder (*gāmakumāriyaṃ*); 1.13.11: a monk should not do the "work of a householder" (*gārikammaṃ*).
148. The classic treatments are Louis Dumont, *Homo Hierarchicus: The Caste System and Its Implications*, trans. Mark Sainsbury, Louis Dumont, and Basia Gulati (Chicago: University of Chicago Press, 1980[1966]), and J. C. Heesterman, *The Inner Conflict of Tradition: Essays in Indian Ritual, Kingship, and Society* (Chicago: University of Chicago Press, 1985). For a brief anthology of relevant Brahmanical sources, see Patrick Olivelle, "Ascetic Withdrawal or Social Engagement," in Donald S. Lopez, Jr., ed., *Religions of India in Practice* (Princeton: Princeton University Press, 1995), 533–546.
149. *Sn.* 828: *ete vivādā samaṇesu jātā, etesu ugghāti nighāti hoti / etam pi disvā virame kathojjaṃ, na h'aññadattha'tthi pasaṃsalābhā //.*
150. *Sn.* 882: *yam āhu saccaṃ tathiyanti eke, tam āhu aññe tucchaṃ musā ti. / evam pi vigayha vivādayanti, kasmā na ekaṃ samaṇā vadanti.*
151. *Sn.* 884: *ekañ hi saccaṃ na dutīyam atthi, yasmiṃ pajāno vivade pajānaṃ / nānā te saccāni sayaṃ thunanti, tasmā na ekaṃ samaṇā vadanti //.* I follow Norman here in his reading of the second *pada*—Norman, *The Group of Discourses*, vol. 2, 331 n. 884.
152. *Sn.* 890: *parassa ce hi vacasā nihīno, tumo sahā hoti nihīnapañño / atha ce sayaṃ vedagū hoti dhīro, na koci bālo samaṇesu atthi //.*

## CHAPTER 5

1. For an overview of the development of "law" within the context of the Dharmaśāstra tradition, including excerpts from relevant primary sources, see Patrick Olivelle, *A Dharma Reader: Classical Indian Law* (New York: Columbia University Press, 2017).
2. Olivelle, *The Āśrama System*, 87.
3. Ibid., 3.
4. Ibid., xxxi. Olivelle cites the fact that Āpastamba does not deal with mixed classes as one reason for believing that it is older than Gautama.

5. *ĀDhS* 1.1.1–3: *athātas sāmayācārikān / dharmajñasamayaḥ pramāṇam / vedāś ca /.*
6. Olivelle, *Dharmasūtras*, xxxiii-xxxiv.
7. *ĀDhS* 1.1.4–5: *catvāro varṇo brāhmaṇakṣatriyavaiśyaśūdrāḥ / teṣāṃ pūrvas-pūrvo janmataḥ śreyān /.*
8. Olivelle, *The Āśrama System*, 4.
9. Personally, I would prefer the term *theoretical construct*, which emphasizes the ideational character of the system and avoids the unnecessary introduction of a Western religious category. In any case, Olivelle's point, which is well taken, is that the *āśrama* system *qua* system should be understood as a normative description used by certain people beginning at a certain point in history, and as such it should not be confused with any actual social institutions it purports to describe, some of which may be older.
10. Olivelle, *The Āśrama System*, 29.
11. Ibid., 98.
12. Ibid., 94.
13. Ibid., 94–98.
14. Olivelle argues (ibid., 91–94) that Āpastamba and Vasiṣṭha accepted the *āśrama* system, but he believes that they do not represent the "liberal Brahmans" against whom Baudhāyana and Gautama argued; rather, they "probably lived during a time when the system had gained widespread acceptance within the mainstream" (ibid., 97). As we will see, none of the four Dharma Sūtras are particularly enthusiastic about the *āśrama* system; Āpastamba, in particular, does not so much accept it as fail to reject it outright as Gautama and Baudhāyana do.
15. Ibid., 97.
16. Ibid., 98.
17. *ye catvāraḥ pathayo devayānā antarā dyāvāpṛthivī viyanti / teṣāṃ yo ajyānimajītimāvahāt tasmai no devāḥ pari datteha sarva iti.*
18. *BDhS* 2.11.9–10, 29: *ye catvāra iti / karmavāda aiṣṭikapāśukasaumikadārvihomāṇām.* The fact that this statement is made twice is likely due to a transposition from verse 29 to verses 9–10: Patrick Olivelle, trans., *Dharmasūtras: The Law Codes of Āpastamba, Gautama, Baudhāyana, and Vasiṣṭha* (Oxford: Oxford University Press, 1999), 387.
19. *eṣa nityo mahimā brāhmaṇasya na karmaṇā vardhate no kanīyān / tasyaivātmā padavittaṃ viditvā na karmaṇā lipyate pāpakeneti.* Interestingly, this very same verse is also quoted at *BDhS* 2.17.7–8, but this time straightforwardly in support of (a classical form of) the *āśrama* system. This portion of Baudhāyana is part of what Olivelle calls "Deutero-Baudhāyana"—a substantial addition to an older Baudhāyana text that, unlike the latter, accepted the *āśrama* system and even provided detailed rules for renunciation. See Olivelle, *The Āśrama System*, 86–87, and Olivelle, *Dharmasūtras*, 127.
20. Olivelle presents some other arguments for his contention that the opponents against which the Dharma Sūtra authors were arguing were Brahmans,

but I find them less convincing. For example, he writes that "[t]he theory of option (*vikalpa*) . . . comes from the Mīmāṃsā tradition" (*The Āśrama System*, 98). In other words, he takes the reference to the *āśramas* as "options" (found, incidentally, only in Gautama) to be a technical term from the Mīmāṃsā tradition—but it is not clear that there was a well-established Mīmāṃsā tradition at the time the Dharma Sūtras were written; or that *vikalpa* could not have been used as a non-technical, ordinary word; or that even if it were meant in a technical sense, that it was not superimposed on the opponents' argument by Gautama himself. Olivelle also argues that "[t]he system attempts to fit itself into the pre-existing framework of life-cycle rituals (*saṃskāra*), giving a new significance to the period of initiatory studentship as a preparatory school for all the adult modes of life" (*The Āśrama System*, 98). But again, this could be due to the Dharma Sūtra authors' own agenda, rather than that of their opponents.

21. Olivelle, "Review of *The Two Sources*," 163.
22. Ibid.
23. Pandurang Vaman Kane, *History of Dharmaśāstra*, vol. 2, part 1 (Poona: Bhandarkar Oriental Research Institute, 1941), 27–28.
24. Michael Witzel, "On the Localization of Vedic Texts and Schools (Material on Vedic *śākhās*, 7)," in G. Pollet, ed., *India and the Ancient World. History, Trade and Culture before A.D. 650. P.H.L. Eggermont Jubilee Volume*, Orientalia Lovaniensia Analecta, vol. 25 (Leuven, 1987), 173–213.
25. Michael Witzel, "Early Sanskritization: Origins and Development of the Kuru State," *Electronic Journal of Vedic Studies* 1, no. 4 (Dec. 1995): 1–26. For more detailed examinations of the linguistic considerations involved in the stratification of Vedic texts, see Michael Witzel, "Tracing the Vedic Dialects," in Collette Caillat, ed., *Dialects dans les litteratures indo-aryennes. Actes du Colloque International organise par UA 1058 sous les auspices du C.N.R.S avec le soutien du College de France, de la Fondation Hugot du College de France, de l'Universite de Paris III, du Ministre des Affaires Etrangeres, Paris (Fondation Hugot) 16–18 Septembre 1986* (Paris: College de France, Institut de Civilisation Indienne, 1989), 97–264, and Michael Witzel, "The Development of the Vedic Canon and its Schools: The Social and Political Milieu (Material on Vedic *śākhās*, 8)," in Witzel, ed., *Inside the Texts, Beyond the Texts*, 257–345.
26. J. C. Heesterman, *The Inner Conflict of Tradition: Essays in Indian Ritual, Kingship, and Society* (Chicago: University of Chicago Press, 1985).
27. Ibid., 199.
28. J. C. Heesterman, *The Broken World of Sacrifice: An Essay in Ancient Indian Ritual* (Chicago: University of Chicago Press, 1993).
29. See, e.g., Michael Witzel, "Early Sanskritization," 10.
30. Kane, *History of Dharmaśāstra*, 36.
31. Smith, *Classifying the Universe*, 28.

32. Ibid., 60–79. Lauren Bausch has also shown that the three functions, rather than the four social classes or *varṇas*, were pervasive in the Vedic literature: Lauren Bausch, "Varṇa as Internal Powers in Vedic Texts," paper presented at the 227th Meeting of the American Oriental Society, Los Angeles, March 2017.
33. See, e.g., *RV* X.71.8: *hṛdā taṣṭeṣu manaso javeṣu yad brāhmaṇāḥ saṃyajante sakhāyaḥ / atrāha tvaṃ vi jahur vedyābhir ohabrahmāṇo vi caranty u tve //*—"When the impulses of the mind are fashioned in the heart, when Brahmans sacrifice together as friends / They leave one behind with knowledge, while others possessing *brahman* ramble through." Note that while this passage indicates that Brahmans were valued for their erudition, it does not imply that there was such a thing as a Brahman who had no Vedic education at all. The Brahman-by-birth (*brahma-bandhu*) of later times was characterized by a total negligence in the performance of Vedic sacrifices, not by a priestly vocation in which he merely lacked expertise.
34. *ŚB* 5.5.4.9; cited by Kane, *History of Dharmaśāstra*, 38, incorrectly as *ŚB* 5.4.6.9.
35. *AB* II.19: *dāsyāḥ putraḥ kitavo'brāhmaṇaḥ . . . vidur vā imaṃ devā*. Cf. *KB* XII.3.
36. Lauren Bausch, "Kosalan Philosophy in the *Kāṇva Śatapatha Brāhmaṇa* and the *Sutta Nipāta*" (unpublished PhD diss., University of California, Berkeley, 2015), 52. The reference is to *BĀU* 4.4.23: *tasmād evaṃvic chānto dānta uparatas titikṣuḥ samāhito bhūtvātmany evātmānaṃ paśyati / sarvam ātmānaṃ paśyati / nainaṃ pāpmā tarati / sarvaṃ pāpmānaṃ tarati / nainaṃ pāpmā tapati / sarvaṃ pāpmānaṃ tapati / vipāpo virajo 'vicikitso brāhmaṇo bhavati / eṣa brahmalokaḥ samrāṭ / enaṃ prāpito 'sīti hovāca yājñavalkyaḥ /.*
37. See, e.g., *AB* VII.15, in which Varuṇa declares the Brahman to be higher than the *kṣatriya*. Even this passage is not particularly early, however; Witzel has shown on independent philological grounds that the second half of the *Aitareya Brāhmaṇa* is a late addition—Michael Witzel, "Tracing the Vedic Dialects," 115.
38. *ŚB* V.4.4.15; V.4.2.7.
39. *JB* I.285.
40. *JUB* 3.28.4. The famous passage on the "three debts" of the Brahman (*TS* 6.3.10.5) does say that the Brahman is "born" (*jāyate*) with three debts, but, as we discussed in the previous chapter, the early rhetoric of "birth" associated with *brahmacarya* makes it unclear whether this passage refers to literal birth or birth as a Brahman. The *JUB* passage, on the other hand, is unambiguous insofar as it speaks of the desire to be born in either a "Brahman lineage" (*brāhmaṇa-kule*) or a "royal lineage" (*rāja-kule*).
41. *AB* VII.29: *ādāyy āpāyy āvasāyī yathākāmaprayāpyo.*
42. Witzel, "Early Sanskritization," 5.
43. Timothy Lubin, "The Transmission, Patronage, and Prestige of Brahmanical Piety from the Mauryas to the Guptas," in Federico Squarcini, ed., *Boundaries, Dynamics and Construction of Traditions in South Asia* (Florence: Firenze University Press, 2005), 77–103.

44. Timothy Lubin, "The householder ascetic and the uses of self-discipline," in Peter Flügel and Gustaaf Houtman, eds., *Asceticism and Power in South and Southeast Asia* (London: Routledge, forthcoming), 8–14.
45. Ibid., 19.
46. Although the one extant version of this *sūtra* in Sanskrit Sanskritizes the name as Ambāṣṭa, Bronkhorst argues that the name could also be Sanskritized as Ambaṣṭha, which is the name of a "mixed caste" derived from a Brahman father and a non-Brahman (usually *vaiśya*) mother—*Greater Magadha*, 354. This would make Ambaṭṭha's name, quite possibly, a joke, which appears to be a common trope in the portrayal of Brahmans in "encounter dialogs" in the early Buddhist *sūtras.*
47. This statement in the *Ambaṭṭha Sutta* is, in a sense, contradicted by the story of Rāma Jāmadagnya killing all of the *kṣatriyas* of the world 21 times over, insofar as, after he does so, *kṣatriya* women go to Brahmans to bear children by them so that they can continue the *kṣatriya* lineage (see, e.g., *MBh.* 1.58.1–9). But this story is, of course, the product of a Brahmanical polemical agenda that was critical of *kṣatriyas* who did not pay proper respect to Brahmans—on which see Robert Goldman, "Masters of the Earth: The Bhṛgus and the Kṣatriyas," in *Gods, Priests, and Warriors: The Bhṛgus of the* Mahābhārata (New York: Columbia University Press, 1977), 93–112. And indeed, even as such, the account of the repopulation of the *kṣatriya* lineage after Rāma Jāmadagnya's genocide clearly belies the Brahmanical claim that *varṇas* are determined strictly by birth, insofar as it accomplishes that repopulation of the *kṣatriya* lineage through a *mixture* of *varṇas*.
48. Freiberger, "Negative Campaigning."
49. *Sn.* 2.7; *DN* 3, 27; *SN* 4.35.132; *AN* 5.192.
50. Note that the only "proof" of birth requested by the Brahman teacher in this text is a *gotra*. Considering that in early India *gotra* does not appear to have been restricted to a distinct Brahman *varṇa*—the Buddha, for example, possesses one—this may indicate that the "birth" esteemed by early Vedic Brahmans may have been a matter of *high* birth in general, rather than birth into a specific *class*. This would help to explain the discussion of mixed marriages in the *Ambaṭṭha Sutta*. Brahmans would accept the son of a *kṣatriya* as a student because he is of high birth, i.e., he possesses a *gotra*, while *kṣatriyas* would not accept the son of a Brahman because of their incestuous commitment to purity of the lineage, already referred to earlier in the story of King Okkāka (Ikṣvāku).
51. *ChU* 4.4.2: *nāham etad veda tāta yad gotras tvam asi. bahv ahaṃ carantī paricāriṇī yauvane tvām alabhe. sāham etan na veda yad gotras tvam asi. jabālā tu nāmāham asmi. satyakāmo nāma tvam asi. sa satyakāma eva jābālo bruvīthā iti.*
52. Black, *Character of the Self*, 54. Black assumes that the issue in this passage is whether Satyakāma is a Brahman or not, and that this is left ambiguous. As much

would seem to be implied by Hāridrumata's exclamation that a non-Brahman would not speak as Satyakāma did, but the technical issue around which the passage revolves is actually not "Brahmanhood" per se, but Satyakāma's *gotra*. It is for his *gotra* that Satyakāma asks his mother, and which she is not able to tell him because she does not know who his father is, and it is for his *gotra* that Hāridrumata asks when Satyakāma comes asking to be his student. Although *gotra* has come to be associated specifically with Brahmans, Brough has demonstrated that this was not always the case. See John Brough, "The Early History of the Gotras," *Journal of the Royal Asiatic Society of Great Britain and Ireland*, no. 1 (Apr. 1946): 32–45, and John Brough, "The Early History of the Gotras (Concluded)," *Journal of the Royal Asiatic Society of Great Britain and Ireland*, no. 1 (Apr. 1947): 76–90. What may be at stake is not so much being a Brahman from birth as coming from an established Aryan lineage, as would be established by a *gotra*. Indeed, even in the encounter dialogs found in the early Buddhist literature in which Brahman interlocutors define Brahmanhood in part in terms of birth, what is emphasized about birth is not Brahman parentage, but rather *purity* going back seven generations. (See, e.g., the *Soṇadaṇḍa Sutta, DN* 4.)

53. Bronkhorst, *Buddhism in the Shadow of Brahmanism*, 40.
54. Chakravarti, *Social Dimensions*, 104; cited in Bronkhorst, *Buddhism in the Shadow of Brahmanism*, 35.
55. Chakravarti, *Social Dimensions*, 98; cited in Bronkhorst, *Buddhism in the Shadow of Brahmanism*, 35.
56. Bronkhorst, *Buddhism in the Shadow of Brahmanism*, 163–164.
57. Āpastamba does mention some classes of people that are presented as "mixed classes" in other Dharma Sūtras, namely, Cāṇḍālas, Paulkasas (elsewhere Pulkasas), and Vaiṇa, but he does not present them as resulting from mixed unions. Rather, they result when a Brahman, Kṣatriya, or *vaiśya* is reborn as a human after sinning heinously in a previous life and spending time in hell (*ĀDhS* 2.2.6–7).
58. *GDhS* 4.16–28; *BDhS* 1.16.6–16, 1.17.1–15, 2.3.29–30, 1.2.13; *VDhS* 18.1–10; *MDhŚ* 10.8–73.
59. *GDhS* 4.19.
60. *GDhS* 4.21.
61. *GDhS* 4.17; *BDhS* 1.17.1, 1.17.7, 1.17.10, 1.17.11; cf. *MDhŚ* 10.12, 10.13, 10.16, 10.19, 10.26, 10.49.
62. *GDhS* 4.19.
63. *BDhS* 1.17.1, 1.17.6.
64. *GDhS* 4.17, 4.18; *BDhS* 1.17.1, 1.17.3; *VDhS* 18.6; cf. *MDhŚ* 10.11, 10.17, 10.26, 10.47.
65. *BDhS* 1.16.9, 1.17.1, 1.17.11; cf. *MDhŚ* 10.19.
66. *BDhS* 1.16.10, 1.17.1, 1.17.12, *VDhS* 18.2; cf. *MDhŚ* 10.19, 10.49 (*veṇa*).

67. *GDhS* 4.16; *BDhS* 1.16.7, 1.17.1, 1.17.3, 1.17.9, 1.17.12; *VDhS* 18.8; cf. *MDhŚ* 10.8, 10.13, 10.15, 10.19, 10.47.
68. *GDhS* 4.17, 4.18; *BDhS* 1.16.8, 1.17.1, 1.17.7; cf. *MDhŚ* 10.11, 10.17, 10.26, 10.47.
69. *GDhS* 4.16; *BDhS* 1.16.7, 1.16.11, 1.16.13, 1.17.3, 1.17.13, 1.17.14, 2.3.29; *VDhS* 18.8; cf. *MDhŚ* 10.8, 10.18, 10.34, 10.36, 10.37, 10.39, 10.48.
70. *GDhS* 4.16, 4.21; *BDhS* 1.17.4, 2.3.30; *VDhS* 18.9; cf. *MDhŚ* 10.8.
71. *GDhS* 3.10; *BDhS* 1.16.8, 1.17.1, 1.17.8, 1.17.10, 1.17.12; cf. *MDhŚ* 10.11, 10.13, 10.17, 10.19, 10.26, 10.33, 10.36, 10.37, 10.47.
72. *GDhS* 4.21.
73. It is not clear how this would have worked on a social level anyway. Insofar as Dharmaśāstric prohibitions against mixing classes were recognized and accepted (which in itself is questionable), illicit unions would presumably have been hidden and difficult to verify in an age before paternity tests. Indeed, Manu seems to acknowledge as much when he says that "Ignobility, cruelty, ferocity, (and) neglect of rites / Make manifest here in the world a man born of a foul womb. // He partakes in the paternal tendencies, or those of the mother, or even both. / In no wise does a person from a bad womb restrain his own nature. // Even in an eminent family, a man of whose birth there be a mixture of wombs / Necessarily joins together with those tendencies to a lesser or greater extent. //" (*MDhŚ* 10.58–60: *anāryatā niṣṭhuratā krūratā niṣkriyātmatā / puruṣaṃ vyañjayantīha loke kaluṣayonijam // pitryaṃ vā bhajate śīlaṃ mātur vobhayam eva vā / na kathaṃcana duryoniḥ prakṛtiṃ svāṃ niyacchati // kule mukhye'pi jātasya yasya syād yonisaṃkaraḥ / saṃśrayaty eva tac chīlaṃ naro'lpam api vā bahu//*). There may be no DNA test to ferret out mixed-breed children, but they inevitably reveal themselves by their acts.
74. *Caṇḍālas* are, in fact, mentioned frequently in the Pali Canon as a despised social group. In several texts, they are mentioned together with other groups that are listed in the Dharma Sūtras as mixed classes (*vena, nesāda, rathakāra, pukkusa*): *Vin.* IV.6, IV.12; *MN* 93, 96, 129; *SN* 1.3.3.1; *AN* 3.1.2.3, 4.2.4.5, 5.4.5.2, 6.2.6.3.
75. The early ascription of Māgadhas and Vaidehas to "mixed class" status may be related to the fact that they are eastern peoples of "Greater Magadha," which, as Bronkhorst has pointed out, was not originally considered part of Āryavarta (Bronkhorst, *Greater Magadha*, 1).
76. *BDhS* 1.2.13: *avantayo'ṅgamagadhāḥ surāṣṭrā dakṣiṇāpathāḥ / upāvṛtsindhusauvīrā ete saṃkīrṇayonayaḥ.*
77. *MDhŚ* 10.15, 10.36, 10.21–23.
78. *MDhŚ* 10.43: *śanakais tu kriyālopādimāḥ kṣatriyajātayaḥ / vṛṣalatvaṃ gatā loke brāhmaṇādarśanena ca //.*
79. Strabo, *Geography*, 15.59; trans. McCrindle, *Ancient India as Described in Classical Literature*, 65–66.
80. *ĀDhS* 1.2.11–16; *GDhS* 2.45–47; *BDhS* 1.3.1–4.

81. Strabo, *Geography*, 15.60; trans. McCrindle, *Ancient India as Described in Classical Literature*, 67.
82. *ĀDhS* 2.21.19, 2.22.1–2: *ata eva brahmacaryavān pravrajati . . . . tasyāraṇyam ācchādanaṃ vihitam. tato mūlaiḥ phalaiḥ parṇais tṛṇair iti vartayaṃś caret.*
83. Strabo, *Geography*, 15.60; trans. McCrindle, *Ancient India as Described in Classical Literature*, 67.
84. Ibid.
85. *yathā vā paneke bhonto samaṇabrāhmaṇā saddhādeyyāni bhojanāni bhuñjitvā te evarūpāya tiracchānavijjāya micchājīvena jīvitaṃ kappenti, seyyathidaṃ . . . vassakammaṃ vossakammaṃ . . . vamanaṃ virecanaṃ uddhaṃvirecanaṃ adhovirecanaṃ sīsavirecanaṃ kaṇṇatelaṃ nettatappanaṃ natthukammaṃ añjanaṃ paccañjanaṃ sālākiyaṃ sallakattiyaṃ dārakatikicchā mūlabhesajjānaṃ anuppadānaṃ osadhīnaṃ paṭimokkho iti vā iti evarūpāya tiracchānavijjāya micchājīvā paṭivirato samaṇo gotamo ti.*
86. For a study of the practices of "doctor monks" (หมอพระ) in the Thai province of Nonthaburi, which include exorcism; the use of medicaments and *yantras* to cure skin rashes; and the use of herbs to cure dog, snake, and insect bites, see Nanda Raksakhom, "การเยียวยารักษาโดยวิธีการทางศาสนา" ["Medical Treatment using Religious Methods"] (BA Senior Thesis, College of Religious Studies, Mahidol University, 2005). The performance of simple astrological and other divinological calculations, which are also proscribed by the *Brahmajāla Sutta*, are, on the other hand, a commonplace among Thai monks.
87. *BDhS* 2.11.12, *VDhS* 7.1. Āpastamba (2.21.1) refers to this *āśrama* as the *mauna* (though later as *parivrāja*—*ĀDhS* 2.21.7), and Gautama (3.2) refers to it, interestingly enough, as the *bhikṣu*. I believe that the latter's use of the word *bhikṣu* lends credence to the argument that Buddhist *bhikkhus* were, colloquially speaking, *paribbājakas*; the categories, in other words, appear to have been interchangeable.
88. *GDhS* 3.11–25: *anicayo bhikṣuḥ. ūrdhvaretāḥ. dhruvaśīlo varṣāsu. bhikṣārthī grāmam iyāt. jaghanyam anivṛttaṃ caret. nivṛttāśīḥ. vāk cakṣuḥkarmasaṃyataḥ. kaupīnāc chādanārthaṃvāsobibhṛyāt.prahīṇamekenirṇijya.nāviprayuktamoṣadhivanaspatīnām aṅgam upāda dīta. na dvitīyām apartu rātriṃ grāme vaset. muṇḍaḥ śikhī vā. varjayed bījavadham. samo bhūteṣu hiṃsānugrahayoḥ. anārambhī.*
89. *BDhS* 2.11.16–20. Baudhāyana says that the *parivrājaka* shaves his head *except* for the topknot, while Gautama says that he may either shave his head or have a topknot.
90. *VDhS* 10.6–13.
91. *ĀDhS* 2.22.7–11.
92. For a more detailed comparison of sources on the characteristics of ancient Indian *parivrājakas*, see Olivelle, *Buddhist Monachism*, 11–24.
93. *MN* 11, 13, 59, 150; *SN* 2.1.3.4, 2.1.7.10, 3.1.9.4, 4.1.8.8, 4.1.15.7, 4.2.2.9, 4.2.2.10, 5.1.1.5, 5.1.5.1–8, 5.2.6.2–4, 5.10.2.1–2; AN 2.33–42, 3.69, 3.94,

7.42–43, 8.83, 9.1, 10.58; *Ud.* 2.4, 4.8, 6.10. *Ud.* 4.8 is fairly unique in that in it the "wanderers of other sects" are actual characters within the plot of the *sutta*, who in fact conspire to frame a *saṅgha* of Buddhist *bhikkhus* for having sex with a female wanderer and then murdering her!

94. *aññtitthiyasamaṇabrāhmaṇaparibbājakānaṃ* (*SN* 2.2.11), *nānātitthiyasamaṇa-brāhmaṇaparibbājakā* (*Ud.* 6.4–6), *aññatitthiyā samaṇabrāhmaṇaparibbājakā* (*SN* 4.8.7).
95. *ṭhānaṃ kho panetaṃ, bhikkhave, vijjati yaṃ aññatitthiyā paribbājakā evaṃ vadeyyuṃ ko panāyasmantānaṃ assāso, kiṃ balaṃ, yena tumhe āyasmanto evaṃ vadetha . . . evaṃvādino, bhikkhave, aññatitthiyā paribbājakā evam assu vacanīyā.*
96. Olivelle, *The Āśrama System*, 96.
97. Āpastamba does present, in the mouths of his opponents, the following quote from a "Purāṇa": "The eighty thousand seers who desired offspring went along the sun's southern course. They obtained cremation grounds. The eighty thousand seers who did not desire offspring went along the sun's northern course. They, indeed, attained immortality" (*ĀDhS* 2.23.4–5: *aṣṭāśī tisahasrāṇi ye prajāmīṣir arṣayaḥ. dakṣiṇenāryamṇaḥ panthānaṃ te śmaśānāni bhejire. aṣṭāśītisahasrāṇi ye prajāṃ neṣir arṣayaḥ. uttareṇāramṇaḥ panthānaṃ te'mṛtatvaṃ hi kalpate*). The second part of the opponents' argument is that celibate religious practitioners have special powers. In reference to these two pieces of evidence—the quote from the "Purāṇa" and the special powers of renunciates—Āpastamba has his opponents summarize their argument by saying, "Therefore, on the basis of *śruti* and visible results, some say that these *āśramas* are superior." (*ĀDhS* 2.23.9: *tasmāc chrutitaḥ pratyakṣaphalatvācca viśiṣṭān āśramān etān eke bruvate*). The Purāṇa quote is clearly referred to here as *śruti*, which Olivelle (*Dharmasūtras*, 67) translates as "vedic testimony," but it seems that the word is not being used here in the technical sense it came to have later, as referring specifically to Vedic revelation. As far as I know, the quote has never been traced, and it is in any case presented as coming from a "Purāṇa," not the Vedas.
98. *BDhS* 2.11.28: *prāhlādir ha vai kapilo nāmāsura āsa. sa etān bhedāṃś cakāra devaiḥ saha spardhamānaḥ. tān manīṣī nādriyeta.*
99. *ĀDhS* 2.23.10: *traividyavṛddhānāṃ tu vedāḥ pramāṇam iti niṣṭhā.*
100. *ĀDhS* 2.21.11–12: *tasya muktam ācchādanaṃ vihitam. sarvataḥ parimokṣam eke.*
101. *BDhS* 2.11.26: *apavidhya vaidikāni karmāṇy ubhayataḥ paricchinnā madhyamaṃpadaṃ saṃśliṣyāmaha iti.*
102. Richard Lariviere, "Dharmaśāstra, Custom, 'Real Law' and 'Apocryphal' Smṛtis," *Journal of Indian Philosophy* 32 (2004), 618.
103. Ibid., 612.
104. Ibid., 616.
105. There is an interesting parallel, I would argue, between Lariviere's understanding of the Dharmaśāstric project and that of the Sanskrit grammarians,

especially when viewed through the lens of Bronkhorst's recent comments on Sanskritization. There is, for both bodies of literature, a certain "scientific" or empirical component—the Dharmaśāstra authors must take into account actual human custom in formulating their accounts of *dharma*, just as the grammarians must take into account actual human speech in formulating their accounts of grammar. Both, however, are overlaid by an ideological agenda that colors the presentation of actual custom or language and at times pushes against it. While that ideological agenda in the Dharmaśāstra literature is obvious, so much so that, Lariviere argues, it obscures its roots in customary law, the ideological agenda of Sanskrit grammar is less obvious and has even been denied—see Pollock, *The Language of the Gods.* Bronkhorst, however, has argued convincingly that Sanskritization was intimately intertwined with the spread of the Brahmanical ideological agenda—Bronkhorst, *Buddhism in the Shadow of Brahmanism*, 46–65.

106. Olivelle, *The Āśrama System*, 91.
107. *ĀDhS* 2.24.1: *prajātim amṛtam.*
108. *VDhS* 8.14: *caturṇām āśramāṇāṃ tu gṛhasthas tu viśiṣyate.*
109. Although none of the Dharma Sūtras explicitly label the practitioners of the celibate *āśramas* as representing "other" or even "rival" groups, it is clear from their critiques of those *āśramas* that they were concerned with issues of Vedic learning and ritual practice, rather than only the issue of whether it is necessary to produce offspring. In other words, it appears that the celibate *āśramas* were problematic not only because they failed to produce offspring—something that could be understood as a fully intra-Brahmanical dispute—but because they did not acknowledge the need for studying the Vedas and performing rituals. As already mentioned above, Āpastamba begins his rebuttal of the opinion that the celibate *āśramas* were superior by stating that the Vedas are to be taken as the standard—a point that hardly seems necessary to make if the opponents were simply "liberal Brahmans." Baudhāyana attributes, as already mentioned, two Vedic quotes to his opponents, but he ends his rebuttal of their position by stating, "The three knowledges, *brahmacarya*, procreation, faith, austerity, sacrifice, gift-giving: We are with only those who do these things; praising something else, one becomes dust and perishes" (*BDhS* 2.11.34: *trayīṃ vidyāṃ brahmacaryaṃ prajātiṃ śraddhāṃ tapo yajñam anupradānam. ya etāni kurvate tair it saha smo rajo bhūtvā dhvaṃsate'nyat praśaṃsann iti*). This appears to quite sharply demarcate a line between a Vedic tradition and a non-Vedic "other." Finally, Vasiṣṭha ends his discussion of the *āśramas* by, as already mentioned, declaring the householder superior to the other three, followed by what I would characterize as a succinct description of his vision of the Brahmanical tradition: "Always performing ablutions, always wearing the sacred thread, always reciting (the Veda), avoiding the food of outcastes, both going (to his wife) in season and making offerings according to the rule, a Brahman does not

fall from *brahmaloka*" (*VDhS* 8.17: *nityodakī nityayajñopavītī nityasvādhyāyī patitānnavarjī. ṛtau ca gacchan vidhivac ca juhvan na brāhmaṇaś cyavate brahmalokād iti*).

110. Again, justifying social customs within a Vedic framework need not imply that social practices were always recorded with complete fidelity to the way in which they were actually practiced, with sophistic arguments provided to legitimize them as such on the basis of the Vedas. Āpastamba, for example, begins his description of the *āśramas* by stating that "all are required not to abandon Vedic learning" (*ĀDhS* 2.21.4: *sarveṣām anūtsargo vidyāyāḥ*). This need not be interpreted as indicating that Āpastamba is only talking about Brahmans who pursue celibate *āśramas* such as that of the *parivrājaka;* in fact, as I have argued, his rebuttal of the claim that celibate *āśramas* are superior appears to presuppose that those opponents question or reject the authority of the Vedas. The assertion that those who enter into various *āśramas* must not abandon the Vedas is, in my opinion, better interpreted as a normativizing fiction—an attempt to reconcile diverse ways of life found in actual practice with Āpastamba's own Vedic ideal.

111. If Olivelle is right in dating Āpastamba before Gautama, then the two Dharma Sūtras that reject the celibate *āśramas* outright—Gautama and Baudhāyana—would fall chronologically right in the middle of the four.

112. The term *āśrama* is actually well suited to a discussion of "lifestyles" from a perspective that favors a lifestyle that produces progeny. As Olivelle explains in his study of the *āśrama* system, the closely related word *śrama* is used most significantly in the Vedas to refer to the "creative activities of Prajāpati"; it, moreover, is used as a synonym for sacrifice and has "clear sexual connotations"—Olivelle, *The Āśrama System*, 10.

## CHAPTER 6

1. This chapter will focus on Buddhist evidence, in which I have greater expertise, and on which more modern scholarly work has been done. As we will see in the next chapter, Buddhist literature may have played an outsized role in a process that ended up affecting Jains in a fairly equal way.
2. On the importance of framing as a narrative device in early Indian literature, see Brian Black and Laurie Patton, eds., *Dialogue in Early South Asian Religions: Hindu, Buddhist, and Jain Traditions* (Surrey, England: Ashgate, 2015), 17–18.
3. By "original," I simply mean the verses as they are preserved in Pali, with the possible exception of v. 836, which is not commented upon by the *Mahāniddesa* (Norman, *Group of Discourses*, 836), and/or their counterparts in the Chinese version. This does not necessarily imply that those verses were composed together at one time by a single author; as we have discussed above, Vetter and Burford have given compelling reasons for believing that the *Aṭṭhaka* is a composite text.

4. *Nidd.* 1.1.766–9, 1.3.782, 1.6.805, 1.6.808, 1.11.864–5, 1.14.915, 1.14.932, 1.15.935, 1.15.947, 1.15.948, 1.16.955, 1.16.957, 1.16. 970, 1.16.973. (I cite from the two *Niddesas* according to whether it is the first [*Mahā*] or second [*Cūḷa*] *Niddesa*, followed by the number of the *sutta*, and ending with the number of the verse according to the *Sutta Nipāta* enumeration that is being commented upon.) Interestingly, none of the references to the four *varṇas* are found in commentaries on *suttas* that Vetter includes within the "core."
5. *Nidd.* 1.2.773, 1.15.939. I have not been able to trace the first quote, but the second is a quote from *MN* 87.
6. The others are *Tissa Metteya* (7), *Pasūra* (8), and *Sāriputta* (16).
7. Burford has noted the irony of the fact that in this *sutta* the Buddha enters into a dispute with Māgandiya in order to express his view that one should not hold any view, because holding views leads to disputes—Burford, *Desire, Death and Goodness*, 54–57.
8. On the pervasiveness of misogynistic themes in early Buddhism, see Liz Wilson, *Charming Cadavers: Horrific Figurations of the Feminine in Indian Buddhist Hagiographic Literature* (Chicago: University of Chicago Press, 1996).
9. *Sn.* 835: *disvāna taṇhaṃ aratiṃ ragañca, nāhosi chando api methunasmiṃ / kim evidaṃ muttakarīsapuṇṇaṃ, pādāpi naṃ samphusituṃ na icche //.*
10. *Sn.* 836: *etādisaṃ ce ratanaṃ na icchasi, nāriṃ narindehi bahūhi patthitaṃ / diṭṭhigataṃ sīlavataṃ nu jīvitaṃ, bhavūpapattiñ ca vadesi kīdisaṃ //.*
11. T. 198: 我所說婬不欲，無法行不內觀，雖聞惡不受厭，內不止不計苦，見外好筋皮裹，尊云何當受是，內外行覺觀是，於黠邊說癡行。
12. The full gloss can be found at the first instance of the word *brāhmaṇa* at v. 790 (subsequently the gloss is abbreviated using the word *pe*): *sattannaṃ dhammānaṃ bāhitattā brāhmaṇo — sakkāyadiṭṭhi bāhitā hoti, vicikicchā bāhitā hoti, sīlabbataparāmāso bāhito hoti, rāgo bāhito hoti, doso bāhito hoti, moho bāhito hoti, māno bāhito hoti. bāhitāssa honti pāpakā akusalā dhammā saṃkilesikā ponobhavikā sadarā dukkhavipākā āyatiṃ jātijarāmaraṇiyā. bāhitvā sabbapāpakāni, [sabhiyāti bhagavā] / vimalo sādhusamāhito ṭhitatto / saṃsāramaticca kevalī so, asito tādi pavuccate sa brahmā //.*
13. *Sn.* 518: *kiṃ pattinam āhu brāhmaṇaṃ, (iti sabhiyo) / samaṇaṃ kena kathañ ca nhātako ti / nāgo ti kathaṃ pavuccati / puṭṭho me bhagavā byākarohi //.*
14. *Sn.* 519–522.
15. The honorific *nāga* is found only once in the *Aṭṭhaka* (*Sn.* 4.9.845), making it less common than *bhikkhu*, *muni*, and *brāhmaṇa*. It is used three times, however, in the *Pārāyaṇa* (*Sn.* 5.4.1058, 5.12.1101, and v. 1131 in the *anugītigāthā*) to refer to the Buddha himself.
16. For a full English translation of this text, see P. V. Bapat, trans., *Arthapada Sutra: Spoken by the Buddha—Translated by the Upāsaka Che-Kien under the Wu Dynasty (222–280 A.D.)*, parts 1 and 2 (Calcutta: Visva-Bharati, 1951).
17. It is of course impossible to know what title exactly the text translated into Chinese originally had. The choice of the Chinese translator to use the character

足 (lit., "foot") in the title would suggest an original Sanskrit *pada*; accordingly, Bapat entitles his translation of the text the *Arthapada Sūtra*. On the other hand, the extant Sanskrit references we have to the text—the two references already mentioned above in the *Divyāvadāna* and a reference to one set of verses as an *artthavargīyaṃ sūtraṃ* in the Sanskrit fragments of the text itself published by Hoernle (Fr. 1, obv., ln. 4)—agree on the title *Arthavargīya*, which is more consistent with the Pali title *Aṭṭhaka Vagga*, at least with respect to the word *Vagga*. The word *aṭṭhaka* in the Pali, however, most likely should be Sanskritized as *aṣṭaka*, in reference to the fact that *suttas* 2-5 of the text—all of which, incidentally, have *aṭṭhaka* in their titles—are each composed of eight verses. This is reflected, however, neither in the Sanskrit references that we have nor in the Chinese translation, where 義 clearly refers to "meaning" or *artha* and has nothing to do with the number eight. Given the fact that only four of the sixteen *suttas* of the *Aṭṭhaka Vagga*/**Arthavargīya* have eight verses, it is possible that early on in the tradition, the reference to "eight" was forgotten and *aṭṭhaka* mistakenly Sanskritized as *artha*. In any case, I refer to the non-Pali text or texts that correspond to the Pali *Aṭṭhaka Vagga* but include prose frame narratives as **Arthavargīya*, simply as a matter of convention since that title is attested in actual Sanskrit sources.

18. Jan Nattier, *A Guide to the Earliest Chinese Buddhist Translations* (Tokyo: The International Research Institute for Advanced Buddhology, Soka University, 2008), 116–117.
19. For a brief description of Sengyou's catalogue, see ibid., 11–13.
20. Translated in ibid., 121; bracketed dates in the original, but tone-marks mine.
21. That is, *arthavargīya* verses. Several of the *sūtras* in the Chinese version also include other verses, but these can be distinguished from the *arthavargīya* verses by the fact that only the latter are translated in the unique six-character style just mentioned. In many cases, the *arthavargīya* verses can also be distinguished by the following words introducing the verses: 說是義足經, "[The Buddha] said this *arthavargīya* [or *arthapada*] *sūtra*."
22. It is of course possible that the change happened in the other direction, but I think it most likely that the Pali order is more original because, as already mentioned, the order of the *suttas* in the *Aṭṭhaka Vagga* is exact according to number of verses. In spite of minor differences in the verses, the Chinese *sūtras* each have the exact same number of verses as their Pali counterparts, and with the exception of the two just mentioned, its *sūtras* are in the same order as the Pali *suttas*, which indicates that both come from a common ancestor with sixteen *sūtras*, each with a fixed number of verses, ordered according to increasing length. The Chinese version deviates from this pattern only slightly—either because two of the *sūtras* were misplaced and added at the end at some point in the transmission of the translation, or because it was translated from an original in an Indian language in which the misplacement had already occurred.

23. A. F. Rudolf Hoernle, "The Sutta Nipata in a Sanskrit Version from Eastern Turkestan," *Journal of the Royal Asiatic Society* 48, n. 4 (Oct. 1916): 709–732. The longest prose fragment (fr. 2, rev. and fr. 3; p. 714–715) refers to a *parivrājaka* named Māgandika, and thus, according to Hoernle, apparently corresponds to the *Māgandiya Sutta* of the *Aṭṭhaka*, which identification is what gave him the first clue to the identification of the fragments (p. 714 n. 3). Hoernle was apparently unaware of the existence of a Chinese translation of the *Arthavargīya* that also included prose sections together with the verses. Although the fragmentary nature of Hoernle's Sanskrit version and the vicissitudes of translation lying behind the Chinese version make a direct comparison of the two difficult, it seems unlikely that the Chinese version was translated from a text that was *exactly* the same as the Sanskrit text from which Hoernle's fragments come; for example, while the Sanskrit fragments refer to Māgandika as a *parivrājaka*, the Chinese version refers to him (摩因提) as a Brahman (梵志).
24. See the *Paramatthajotikā II* commentary on *Sn.* 4.10: *kā uppatti? imassa suttassa ito paresañ ca pañcannaṃ kalahavivādacūḷabyūhamahābyūhatuvaṭakātt adaṇḍasuttānaṃ sammāparibbājanīyassa uppattiyaṃ vuttanayeneva sāmaññato uppatti vuttā. visesato pana yatheva tasmiṃ mahāsamaye rāgacaritadevatānaṃ sappāyavasena dhammaṃ desetuṃ nimmitabuddhena attānaṃ pucchāpetvā sammāparibbājanīyasuttam abhāsi, evaṃ tasmiṃ yeva mahāsamaye "kiṃ nu kho purā sarīrabhedā kattabban"ti uppannacittānaṃ devatānaṃ cittaṃ ñatvā tāsaṃ anuggahatthaṃ aḍḍhateḷasabhikkhusataparivāraṃ nimmitabuddhaṃ ākāsena ānetvā tena attānaṃ pucchāpetvā imaṃ suttam abhāsi.*
25. For these reasons, I cannot agree with Bapat's assessment that the Pali commentary provides an "identical introductory story" to that found in the *Yìzújīng*—Bapat, *Arthapada Sutra*, 1 n. 2.
26. Bapat, *Arthapada Sutra*, 16 n. 1.
27. The practice of embedding verses within a prose narrative is found in many Pali texts, sometimes fully within the canonical boundary, but in other cases straddling the canonical-commentarial divide. The *Sagāthā Vagga* of the *Saṃyutta Nikāya*, which we already discussed earlier in this chapter, is an example in which canonical *sutta*s are composed of verses embedded in prose narratives (hence the name *Sagāthā*, "with verses"). Most examples, however, are found in the *Khuddaka Nikāya*, where the *Aṭṭhaka* itself is found. Many of the canonical *suttas* of the *Sutta Nipāta* in which the *Aṭṭhaka* is found include prose narration along with their verses; the *Aṭṭhaka* is, in fact, unique insofar as it is the only *vagga* of the *Sutta Nipāta* that does *not* contain any prose. The *Udāna* and *Itivuttaka* are entire collections whose *suttas* consist of prose narrations that describe the circumstance in which the Buddha said something in verse. Other collections in the *Khuddaka* also associate prose narratives with verse, but in those cases, the tradition considers only the verses to be canonical and the prose to be extra-canonical commentary. The most well-known of these is of course

the *Jātaka*, which is in fact better known for its extra-canonical prose "commentary" than its canonical verses since in most cases the actual story of the Buddha's former birth is only intelligible from the former. The same is true of the *Dhammapada*—the canonical verses which are so well-known in the West from repeated translation into Western languages are supplemented in the commentary with extensive prose narratives that serve to contextualize those verses; as we have already seen, this is one of the places in the Pali tradition where the complete story of Māgandiya offering his daughter to the Buddha is preserved.

Of these examples, the *Udāna* provides an interesting counterpoint to the *Aṭṭhaka* as an illustration of the process by which prose narratives and verses were combined differently by different traditions. While the Pali *Udāna* collection consists entirely of prose narratives with embedded verses, most of the other extant *Udāna* collections, including a Sanskrit version, a Tibetan translation, and one (T. 213) of two translations found in the Chinese Canon, include only verses—see Bhikkhu Anālayo, "The Development of the Pāli *Udāna* Collection," *Buddhist Studies (Bukkyō Kenkyū)* 37 (March 2009), 39–40 and 63 n. 2–4. The second Chinese translation of an *Udāna* collection (T. 212) *does* include prose narratives (Ibid., 40), but it includes prose narratives only for some verses (providing in other cases only a word-commentary), and even when a prose narrative is present, it more often than not does not correspond to the narrative found in the Pali version (Ibid., 41–46). In fact, only in the case of the first three *udānas* is there an exact correspondence between both the verses and the prose narrative in the Pali and T. 212. Through a detailed study and comparison of the Pali *Udāna* and T. 212, Bhikkhu Anālayo has shown that the *udānas* were most likely circulated without prose at first; that they grew as verse collections differently in different traditions; and moreover that even when prose was added, it was done so independently and in different ways by different traditions (Ibid., 55–57). Anālayo notes in his conclusion that "[t]he case of the Pāli *Udāna* collection thus appears to be in some respects the reverse of the case of the *Aṭṭhakavagga*" (Ibid., 56)—that is, while the Pali tradition, unlike other traditions, kept the *Aṭṭhaka* verses free of prose, it preserved the *Udāna* verses completely embedded in prose, unlike most other traditions, which did not. More importantly, though, Anālayo's study shows that even when two traditions do attach prose to a set of verses, they can do so independently even while drawing upon a common tradition.

28. For references to Pali and other parallels to the stories in the *Yìzújīng*, see the notes at the beginning of each *sūtra* in Bapat, *Arthapada Sutra*.
29. This word for *brāhmaṇa* is a "translation" that contains a transcription within it. It is based on a putative etymology of *brāhmaṇa* as deriving from *brahma* and *manas* (i.e., "one who has the intellect of *brahman* [or Brahmā]"), with the character 梵 transcribing *brahma* and the character 志 translating *manas*. In later translations, *fànzhì* came to be replaced as a translation for *brāhmaṇa* by *póluómén* (婆羅門), which is pure transcription.

30. Interestingly, Zhī Qiān does not include *fànzhì* in his translation here either, but he does include *shāmén* (沙門) as a transcription for *śramaṇa*: 悉無能說到處，眾學沙門遊心，悉令求所在處，如觸冒知如去.

31. Strictly speaking, the same is true of Sanskrit/Pali, insofar as the subject is implicit in the inflection of the verb; an explicit subject is usually included for emphasis. In this respect, the *Aṭṭhaka* puts routine emphasis on the subject when it is the ideal person by making varied use of different honorific terms, including *bhikkhu, muni,* and *brāhmaṇa*. Zhī Qiān's translation simply shows a tendency to efface this variegated emphatic reference to the ideal person, and prefers to leave the subject implicit.

32. In *sutta* 4 of the *Aṭṭhaka, brāhmaṇa* occurs twice, in v. 790 and 795. We have already looked at the Chinese for the relevant *pāda* in v. 790 (a) in the context of our discussion of the way in which the *Yìzújīng* mirrors the *Mahāniddesa*'s practice of reinterpreting the teaching against all views as only referring to *wrong* views: 從異道無得脫, "Following another path, one does not obtain liberation." I have rendered the subject of "obtain" here as "one" because the subject—presumably *brāhmaṇa* in the original—is omitted in the Chinese. The Chinese counterpart to v. 795, however, is the one verse, already mentioned, where Zhī Qiān explicitly translates *brāhmaṇa* in his translation. The relevant *pāda* (a) is 無所有為梵志, "Without attachments, he is a Brahman."

    The word *brāhmaṇa* also occurs twice in *sutta* 5 of the *Aṭṭhaka*, in the final two verses, 802–803. The Chinese equivalents to these verses are discernible, but obscured by what likely are mistranslations. The relevant portion of v. 802 is the second hemistich, which reads, *taṃ brāhmaṇaṃ diṭṭhim anādiyānaṃ, kenīdha lokasmiṃ vikappayeyya*, "Who here in the world could have doubts about that Brahman who has not taken a view?" The Chinese, however, reads, 慧觀法竟見意，從是得捨世空, which I interpret as "With wisdom he looks at *dharma* and completely sees the meaning; from this, he attains [Awakening?] and abandons the empty [things] of the world." The first sign that there is a problem of translation here is the phrase 從是 ("from this") for *kena*, when in fact *kena* is a question word referring to a person ("by whom?"). The character 世 ("world") appears to reflect the locative *lokasmiṃ*, but it is used in a context that does have support in the Pali text. In the first *pāda*, Zhī Qiān uses two verbs meaning "to see" (觀 and 見), although none are found in th Pali—perhaps he was misled by the noun *diṭṭhim*, which is derived from a verb meaning "to see." The character 慧 ("wisdom") is difficult to explain, but may possibly be meant as a translation of *taṃ brāhmaṇaṃ*.

    The Chinese counterpart to v. 803 is easier to reconcile with the Pali, but also appears to involve mistranslation. The relevant *pāda* in Pali reads, *na brāhmaṇo sīlavatena neyyo*, "A Brahman is not to be inferred by morality or vows." The Chinese, on the other hand, reads, 但守戒求為諦, "Only maintaining vows, he seeks for the truth." It is not clear to me where "he seeks for the truth" comes from, but more importantly, Zhī Qiān says that the ideal person *maintains* vows, when the Pali in fact says quite the opposite, that he is *not* to be inferred by morality or vows. In any case, as in v. 790 above, *brāhmaṇa* appears to have been simply omitted from the translation as an implicit subject.

The Chinese counterpart to v. 843 in *sutta* 9 is of particular interest because here we find what is almost certainly an interpretative translation of *brāhmaṇa* that holds it to be metaphorical. The relevant *pāda* (a) reads, 有諦人當何言, "What should the person who has truth say?" The Pali, however, reads, *saccan ti so brāhmaṇo kiṃ vadeyya*, "Why should that Brahman say, 'True'?" It appears that Zhī Qiān has taken *kiṃ* to mean "what?" when here it actually means "why?" This renders the content of what the Brahman says (or rather does not say)—namely, *saccan ti* ("True")—superfluous, and so it appears that Zhī Qiān has somehow taken it as descriptive of "that Brahman" (*so brāhmaṇo*), resulting in the phrase "the person who has truth" (有諦人).

There are two verses in *sutta* 13 of the *Aṭṭhaka*, 907 and 911, that contain the word *brāhmaṇa*. The first of these has no counterpart in the Chinese. There is a verse in the corresponding Chinese *sūtra* (12) between the verses that correspond to v. 906 and v. 908 in the Pali, but as Bapat notes, it is completely different from Pali v. 907—Bapat, *Arthapada Sutra*, 110. The second of the two Pali verses, however, does have a clear equivalent, the relevant *pāda* (a) of which reads, 慧意到無所至, "The one with wise thoughts attains anything without exception." The overall sense of the translation is difficult to reconcile with the Pali—*na brāhmaṇo kappam upeti saṅkhā*, "The Brahman does not attain a proper definition"—although the sense of "attaining" may likely derive from the verb *upeti*. More importantly, though, we find here once again what is probably an interpretive translation of *brāhmaṇa*. As already stated above, the standard translation Zhī Qiān uses for *brāhmaṇa* is *fànzhì* (梵志), which is based on an assumed etomylogical derivation of the word from *brahma* and *manas*, and uses 梵 to transcribe *brahma* and 志 to translate *manas*. In this verse, it appears that Zhī Qiān is using 慧意 to translate the supposed etomylogical roots of *brāhmaṇa* even more explicitly—慧 ("intelligent") is for *brahma*, and 意 ("thought") is for *manas*. He is thus interpreting *brāhmaṇa* here as literally a "person of intelligent thoughts."

The final instance of *brāhmaṇa* in the *Aṭṭhaka* is in v. 946 of *sutta* 15, which has its parallel in *sūtra* 16 of the *Yìzújīng*. The relevant portion is the first hemistich, which in Pali reads, *saccā avokkamma muni, thale tiṭṭhati brāhmaṇo*, "Not having deviated from the truth, the sage stands on dry ground, a Brahman." The Chinese translation, again, appears to be somewhat garbled: 乘諦力黠已駕，立到彼慧無憂, "Riding the power of truth, he already is able to control his craftiness. He immediately reaches the other [shore]; there is no concern about wisdom." Nevertheless, we can still see the connection to the Pali in the characters 諦 ("truth") for *saccā* and 立 (which can also mean "to stand") for *tiṭṭhati*. The word *brāhmaṇo*, together with its appositive *muni*, appears to have been omitted as an implicit subject, or else incorporated in the sense of "wisdom" (慧).

33. The name given for this Brahman in the Chinese is *Mójié* (摩竭), a standard transcription for *makara*, which refers to a sea monster or monster-like sea-borne animal (such as a crocodile). Bapat prefers to read *Mójié* as a transcription for Māgadha, however, since it is also attested as a transcription for Magadha (the *janapada*). I nonetheless prefer the reading *makara*, which is consistent with the tendency of early Buddhist texts, as we discussed earlier in this chapter, to give Brahmans "funny" names.
34. T. 198: 見摩竭者，悉得解脫；今見死屍亦解脫；後聞名者亦解脫.
35. T. 198: 是曹梵志，非一世癡冥。過去久遠.
36. T. 198: 是時鏡面王者，即我身是；時無眼人者，即講堂梵志是.
37. Bapat suggests, plausibly, that this name may be a translation of *dharmadarśī*—Bapat, *Arthapada Sutra*, 104.
38. T. 198: 是時，座中有梵志，名法觀，亦在大眾中。因緣所計，見於泥洹脫者有支體，以故生意疑信因緣。佛知法觀梵志所生疑，是時便作一佛，端正形類無比，見者悉喜，有三十二大人相，金色復有光，衣法大衣，亦如上說。
39. See Bapat, *Arthapada Sutra*, 106–114, for a full accounting of the differences.
40. This would presumably be an early example of the Buddha being portrayed as producing a *nirmāṇakāya* (lit., "constructed body")—not as a divine *sambhogakāya* creating a phantasm of himself to play out the life of the "historical" Buddha, as we find in the developed Mahāyāna doctrine of the Three Bodies, but as a human (but fully Awakened) being making use of his special powers to construct an ethereal body. See David Gordon White, *Sinister Yogis* (Chicago: University of Chicago Press, 2009), 177–182.
41. This *sutta* is a bit of an outlier among the "Brahman-texts" of the *Aṭṭhaka* insofar as it is not included among the "core" *sutta*s identified by Vetter; as such, the Brahman in this *sutta* represents an ideal much closer to what one would expect according to mainstream early Buddhist doctrine than what we find in the "core" *sutta*s. Overall, the *sutta* takes up fairly ordinary themes such as abandoning desire and becoming free from attachments, but it begins with a brief reference to the fear that comes from those who have "taken up the stick" (*attadaṇḍā*)—from which the Pali title (*attadaṇḍasuttaṃ*) is derived. The **Arthavargīya* from which the *Yìzújīng* was translated appears to interpret the verses as a whole as an exhortation against violence, and thus it introduces them with a long prose narrative in which a king, because of a perceived slight, slaughters all of the Sakyas, prompting the Buddha to predict that he will pay dearly for this sin in future lifetimes. Although this narrative serves as another interesting example of how framing can be used in general to interpret a set of verses—in this case, by emphasizing the theme of violence—it does not introduce Brahmans as characters in any significant way, and thus it essentially ignores the use of the word *Brahman* in the verses.
42. The gloss is word-for-word the same as found in the *Mahāniddesa*, except that in the case of v. 1063, in the dialog with Dhotaka, the word *bhagavā* is added at

the beginning to make clear that the Brahman being referred to is the Buddha himself.

43. *Sn.* 1026: *avijjā muddhāti jānāhi, vijjā muddhādhipātinī / saddhāsatisamādhīhi, chandavīriyena saṃyutā //.*

44. See the gloss on the vocative *brāhmaṇa* in v. 1140: *brāhmaṇā ti gāravena mātulaṃ ālapati.*

45. Interestingly, this and the immediately preceding verse, in which Bāvarī asks the question, are in *tuṭṭhubha,* while the rest of the *vatthu-gāthā* is in *vatta.*

46. See *Paramatthajotikā II,* commentary on the *vatthu-gāthā* of the *Pārāyaṇa,* v. 1013.

47. *idam avoca bhagavā magadhesu viharanto pāsāṇake cetiye.*

48. Thus, Piṅgiya's dialog with the Buddha is entitled *piṅgiya-māṇava-pucchā.* The manuscript traditions of the *Cūḷaniddesa* are not, however, consistent about the titles of the individual dialogs in the *Pārāyaṇa*—see W. Stede, ed., *Niddesa,* vol. 3 (London: Pali Text Society, 1918), xx-xxi.

49. *yathā ahū vakkali muttasaddho, bhadrāvudho āḷavi gotamo ca / evam eva tvam pi pamuñcassu saddhaṃ / gamissasi tvaṃ piṅgiya maccudheyyassa pāraṃ //.* See Norman, *Group of Discourses,* 389–390 n. 1146, for a discussion of the difficulties in translating *muttasaddho.*

50. A monk by the name of Vakkali is referred to in two other places: *SN* 3.1.9.5 and *AN* 1.208.

51. N. A. Jayawickrama, "The Vaggas of the Sutta Nipāta," *University of Ceylon Review* 6 (1948), 243–249.

52. Bāvarī is referred to in the *Cūḷaniddesa* in the commentaries on v. 1084, the prose section at the beginning of the first epilogue, v. 1134, v. 1135, and v. 1138. In the last of these commentaries, the *Niddesa* author tells us that Piṅgiya was Bāvarī's nephew (*piṅgiyā ti bāvarī taṃ nattāraṃ nāmena ālapati*), which provides additional confirmation that the *Niddesa*'s information on Bāvarī was not simply based on the *vatthu-gāthā,* since the latter makes no mention of Piṅgiya's relationship to Bāvarī.

53. Jayawickrama writes, "The probability is that both the v.g. and Nd 2 were not separated from each other by a long interval of time, and that the subject matter of the v.g. may have existed in some form before Nd 2 was compiled, and that the latter was influenced by it"—Jayawickrama, "Vaggas of the Sutta Nipāta," 248.

54. See Norman, *Group of Discourses,* 359 n. 976–1031. The relevant fragment, which Norman cites, is Turfan fragment no. 1582, published in Heinz Bechert and Klaus Wille, eds., *Sanskrithandschriften aus den Turfanfunden,* vol. 6 (Stuttgart: Franz Steiner Verlag Wiesbaden GMBH, 1989), 199–200. Other fragments from the *Pārāyaṇa* (or, more properly speaking, fragments that show parallels to certain parts of the *Pārāyaṇa*) are found in the same volume on p. 198 and in Lore Sander and Ernst Waldschmidt, eds., *Sanskrithandschriften aus den Turfanfunden* 4 (Wiesbaden: Franz Steiner Verlag GMBH, 1980), p. 236–238.

55. I am, of course, ignoring the titles of the dialogs, which, as I have already discussed, follow the story in the *vatthu-gāthā* by referring to the 16 interlocutors as *māṇava*, but, based on the inconsistent evidence provided by *Niddesa* manuscripts, are almost certainly late. The actual *verses* contained in these 16 dialogs provide almost no information about the interlocutors' identities other than their names; the one exception, which we already looked at earlier, is v. 1100 in the *Jatukaṇṇi-māṇava-pucchā* (11), in which the Buddha refers to his interlocutor with the vocative *brāhmaṇa*. This verse (along with the two immediately preceding, which also present the Buddha's words) is in the *vatta* meter, unlike v. 1096–7 (which present Jatukaṇṇī's question), which are in *tuṭṭhubha*. Although we can of course only speculate, it is possible that additions, such as the *vatta* verses of this dialog, were made by the same person who wrote the first epilogue, which is also in *vatta* meter, to a pre-existing text or texts to "fill out" a desired scheme of 16 question-and-answer dialogs.
56. *idam avoca bhagavā magadhesu viharanto pāsāṇake cetiye.*
57. *paricārakasoḷasānaṃ brāhmaṇānaṃ ajjhiṭṭho puṭṭho puṭṭho pañhaṃ byākāsi.*
58. *ajito tissametteyyo, puṇṇako atha mettagū / dhotako upasīvo ca, nando ca atha hemako // todeyya-kappā dubhayo, jatukaṇṇī ca paṇḍito / bhadrāvudho udayo ca, posālo cāpi brāhmaṇo / mogharājā ca medhāvī, piṅgiyo ca mahāisi // ete buddhaṃ upāgacchuṃ, sampannacaraṇaṃ isiṃ / pucchantā nipuṇe pañhe, buddhaseṭṭhaṃ upāgamuṃ //.*
59. Vetter, "Some Remarks," 38.
60. Verse 1009, which immediately follows the list of the 16 Brahmans in the *vatthu-gāthā*, nods to the grandiose titles given to them in the list by saying that they "all had their separate groups, [and were] famous throughout the world" (*paccekagaṇino sabbe sabbalokassa vissutā*). This seems contrived, however; how can these 16 Brahmans be both *māṇavas* and famous teachers in their own right?
61. The result is a jarring disjunction between v. 1130, the last verse of the first epilogue, and v. 1131, the first verse of the second epilogue.
62. Even the internal composition of the *anugīti-gāthā* is somewhat suspect. For one thing, it exhibits a remarkable heterogeneity of meters—v. 1131–2, 1135–41, and 1147–8 are in *vatta*; v. 1133–4, 1142–4, and 1146 are in *tuṭṭhubha*; while v. 1145 and 1149 are mixed. This is not conclusive in and of itself, but it is suggestive. In addition, while I have been emphasizing v. 1142–1144 (all in *vatta*), in which Piṅgiya clearly states that he is not physically with the Buddha and can only return to him in his mind because of his feebleness in old age, these are immediately preceded by verses in *tuṭṭhubha* in which he tells his interlocutor, "I am not absent from him [i.e., the Buddha] even for a moment, Brahman" (v. 1140: *nāhaṃ tamhā vippavasāmi muhuttam api brāhmaṇa*).
63. Vetter, "Some Remarks," 38.
64. *Sn*. 5.4.1054, 5.4.1057, 5.5.1061, 5.5.1067, 5.7.1083.
65. *paricārakasoḷasānaṃ brāhmaṇānan ti piṅgiyo brāhmaṇo bāvarissa brāhmaṇassa paddho paddhacaro paricārako sisso. piṅgiyena te soḷasā ti — evam pi paricārakasoḷasānaṃ brāhmaṇānaṃ.*

66. *atha vā, te soḷasa brāhmaṇā buddhassa bhagavato paddhā paddhacarā paricārakā sissā ti — evam pi paricārakasoḷasānaṃ brāhmaṇānaṃ.*
67. One could argue that a counterexample is provided by the *Puṇṇaka-māṇava-pucchā* (3), in which Puṇṇaka asks about sacrifice, and the Buddha explains that sacrifice does not lead to the "far shore." We have already encountered this dialog as one of the dialogs in which the word *brāhmaṇa* appears, but used together with the word *khattiya* in apparent reference to a particular social group, rather than the ideal person. There is no particular association between Brahmanhood and the practice of sacrifice here, however; Brahmans are simply mentioned together with seers (*isayo*), human beings (*manujā*) and *khattiyas* as among those who have sacrificed to gods in the past.

## CHAPTER 7

1. Bronkhorst, *Buddhism in the Shadow of Brahmanism*, 163–164.
2. Ibid., 164.
3. Ibid., 164–165.
4. *MBh.* 1.56.33: *yad ihāsti tad anyatra yan nehāsti na tat kva cit*: "What is here is (found) elsewhere; what is not here is not (found) anywhere."
5. Recent studies addressing the *Mahābhārata* as a response to Buddhism, the *śramaṇa* movements in general, and the reign of Aśoka include Nicholas Sutton, "Aśoka and Yudhiṣṭhira: A Historical Setting for the Ideological Tensions of the *Mahābhārata*," *Religion* 27 (1997): 331–341; James L. Fitzgerald, "Making Yudhiṣṭhira the King: the Dialectics and the Politics of Violence in the *Mahābhārata*," *Rocznik Orientalistyczny* 54, no. 1 (2001): 63–92; Madeleine Biardeau, *Le Mahābhārata: Un récit fondateur du brahmanisme et son interpretation*, 2 vols. (Paris: Editions de Seuil, 2002); James L. Fitzgerald, *The Mahābhārata, Volume 7* (Chicago: University of Chicago Press, 2004), 100–142; Alf Hiltebeitel, "Buddhism and the Mahābhārata. Boundary Dynamics in Textual Practice," in Federico Squarcini, ed., *Boundaries, Dynamics, and Construction of Traditions in South Asia* (London: Anthem Press, 2011), 107–131.
6. In choosing to refer to this genre of texts as "encounter dialogs,"* I have attempted to use a fairly neutral term so as to leave the category open to as wide a relevant variety of texts as possible. Many encounter dialogs, indeed those that have most commonly caught scholars' attention as purported evidence of the antagonism between early Buddhism and Brahmanism, are not simply dialogs but *debates*; that is, the Buddha encounters a Brahman and debates with him over the tenets advanced by Neo-Brahmanism—the *varṇa* system, Brahmanical superiority, the importance of knowledge of the Vedas and ritual, and so on. In other cases, however, the dialog is simply a dialog—as, for example, when a Brahman such as Jāṇussoṇi approaches the Buddha and simply asks a question, which the Buddha answers by giving a sermon. Even in these latter cases, however, the

juxtaposition of an interlocutor identified as a Brahman next to the Buddha who is not so identified serves to establish a Buddhist identity as separate from that of the Brahmans.

*Incidentally, the term *encounter dialogue* has also been used by John McRae to refer to Chan *gong'ans* in which a teacher has an encounter with a student: John R. McRae, *Seeing Through Zen: Encounter, Transformation, and Genealogy in Chinese Chan Buddhism* (Berkeley: University of California Press, 2003), 18–19, 74–100. In using the same term (which is in any case unintentional), I do not mean to imply any relationship or even comparison between the *sūtras* I am referring to in the early Buddhist tradition and the Chinese *gong'ans* that McRae is referring to. Obviously, however, there are certain similarities that would lead each of us independently to choose the words *encounter* and *dialog* to describe the texts we are dealing with.

7. Brian Black, "Rivals and Benefactors: Encounters Between Buddhists and Brahmins in the Nikāyas," *Religions of South Asia* 3, no. 1 (2009): 25–43.
8. Chakravarti, *Social Dimensions*, 98; cited in Bronkhorst, *Buddhism in the Shadow of Brahmanism*, 35.
9. These are the three knowledges obtained by the Buddha at his Awakening; see, e.g., *MN* 36.
10. Although a full exploration of the issue is beyond the scope of this book, it is possible that the encounter dialog genre as a whole actually developed out of the *Brāhmaṇa Saṃyutta* of the *Saṃyutta Nikāya*. The *Brāhmaṇa Saṃyutta* is part of the *Sagāthā Vagga*, a major division of the *Saṃyutta Nikāya* in which all *suttas* incorporate verses (*gāthā*) within them and are organized into sub-*vaggas* according to the type of interlocutor involved (in this case, Brahmans). The fact that some of these verses are found elsewhere in other contexts implies that the *suttas* of the *Sagāthā Vagga* were created somewhat formulaically by embedding preexisting verses within short prose narratives involving variations on certain "stock characters." According to a theory proposed by the Taiwanese scholar-monk Yìnshùn, the *Saṃyuktāgama* (Skt. for the collection referred to in Pali as the *Saṃyutta Nikāya*) was the earliest canonical collection created, organized according to the first three Buddhist *aṅgas* (*sūtra, geya,* and *vyākaraṇa*); out of this early collection, the other Nikāya/Āgama traditions developed as larger *sūtras* were produced according to *Saṃyukta* models—Yìnshùn 印順, *Yuanshi fojiao shengdian zhi jicheng* 原始佛教聖典之集成 [The compilation of the scriptures of original Buddhism] (Zhubei: Zhengwen, 2002); English summary in Choong Mun-keat, *The Fundamental Teachings of Early Buddhism: A comparative study based on the Sūtrāṅga portion of the Pāli Saṃyutta-Nikāya and the Chinese Saṃyuktāgama* (Wiesbaden: Harrassowitz Verlag, 2000), 9–11. This theory has been taken up and elaborated upon by Bhikkhu Sujāto, "Aṅgas in the Nikāyas & Āgamas," in *A History of Mindfulness: How Insight Worsted Tranquility in the Satipaṭṭhāna Sutta* (n.p.: Santipada, 2012), 82–108. Further

information on this theory and its relevance for the study of encounter dialogs can be found in Nathan McGovern, "Comparative Nikāya/Āgama Studies and the Development of the Nikāya/Āgamas," in "Buddhists, Brahmans, and Buddhist Brahmans: Negotiating Identities in Indian Antiquity" (PhD diss., University of California, Santa Barbara, 2013), 402–462.

11. *DN* 3, *Ambaṭṭha Sutta; DN* 4, *Soṇadaṇḍa Sutta; DN* 5, *Kūṭadanta Sutta; DN* 12, *Lohicca Sutta; DN* 13, *Tevijja Sutta; DN* 27, *Aggañña Sutta. DN* 6, *Mahāli Sutta,* has the form of an encounter dialog insofar as it involves Brahmans visiting the Buddha, but they end up being superfluous to the narrative, which is taken from the following *sutta, DN* 7, *Jāliya Sutta. DN* 10, *Subha Sutta,* is not strictly speaking an encounter dialog in that the Buddha does not appear in it at all—indeed, it takes place after the Buddha's death—but it nonetheless has a similar structure, with a Brahman youth (*māṇava*) named Subha meeting with the Buddha's disciple Ānanda.

12. These three *suttas* have been fruitfully studied in tandem by Brian Black as supporting the arguments of Tsuchida Ryutaro and Oliver Freiberger that early Buddhism was not as opposed to Brahmanism as sometimes supposed: see Black, "Rivals and Benefactors." For an extended study of the *Ambaṭṭha Sutta,* see also Alf Hiltebeitel, *Dharma: Its Early History in Law, Religion, and Narrative* (Oxford: Oxford University Press, 2001), 108–123.

13. For a detailed comparison of this formula in all available versions, see Konrad Meisig, *Das Śrāmaṇyaphala-Sūtra: Synoptische Übersetzung und Glossar der chinesischen Fassungen verglichen mit dem Sanskrit und Pāli* (Wiesbaden: Otto Harrassowitz, 1987), 39–52.

14. These three versions are the well-known Theravāda version preserved in Pali, a likely Dharmaguptaka version preserved in Chinese (T. 1), and a likely Sarvāstivāda version preserved in a recently discovered Sanskrit manuscript. On the sectarian affiliation of the Chinese version, see Mayeda Egaku, "Japanese Studies on the Schools of the Chinese Āgamas," in *Genshi bukkyō seiten no seiritsushi kenkyū* [A History of the Formation of Original Buddhist Texts] (Tokyo: Sankibō Busshorin, 1964), 97. On the Sanskrit *Dīrghāgama,* see Jens-Uwe Hartmann, "Zu einer neuen Handschrift des Dīrghāgama," in Christine Chojnacki et al., eds., *Vividharatnakaraṇḍaka: Festschrift für Adelheid Mette,* Indica et Tibetica, vol. 37 (Swisstal-Odendorf: Indica et Tibetica Verlag, 2000), 359–367; Jens-Uwe Hartmann, "Further Remarks on the New Manuscript of the Dīrghāgama," *Journal of the International College for Advanced Buddhist Studies* 5 (2002): 133–150; and Jens-Uwe Hartmann, "Contents and Structure of the Dīrghāgama of the (Mūla)-Sarvāstivādins," *Annual Report of the International Research Institute for Advanced Buddhology at Soka University* 7 (2004): 119–137; Jens-Uwe Hartmann and Klaus Wille, "The Manuscript of the *Dīrghāgama* and the Private Collection in Virginia," in Paul Harrison and Jens-Uwe Hartmann, eds., *From Birch Bark to Digital Data: Recent Advances in Buddhist Manuscript*

*Research* (Vienna: Verlag der Österreichischen Akademie der Wissenschaften, 2014), 137–155.

15. For further details, see McGovern, "Buddhists, Brahmans, and Buddhist Brahmans," 427–429.
16. A *brahmadeyya* is a grant of land to a Brahman or Brahmans by a king. It is likely that these grants were not so much of the land as such, but rather of tax benefits over the population on that land: Bronkhorst, *Buddhism in the Shadow of Brahmanism*, 92. The Pali (*DN* 4) and Chinese (*DĀ* 22) versions of the *Soṇadaṇḍa Sutta* agree that the Brahman interlocutor lived in Campā, which was a *brahmadeyya* land grant, but they disagree as to the donor: Bimbisāra of Magadha according to the Pali, Prasenajit of Kośala according to the Chinese. Likewise, the Pali (*DN* 5) and Chinese (*DĀ* 23) versions of the *Kūṭadanta Sutta* agree that Kūṭadanta lived in a *brahmadeyya* grant called Khānumata, but they show the same disagreement over the donor: Bimbisāra in the Pali and Prasenajit in the Chinese. The Pali and Chinese versions of the *Ambaṭṭha Sutta*, on the other hand, are in complete agreement that the Brahman Pokkharasāti lived in Ukkhaṭṭha, which was given to him as *brahmadeyya* by Prasenajit (P. Pasenadi).
17. *Vin*. I.35, I.242, I.245, III.1; *DN* 3, 4, 5, 6, 12; *MN* 41, 42, 60, 82, 91, 92, 95, 150; *SN* 5.11.1.7; *AN* 3.63, 3.65. A short version is found in *DN* 2, 13; *MN* 75, 98, 140.
18. *taṃ kho pana bhavantaṃ gotamaṃ evaṃ kalyāṇo kittisaddo abbhuggato — iti pi so bhagavā arahaṃ sammāsambuddho vijjācaraṇasampanno sugato lokavidū anuttaro purisadammasārathi satthā devamanussānaṃ buddho bhagavā. so imaṃ lokaṃ sadevakaṃ samārakaṃ sabrahmakaṃ sassamaṇabrāhmaṇiṃ pajaṃ sadevamanussaṃ sayaṃ abhiññā sacchikatvā pavedeti. so dhammaṃ deseti ādikalyāṇaṃ majjhekalyāṇaṃ pariyosānakalyāṇaṃ, sātthaṃ sabyañjanaṃ. kevalaparipuṇṇaṃ parisuddhaṃ brahmacariyaṃ pakāseti. sādhu kho pana tathārūpānaṃ arahataṃ dassanaṃ hotī ti*: "Now, regarding the Venerable Gotama a good reputation has gone forth thus: 'That Blessed One is worthy, fully Awakened, endowed with knowledge and conduct, well-gone, knower of the world, the unexcelled charioteer of people who are to be trained, instructor of gods and men, the Awakened, the Blessed One. Having realized for himself by higher knowledge, he declares this world with the gods, with the Māras, with the Brahmās; [he declares] the people with the *samaṇas* and Brahmans, with the gods and men. He preaches the *dhamma*, which is good in the beginning, good in the middle, good in the end, with meaning and articulation. He proclaims a wholly perfect, completely pure *brahmacariya*. Well indeed is it to see such worthies.' "
19. These Brahmans are called *brāhmaṇagahapatikā*, "Brahman householders," indicating explicitly that they represent the householder conception of Brahmanhood.
20. *. . . ubhato sujāto mātito ca pitito ca, saṃsuddhagahaṇiko yāva sattamā pitāmahayugā akkhitto anupakkuṭṭho jātivādena*: ". . . is well born on both the mother's side and

the father's side, of pure descent up to the seventh generation, undisturbed, irreproachable with respect to the matter of birth."

21. As found in *DN* 3, 14, 30; *MN* 91, 92: *yehi samannāgatassa mahāpurisassa dveva gatiyo bhavanti anaññā. sace agāraṃ ajjhāvasati, rājā hoti cakkavattī dhammiko dhammarājā cāturanto vijitāvī janapadatthāvariyappatto sattaratanasamannāgato. tassimāni sattaratanāni bhavanti. seyyathidaṃ — cakkaratanaṃ hatthiratanaṃ assaratanaṃ maṇiratanaṃ itthiratanaṃ gahapatiratanaṃ pariṇāyakaratanameva sattamaṃ. parosahassaṃ kho panassa puttā bhavanti sūrā vīraṅgarūpā parasenappamaddanā. so imaṃ pathaviṃ sāgarapariyantaṃ adaṇḍena asatthena dhammena abhivijiya ajjhāvasati. sace kho pana agārasmā anagāriyaṃ pabbajati, arahaṃ hoti sammāsambuddho loke vivaṭacchado*: ". . . endowed with which a Great Man has only two courses, no other. If he dwells in a house, he becomes a wheel-turning king, a righteous *dhamma*-king, conqueror of the four directions, one who has attained the security of his country, endowed with seven treasures. He has these seven treasures: the treasure of the wheel, the treasure of elephants, the treasure of horses, the treasure of women, the treasure of householders, the treasure of advisers, just these seven. And he has over a thousand sons, who are brave, heroic, crushing the armies of others. He dwells having conquered this earth bounded by the ocean, not with the rod, not with the sword, (but) with *dhamma*. But if he goes forth from the house into homelessness, he becomes a Worthy, a Perfectly Awakened One, who has drawn away the veil of the world."

22. The PTS Dictionary prefers "ox tooth," taking *kūṭa* as meaning "ox." Rhys Davids, however, translated the name as "pointed tooth," apparently extrapolating from the possible meaning of *kūṭa* as "pinnacle" or "point." Since *kūṭa* has a third meaning, that is, "false," or a "lie" or "deceit," I suggest here yet another possible translation—"false tooth"—although I leave it open as to whether this would mean that the Brahman had dentures or simply was a liar.

23. Bronkhorst, *Greater Magadha*, 354.

24. Indeed, in encounter dialogs the Brahman interlocutor is often introduced using what I call the "Triple Veda" formula, which specifically lauds the interlocutor for his Vedic learning. This formula is found in 11 *suttas* in the Pali Canon: *DN* 3, 4, 5; *MN* 91, 92, 93, 95, 100; *AN* 3.58, 3.59, 5.192; *Sn.* 3.7. The formula is as follows: . . . *tiṇṇaṃ vedānaṃ pāragū sanighaṇḍukeṭubhānaṃ sākkharappabhedānaṃ itihāsapañcamānaṃ, padako, veyyākaraṇo, lokāyatamahāpurisalakkhaṇesu anavayo*, "[The Brahman in question is] perfected in the three Vedas—together with their vocabularies and rituals, with their phonology and etymology, and the oral tradition (*itihāsa*) as a fifth—skilled in philology and grammar, not lacking in the Lokāyata and marks of a Great Man."

25. In taking up this theme, the *Kūṭadanta Sutta* may be following a precedent set by the *Saṃyutta* collection of encounter dialogs in the *Brāhmaṇa Saṃyutta*.

Two *suttas* in that collection (*SN* 1.7.8–9) involve the Buddha encountering a Brahman who is in the course of performing a Vedic sacrifice.

26. Black, "Ambaṭṭha and Śvetaketu."
27. The concept of the head splitting if one cannot give an answer in debate appears to be pan-Indian and trans-sectarian, as it is also found in Brahmanical sources. On the "motif of head shattering" in Brahmanical literature, see Black, *Character of the Self*, esp. 80–88. For a comparative study, see Michael Witzel, "The Case of the Shattered Head," *Studien zur Indologie und Iranistik* 13/14 (1987): 363–416.
28. Hiltebeitel, apparently accepting naively Brahmanical claims to purity of lineage, calls this claim by the Buddha "highly dubious": Hiltebeitel, *Dharma*, 116. Bronkhorst, on the other hand, has shown that some Brahmanical texts do indeed countenance the acceptance of a son of a Brahman father and *kṣatriya* mother as a Brahman: Bronkhorst, *How the Brahmins Won*, 114–117. As I have argued in Chapter 5, Buddhist arguments against Brahmanical claims to purity should be taken seriously even when they do conflict with Brahmanical self-representations.
29. Bronkhorst, *Greater Magadha*, 354.
30. *khattiyo seṭṭho janetasmiṃ, ye gottapaṭisārino / vijjācaraṇasampanno, so seṭṭho devamānuse //*. Interestingly, we do indeed find this verse elsewhere, attributed, as claimed here, to a Brahmā (specifically Sanaṅkumāra in the Theravāda tradition). In a *sutta* of the *Brahmā Saṃyutta*, in the *Sagāthā Vagga* of the *Saṃyutta Nikāya*, Brahmā Sanaṅkumāra appears to the Buddha, utters this very verse, and the Buddha expresses his approval (*SN* 1.6.2.1; cf. *SĀ* 1190 and *SĀ2* 103).
31. On the theme of Brahmans in the Buddha's day not living up to the example of the Vedic *ṛṣis*, see also *Sn*. 2.7.
32. A Chinese translation of the *Madhyamāgama*, probably belonging to the Sarvāstivāda school, is preserved at T. 26 (*Zhōng Āhán Jīng* 中阿含經). Like its Pali counterpart, the Chinese *Madhyamāgama* contains a *Brāhmaṇa Varga*, but this *Brāhmaṇa Varga* is quite different in its contents from the *Brāhmaṇa Vagga* of the Pali *Majjhima Nikāya*, containing twice as many *sūtras* overall (20 instead of 10), but only four in common with the Pali collection. The Sarvāstivāda collection appears to have been open to almost any *sūtra* that referred to Brahmans in some way, while the Theravāda version was generally limited to substantive "encounter dialogs." See McGovern, "Buddhists, Brahmans, and Buddhist Brahmans," 520–531.
33. *Mahāsālā* literally means "great hall" and refers to the great wealth of these Brahmans. On the term *mahāsālā*, see Tsuchida, "Two Categories of Brahmins," 54–62.
34. Interestingly, this *sutta* puts great emphasis on the supposed fact that Brahmans of old, unlike contemporary Brahmans, did not kill *cows*. Ironically, one of the oldest texts to speak of the "holy cow," therefore, would be this, a Buddhist text.
35. Interestingly, the process described here, though expressed in extremely polemical terms, does bear a certain resemblance to the historical process by which

the *śrauta* ritual was codified for the sake of state legitimation, as described by modern scholars such as Jan Heesterman and Michael Witzel. I am of course not suggesting that the Buddha's account here in the *Brāhmaṇadhammika Sutta* is "historical," but rather that it is offering a polemical account of an *actual historical process*—namely, the development of the *śrauta* ritual and concomitant growth of a specialized class of ritual specialists to administer it.

36. Dundas, *The Jains*, 75.
37. See, for example, Black, "Ambaṭṭha and Śvetaketu"; Black, "Rivals and Benefactors"; Freiberger, "Negative Campaigning"; and Hiltebeitel, *Dharma*, 108–124.
38. The *jaṭilas* are a complicated issue because, as I argued in Chapter 4, *jaṭila* was likely a slang term rather than an emic designation. There is little reason to believe that the blandly descriptive "forest dwellers" (*vānaprastha*) employed by the Dharma Sūtra authors was an emic designation either; instead, it seems quite plausible that the practitioners designated by these two terms simply considered themselves Brahmans. Since they were not reduced to non-Brahmanical status by the process we have been examining in this chapter, it did not become necessary for them to adopt a different designation for themselves, as did the Buddhists and Jains.
39. According to Vincent Eltschinger, *Buddhist Epistemology as Apologetics: Studies on the History, Self-understanding and Dogmatic Foundations of Late Indian Buddhist Philosophy* (Vienna: Verlag der Österreichischen Akademie der Wissenschaften, 2014), 71, cited by Bronkhorst, *Buddhism in the Shadow of Brahmanism*, 191–193, direct philosophical confrontation between Buddhists and Brahmans did not begin until the end of the 5th century CE. While this represented a significant shift on both sides, the Buddhists at least possessed older scriptures that referred routinely to the Brahmans as opponents. As we discussed at the beginning of this chapter, Brahmanical scriptures, whether *śruti* or *smṛti*, generally speaking did not return the favor; thus, the emergence of direct philosophical confrontation with Buddhists represented for them a fairly novel acknowledgment of the Buddhists' existence.
40. Bronkhorst, *Buddhism in the Shadow of Brahmanism*, 74–97.
41. For a study of Brahmanical ascetic literature and translation of several texts in that genre, see Patrick Olivelle, *Saṃnyāsa Upaniṣads: Hindu Scriptures on Asceticism and Renunciation* (New York: Oxford University Press, 1992).
42. Olivelle, *The Āśrama System*.
43. Bronkhorst, *Greater Magadha*.

## CHAPTER 8

1. On the *Isibhāsiyāiṃ*, see Dundas, *The Jains*, 17–19. For an edition of the Ardhamāgadhī text, with an introduction and translation into Hindi and English, see Mahopadhyay Vinaysagar, ed. and trans., *Isibhasiyaim Suttaim (Rishibhashit*

*Sutra)*, trans. Kalanath Shastri and Dinesh Chandra Sharma (Jaipur: Prakrit Bharati Academy, 1988). In his introduction, Vinaysagar attempts to identify as many of the seers in the text as possible, including the ones mentioned above. In some cases the identifications are rather uncertain, as in the case of "Maskarin Gośāla" (identified with a seer whose name is given as Maṅkhaliputta in the Ardhamāgadhī) and "Śāriputra" (identified with a certain "Sātiputta Buddha"). Although the the identification of the latter is somewhat dubious given that there is no philological explanation for an *r* transforming into a *t*, the identification of this seer with some sort of "Buddhist" figure is made plausible for two other reasons. First, of course, is the fact that he is referred to as "Buddha," a title given to none of the other seers in the text. Second, the actual content of the verses attributed to this seer has a vaguely Buddhist ring to it, in particular *Isi.* 38.2–4, which seems to refer to the middle path.

2. I say this advisedly, aware that the antiquity of the Upaniṣads has been questioned, in particular by Bronkhorst. Certainly some of the later Upaniṣads postdate Buddhism, and Bronkhorst may be right in questioning the antiquity of even the *Bṛhadāraṇyaka* and *Chāndogya Upaniṣads* in the form they come down to us. But as with all early Buddhist, Jain, and Brahmanical texts, I think we should understand these texts as they come down to us as a sectarianization of older figures and their teachings. I am not convinced by Bronkhorst's argument that the teachings on karma, *ātman*, and rebirth in the earliest Upaniṣads are borrowed from a separate source, the culture of Greater Magadha. Bronkhorst does rightly point out that Brahmanism appeared uncomfortable with these ideas for some time afterward, but I believe that this was a result of a reaction against the extremes to which Buddhists and Jains took them, rather than of an aberrant "borrowing" of them from the latter.
3. On the continuities between late Vedic and early Buddhist thought, much to be anticipated is the publication of the work of Lauren Baush, "Kosalan Philosophy in the *Kāṇva Śatapatha Brāhmaṇa* and the *Sutta Nipāta*."
4. Alexander Wynne, *The Origin of Buddhist Meditation* (London: Routledge, 2007).
5. For an overview, see ibid., 8.
6. Although some scholars have read the evidence in this way, there are certain complications involved. On Mahāvīra's relationship to Pārśva, see Dundas, *The Jains*, 30–33.
7. The classic study of the Ājīvakas is A. L. Basham, *History and Doctrines of the Ājīvakas: A Vanished Indian Religion* (Delhi: Motilal Banarsidass, 2002[1951]). For a recent study of the relationship between Mahāvīra, Gosāla, and other even less well-understood ascetic figures in ancient India, see Piotr Balcerowicz, *Early Asceticism in India: Ājīvikism and Jainism* (Oxford: Routledge, 2016).
8. Bronkhorst, *Greater Magadha*, 38–45.

9. Daniel Boyarin, *The Jewish Gospels: The Story of the Jewish Christ* (New York: The New Press, 2012).
10. Boyarin, *Border Lines.*
11. Elaine Fisher, *Hindu Pluralism: Religion and the Public Sphere in Early Modern South Asia* (Oakland: University of California Press, 2017).

# *Bibliography*

ELECTRONIC RESOURCES FOR PRIMARY TEXTS

*CBETA* 中華電子佛典協會. www.cbeta.org.
*Göttingen Register of Electronic Texts in Indian Languages.* gretil.sub.uni-goettingen.de.
Yuttadhammo. *Digital Pali Reader.* pali.sirimangalo.org.

For further information on the citation of primary texts, see the end of the Introduction. For a full list of primary texts cited, see the Abbreviations.

BOOKS AND ARTICLES

Adcock, C. S. *The Limits of Tolerance: Indian Secularism and the Politics of Religious Freedom.* Oxford: Oxford University Press, 2014.

Adikaram, E. W. *Early History of Buddhism in Ceylon, or "State of Buddhism in Ceylon as Revealed by the Pāli Commentaries of the 5th Century A.D."* Colombo: M. D. Gunasena and Co., 1946.

Allon, Mark. "The Oral Composition and Transmission of Early Buddhist Texts." In *Indian Insights: Buddhism, Brahmanism and Bhakti. Papers from the Annual Spalding Symposium on Indian Religion,* edited by Sute Hamilton and Peter Connolly, 39–61. London: Luzac Oriental, 1997.

Almond, Philip C. *The British Discovery of Buddhism.* Cambridge, England: Cambridge University Press, 1988.

Anālayo Bhikkhu. "Comparative Notes on the Madhyama-Āgama." *Fuyan Buddhist Studies* 2 (2007): 33–56.

Anālayo Bhikkhu. "The Development of the Pāli *Udāna* Collection." *Buddhist Studies (Bukkyō Kenkyū)* 37 (March 2009): 39–72.

Anālayo Bhikkhu. *A Comparative Study of the* Majjhima-nikāya. 2 vols. Taipei: Dharma Drum Publishing, 2011.

Appleton, Naomi. *Shared Characters in Jain, Buddhist and Hindu Narrative: Gods, Kings and Other Heroes.* London: Routledge, 2017.

Asad, Talal. *Genealogies of Religion: Discipline and Reasons of Power in Christianity and Islam*. Baltimore: Johns Hopkins University Press, 1993.

Bailey, Greg, and Ian Mabbett. *The Sociology of Early Buddhism*. Cambridge, England: Cambridge University Press, 2003.

Balcerowicz, Piotr. *Early Asceticism in India: Ājīvikism and Jainism*. Oxford: Routledge, 2016.

Bandhu, Vishva. *A Vedic Word-Concordance*. Vol. 5 (Index). Part 1. Hoshiarpur: V.V.R. Institute, 1964.

Bapat, P. V., trans. *Arthapada Sutra: Spoken by the Buddha—Translated by the Upāsaka Che-Kien under the Wu Dynasty (222–280 A.D.)*. 2 parts in 1 vol. Calcutta: Visva-Bharati, 1951.

Bareau, André. *Recherches sur la biographie du Buddha dans les Sūtrapiṭaka et les Vinayapiṭaka anciens: de la quête de l'éveil à la conversion de Śāriputra et de Maudgalyāyana*, Publications de l'Ecole Française d'Extrême-Orient, vol. 53. Paris: Ecole Française d'Extrême-Orient, 1963.

Basham, A. L. *History and Doctrines of the Ājīvikas: A Vanished Indian Religion*. Delhi: Motilal Banarsidass, 2002 [1951].

Bausch, Lauren. "Kosalan Philosophy in the *Kāṇva Śatapatha Brāhmaṇa* and the *Sutta Nipāta*." Unpublished PhD diss., University of California, Berkeley, 2015.

Bausch, Lauren. "Varṇa as internal powers in Vedic Texts." Paper presented at the 227th Meeting of the American Oriental Society, Los Angeles, March 2017.

Bayart, Jean-François. *The Illusion of Cultural Identity*. Trans. Steven Rendall, Janet Roitman, Cynthia Schoch, and Jonathan Derrick. Chicago: University of Chicago Press, 2005.

Bechert, Heinz. *The Dating of the Historical Buddha*. 2 vols. Göttingen: Vandenhoeck and Ruprecht, 1991–1992.

Bechert, Heinz, and Klaus Wille, eds. *Sanskrithandschriften aus den Turfanfunden*. Vol. 6. Stuttgart: Franz Steiner Verlag Wiesbaden GMBH, 1989.

Biardeau, Madeleine. *Le Mahābhārata: Un récit fondateur du brahmanisme et son interprétation*. 2 vols. Paris: Éditions du Seuil, 2002.

Black, Brian. *The Character of the Self in Ancient India: Priests, Kings, and Women in the Early Upaniṣads*. Albany, NY: SUNY Press, 2007.

Black, Brian. "Rivals and Benefactors: Encounters Between Buddhists and Brahmins in the Nikāyas." *Religions of South Asia* 3, no. 1 (2009): 25–43.

Black, Brian. "Ambaṭṭha and Śvetaketu: Literary Connections Between the Upaniṣads and Early Buddhist Narratives." *Journal of the American Academy of Religion* 79, no. 1 (March 2011): 136–161.

Black, Brian, and Laurie Patton, eds. *Dialogue in Early South Asian Religions: Hindu, Buddhist, and Jain Traditions*. Surrey, England: Ashgate, 2015.

Bodhi, Bhikkhu, trans. *The Connected Discourses of the Buddha: A New Translation of the* Saṃyutta Nikāya. Boston: Wisdom Publications, 2000.

Bodhi, Bhikkhu, trans. *The* Suttanipāta: *An Ancient Collection of the Buddha's Discourses Together with Its Commentaries*. Somerville, MA: Wisdom Publications, 2017.

Böhtlingk, Otto, and Rudolph Roth. *Sanskrit-Wörterbuch*. Vol. 5. St. Petersburg: Kaiserlichen Akademie der Wissenschaften, 1858.

Boyarin, Daniel. *Border Lines: The Partition of Judeo-Christianity*. Philadelphia: University of Pennsylvania Press, 2004.

Boyarin, Daniel. *The Jewish Gospels: The Story of the Jewish Christ*. New York: The New Press, 2012.

Bronkhorst, Johannes. "Dharma and Abhidharma." *Bulletin of the School of Oriental and African Studies* 48, no. 2 (1985): 305–320.

Bronkhorst, Johannes. *The Two Sources of Indian Asceticism*. Bern: Peter Lang, 1993.

Bronkhorst, Johannes. *The Two Traditions of Meditation in Early India*. Delhi: Motilal Banarsidass, 1993.

Bronkhorst, Johannes. *Greater Magadha: Studies in the Culture of Early India*. Leiden: Brill, 2007.

Bronkhorst, Johannes. *Buddhism in the Shadow of Brahmanism*. Leiden: Brill, 2011.

Bronkhorst, Johannes. *How the Brahmins Won: From Alexander to the Guptas*. Leiden: Brill, 2016.

Brough, John. "The Early History of the Gotras." *Journal of the Royal Asiatic Society of Great Britain and Ireland*, no. 1 (Apr. 1946): 32–45.

Brough, John. "The Early History of the Gotras (Concluded)." *Journal of the Royal Asiatic Society of Great Britain and Ireland*, no. 1 (Apr. 1947): 76–90.

Burford, Grace G. *Desire, Death and Goodness: The Conflict of Ultimate Values in Theravāda Buddhism*. New York: Peter Lang, 1991.

Burnouf, Eugène. *Introduction to the History of Indian Buddhism*. Trans. Katia Buffetrille and Donald S. Lopez, Jr. Chicago: University of Chicago Press, 2010.

Cameron, Euan. *Enchanted Europe: Superstition, Reason, and Religion, 1250–1750*. Oxford: Oxford University Press, 2010.

Chakravarti, Uma. *The Social Dimensions of Early Buddhism*. Delhi: Oxford University Press, 1987.

Cohen, Richard S. "Nāga, Yakṣiṇī, Buddha: Local Deities and Local Buddhism at Ajanta." *History of Religions* 37, no. 4 (May 1998): 360–400.

Collins, Steven. "The Discourse on What is Primary (Aggañña-Sutta): An Annotated Translation." *Journal of Indian Philosophy* 21 (1993): 301–393.

Coomaraswamy, Ananda K. "Some Pāli Words." *Harvard Journal of Asiatic Studies* 4, no. 2 (Jul. 1939): 116–190.

Cousins, Lance S. "The Dating of the Historical Buddha: A Review Article." *Journal of the Royal Asiatic Society* 6, no. 1 (1996): 57–63.

Cousins, Lance S. "The Early Development of Buddhist Literature and Language in India." *Journal of the Oxford Centre for Buddhist Studies* 5 (2013): 89–135.

Cousins, Lance S. "Pali Oral Literature." In *Buddhist Studies Ancient and Modern*, edited by P. Denwood and A. Piatigorsky, 1–11. London: Curzon Press, 1983.

Cowell, E. B. *The Jātaka, or Stories of the Buddha's Former Births*. Trans. Robert Chalmers et al. 6 vols. in 3 physical vols. Delhi: Motilal Banarsidass Publishers, 1994 [1895].

Dehejia, Vidya. "On Modes of Visual Narration in Early Buddhist Art." *The Art Bulletin* 72, no. 3 (Sept. 1990): 374–392.

de Jong, J. W. "A Brief History of Buddhist Studies in Europe and America (Part I)." *Eastern Buddhist* 7, no. 1 (1974): 55–106.

de Jong, J. W. "A Brief History of Buddhist Studies in Europe and America (Part II)." *Eastern Buddhist* 7, no. 2 (1974): 49–82.

Donner, Fred M. "From Believers to Muslims: Confessional Self-Identity in the Early Islamic Community." *Al-Abḥāth* 50–51 (2002–2003): 9–53.

Donner, Fred M. *Muhammad and the Believers at the Origins of Islam*. Cambridge, MA: Belknap Harvard University Press, 2010.

Dumont, Louis. *Homo Hierarchicus: The Caste System and its Implications*. Trans. Mark Sainsbury, Louis Dumont, and Basia Gulati. Chicago: University of Chicago Press, 1980 [1966].

Dundas, Paul. *The Jains*. 2nd ed. London: Routledge, 2002.

Eltschinger, Vincent. *Buddhist Epistemology as Apologetics: Studies on the History, Self-understanding and Dogmatic Foundations of Late Indian Buddhist Philosophy*. Vienna: Verlag der Österreichischen Akademie der Wissenschaften, 2014.

Fisher, Elaine. *Hindu Pluralism: Religion and the Public Sphere in Early Modern South Asia*. Oakland: University of California Press, 2017.

Fitzgerald, James, trans. *The Mahābhārata*. Vol. 7. Chicago: University of Chicago Press, 2004.

Fitzgerald, James, trans. "Making Yudhiṣṭhira the King: The Dialectics and the Politics of Violence in the *Mahābhārata*." *Rocznik Orientalistyczny* 54, no. 1 (2001): 63–92.

Flint, Valerie I. J. *The Rise of Magic in Early Medieval Europe*. Princeton: Princeton University Press, 1991.

Freiberger, Oliver. "The ideal sacrifice. Patterns of reinterpreting brahmin sacrifice in early Buddhism." *Bulletin d'Etudes Indiennes* 16 (1998): 39–49.

Freiberger, Oliver. "Negative Campaigning: Polemics Against Brahmins in a Buddhist *Sutta*." *Religions of South Asia* 3, no. 1 (2009): 61–76.

Fynes, Richard. "Review of *Greater Magadha* by Johannes Bronkhorst." *Journal of the Oxford Centre for Buddhist Studies* 1 (Oct. 2011): 212–215.

Glass, Andrew. *Four Gāndhārī Saṃyuktāgama Sūtras: Senior Kharoṣṭhī Fragment 5*. Gandhāran Buddhist Texts. Vol. 4. Seattle: University of Washington Press, 2007.

Goldman, Robert. *Gods, Priests, and Warriors: The Bhṛgus of the* Mahābhārata. New York: Columbia University Press, 1977.

Gombrich, Richard. "How the Mahāyāna Began." *Journal of Pali and Buddhist Studies* 1 (March 1988): 29–46.

Gombrich, Richard. "The Buddha's Book of Genesis?" *Indo-Iranian Journal* 35 (1992): 159–178.

Gombrich, Richard. "Recovering the Buddha's Message." In *Buddhism: Critical Concepts in Religious Studies*, edited by Paul Williams. Vol. 1, 113–128. New York: Routledge, 2005.

Gombrich, Richard. *How Buddhism Began: The Conditioned Genesis of the Early Teachings*. New Delhi: Munshiram Manoharlal Publishers, 2007.

Gombrich, Richard. *What the Buddha Thought*. London: Oxford Center for Buddhist Studies, 2009.

Gómez, Luis O. "Proto-Mādhyamika in the Pāli Canon." *Philosophy East and West* 26, no. 2 (Apr. 1976): 137–165.

Hacker, Paul. *Inklusivismus: Eine Indische Denkform*. Edited by Gerhardt Oberhammer. Vienna: De Nobili Research Library, 1983.

Halbfass, Wilhelm. *India and Europe: An Essay in Understanding*. Albany, NY: SUNY Press, 1988.

Hartmann, Jens-Uwe, and Klaus Wille. "The Manuscript of the *Dīrghāgama* and the Private Collection in Virginia." In *From Birch Bark to Digital Data: Recent Advances in Buddhist Manuscript Research*, edited by Paul Harrison and Jens-Uwe Hartmann, 137–155. Vienna: Verlag der Österreichischen Akademie der Wissenschaften, 2014.

Heesterman, J. C. *The broken world of sacrifice: an essay in ancient Indian ritual*. Chicago: University of Chicago Press, 1993.

Heesterman, J. C. *The inner conflict of tradition: essays in Indian ritual, kingship, and society*. Chicago: University of Chicago Press, 1985.

Hiltebeitel, Alf. *Rethinking the Mahābhārata: A Reader's Guide to the Education of the Dharma King*. Chicago: University of Chicago Press, 2001.

Hiltebeitel, Alf. "Buddhism and the *Mahābhārata*: Boundary dynamics in textual practice." In *Boundaries, Dynamics, and Construction of Traditions in South Asia*, edited by F. Squarcini, 107–131. Florence: Firenze University Press, 2005.

Hiltebeitel, Alf. *Dharma: Its Early History in Law, Religion, and Narrative*. Oxford: Oxford University Press, 2011.

Hinüber, Oskar von. "Die neun Aṅgas: Ein früher Versuch zur Einteilung buddhistischer Texte." *Wiener Zeitschrift für die Kunde Südasiens* 38 (1994): 121–135.

Hinüber, Oskar von. *A Handbook of Pāli Literature*. Berlin: Walter de Gruyter, 2000.

Hinüber, Oskar von. "Hoary Past and Hazy Memory: On the History of Early Buddhist Texts." *Journal of the International Association of Buddhist Studies* 29, no. 2 (2006 [2008]): 193–210.

Hoernle, A. F. Rudolf. "The Sutta Nipata in a Sanskrit Version from Eastern Turkestan." *Journal of the Royal Asiatic Society* 48, no. 4 (Oct. 1916): 709–732.

Horner, I. B. *The Book of the Discipline (Vinaya-Piṭaka)*. 6 vols. Oxford: The Pali Text Society, 1982–1992 [1938–1966].

Hultzsch, E. *Inscriptions of Aśoka*. Corpus Inscriptionum Indicarum. Vol. 1. Tokyo: Meicho-Fukyū-kai, 1977.

Inden, Ronald. "Changes in the Vedic Priesthood." In *Ritual, State and History in South Asia: Essays in honour of J.C. Heesterman*, edited by A. W. van den Hoek et al., 556–577. Leiden: Brill, 1992.

Ireland, John D., trans. *The Udāna and the Itivuttaka: Two Classics from the Pāli Canon*. Kandy: Buddhist Publication Society, 1997.

Jacobi, Hermann. *Gaina Sûtras*. 2 vols. Sacred Books of the East. Vol. 22–23. Oxford: Clarendon Press, 1884.

Jayawickrama, N. A. "The Vaggas of the Sutta Nipāta." *University of Ceylon Review* 6 (1948): 243–249.

Jones, J. J., trans. *The Mahāvastu*. London: Luzac and Company, 1949.

Jurewicz, Joanna. "Playing with Fire: The *pratītyasamutpāda* from the Perspective of Vedic Thought." *Journal of the Pali Text Society* 26 (2000): 77–103.

Kane, Pandurang Vaman. *History of Dharmaśāstra*. Vol. 2. Part 1. Poona: Bhandarkar Oriental Research Institute, 1974.

Karttunen, Klaus. *India and the Hellenistic World*. Helsinki: Finnish Oriental Society, 1997.

King, Richard. *Orientalism and Religion: Postcolonial Theory, India and 'The Mystic East.'* London: Routledge, 1999.

Lamotte, Étienne. *History of Indian Buddhism: From the Origins to the Śaka Era*. Trans. Sara Webb-Boin. Louvain-la-Neuve: Université Catholique de Louvain, 1988 [1958].

Lariviere, Richard. "Dharmaśāstra, Custom, 'Real Law' and 'Apocryphal' Smṛtis." *Journal of Indian Philosophy* 32, no. 5–6 (Dec. 2004): 611–627.

Lopez, Donald S., Jr. "Buddha." In *Critical Terms for the Study of Buddhism*, edited by Donald S. Lopez, Jr. Chicago: University of Chicago Press, 2005.

Lubin, Timothy. "The Transmission, Patronage, and Prestige of Brahmanical Piety from the Mauryas to the Guptas." In *Boundaries, Dynamics and Construction of Traditions in South Asia*, edited by Federico Squarcini, 77–103. Florence: Firenze University Press, 2005.

Macdonell, Anthony. *A Vedic Grammar for Students*. Delhi: Motilal Banarsidass, 1993.

MacMullen, Ramsay. *Christianizing the Roman Empire: A.D. 100–400*. New Haven: Yale University Press, 1984.

Maes, Claire. "Dialogues With(in) the Pāli Vinaya: A Research into the Dynamics and Dialectics of the Pāli Vinaya's Ascetic Others, with a Special Focus on the Jain Other." Unpublished PhD diss., Universiteit Ghent, 2015.

Malamoud, Charles. "Théologie de la dette dans les Brāhmaṇa." *Puruṣārtha: Science Sociales en Asie du Sud* 4 (1980): 39–62.

Manné, Joy. "Categories of Sutta in the Pāli Nikāyas and their Implications for our Appreciation of the Buddhist Teaching and Literature." *Journal of the Pali Text Society* 15 (1990): 29–87.

Masefield, Peter, trans. *The Udāna*. Oxford: Pali Text Society, 1994.

Masuzawa Tomoko. *The Invention of World Religions*. Chicago: University of Chicago Press, 2005.

Mayeda Egaku. "Japanese Studies on the Schools of the Chinese Āgamas." In *Genshi bukkyō seiten no seiritsushi kenkyū* [A History of the Formation of Original Buddhist Texts], 94–103. Tokyo: Sankibō Busshorin, 1964.

McClish, Mark. "Political Brahmanism and the State: A Compositional History of the *Arthaśāstra*." PhD diss., University of Texas at Austin, 2009.

McCrindle, John W. *Ancient India as Described by Megasthenês and Arrian*. Calcutta: Thacker, Spink, and Co., 1877.

McCrindle, John W. *Ancient India as Described in Classical Literature*. St. Leonards: Ad Orientem, 1971 [1901].

McGovern, Nathan. "Brahmā: An Early and Ultimately Doomed Attempt at a Brahmanical Synthesis." *Journal of Indian Philosophy* 40, no. 1 (Feb. 2012): 1–23.

McGovern, Nathan. "Buddhists, Brahmans, and Buddhist Brahmans: Negotiating Identities in Indian Antiquity." Ph.D. dissertation, University of California, Santa Barbara, 2013.

McGovern, Nathan. "On the Origin of the 32 Marks of a Great Man." *Journal of the International Association of Buddhist Studies* 39 (2016): 207–247.

McGovern, Nathan. "The Contemporary Study of Buddhism." In *The Oxford Handbook of Contemporary Buddhism*, edited by Michael Jerryson, 701–714. New York: Oxford University Press, 2017.

Meisig, Konrad. *Das Śrāmaṇyaphala-Sūtra: Synoptische Übersetzung und Glossar der chinesischen Fassungen verglichen mit dem Sanskrit und Pāli*. Wiesbaden: Otto Harrassowitz, 1987.

Müller, F. Max. *Comparative Mythology: An Essay*. Edited by Abram Smythe Palmer. London: George Routledge and Sons, n.d.

Nakamura Hajime. *Indian Buddhism: A Survey with Bibliographical Notes*. Delhi: Motilal Banarsidass, 2007.

Nakano, Gishō, and N.A. Jayawickrama. "Ācārya." In *Encyclopedia of Buddhism*, edited by G.P. Malalasekera, vol. 1, 163–168. Government of Ceylon, 1961.

Ñāṇamoli, Bhikkhu, and Bhikkhu Bodhi. *The Middle Length Discourses of the Buddha: A New Translation of the* Majjhima Nikāya. Boston: Wisdom Publications, 1995.

Nanda Raksakhom. "การเยียวยารักษาโดยวิธีการทางศาสนา" ["Medical Treatment using Religious Methods"]. BA Senior Thesis, College of Religious Studies, Mahidol University, 2005.

Nattier, Jan. *A Guide to the Earliest Chinese Buddhist Translations*. Tokyo: The International Research Institute for Advanced Buddhology, Soka University, 2008.

Nigam, Aditya. *The Insurrection of Little Selves: The Crisis of Secular-Nationalism in India*. New Delhi: Oxford University Press, 2006.

Norman, K. R., trans. *The Elders' Verses I: Theragāthā*. London: Luzac and Company, 1969.

Norman, K. R., trans. *The Elders' Verses II: Therīgāthā*. London: Luzac and Company, 1971.

Norman, K. R. "A note on *Attā* in the *Alagaddūpama Sutta*." In *Studies in Indian Philosophy: A Memorial Volume in Honour of Pandit Sukhlaji Sanghvi, LD series* 84, 19–29. Ahmedabad, 1981.

Norman, K. R. "Theravāda Buddhism and Brahmanical Hinduism: Brahmanical Terms in a Buddhist Guise." *The Buddhist Forum* 51 (1991): 193–200.

Norman, K. R., trans. *The Group of Discourses (Sutta Nipāta)*. Vol. 2. Oxford: Pali Text Society, 1992.

O'Flaherty, Wendy Doniger, trans. *The Rig Veda*. London: Penguin Books, 1981.

O'Hanlon, Rosalind. *Caste, Conflict, and Ideology: Mahatma Jotirao Phule and Low-Caste Protest in Nineteenth-Century Western India*. Cambridge, England: Cambridge University Press, 1985.

Ohira Suzuko. *A Study of the Bhagavatīsūtra: A Chronological Analysis*. Ahmedabad: Prakrit Text Society, 1994.

Oldenberg, Hermann. *Buddha: His Life, His Doctrine, His Order*. Trans. William Hoey. London: Williams and Norgate, 1892.

Oldenberg, Hermann. *Die Religion des Veda*. Berlin: Verlag von Wilhelm Herz, 1894.

Olivelle, Patrick. *The Origin and Early Development of Buddhist Monachism*. Colombo: Gunasena, 1974.

Olivelle, Patrick. *Saṃnyāsa Upaniṣads: Hindu Scriptures on Asceticism and Renunciation*. New York: Oxford University Press, 1992.

Olivelle, Patrick. *The Āśrama System: The History and Hermeneutics of a Religious Institution*. New Delhi: Munshiram Manoharlal Publishers, 1993.

Olivelle, Patrick. "Ascetic Withdrawal or Social Engagement." In *Religions of India in Practice*, edited by Donald S. Lopez, Jr., 533–546. Princeton: Princeton University Press, 1995.

Olivelle, Patrick. "Review of *The Two Sources of Indian Asceticism* by Johannes Bronkhorst." *Journal of the American Oriental Society* 115, no. 1 (1995): 162–164.

Olivelle, Patrick, trans. *The Early Upaniṣads*. New York: Oxford University Press, 1998.

Olivelle, Patrick, trans. *Dharmasūtras: The Law Codes of Āpastamba, Gautama, Baudhāyana, and Vasiṣṭha*. Oxford: Oxford University Press, 1999.

Olivelle, Patrick, ed. and trans. *Dharmasūtra Parallels: Containing the Dharmasūtras of Āpastamba, Gautama, Baudhāyana, and Vasiṣṭha*. Delhi: Motilal Banarsidass Publishers, 2005.

Olivelle, Patrick, trans. *Manu's Code of Law: A Critical Edition and Translation of the* Mānava-Dharmaśāstra. Oxford: Oxford University Press, 2005.

Olivelle, Patrick, ed. *Between the Empires: Society in India 300 BCE to 400 CE*. Oxford: Oxford University Press, 2006.

Olivelle, Patrick. *A Dharma Reader: Classical Indian Law*. New York: Columbia University Press, 2017.

Pandian, M. S. S. *Brahmin and Non-Brahmin: Genealogies of the Tamil Political Present.* Ranikhet, India: Permanent Black, 2007.

Pérez-Remón, Joaquín. *Self and Non-Self in Early Buddhism.* The Hague: Mouton Publishers, 1980.

Pollock, Sheldon. *The Language of the Gods in the World of Men: Sanskrit, Culture, and Power in Premodern India.* Berkeley: University of California Press, 2006.

Reynolds, Frank E., and Charles Hallisey. "The Buddha." In *Buddhism and Asian History,* edited by Joseph M. Kitagawa and Mark D. Cummings, 29–49. New York: Macmillan Publishing Company, 1989.

Rhys Davids, T. W. *Dialogues of the Buddha.* 3 vols. London: Oxford University Press, 1899.

Rhys Davids, T. W. *Buddhist India.* New York: G.P. Putnam's Sons, 1903.

Rhys Davids, T. W. "The Early History of the Buddhists." In *The Cambridge History of India,* vol. 1, edited by E. J. Rapson, 171–197. Cambridge, England: Cambridge University Press, 1922.

Rhys Davids, T. W. *The Questions of King Milinda.* Vol. 1. New York: Dover Publications, 1963 [1890].

Rotman, Andy, trans. *Divine Stories: Divyāvadāna.* Part 1. Boston: Wisdom Publications, 2008.

Ruegg, David Seyfort. *The Symbiosis of Buddhism with Brahmanism/Hinduism in South Asia and of Buddhism with "Local Cults" in Tibet and the Himalayan Region.* Wien: Verlag der Österreichischen Akademie der Wissenschaften, 2008.

Salomon, Richard. *Indian Epigraphy.* New York: Oxford University Press, 1998.

Samuel, Geoffrey. *The Origins of Yoga and Tantra: Indic Religions to the Thirteenth Century.* Cambridge, England: Cambridge University Press, 2008.

Sander, Lore, and Ernst Waldschmidt, eds. *Sanskrithandschriften aus den Turfanfunden.* Vol. 4. Wiesbaden: Franz Steiner Verlag GMBH, 1980.

Sarbacker, Stuart Ray. *Samādhi: The Numinous and Cessative in Indo-Tibetan Yoga.* Albany, NY: SUNY Press, 2005.

Schlieter, Jens. "Did the Buddha Emerge from a Brahmanic Environment? The Early Buddhist Evaluation of 'Noble Brahmins' and the 'Ideological System' of Brahmanism." In *Dynamics in the History of Religions between Asia and Europe: Encounters, Notions, and Comparative Perspectives,* edited by Volkhard Krech and Marion Steinicke, 137–148. Leiden: Brill, 2012.

Schopen, Gregory. "Archaeology and Protestant Presuppositions in the Study of Indian Buddhism." *History of Religions* 31 (1991): 1–23.

Schopen, Gregory. "Two Problems in the History of Indian Buddhism: The Layman/Monk Distinction and the Doctrines of the Transference of Merit." In *Bones, Stones, and Buddhist Monks: Collected Papers on the Archaeology, Epigraphy, and Texts of Monastic Buddhism in India,* 23–55. Honolulu: University of Hawai'i Press, 1997.

Schopen, Gregory. "Mahāyāna in Indian Inscriptions." In *Figments and Fragments of Mahāyāna Buddhism in India*. Honolulu: The University of Hawai'i Press, 2005 [1979].

Smith, Brian K. *Classifying the Universe: The Ancient Indian* Varṇa *System and the Origins of Caste*. New York: Oxford University Press, 1994.

Smith, Jonathan Z. "Religion, Religions, Religious." In *Critical Terms for Religious Studies*, edited by Mark C. Taylor, 269–284. Chicago: University of Chicago Press, 1998.

Stede, W., ed. *Niddesa*. Vol. 3. London: Pali Text Society, 1918.

Strong, John S. *The Legend of King Aśoka: A Study and Translation of the* Aśokāvadāna. Delhi: Motilal Banarsidass, 1983.

Sujāto, Bhikkhu. *A History of Mindfulness: How Insight Worsted Tranquility in the Satipaṭṭhāna Sutta*. N.p.: Santipada, 2012.

Sutton, Nicholas. "Aśoka and Yudhiṣṭhira: A Historical Setting for the Ideological Tensions of the *Mahābhārata*." *Religion* 27 (1997): 331–341.

Tambiah, Stanley. *World Conqueror & World Renouncer: A Study of Buddhism and Polity in Thailand Against a Historical Background*. Cambridge, England: Cambridge University Press, 1976.

Thapar, Romila. *From Lineage to State: Social Formations in the Mid-First Millennium B.C. in the Ganga Valley*, in *History & Beyond*. New Delhi: Oxford University Press, 2000.

Tsuchida Ryutaro. "Two categories of Brahmins in the early Buddhist period." *The Memoirs of the Toyo Bunko* 49 (1991): 51–95.

Turnour, George. *The Maháwanso*. Vol. 1. Ceylon: Cotta Church Mission Press, 1837.

van Buitenen, J. A. B., trans. *The Mahābhārata*. Vols. 1–3. Chicago: Chicago University Press, 1973–1978.

van der Veer, Peter. "The Concept of the Ideal Brahman as an Indological Construct." In *Hinduism Reconsidered*, edited by Günther-Dietz Sontheimer and Hermann Kulke, 153–172. New Delhi: Manohar Publishers and Distributors, 2005 [1989].

Vetter, Tilmann. *The Ideas and Meditative Practices of Early Buddhism*. Leiden: Brill, 1988.

Vetter, Tilmann. "Some Remarks on Older Parts of the Suttanipāta." In *Earliest Buddhism and Madhyamaka: Panels of the VIIth World Sanskrit Conference*, edited by Schmidthausen and Ruegg, 36–56. Leiden: Brill, 1990.

Vinaysagar, Mahopadhyay, ed. and trans. *Isibhasiyaim Suttaim (Rishibhashit Sutra)*. Trans. Kalanath Shastri and Dinesh Chandra Sharma. Jaipur: Prakrit Bharati Academy, 1988.

Waldschmidt, Ernst, et al., eds. *Sanskrithandschriften aus den Turfanfunden*. Verzeichnis der Orientalischen Handschriften in Deutschland. Vol. 10. Parts 1–10. Stuttgart: Franz Steiner Verlag, 1965–2008.

Walser, Joseph. "When did Buddhism Become Anti-Brahmanical? The Case of the Missing Soul." *Journal of the American Academy of Religion* 86, no. 1 (March 2018): 94–125.

Walshe, Maurice. *The Long Discourses of the Buddha: A Translation of the* Dīgha Nikāya. Boston: Wisdom Publications, 1995.

Warder, A. K. *Pali Meter*. London: Luzac, 1967.

Wedemeyer, Christian K. *Making Sense of Tantric Buddhism*. New York: Columbia University Press, 2013.

White, David Gordon. *Myths of the Dog-Man*. Chicago: University of Chicago Press, 1991.

White, David Gordon. *Sinister Yogis*. Chicago: University of Chicago Press, 2009.

Wilson, Liz. *Charming Cadavers: Horrific Figurations of the Feminine in Indian Buddhist Hagiographic Literature*. Chicago: University of Chicago Press, 1996.

Witzel, Michael. "The Case of the Shattered Head." *Studien zur Indologie und Iranistik* 13/14 (1987): 363–416.

Witzel, Michael. "On the Localization of Vedic Texts and Schools (Material on Vedic *śākhās*, 7)." In *India and the Ancient world. History, Trade and Culture before A.D. 650. P.H.L. Eggermont Jubilee Volume*, edited by G. Pollet, Orientalia Lovaniensia Analecta, vol. 25, 173–213. Leuven, 1987.

Witzel, Michael. "Tracing the Vedic Dialects." In *Dialects dans les littératures indo-aryennes. Actes du Colloque International organisé par UA 1058 sous les auspices du C.N.R.S avec le soutien du College de France, de la Fondation Hugot du College de France, de l'Université de Paris III, du Ministre des Affaires Etrangères, Paris (Fondation Hugot) 16–18 Septembre 1986*, edited by Collette Caillat, 97–264. Paris: College de France, Institut de Civilisation Indienne, 1989.

Witzel, Michael. "Early Sanskritization: Origins and Development of the Kuru State." *Electronic Journal of Vedic Studies* 1, no. 4 (Dec. 1995).

Witzel, Michael. "The Development of the Vedic Canon and its Schools: The Social and Political Milieu (Material on Vedic *śākhās*, 8)." In *Inside the Texts, Beyond the Texts: New Approaches to the Study of the Vedas*, edited by Michael Witzel, Opera Minora, vol. 2, 257–345. Cambridge, MA: Harvard University Department of Sanskrit and Indian Studies, 1997.

Wolf, Kenneth. *The Poverty of Riches: St. Francis of Assisi Reconsidered*. Oxford: Oxford University Press, 2003.

Woodward, F. L., and E. M. Hare, trans. *The Book of the Gradual Sayings (Aṅguttara Nikāya), or More-Numbered Suttas*. 5 vols. Oxford: The Pali Text Society, 1996–2001.

Wynne, Alexander. *The Origin of Buddhist Meditation*. London: Routledge, 2007.

Yìnshùn 印順. *Yuanshi fojiao shengdian zhi jicheng* 原始佛教聖典之集成 [The compilation of the scriptures of original Buddhism]. Zhubei: Zhengwen, 2002.

# *Index*

**Note:** An italicized t after a page number refers to a table


Adcock, C. S., 27
Adigal, Maraimalai, 28
Aggikabhāradvāja, encounter dialog about, 53–54
*Ahi-nakula,* 3, 225**n4**. *See also* Snake and mongoose
Alcott, Henry Steel, 28
Almond, Philip, 9, 10
*Ambaṭṭha Sutta,* 199–207
condemnation of Neo-Buddhism in, 203–204, 208–209, 210–212
*Aṅguttara Nikāya,* 118, 147, 208
*Āpastamba Dharma Sūtra,* 153, 163–164
and the *āśrama* system, 137, 151, 159, 160, 162
householder Brahman ideology, 134–135, 136–137
and the *varṇa* system, 136–137, 146, 150, 151
**Arthavargīya,* 166, 169–170, 172–182
*sutta* order in, 173–174
translation problems with, 177
Aryan invasion theory, 27–28
Arya Samaj, 27
Ascetics, 18, 77, 113, 115, 155, 218
Aśoka, 46–48, 50, 80
*dhamma,* definition of, 79–80
early historical documents of, 41–42, 234**n2**
ideology of kingship, 49, 237**n37**
*Āśrama* system, 163–164, 272**n109**, 272**n112**
in *Āpastamba Dharma Sūtra,* 137, 151, 159, 160, 162
in *Baudhāyana Dharma Sūtra,* 138–139, 156–157, 158–159, 162, 216
*brahmacarya* and, 103–104, 111–112
categories of, in colloquial discourse, 151–158
four ways of life and, 83, 103, 104, 135–136, 215
Neo-Brahmanism and, 25, 110–111, 214–216, 223
originating from "liberal" Brahmans, 138–140, 152, 161, 264**n14**
in the Pali Canon, 156–157
polemical systemization of actual social practice by, 158–162, 164, 196
as theological construct, 137–140
*Assalāyana Sutta,* 48, 207–208
*Aṣṭādhyāyī* (Pāṇini), 3, 67
*Atharva Veda,* 105–108

Atomism, theory of, 75, 120
*Attadaṇḍa Sutta*, 91
*Aṭṭhaka/*Arthavargīya*. *See* *Arthavargīya*
*Aṭṭhaka Vagga*, 166. *See also* individual *suttas* of
antiquity of, 59–60
Brahman references in, 87–91, 93–94, 130, 165, 191–192
Chinese translation of, 172–182
*Mahāniddesa* commentary on, 167–172
and *Pārāyaṇa Vagga*, comparisons with, 58–60, 62, 182–183
Awakened Buddhist, 192
*Āyāraṅga Sutta*, 62
Brahman references in, 87–89, 91–93, 94, 98
celibacy in, 100–101
householders in, 127

Bailey, Greg, 18, 52, 68
*Baudhāyana Dharma Sūtra*, 136, 150, 160
*āśrama* system in, 138–139, 156–157, 158–159, 162, 216
renunciatory ideal of, 134
Bāvarī, narrative of, 183–185, 187, 190–191
Bayart, Jean-François, 23
Bechert, Heinz, 44
Bestial sciences, 154–155
Bhāradvāja, encounter dialog about, 55–56
Birth, Brahmanism based on, 26, 55–57. *See also Varṇa* system
Black, Brian, 196, 203
Blind men and elephant parable, 175, 176, 179
Boyarin, Daniel, 32, 222, 223
*Brahmacarya*, 86–87, 99–112, 129, 215. *See also* Celibacy as Brahmanical
in the *āśrama* system, 103–104, 111–112
and householdership, 151, 155–156, 163–164
in Pali Canon, 101–102
*Brahmajāla Sutta*, 69, 72, 154–155
*Brāhmaṇadhammika Sutta*, 208–209
*Brāhmaṇa Saṃyutta*, 55–56, 182
paradigm of, 198–199
Brahmanical identities, 88, 99, 117, 138, 139, 218
Brahmanical literature, 24–25
Brahmanism, 2, 15–22. *See also Āśrama* system; Brahmans; *Varṇa* system
birth, based on, 26, 55–57
chronological relationship with Buddhism, 6–8, 15
early texts' description of, 12–13
and Hinduism, 3–5
historical development of, 16–18, 20–21
and Jainism, 4, 24, 85–87, 139–140, 165
study of, 22–27
theological construct of *āśrama* system, 137–140
Brahmans, 1–2, 18, 86–87. *See also* Brahmanism; Householders; *Śramaṇas* and Brahmans
the Buddha as, 24, 51–52, 96–97, 190
Buddha's comparison of old *vs.* new, 208–209
and Buddhism, 51–58, 85–87, 139–140, 165
Buddhist nun as, 249**n1**
critiques and criticisms of, 27–28
encounter dialogs on, 54–57
householders, 122–129, 133–164, 194, 218
ideal persons as, 24, 85–86, 88–89, 90–92, 98–99
Jainism, as founders of, 87–99
modern status of, 28–29
polemical model of, 51–58

*British Discovery of Buddhism* (Almond), 9
*The Broken World of Sacrifice* (Heesterman), 142
Bronkhorst, Johannes, 48, 80, 110, 120, 125
  Greater Magadha Theory, 19, 21–22, 71–72, 216
  ideological movement of Brahmanism, 13, 17, 19–22, 226**n16**
  modern American political analogy, 194–195
  on spread of Brahmanism, 147–148, 195
Buddha. *See also* Buddhism
  and Aggikabhāradvāja, encounter dialog about, 53–54
  and Bhāradvāja, encounter dialog about, 55–56
  as a Brahman, 24, 51–52, 96–97, 190
  on Brahmans, comparison of old *vs.* new, 208–209
  celibacy, teachings on, 101–102
  dates of life and death of, 43–45, 49–50
  Enlightenment of, 73–74
  European religious narrative about, 8–9, 10
  high birth of, 126
  and *jaṭilas*, 18, 116
  marriage offer to, 168–170, 173–175
  meditation, study of, 220–221
  misogyny of, 168–169
  as reformer, 9, 126, 227**n22**
  reincarnation, belief in, 71, 77–78
  relics of, 50
  and Soṇadaṇḍa, encounter dialog about, 54–55
  teachings on wrong views, 72–77
  third sermon, 116, 258–259**n103**
  and Vāseṭṭha, encounter dialog about, 55–56
*Buddha: His Life, His Doctrine, His Order* (Oldenberg), 9
Buddhaghosa, 45, 170, 176
  commentary on *Kāma Sutta*, 175–176
  commentary on *Māgandiya Sutta*, 169–170, 175, 185
Buddhism, 2, 4, 5, 15–22. *See also* Buddha
  and *brahmacarya*, 99
  and Brahmans, 51–58, 85–87, 139–140, 165
  chronological relationship with Brahmanism, 6–8
  elitist movement of, early, 126–127, 262**n143**
  founding Brahmans of, 87–99
  and hierarchy of human beings, 118–119
  Hinduism and, 16
  oral literature, chronology of, 50–51
  oral literature of, early, 42–51, 234**n16**
  oral literature of, treating diachronically, 58–60, 62
  and *śramaṇas*, 130
  and the world religions paradigm, 31
*Buddhism in the Shadow of Brahmanism* (Bronkhorst), 20, 148
*Buddhist India* (Rhys Davids), 11
Buddhist nun as Brahman, 249**n1**
Buddhist *sūtras*, 20, 46, 65–66, 191, 197. *See also* Encounter dialogs; Teachings on wrong views; individual texts
Buddhology, 5, 11–15
  and Brahmanical *vs.* Buddhist texts, 11–13, 227–228**n27**
  geographical diversity of India and, 14
Buffetrille, Katia, 6, 8
Burford, Grace, 167
  diachronic analysis of texts, 60, 166, 242**n78**

Burnouf, Eugène, 9, 11, 226**n16**
  and chronology of Brahmanism and Buddhism, 5, 6–8, 10, 15, 85

*Cakravartin*, 48–49, 237**n37**
*Caṅkī Sutta*, 208
Catholicism, sentiment against, 9, 15–16
Celibacy as Brahmanical, 99–102, 108–109, 112–113, 118, 129, 213–214, 216. *See also Brahmacarya*
  in the Dharma Sūtras, 162, 272**n109**, 272**n112**
  and householders, 128–129, 154, 159, 218
  Neo-Brahmanism and, 25
Chakravarti, Uma, 18, 123–124, 125, 126
Chinese *sūtra* and Pali *sutta*, compared, 174*t*
Chinese translation of *Aṭṭhaka Vagga*, 172–182
Christianity, 222, 233**n86**
  and characteristics of religions, 30, 31–32
*Classifying the Universe: The Ancient Indian* Varṇa *System and the Origins of Caste* (Smith), 143
Crop loss parable, 176
*Cūḷabyūha Sutta*, 130–131
Cultural identities, historic fabrications of, 23

Dakake, Maria, 33
"Deutero-Baudhāyana," 134
Dhamma, 49, 79–80
Dharma Sūtras, 25, 62–63, 83, 103, 160–162
  *Āpastamba*, 134–135, 136–137, 150, 151, 153, 159, 160, 162, 163–164
  the *āśrama* system in, 138–139, 151–152, 155, 158–159, 161–162, 214, 216, 272**n109**, 272**n112**
  *Baudhāyana*, 134, 136, 138–139, 150, 156–157, 158–159, 162
  *Gautama*, 156–157, 158, 162, 216
  householders in, 122–123, 124, 128, 222
  householders supremacy in, 133–134, 136–137
  *jaṭilas* and *vānaprastha* in, 113, 114–115, 116, 117–118
  *Vasiṣṭha*, 136, 156–157, 162
*Dīgha Nikāya*, 101–102, 199–207
Donner, Fred, 33
*Dvandva* compound, 67–69, 82

Early Vedic period, 141
Elitist movement of early Buddhism, 126–127, 262**n143**
Encounter dialogs, 72, 125, 194, 207–210, 244**n11**
  Aggikabhāradvāja, 53–54
  Bhāradvāja, 55–56
  *Brāhmaṇa Saṃyutta* paradigm, 198–199
  *Dīgha Nikāya*, 199–207
  genre of, 196–198, 283–284**n6**, 284**n10**
  in Jain literature, 209–210
  on Neo-Brahmanism, 196–197, 199, 202, 207, 210, 211–212
  Soṇadaṇḍa, 54–55
  *śramaṇa*s and Brahmans, 211–212, 213
  undermining of teachings, 211
  *varṇa* system in, 197, 207
  Vāseṭṭha, 55–56
Enlightenment, 73–74, 77, 245**n18**
Entrances to ruin, 206
*Esukārī Sutta*, 208
European religious narrative, 8–9, 10
Exchange relationship, 262**n144**

"Fame of Gotama" formula, 200, 201
"Far shore" dialogs, 184

Fire
 Buddha's third sermon, 116, 258–259**n103**
 and *jaṭilas*, association with, 115–116
 metaphor of early Buddhism, 19
"First Indian state," 141–142
"Forest dweller" practitioners, 113, 153, 155, 156, 256–257**n86**. *See also Jaṭilas*
Four lifestyles *(varṇa)*. *See Varṇa* system
Four ways of life *(āśrama)*. *See Āśrama* system

*Gautama Dharma Sūtra*, 156–157, 158, 162, 216
*Ghoṭamukha Sutta*, 208
*Going to the Far Shore*, 184
Gombrich, Richard, 19, 52, 59, 70
Gómez, Luis, 88, 89, 172
Greater Magadha, 19, 21–22, 71–72, 216
*Greater Magadha* (Bronkhorst), 19
"Great Man," Buddha as, 48
 32 marks of, 180, 181, 184, 187, 191, 201, 206–207
Gṛhya Sūtras, 110, 145, 146, 151

Hacker, Paul, 32
Head-splitting, metaphorically, 183–184, 191
Heesterman, Jan, 142
Heterogenetic approach to scholarship, 15
Hierarchy of human beings of Pūraṇa Kassapa, 118–119
Hinduism, 2, 223
 and Brahmanism, 4–5
 and British colonialism, 225–226**n6**
 and Buddhism, 16
 and European religious narrative, 9
 as a modern world religion, 27–28
*Histoire du Bouddhisme Indien* (Lamotte), 13

Householders, 122–129
 *brahmacarya* and, 151, 155–156, 163–164
 Brahmans as, 133–164, 194, 218
 children of, 152–153
 Neo-Brahmanism and, 133, 165, 206, 218, 222
 in Pali Canon, 124, 127
 relationships with Buddhist monks, 127–128
 and *śramaṇas*, 131–132
Householder supremacy, 133–134, 136–137, 164
*How Buddhism Began* (Gombrich), 19
*How the Brahmins Won* (Bronkhorst), 19–20

Ideal persons, 24, 85–86, 88–89, 90–92, 93, 98–99, 130, 178, 181–183
Identities
 Brahmanical, 24–25, 88, 99, 117, 138, 139, 218
 cultural, 23
 illusions of, 23–24
 religious, 31–33
Identity formation, 4
*The Illusion of Cultural Identity* (Bayart), 23
Inclusivism, 32, 223, 233**n86**
*Indika* (Megasthenes), 42
Indology and Buddhology, 5, 11, 16, 17, 32
*Introduction à l'histoire du Buddhisme indien* (Burnouf), 6

Jainism, 2
 and *brahmacarya*, 99
 and Brahmanism, 4, 24, 85–87, 139–140, 165
 and Neo-Brahmanism, 209–210
 and *śramaṇas*, 130
 Jains as Brahmans, 87–99

Jain literature. *See also Āyāraṅga Sutta; Sūyagaḍaṃga Sutta*
Brahman and *śramaṇa* references in, 66, 219
celibacy, practice of, 100–101
earliest texts of, 62
encounter dialogs in, 209–210
teachers in, 102, 221
Jātakas, 113–117, 202–203
*Jaṭilas*, 113–121, 129, 156, 206
Buddha's opinion of, 18, 116
fire, association with, 115–116
Jayawickrama, N. A., 187
*The Jungle Book* (Kipling), 1
Justice Party, 28

*Kāma Sutta*, 176
Kambojas, 48
Kane, Pandurang Vaman, 140–141, 142–143
Karma, 74–75, 118, 120, 216, 221
burning off of, 74, 120
Kleitarchos, 42
*Kūṭadanta Sutta*, 199–203, 209

Lamotte, Étienne, 13
Lariviere, Richard, 160–161
Late Vedic period, 141, 142
"Liberal" Brahmans, 140, 159, 160, 161
and *āśrama* system, origin of, 138–140, 152, 161, 264**n14**
"Long chronology," 43–44
Lopez, Donald S., 6, 8
Lubin, Timothy, 109, 110
Luther, Martin, 9
"Lutheran model" of Buddhist origins, 5, 8–11

Mabbett, Ian, 18, 52, 68
Māgandiya as Brahman, 168–170, 179–180
*Māgandiya Sutta*, 90, 179–180
in *Mahāniddesa*, 167–168
marriage offer to the Buddha in, 175–176
*Mahābhārata*, 17, 195–196
*Mahāniddesa*
and *Aṭṭhaka Vagga*, commentary on, 167–172
discussion with Brahman Māgandiya, 168–170
gloss on word *Brahman* in, 170–172, 179
*Mahāparinibbāna Sutta*, 49, 50
*Mahāsīhanāda Sutta*, 81–82
Mahāvīra, 92–94, 98, 121, 221
*Makara the Brahman Sūtra*, 177–178
Manu, 136, 150, 164, 215
Marketing strategy, 18, 52, 57, 85, 86, 103
"Marks of a Great Man." *See* 32 marks of a Great Man
Masuzawa, Tomoko, 31
Mātaṅga, 54, 238**n48**
Maurya, Candragupta, 42, 48, 152
Mauryan period of history, 41–42, 49, 60–61
Meditation, 16, 17
Buddha's study of, 220–221
Megasthenes, 152–154, 155, 158
social groups of India of, 42, 234**n7**
Middle Vedic period, 141–142
Misogyny of Buddha, 168–169
Mixed castes, concept of, 136, 149, 150, 151, 269**n73**

Nandas, 49
Neo-Brahmanism, 26, 191
appropriation of Brahman definition, 193–194, 195–196, 213, 218
and *āśrama* system, 25, 110–111, 214–216, 223
and Brahmans, counterpoint to, 181–182

and celibacy, 25
condemnation of in *Ambaṭṭha Sutta*, 203–204, 206
and encounter dialogs, 196–197, 199, 202, 207, 210, 211–212
and householdership, 133, 165, 206, 218, 222
and Jainism, 209–210
use of terminology, 21, 231–232**n66**
Non-Brahmin Manifesto of 1916, 28
Norman, K. R., 59, 70–71, 251–252**n36**
Normative life cycle, 135, 136

Oldenberg, Hermann, 9–10, 16, 126
Olivelle, Patrick, 16, 82–83, 134, 139
*āśrama* system, 103, 104, 135–136, 137–139, 140, 151–152, 215
Oppositional compounds, 3, 34, 39, 66, 67–68, 213
Oral literature. *See also Tripiṭaka*
early Buddhist, 42–51, 58–60, 61, 234**n16**
"Orders of life" of Jainism, 103
Orthogenetic approach to scholarship, 15

Pali Canon, 8
analysis of, 18, 20
the *āśrama* system in, 156–157
*brahmacarya* in, 101–102
celibacy, practice of, 101–102
"Fame of Gotama" formula in, 200
gods mentioned in, 226**n16**
householders in, 124, 127
*jaṭilas* and *vānaprastha* in, 113, 115
oral origins of, 33–34, 51–52, 57
parallel texts to, 235**n17**
*śramaṇas* and Brahmans in, 78–79
Pali Text Society, 11
*Pali Tipiṭaka*, 45–46. *See also* Pali Canon
Pāṇini's grammar, 3, 67
*Paramaṭṭhaka Sutta*, 178
*Pārāyaṇa Vagga*, 62, 77–78, 166–167, 251**n31**
and *Aṭṭhaka Vagga*, compared, 58–60, 62, 182–183
Brahman references in, 87–89, 94–95, 97–98, 165, 191–192
framing in, 182–191
inner-frame of, 189–190
outer frame of, 190–191
*Paribbājaka*, 72, 156–158, 206, 244**n9**
*Parivrājaka*, 103–104, 156
*Pasūra Sutta*, 130
Patañjali
*ahi-nakula*, 225**n4**
on oppositional compounds, 3, 34, 39, 66, 67–68, 213
and the snake and mongoose, 2–3, 67
Phule, Jyotirao, 27–28
"Physician" practitioners, 154
Piṅgiya, story of, 184–186, 189, 282**n62**
Political analogy for Neo-Brahmans, 194–195, 213
Pollock, Sheldon, 17
Protestant Reformation model, 9, 11, 30. *See also* Luther, Martin
*Purābheda Sutta*, 93–94, 95, 96
Pūraṇa Kassapa, 74–75, 118–119, 120
*Puruṣa Sūkta*, 143, 144, 150

Ramasamy, Periyar E. V., 28
Rebirth, 77, 95, 110, 216, 219–220
Reformer, Buddha as, 9, 126, 227**n22**
Reincarnation, 71, 77–78. *See also* Rebirth
Religion, defining, 29–30
Religious identities, 31–33
Renouncers *vs.* householders, 122–129, 134
Rhetoric, perils of, 212–216

Rhys Davids, Thomas William, 11–13
Christian New Testament, comparisons with, 47, 227**n27**, 236–237**n31**
"Rich man's poverty," 262**n143**
Rikki-Tikki-Tavi, 1
Roy, Rammohan, 27
Ryutaro, Tsuchida, 18

Sacrifices, Buddha advice on, 202–203, 209
Śākya, 7
*Sāmaññaphala Sutta,* 74–76, 120
*Sammāparibbājanīya Sutta,* 175
*Saṃsāra,* 78, 116, 220
*Saṅgārava Sutta,* 72–73
Sanskrit cosmopolis, 17
Saraswati, Dayananda, 27
Schopen, Gregory, 45
Sees-Dharma, 180–181
Self-Respect Movement, 28
"Short chronology," 44
Six "heretical" teachers, 74–76, 118–120
Smith, Brian K., 143, 228**n27**
Snake and mongoose, 2–4
grammar of an opposition, 67–70, 243**n1**
in the Mauryan dynasty, 41–42
tracing ancient history of, 40, 51, 165–166, 192, 212–213
and the "true Brahman," 51–52
undermining model of, 16, 24
*Social Dimensions of Early Buddhism* (Chakravarti), 18
*Society at the Time of the Buddha* (Wagle), 18
*The Sociology of Early Buddhism* (Bailey and Mabbett), 18
Soṇadaṇḍa, encounter dialog about, 54–55
*Soṇadaṇḍa Sutta,* 54, 199–203, 207
*Śramaṇa-brāhmaṇa* compound, 34, 66, 67–70
as a single category, 77–82
in teachings on wrong views, 72–77
*Śramaṇas*
early appearance of the word, 43, 82–83
end of Brahman connection, 129–132
*Śramaṇas* and Brahmans, 217–219
celibacy of, 112–113
conflict between, 2, 10, 16, 39–40
emergence of opposition between, 58–60, 61–62
in encounter dialogs, 211–212, 213
overlap of, 25
in Pali Canon, 78–79
in teachings on wrong views, 197
as undifferentiated worthy recipients, 77–82
*Śrauta* ritual, 142
Strabo, 42, 153–154
Subha Sutta, 208
*Suddhaṭṭhaka Sutta,* 177–178
*Sūyagaḍaṃga Sutta,* 62, 76–77
Brahman references in, 87–89, 94, 95–96
celibacy in, 100–101
householders in, 127–128

"Tathāgata Arises" formula, 199–200, 202, 206
Teachings on wrong views, 70–77, 197, 223, 244**n11**
Thass, Iyothee, 28
Theological construct of *āśrama* system, 137–140, 264**n9**
Theology of debts, 105
Theoretical construct, 264**n9**
Third sermon of Buddha, 19, 116
32 marks of a Great Man, 180, 181, 184, 187, 191, 201, 206–207